THE GEORGE GUND FOUNDATION
IMPRINT IN AFRICAN AMERICAN STUDIES

The George Gund Foundation has endowed
this imprint to advance understanding of
the history, culture, and current issues
of African Americans.

The publisher gratefully acknowledges
the generous contribution to this book provided by
the African American Studies Endowment Fund of
the University of California Press Foundation,
which is supported by a major gift from
the George Gund Foundation.

TWILIGHT PEOPLE

Twilight People

*One Man's Journey
to Find His Roots*

David Houze

University of California Press

Berkeley Los Angeles London

University of California Press, one of the most distinguished
university presses in the United States, enriches lives around
the world by advancing scholarship in the humanities, social
sciences, and natural sciences. Its activities are supported by
the UC Press Foundation and by philanthropic contributions
from individuals and institutions. For more information, visit
www.ucpress.edu.

University of California Press
Berkeley and Los Angeles, California

University of California Press, Ltd.
London, England

Photographs supplied by the author unless otherwise indicated.

Library of Congress Cataloging-in-Publication Data

Houze, David. 1965–
     Twighlight people : one man's journey to find his roots /
David Houze.
          p.   cm.
     "The George Gund Foundation imprint in African Amer-
ican Studies."
     Includes bibliographical references and index.
     ISBN 0-520-24398-6 (cloth : alk. paper)
     1. Houze, David. 1965–.   2. African Americans—
Biography.   3. African Americans—Civil rights—Southern
States—History—20th century.   4. Civil rights movements—
Southern States—History—20th century.   5. Southern
States—Race relations.   6. Apartheid—South Africa.
7. South Africa—Race relations.   8. Brothers and sisters.
I. Title.
E185.92.H68   2006
916.804'6508996073—dc22   2005035322

Manufactured in the United States of America

15   14   13   12   11   10   09   08   07   06
10   9   8   7   6   5   4   3   2   1

The paper used in this publication meets the minimum requirements of ANSI/NISO Z39.48-1992 (R 1997) (*Permanence of
Paper*).

For my mother, Yvonne,
and my brother Xavier

✳

In memory of
Robert "Robbie" Brooks
and Nick Nicholas

CONTENTS

AUTHOR'S NOTE

When I set out to write this book, I envisioned a project that embraced the best of academic research, journalistic reportage and personal memoir. While the practices and standards of the first two areas are relatively straightforward, my experience with the third area—the memoir—has been a bit more complicated. My approach has been especially charged with an impulse toward truth-telling, a desire to relay the facts to the best of my ability; but a few issues have continued to needle me. First, some instances of dialogue in the book, though based on interviews and memory, are recreations stemming from actual circumstances and events. Second, a few names have been changed, either to protect identities or because they were blurred by the onslaught of time. And finally, although I am mindful of the sanctity of quotation marks among journalists and scholars alike, I have, in an effort to provide a uniform, accessible reading experience, taken the liberty of using quotation marks in those instances of recreated dialogue or conversation. After all, according to William Zinsser in his classic *On Writing Well,* "To write good memoir you must become the editor of your own life, imposing on an untidy sprawl of half-remembered events a narrative shape and an organizing idea." I hope the efforts I have made to make sense of my life do not distract from the journey on which I invite you to accompany me.

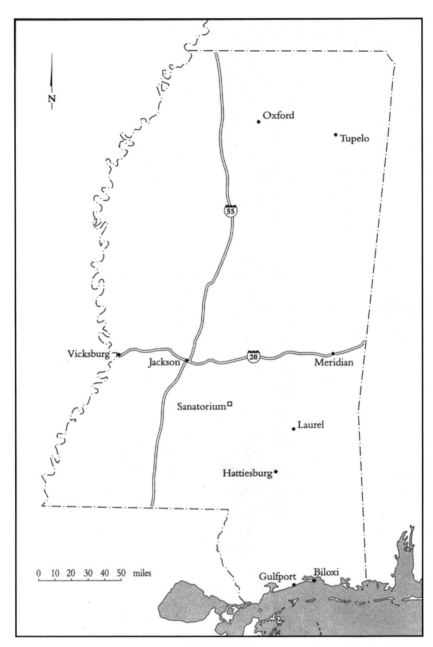

MISSISSIPPI

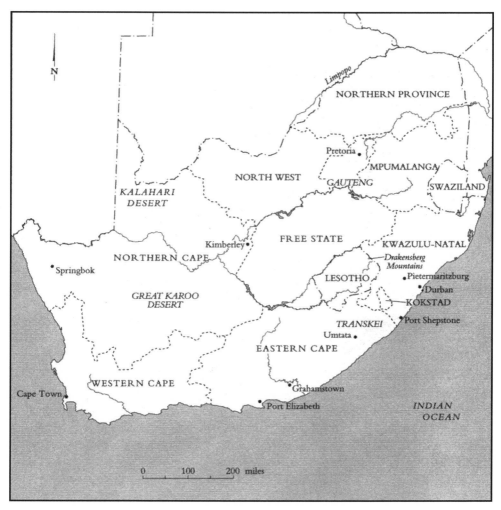

SOUTH AFRICA

Coloured people have been a twilight people
for too long, and too long others have said
what we are supposed to be, where we come
from and where we should be politically.
Nobody asks *us* where we want to be.

PETER MARAIS
Cape Town legislator

We all live here now
in the twilight
where shadows and light bob and weave
twist and try to break each other's necks.

MONGANE WALLY SEROTE
South African poet

PROLOGUE

One of the unwritten rules of the universe has to be that the harder you look for something, the more elusive it proves to be. But sooner or later, you do find what you've always been looking for, you do claim the proverbial prize—at least that's what I told myself to justify my aching knees and the sweat now starting to trickle down my face. All around me, dog-eared books on South African history, discarded fast-food wrappers, and dirty clothes littered my closet-size room at the newly built Stratford Inn, a single room occupancy hotel near downtown Atlanta. As I frantically searched for a photograph, the usual assortment of crackheads and alcoholics argued down the hallway.

Goddamn motherfucker, keep yo' motherfuckin' hands off my goddamn cigarettes!

Bitch, ain't nobody studyin' 'bout yo' skanky ass! And you better git out my fuckin' face.

The acrid smells of cigarette smoke and rancid bacon grease mixed with the howls of manic laughter now threatening to erupt into physical violence. Just another day in paradise, I brooded, while flinging the contents of a worn duffel bag all over the floor.

As the commotion from the derelicts surged and finally subsided, I found the grainy black-and-white snapshot. It was tucked in a box containing the detritus of my life: old newspapers, copies of passport applications, my diploma from the University of Georgia. Three little girls, dressed identically in gray dresses and black patent-leather shoes, stared into the camera at Crown Studios in Durban, South Africa, in 1965, the year I was born. The photograph had always been a source of mystery and wonderment for me, as if the faces depicted there would one day reveal their secrets. Only hours earlier, my mother had confirmed what I had suspected but had not been able to establish for many years: these three smiling children were my sisters.

I had phoned my mother, who lived in Detroit, from the *Atlanta*

Journal-Constitution office, where I had a job. She was worried about me. I seemed to be floundering, only a year after graduating from college in 1991. The past year had been spent frantically and futilely searching for work as a journalist in an economy mired in recession. After we exchanged a few banalities, I told my mother that I was thinking about going to South Africa, since I had few prospects in Atlanta.

"What do you think?" I asked her.

After issuing her standard rebuke—"Boy, you just don't know what to do with yourself, do you?"—she remained silent while I made the case for fleeing to South Africa. Despite the Stratford's brand-new fixtures and recent paint, I was living in what amounted to a hotel for paupers, prostitutes, transients, and drug addicts in a grubby area of Atlanta, one of the nouveau flophouses sprouting up around the city. My eighty-five-dollar-a-week room at the Stratford contained a full-size bed, a small desk and chair, a sink and mirror, and a prison-regulation toilet and shower wedged into a corner. Outside my door, the crackheads and drunks enjoyed congregating in the hallways, a kind of traveling party that always seemed to end up in a room three doors down from mine.

In keeping with this depressing situation, my health was slowly deteriorating: I had a mouthful of rotting teeth; the eyeglasses I relied on were jury-rigged with tape and paperclips; and I had lately been stricken with a mysterious skin rash. On top of all this, a drug dealer named Rat had pulled a gun on me during a dispute over money in a crack house near the Atlanta–Fulton County Stadium a few days earlier.

I worked only part time at the *Atlanta Journal-Constitution,* doing grunt work—taking dictation, delivering faxes, and making "really good coffee," according to the crusty old city editor. At night, I flipped burgers and worked the fry station at Flamingo Joe's Café in Peachtree Center. My latest foray into the hot grease and barely controlled anarchy of cooking hadn't exactly made me confident that I would be able to use my newly minted bachelor's degree in journalism in any meaningful way any time soon.

Besides the discontent with my jobs and living situation, I had never really gotten over an almost abnormal fascination with the country that claimed me by blood and ancestral ties. Despite the misery of my current existence, I took some comfort in being freakishly conversant with the minutiae and esoterica of South African history, politics, and culture gleaned from the books and articles, now strewn across the floor of my room, that I managed to borrow from the public library or purchase instead of food or medical care. South Africa haunted me, dogged me, challenged me, and frustrated me.

My mother listened intently to my litany of restlessness. "So when are you thinking about leaving?" she asked.

"As soon as I can get a ticket and"—I added craftily—"get in touch with somebody over there. Do you know of anybody I can call?"

She paused but seemed to take the bait. "Well, you can get in touch with a lady named Bessie Keachie," she volunteered, haltingly. "I lost her number a long time ago—o-oh, Lawd, it's been a long time—but she's the lady I kept in touch with because she took care of your sisters."

"Sisters?!" I sputtered. Editors and reporters on the city desk glanced over curiously at me. I lowered my voice and continued. "You mean I really do have sisters over there?"

"Yes, you do," she replied matter-of-factly, instantly invalidating all the denials and dodges she had offered over the years as I had nagged her for this precise information.

This revelation was like finding out that a brain tumor once deemed inoperable could be safely removed. I had lived with the burden of not knowing much about myself or my family for so long that this news seemed unreal and oddly timed. Maybe my mother felt sorry for me because I was working two dead-end jobs at age twenty-six. Maybe she felt guilty for never really confirming or disavowing the existence of three daughters in South Africa. Whatever the case, I felt immense joy and relief and wholeness.

"Why didn't you tell me all about this before, Ma?" I whispered.

She paused before answering. "I guess there's a time for everything, David."

She gave me what details she could about Bessie Keachie, whom she now referred to as Auntie Bessie. She had not spoken to Auntie Bessie in twenty-five years, but she remembered that she lived in Durban, on Mimosa Road, in Greenwood Park. Aunt Bessie had helped to rear the three girls—my newfound sisters—after my mother and I left South Africa, and she would know how to contact them.

My mother made me promise that I would call her before I left the country. I said I would, and she ended the phone call by saying, "I love you, David." The phrase sounded genuine but awkward—like a pre-emptive strike of some kind, to protect her against what I might discover—because we had rarely spoken those words to each other during my childhood.

My mother and I had clashed since I was a boy. For years, as a child, I had called her by her name, Yvonne, rather than using a more endearing term like "mommy" or "mother." I didn't begin calling her "Ma," and that somewhat tentatively, until I was nearly fourteen. Until then, she was just Yvonne, not really my mother, though I couldn't articulate my reasons for this lapse in the mother-son covenant. I remember one of my mother's friends pulling me aside and scolding, "David, this is your mother. Don't you think it's about time you started acknowledging her as such?" I agreed with the well-intentioned woman, but I was secretly terrified at the prospect. Calling my mother by anything other than her name just didn't feel right.

The novelty of calling my mother "Ma" lasted about a week, and we soon returned to our uneasy and often antagonistic relationship. I was angry with her for a lot of things. I felt that she had neglected me since my father's death in 1974; I was tired of being jerked around from city to city in her endless effort to fill the void left by his death; and I was sickened because I believed that she had abandoned my brother Xavier after he had been diagnosed with mental retardation. But most of all, I seethed with resentment and bitterness over her refusal to tell me anything about South Africa, where I was born, or about who and what we had left behind when we showed up in Meridian, Mississippi, in 1966.

Now, in 1992, I stared at the photograph of the girls, identified as Antoinette, Adrienne, and Geraldine, dressed in matching outfits and wearing bemused facial expressions. Where was I when the photo was taken? I wondered. Did the girls know of my existence? Did these three smiling cherubs have any idea that their mother would soon disappear from their lives?

Going back to South Africa seemed to be the only way to answer these questions. I was rudderless in Atlanta, ensnared in a spiral of hopelessness and slowly succumbing to the squalid reality of life among the drifters at the Stratford Inn. More than anything, I needed to discover where my life had begun. But to bring to light what had happened twenty-five years earlier on the shores of South Africa, I first needed to revisit and conjure Meridian, Mississippi, another southern place forever part and parcel of my memory and identity, a place where the seeds of a now slowly ripening self-discovery had first been sown.

I

From Down South
to Down South

An invented past can never be used; it cracks
and crumbles under the pressures of life like
clay in a season of drought.

JAMES BALDWIN
The Fire Next Time

To South Africans of color such as my mother, who came of age in the years after 1948, when the white minority government launched the social experiment known as apartheid, the United States beckoned as a country of promise and opportunity, a faraway place relatively free of the racialized degradation South Africa had come to epitomize. Americans, especially black Americans, were glamorous and well off and lived in beautiful homes, my mother and many in her generation believed. Although they understood that whites ran most things in America, too, it was hard to conceive of a life as oppressive as that experienced by people of color under the strictures of South African *baaskaap,* or white domination.

As she planned to leave, my mother believed that she was escaping a country on the verge of self-destruction, its trauma highlighted by events that were increasingly capturing the world's attention. In 1966, thousands of people had been evicted from District Six, a multiracial area in central Cape Town, and dumped on the barren wastelands of the Cape Flats. In May 1966, anti-apartheid activist Bram Fischer was sentenced to life in prison for his work with the African National Congress (ANC) and its military wing, Umkhonto we Sizwe (Spear of the Nation), and the South African Communist Party. A month later, U.S. Senator Robert F. Kennedy toured the country, speaking out against apartheid, meeting with ANC president-general Albert Luthuli, and criticizing the government in a historic speech at the University of Cape Town. In July 1966, the government banned nearly one thousand people under the Suppression of Communism Act and the Riotous Assemblies Act.

In September 1966, Prime Minister Hendrik F. Verwoerd, the architect of apartheid, was assassinated in parliament by a deranged coloured messenger. The effect of Verwoerd's death—he was stabbed in the heart as he sat in the legislative chamber—"was as though a lid had been lifted off the bubbling cauldron," according to historian Douglas Brown. On

December 20, 1966, the United Nations General Assembly took a first step toward imposing economic sanctions on South Africa, in a draft resolution that named the country as a threat to international peace. And that same year, the widely publicized case of Sandra Laing illuminated the devastating impact of apartheid policies on individual human lives.

Laing was a victim of the 1950 Population Registration Act, under which every child was classified by race. A fifteen-year-old girl brought up in a white family, she was expelled from her all-white school because of suspicions that she was of mixed race, or coloured. Though her parents successfully fought the government's Race Classification Board to have their daughter reclassified as white, they themselves eventually disowned her when she ran off to a township with a black man and had children.

At the age of eighteen, Laing applied for an identity document necessary to place her children in school. The authorities confirmed that she was white—and promptly threatened to take away her children because they were not white, but coloured. The only way Laing could be classified as coloured and keep her children was to seek her father's permission. But he was still bitter over her decision to elope with a black man and refused to endorse her application. Told by the authorities that she could apply for reclassification without her father's permission when she reached age twenty-one, Laing nonetheless spent another six years as a person without an identity, unable to function in society and cut off from her white family. She was a casualty of South Africa's ruthless pursuit of racial purity, its assault on any reminder of the country's problematic mixed-race heritage.

With these events as a backdrop, my mother found herself peering out the smudged oval of an airplane window, scrutinizing the airport buildings in Durban in December 1966. Uncertainty, mixed with exhilaration, flooded her thoughts. She and I—though I was only a toddler—were beginning our journey to America. She didn't know what to expect in Mississippi, her destination, but she was sure it would be weird. That was to become her official impression of our trip. From the moment we boarded the plane in Durban, en route to New York, she couldn't get over how very strange everything seemed: the people, the way they sounded when they spoke English (if they spoke English at all), the way they looked at her.

Our first stop was at the Ivory Coast airport. Yvonne was shocked when she saw black faces everywhere and realized that black people were actually running things. Under the iron-fisted racial hierarchy of apartheid, most blacks were relegated to jobs such as domestics, gardeners, and mineworkers. Yvonne had never seen or heard of black people confidently in charge of anything other than cooking, cleaning, and caring for the babies of whites, Indians, and even some coloureds. In Ivory Coast, it seemed, the black men who came on board in their smart, crisp uniforms for some unknown purpose and the black workers who scrambled to ready the airplane for the next leg of our journey were clearly in charge.

The next layover, in Paris, confirmed her sense of unreality. It was all new, all strange, all weird, she thought, as we made our way through the maelstrom of Charles de Gaulle Airport: the customs agents assaulting her with rapid-fire French, the swirls and eddies of people jostling us as we made our way through the vast airport.

We stayed in Paris that night. On our way back to the airport, Yvonne couldn't help noticing the broken-down homes on the side of the highway. French people were supposed to be so cultured—at least that's what she'd heard in South Africa—yet here they were living in these awful shacks! Yvonne told me later that she wondered what she was getting herself into, what other surprises were in store for her on the other side of the world.

In Paris, we boarded a flight to New York's Kennedy Airport. On our arrival, Yvonne surrendered a sealed envelope containing chest X-rays to the immigration officials. After being cleared for entry, we stood in the arrival area and waited for her husband. My father, a stocky, caramel-colored man, whom I barely knew—he had been in and out of South Africa since my birth a year and a half earlier—but would come to know as Daddy, soon found us.

He had met Yvonne in Durban two years earlier, when she was living with Auntie Bessie and Bessie's husband, Raymond, a cab driver, in Greenwood Park. Daddy was a merchant marine on shore leave in Durban, and Raymond brought him home for dinner. Yvonne and Daddy became close, seeing each other whenever he was in port and corresponding by letter when he was away at sea. They were married in Durban on August 8, 1966. Their marriage certificate lists my father as an "American Negro" and my mother as "Coloured."

"I was worried about y'all 'cause of all the snow and the bad weather," he said, hugging and kissing Yvonne and me. "Did y'all have any problems on the way?"

"No, we alright, Dave," Yvonne replied.

"Don't worry, everything's gonna be fine," Daddy assured Yvonne. "Come on," he urged, shepherding us through the airport, "we've got to catch another plane."

Our next flight took us to Atlanta, where more wintry weather grounded our connecting flight to Jackson, Mississippi.

"There's no snow where we're going," Daddy told Yvonne. "And my mama's gonna be at the airport to pick us up when we get there, so don't worry about nothin'."

As we piled into a taxi for a hotel near the Atlanta airport, Daddy told Yvonne we were going to be staying with my new grandma for a little while, in Meridian, Mississippi, the place where he had grown up—the place he had escaped when he was fifteen. That night at the hotel, Yvonne watched television for the first time and was introduced to American culture the next morning by Mr. Green Jeans on the *Captain Kangaroo* show. The apartheid government had banned television in South Africa, believing it to be subversive.

Sure enough, my new grandma was there to meet us at the Jackson airport. As soon as we stepped off the plane, she was bounding through the arrival lounge to see the wife and little boy whom my father, her only child, had brought all the way from overseas.

She was a big woman with a short salt-and-pepper Afro and a wide smile. She gave my Daddy a big bear hug and then turned to my mother and me.

"Well, now, looka here," she gushed. "I sure am glad to see y'all." She shook Yvonne's hand and pulled me to her bosom, while taking stock of us: Yvonne with her olive complexion, long whip of black hair, and exotic bracelets and earrings; and me with my shock of black, curly hair and saucer-wide eyes. Grandma had never spoken to my mother before and had become aware of our existence only through a few photographs Daddy had sent her from South Africa. Now she had come face to face with the mysterious woman from South Africa, the foreign woman who, she thought, had caused her son to divorce a perfectly good Mississippi woman—the mother of two of his children, no less.

All along the highway on our drive to Meridian, Yvonne saw nothing but shacks and poor, bedraggled black people, in a landscape of sprawling fields and grinding poverty. This was not at all what she had expected. My mother wanted adventure and excitement. In South Africa, everybody thought that all Americans were rich and sophisticated. Now that we were traveling ninety miles east across central Mississippi to Meridian, Yvonne felt torn—grateful to Daddy for giving us a new life, but shocked and disappointed that this new place, Mississippi, was not the America she had dreamed of as a little girl growing up in the Transkei town of Kokstad.

✴

Mississippi had failed to live up to the dreams of thousands of black people who huddled in those shacks and shanties. "Mississippi is the nation's neediest state, ranking fiftieth in most economic and educational categories," wrote Sally Belfrage in 1965. "Per capita income in 1960 was $1,285, 47.2 per cent below the national average. For every $218 paid per Mississippian to the federal government, $327 went the other way: the state has become a national charity case."

Speeding across the belly of the state in Grandma's weathered gray Pontiac, we were venturing into a barely dampened firestorm—riding deeper into a state deemed the most racist in the United States. James W. Silver had observed, "Within its borders the closed society of Mississippi comes as near to approximating a police state as anything we have yet seen in America." And, as I would come to learn over the years, Mississippi was then the focus of the nation and the world as the forces of segregation vied with the civil rights movement.

The lonely and shadowed hollows teeming with buttercups and milkweeds, the red clay hills, the hay-scattered fields, and the isolated dirt roads could not obscure the violence ripping through the state. The year had begun with the assassination of Vernon Dahmer, a Hattiesburg businessman and a local leader of the National Association for the Advancement of Colored People (NAACP), who died in a house fire set by members of the Ku Klux Klan. Hattiesburg, a railroad and timber town located just south of Meridian, was an early incubator of the civil rights movement in Mississippi, with the arrival of members of the Student Nonviolent Coordinating Committee (SNCC) in 1962.

Dahmer had established himself in the local lumber trade and was well respected by both blacks and whites. But he had drawn the ire of Klan Imperial Wizard Sam Bowers for spearheading local NAACP voter registration efforts. When the Klan arrived on the night of January 10, 1966, to burn him out of his house, Dahmer grabbed his shotgun and provided cover while his family escaped the flames. He exchanged gunfire with the Klan members, who used Molotov cocktails and torches to force him out. Dahmer was eventually pulled from the charred house by friends and family and later died from his injuries at a nearby hospital. Four Klansmen were arrested for Dahmer's murder, but only three were sentenced to life in prison. The fourth, Imperial Wizard Sam Bowers, was freed after a succession of mistrials and hung juries.

Such travesties had been historically and routinely inflicted on black people, far from the normative gaze of American democracy. The southern landscape is littered with the wreckage of brutal slavery, post–Civil War Reconstruction, the inequities of sharecropping, Jim Crow segregation, backbreaking poverty, and ever-present violence. A random tug at the bloodied fabric of Mississippi history turns out a devil's assortment of lynchings, castrations, mutilations, shootings, rapes, and bludgeonings— a sad inventory of white southerners' determination to guard against, in the final analysis, the perceived threat of black male sexuality. According to historian John Dittmer, "Lynching had always been the ultimate form of social control, and neither youth, old age, nor social class offered protection to Negroes who did not stay in their place."

One of the most gruesome examples of brutality meted out to Negroes who strayed from their place in the shadows was the tragic murder of fourteen-year-old Emmett Till. In the summer of 1955, Till's mother, Mamie Till Bradley, who had been part of the mass migration from Mississippi to Chicago, sent her son back south to spend time with her great-uncle, Moses "Preacher" Wright, in Money, Mississippi.

Young Till was about five feet four inches tall, 160 pounds, with a solid build. He stuttered as a result of a bout with polio. His classmates in Chicago knew him as "Bobo," a trickster, a snappy dresser, and a risk-taker. He was also known to carry a photograph of a white girl in his wallet, which he bragged about to fellow students.

When, on a dare, Till called out, "Bye, baby!" to a white woman at a café and then wolf-whistled at her, he had no idea that he had violated the "sanctity of white southern womanhood." He could not have known, when the woman's husband, Roy Bryant, and brother-in-law, J. W. Milam, later got wind of his transgression and abducted him from his great-uncle's cabin, that what may have been permissible in cosmopolitan Chicago was a deadly sin in Mississippi. And surely the boy was naïve when, as the white men beat him within an inch of his life, he produced the photograph of the white girl from Chicago to show that he was used to talking to white women.

The teenager's badly beaten corpse was found bobbing in the Talla-hatchie River. A seventy-four-pound cotton gin fan, attached by barbed wire, had been strung around his neck. His hideously bloated tongue was bulging from his mouth; one of his eyes hung by nerve tendrils against his cheek; and a bullet hole gaped above his right ear. The boy's body had been so pulverized and was in such horrifying shape that Mississippi authorities rushed to seal and bury his coffin.

Till's mother, however, would have none of that, insisting that she wanted the country and the world to witness the barbarity that had been inflicted on her son. In a front-page interview in the *Jackson Daily News* on September 1, 1955, Till Bradley vowed, "The entire state of Mississippi is going to pay for this." Although Bryant and Milam were brought to trial for Till's murder, an all-white, all-male jury acquitted them, leaving unanswered the question of the involvement of others.

The acquittal sparked a wave of outrage and revulsion at Mississippi throughout the country and the world. This outrage was exacerbated when the men described the boy's murder in an exclusive interview with *Look* magazine in 1956. As the rest of the country lurched into the second half of the twentieth century, however haltingly, Mississippi seemed to some to be irredeemably evil and beyond the pale.

Until Emmett Till's murder, Mississippi had been able to fend off the sporadic outside attempts to radicalize rural blacks in the quest for political and economic justice. But both political and economic forces were setting change in motion. The desolation that set in with the introduction of the mechanical cotton picker threatened the sharecropping system and its concomitant domination of black farmers by white landowners. As Nicholas Lemann argues in *The Promised Land,* his masterful rendering of the great northern migration of southern blacks, "The advent of the cotton picker made the maintenance of segregation no longer a matter of necessity for the economic establishment of the South, and thus it helped set the stage for the great drama of segregation's end."

While thousands of blacks left the South in a mass exodus for northern cities such as Chicago and Detroit, Mississippi continued to enshroud itself in a romantic haze of nostalgia about its way of life. Ignored by the rest of the country—no major presidential candidate had visited the state in nearly a century—white Mississippi made much of its august past and reveled in its self-centered existence. Its people seemed gracious and genteel to a fault, and not much stirred in the sleepy little towns complacently wasting away without regard to events in the rest of the country. Such elaborate courteousness—"Y'all come see us, ya heah?" became the constant refrain of Mississippi hospitality—only partially obscured a vigilant commitment to social and racial mores that were often enforced with violence and reinforced by an irrational hatred of "outside agitators."

Busloads of these "agitators" began pouring into Mississippi and Alabama in 1961. Dubbed the Freedom Riders, hundreds of college students from across the country helped the civil rights movement gain momentum in its assault on segregated bus and train terminals. As Lemann noted, "The Southern civil rights movement didn't become truly galvanized at the small-town level until 1961, when a series of sit-ins and, especially, the journey of the Freedom Riders, who traveled throughout the South sitting in at segregated bus stations, generated national newspaper and television coverage and dramatically demonstrated the courage of the people in the movement and the gruesome violence of the white resistance." In an editorial in the *Meridian Star,* Thurman Sensing, an official with a local group called the Southern Industrial Council, expressed the sense of alarm provoked by the Freedom Riders: "Nothing in the American experience has prepared the nation for the invasion of the State of Mississippi now in progress by youths trained and organized by the National Council of Churches and the Student Non-Violent Coordinating Committee."

Meridian was a frequent stopover for the Freedom Riders, and the fury of the white mobs waiting to greet them and the level of invective hurled at them were no less intense than in Jackson and Birmingham. Typically, the students were not allowed to leave their buses at the downtown Trailways bus terminal; police cleared the waiting rooms and formed a *cordon sanitaire* around the station to squelch any gatherings of local black residents who showed up to express their solidarity and get a glimpse of the earnest-looking white and black students from up north.

The Freedom Riders sent shock waves throughout Mississippi and the federal government. President John F. Kennedy sought to placate civil rights leaders and avoid a collision between the activists and segregationists. According to Dittmer, "The president and his brother were convinced that strong federal support for civil rights activists would bring on another civil war in Mississippi, with dire consequences for the South and the nation." Meanwhile, even some black citizens were conflicted over the massive influx of students and activists into the state. The Klan was still active, and fear remained a powerful disincentive to cooperate with groups like the Council of Federated Organizations (COFO), the Congress of Racial Equality (CORE), and SNCC in their campaigns against Mississippi apartheid.

By July 1961, Attorney General Robert Kennedy had filed two suits in Mississippi charging that black citizens had been denied the right to vote. The lawsuits were the first salvos in the widening battle for voting rights in the state, which would culminate in passage of the 1964 Civil Rights Act. But the years leading up to the historic voting rights legislation were pockmarked with mounting incidents of mayhem and resistance to federal oversight. Church bombings, mysterious shootings, voter registration rallies interrupted by gunfire, bloody attempts to integrate white swimming pools—Mississippi was caught up in what seemed to be a never-ending ruckus over racism.

Meridian's white civic and business leaders received at least one vote of confidence, however, in January 1962, when an official of the Dale Carnegie Institute who had traveled extensively in South Africa urged them to stay the course. According to the *Meridian Star,* Dr. Stewart McLelland told the weekly meeting of the all-white Kiwanis Club that the United States and Mississippi should continue to stand firm on segregation, following the role model of South Africa. "The Republic of South Africa is a friend of the U.S. and we need to retain that friendship," McLelland advised the politicians and businessmen. He went on to describe the unique position of whites in South Africa and explained that the country was blessed with total segregation. For those unfamiliar with the South African predicament, the learned professor explained that the country had been originally settled by whites and that the blacks had moved in later. Blacks were simply unable and unqualified to compete with whites economically, McLelland asserted; therefore it followed that voting rights for blacks were simply unthinkable.

Many local leaders were nonetheless desperately seeking an easing of the tensions precipitated by the expanding civil rights movement, the activities of the Freedom Riders, the increasing attention of the federal government, and the activism of Martin Luther King Jr. But any hope of detente between the civil rights activists and the segregationists was dashed in 1963 with the assassination of Medgar Evers, the state field secretary of the NAACP, who was gunned down in the driveway of his home in Jackson. Evers had predicted that Mississippi would become the focus of intensified movement activity. In a twist of fate, his death accelerated that activity, prompting organizations such as CORE and SNCC to wage an all-out war against Mississippi segregation.

Meridian had been a peripheral target in 1961 when the Freedom Riders started passing through en route to Jackson (the state capital) and Birmingham. But the city was now directly in the crosshairs of the movement as it geared up for what would become known as Freedom Summer.

❋

Meridian had been an important railroad town during the Civil War and served as the temporary state capital when Jackson was occupied by Union troops. Author Earl Bailey described the town's growth: "From the beginning, railroads and railroad men dominated Meridian's development. Merging rails had given the town an excuse for being, and one of its co-founders, a pioneer railroad man, then gave the town its name, which he meant to be synonymous with 'junction.'" The city's location in east central Mississippi, near the Alabama line, away from the main battlefields in Vicksburg and Jackson, had spared it from complete destruction by Grant's forces, though the Union Army general did order the demolition of the town's rail facilities and other buildings.

Four railways, two airline services, four bus lines, eight major freight lines, one major petroleum pipeline, and a network of three national and three state highways added to the city's sense of centrality. City leaders called Meridian the "Queen City" and the "Heart of the South," expressing pride that it was a place where life was slow and religion and faith were treasured. Sports enthusiasts and hunters reveled in the city's outlying forests, lakes, and parks.

Nevertheless, Meridian had fallen on hard times by the second half of the twentieth century. As journalist Jack Nelson observed: "At its zenith a bustling rail junction, retail and marketing hub for cotton and lumber, downtown Meridian by the 1960s was parched and down at the heels. The streets were nearly devoid of trees. Weeds poked through cracks in the sidewalk. . . . The once-elegant hotels, which had accommodated hundreds of travelers at night and boasted of their sumptuous dining rooms, now were vacant and sad."

Until the early 1960s, the city's whites and blacks existed in a kind of uneasy mutual dependence: they were bound together by the land and by a tradition of peonage that largely excluded brazen racism, though segregation in public accommodations was a fact of life. Blacks had always worked for stores and other businesses in Meridian, but those jobs had been on the docks and in the storerooms; no one was waited on by a black clerk at the downtown Woolworth's or Kress store. Blacks began breaching the old rules of social etiquette, however, by seeking service at restaurants such as Weidmann's in downtown Meridian, on Twenty-second Avenue. On one occasion during the long, torrid summer of 1964, three black patrons entered this century-old steak house and were turned back at the door by the manager, Thomas (Shorty) McWilliams, who told them, "We can't accommodate you."

Freedom Summer also stirred the city's Ku Klux Klan network, which encompassed nearby Neshoba and Newton counties. The ever-vigilant *Meridian Star* fretted over the coming onslaught on the state's way of life and the "horrors of integration," lamenting: "Truly Mississippi has come upon evil days; we have been delivered into the hands of the Philistines."

*

Michael (Mickey) Schwerner and his wife, Rita, native New Yorkers in their early twenties, arrived in Meridian on January 19, 1964, to work for CORE and COFO, the two groups coordinating movement activities in the state. The couple's first stop in Mississippi was Jackson, where civil rights leader Bob Moses briefed them on their assignment: Mickey and Rita were the first white civil rights activists dispatched from the capital to set up a permanent base in Meridian. As the second largest city in the state, Meridian was seen as strategically important in the overall southern civil rights campaign.

Schwerner was an intense young man with large eyes, an infectious grin, and a goatee; he was always dressed in sweatshirts, jeans, and sneakers. He and Rita, a serious woman with a kind face and reddish brown hair, finally found a place to live in a tiny four-bedroom house at 1308 Thirty-fourth Avenue, although the landlord was initially reluctant to rent to them because of their movement connection. Despite death threats and police intimidation, the Schwerners settled in and found office space for the campaign at 2505 1/2 Fifth Street, a run-down suite of rooms above the Fielder and Brooks drugstore. Mickey told his colleagues in CORE,

"Mississippi is the decisive battleground for America. Nowhere in the world is the idea of white supremacy more firmly entrenched or more cancerous than in Mississippi."

The newly christened Meridian Community Center became a model Freedom Summer office, containing a small library, a recreation room, and a conference room where the Schwerners conducted voter registration classes. Mickey began canvassing the city for volunteers, but many black residents at first distrusted the whites who had suddenly appeared in their neighborhoods—they didn't want any trouble or attention from the police or the Klan. Soon, though, one of the boys from a nearby neighborhood started hanging out at the center, volunteering to help Mickey and Rita put up bookshelves, paint walls, and set up meetings for those brave enough to learn about their voting rights. His name was James (J. E.) Chaney, and he immediately threw himself into the movement.

Chaney, a slender youth known as a loner, was one of five children from a broken home. He had been a rebel and a troublemaker from an early age, when officials at Harris High School reprimanded him for wearing handcrafted NAACP buttons. Chaney had also unwittingly joined one of the first Freedom Rides in 1962, when he boarded a Trailways bus in Tennessee and sat next to one of the new breed of civil rights activists who were challenging segregation on the highways. When the bus arrived in Meridian, Chaney's father pulled him off and away from the threat of arrest and attack by segregationists milling around the station. Now Chaney jumped at the opportunity to help Mickey and Rita and told his mother, who expressed concern about his involvement, that he had finally found a way to make a difference.

In addition to setting up the community center, Mickey was charged with the task of integrating at least one of the city's downtown stores. He and Chaney and a handful of black residents began passing out leaflets calling for sales jobs for blacks at the city's major stores: Kress, Woolworth's, and J. J. Newberry. Police arrested Schwerner after he led a boycott of downtown businesses, but he was quickly released. The city's power structure wanted to deflect any adverse publicity; the mayor and business leaders believed that the "outside agitators" would go away if they were ignored.

Meanwhile, Klansmen in Meridian and surrounding Lauderdale County had taken notice of Schwerner and resolved to eliminate him. "The Jew-boy with the beard at Meridian" and his wife were seen as race mixers, who were threatening to upset the balance of power in the city, where blacks had always known their place in the shadows. The Klansmen closely monitored Schwerner's movements and planned to murder him when he ventured outside the Meridian city limits. Sooner or later, they hoped, Schwerner would want to reach out to rural blacks in one of the nearby counties. When he crossed the city line—into nearby Neshoba or Newton County, where the Klan operated with impunity—they would be waiting.

On Sunday, June 21, 1964, Schwerner, Chaney, and Andrew Goodman, a Freedom Summer volunteer who had been in Meridian for just a little more than twenty-four hours, set off to investigate the burning of a black church in nearby Neshoba County, about twelve miles east of the town of Philadelphia, in the Longdale community. Goodman was a handsome and gregarious college student from New York City. Along with Schwerner and Chaney, he was fresh from a three-day volunteer orientation and training session at the Western College for Women in Oxford, Ohio; now he was eager to hit the ground in Mississippi. He sat in the back seat of a blue Ford Fairlane station wagon with Chaney at the steering wheel and Schwerner poring over a map in the front passenger seat.

Schwerner had informed CORE officials and the FBI agent assigned to Meridian of the trio's trip to the site of the church bombing. Normally, he checked in with the movement office after completing a trip. But by that Sunday evening, CORE and COFO officials in Meridian and Jackson had not heard from the men and reported their disappearance.

Over the next few days, Meridian became the center of the civil rights movement. Helicopters and sailors from the Meridian naval station searched the thirty-mile stretch between the city and Philadelphia, Mississippi; FBI agents trudged through thickets near the area where the men had last been seen; and camera crews from the major television networks filled the hotels in Meridian. President Lyndon Johnson told a news conference in Washington that he was keeping in touch with the FBI as they scoured the search area and that agents would do everything possible to find the missing men. Neshoba County Chief Deputy Sheriff Cecil Price told the FBI that he had arrested the men Sunday afternoon for speeding but had released them at around ten thirty that evening. Price told investigators that he had watched the Ford station wagon disappear down Highway 19 South on the way to Meridian. Price's boss, Sheriff Lawrence

Rainey, disavowed any knowledge of what had happened to the men and speculated that they had left the state.

Nearly three months of intensive searches and national and international scrutiny finally yielded the bodies of the three men, buried beneath an earthen dam about six miles southwest of Philadelphia. Investigators would later learn the awful truth of what had happened to the civil rights workers after they were released from the jail in Philadelphia. Deputy Sheriff Price had delivered them into the hands of fellow Klan members, who drove them to Rock Cut Road, on the outskirts of Meridian. Schwerner was shot and killed first; Goodman was executed next. Chaney apparently struggled with the posse before he was severely beaten and shot three times at close range. The Klansmen then used a bulldozer to bury the bodies beneath the tons of dirt in the dam.

Reaction in Mississippi and in Meridian to the murders ranged from defiance to ambivalence. Only a week after the bodies were unearthed, the *Meridian Star* reported that Governor Paul Johnson told a cheering crowd at the Neshoba County Fair in Philadelphia that the state "must outmaneuver those who would destroy us and our way of life." Speaking two miles from the clay dirt pond where the slain civil rights workers were found, Johnson sent a message to the nation and the world, saying, "Our people are not going to be browbeaten and they're not going to be run over."

Months later, Sheriff Rainey and Deputy Price were charged with conspiracy in the murders. Although seven Klan members, including Imperial Wizard Sam Bowers and Price, were charged with federal civil rights violations and served prison terms ranging from three to six years, Rainey escaped punishment. The state of Mississippi never prosecuted anyone for the slayings. To the Meridian establishment, who had never wanted trouble from "outside agitators," what happened to Schwerner, Goodman, and Chaney on the edge of Meridian might just as well have happened on the moon.

But the Klan had not finished terrorizing the city. Its members, at the urging of Sam Bowers, blamed Meridian's prosperous Jewish community for recruiting the Freedom Riders and supporting the civil rights movement. In the same way that blacks and their churches and schools had been targets of the Klan's bombing and arson campaign, Jews and their homes and synagogues now came under attack. The Klan's main target was Meyer Davidson, a Meridian businessman from a prominent family. The local police and the FBI advised him of the danger posed by the Klan; and, with his cooperation, they devised a plan to entrap a team of bombers who had been sent to Meridian to attack Davidson's home. On Saturday, June 29, 1968, the trap was sprung, and downtown Meridian exploded in a fusillade of bullets that left one of the would-be assassins dead and the other wounded. No law enforcement officers were killed, and the local Klan suffered a mortal blow.

✳

People in Grandma's neighborhood, around Forty-fifth and Forty-sixth avenues in south central Meridian, felt sorry for the three murdered boys, but many were too preoccupied with their own survival to get really worked up about the murders. The neighborhood was pinned between the railroad tracks at the end of Forty-sixth Avenue and bordered by the muddy Sowashee Creek. It contained a smattering of ranch-style brick houses and a depressing abundance of shacks. Sidewalks were nonexistent in the neighborhood; well-worn paths connecting the community of run-down houses complemented the barely paved streets.

With a few exceptions, including Grandma's house, most homes in this neighborhood lacked indoor plumbing and electricity. As late as 1970, people could be seen hoisting huge metal pans to collect water from the communal pumps outside, which were invariably in marshy areas that attracted mosquitoes and flies. One of those pumps was right across the street from Grandma's house, and it drew constant foot traffic. People took the water they collected back to the shacks and used it for drinking water, baths, laundry, and dishwashing. Many of the shacks contained claw-foot tubs, sometimes standing right in the kitchen, where it was not unusual to see children bathing, dishes being washed, and water being heated on a wood-burning stove for cooking and laundry.

Tending the stove was another source of worry for these families. From morning to evening, smoke belched from the rooftops and makeshift chimneys of the shacks. The massive black wood-burning stove had to be fed constantly to keep pace with the family's needs throughout the day. The person who drew stove duty had to be skillful in starting and maintaining the hearth. First thing in the morning, the fire had to be stoked using newspaper if the stove had grown cold overnight; then it took fresh kindling to get the pots boiling for grits or oatmeal and water for baths.

Loading the wood was tricky: every part of the hulking, cabinet-like stove could burn fingers or other body parts. The doors in its belly were pried open with a steel rod, and the pieces of wood were rammed inside.

Once the day began—the baths taken and the breakfasts of eggs, grits, bacon, and skillet bread consumed—many of the grown-ups went to work in the slaughterhouses, stockyards, and timber mills around Meridian and Lauderdale County. The people who lived in the brick houses were either retired or worked as schoolteachers or low-level clerks in the city's bureaucracy. Groups of freshly scrubbed children made the trek to Oakland Heights Elementary School. Others trudged across Fifth Street to Carver or Kate Griffin Junior High School, while high school students had to walk up to Fifth Street to catch the only bus to Meridian High School. The smallest children, those headed to Oakland Heights, had to make their way to school as best they could, without a bus; at this time of the morning, only the city garbage trucks, with black men swinging off their backs, were making their rounds in the neighborhood.

Few people in the neighborhood owned cars, other than those who lived in the brick houses. Every now and then, a rickety pickup truck rumbled along the stretch of shacks, with children piled in the back and the cab packed with three or four riders. But, for the most part, walking was the standard form of transportation. Men dressed in overalls and worn brogans carried lunch pails and made their way toward Fifth and Eighth streets, the main arteries into commercial and industrial Meridian. Women pushing shopping carts taken from the grocery stores on Eighth Street went about their daily errands. Meridian had no public transportation system, and taxis, which tended to hang out at the Trailways bus station, were a luxury few could afford.

There were no stores in the neighborhood. The nearest curb market was Garrett's on Fifth Street, but the place stocked only chips, beer, candy, maybe some bologna or luncheon meat, and crackers. The major food stores were on Eighth Street—the IGA, the A&P, and a Winn-Dixie, if you were willing to travel a bit farther down the road to College Park Plaza. For a time, Grandma operated an eatery out of a one-room hut in her front yard at 4516 Third Street. She sold hot dogs, hamburgers, candy, cookies, soda pop, pickled pigs' feet, boiled eggs, and other small treats. Everybody in the neighborhood knew they could always get a bottle of "Co-Cola" and a bag of peanuts at "Miss Alma's" snack stand—and sometimes they could get it on credit until the first or third of the month when the welfare and Social Security checks arrived.

People tended to congregate on their porches at the end of the day. Children did their homework, women shelled field peas or husked corn, men got caught up in card games of Spades or Tonk, passing around a bottle of beer or liquor. Much of the activity in the neighborhood was observed from those porches, reflected in the gossip:

Honey, did you see what that child was wearing yesterday? She might as well justa showed her ass.

I heard Robert Earl and Carrie Ann was fighting again; they sho' do love to show out, don't they?

Did you hear about Clarence getting drunk and spending all his paycheck at the pool hall? I feel sorry for his wife, that po' woman.

The evenings on the porches helped to make everyone, even the neighbors who lived in the brick houses with the fancy carports, feel connected. Everybody spoke to one another and kept up a constant dialogue on the state of affairs in the neighborhood.

Weekends were when the neighborhood came alive, especially if checks had just arrived. First thing Saturday morning, entire families trudged to the grocery stores to spend their precious money on cheap cuts of pork, ground beef, chicken, sugar, coal oil for the kerosene lamps, and big vats of lard for cooking. Many families grew their own vegetables behind their shacks, or they waited for one of the men pushing a wheelbarrow or cart overflowing with vegetables and fruit for sale to come around. Saturdays were also the days for doing laundry. After many trips to the water pump, women and children slaved over a big metal tub, running the clothes over the rough teeth of a wooden washboard. Those who could afford it made the trip to one of the washhouses on Forty-ninth Avenue or Fifth Street.

In the afternoon, the sweet and tangy smell of barbecue floated through the neighborhood. Ribs and chicken and sausage sizzled on old barrels sliced in half and fired with charcoal and lighter fluid. Wizened old men supervised the barbecue, drinking beer or sharing a bottle of whiskey with buddies who happened by to shoot the breeze. The women sat around in lawn chairs, their job done after preparing great bowls of potato salad and jugs of Kool-Aid for the children, who played horseshoes in the dirt or hopscotch in the streets. Other families chose to fry up catfish, bass, or perch, along with french fries and hush puppies and okra.

The Saturday afternoon smells in Grandma's neighborhood made the mouth water and the eyes itch from all the smoke wafting around. Stray dogs that hadn't been seen in days suddenly returned to wait around for the inevitable scraps.

Saturday afternoons were reserved for cookouts and family gatherings, but at night the streets came alive with raucousness. Della's Café down on Forty-sixth Avenue was where the neighborhood people ventured to listen to crooners like Al Green and David Ruffin on the jukebox, eat fried chicken sandwiches or pickled pigs' feet, play pool, and drink cans of Pabst, Budweiser, and Schlitz. Della also sold pints of gin and whiskey. Every now and then, children would dart in and out to buy penny cookies and candy or a bag of chips and a Coke. The old run-down café, a wooden shack piled onto bricks, looked as sturdy as a heap of toothpicks, but it hosted a never-ending stream of traffic into the early hours of Sunday. Occasionally, gunshots rang out or fights broke out. Della was a big, no-nonsense woman who usually wore a head rag and kept a lipful of snuff. And Della didn't tolerate fights or foolishness in her café; she kept a pistol and a baseball bat on hand in case she needed to "go upside somebody head."

Before the roosters started waking up the neighborhood on Sunday morning, Della's had closed, and most people made their way to the neighborhood church, Bethel Baptist, which sat on the corner of Forty-fifth and Third, right across the street from Grandma's house. With its T-shaped white façade and porchlike entrance, the church was the most imposing structure in the neighborhood. There was no parking lot, so churchgoers with cars had to park on the street or on the shoulder of yards. Church services began with Sunday school, which was dutifully attended by groups of well-washed children. Shortly after Sunday school, the pastor preached a blistering sermon on the wages of sin to an attentive congregation.

After church, everyone returned home to sit down for the ritual of Sunday dinner—pot roast and potatoes, perhaps, or chicken and dressing or smothered pork chops. The pots of black-eyed peas or lima beans that had been simmering on the stove throughout the church service were brought to the table and served with big, buttery chunks of corn bread. Everything was washed down with hefty pitchers of sweet iced tea. Invariably, the rest of the day was devoted to naps and trying to get ready for Monday and another week of much the same routine.

When we pulled into Grandma's driveway on that Sunday night in December 1966—a few days after Christmas—we had missed most of that day's ritual. Yvonne and Daddy and I were too tired to do anything but fall into the bed Grandma had prepared for us. But over the years of my childhood, I would spend many Sundays in Grandma's house at 4516 Third Street, a place where I would come of age and begin to suspect that my life extended far beyond the railroad tracks and the alleys that defined existence for most of the people in that neighborhood.

✳

As we settled into Grandma's house, she began getting up early every morning to make breakfast, usually grits, eggs, sausage, and biscuits. Yvonne ate the eggs, sausage, and biscuits, but she picked at the grits.

"What is this?" she whispered to Daddy. "I never eaten anything like this before."

Daddy chuckled and said, "Those are what's called grits, kinda like a cereal made out of corn meal."

Yvonne did not seem satisfied. She had tasted pap before, which was a South African dish of stiff corn porridge, but only blacks ate the stuff; coloured (mixed-race) people, the South African racial group with which she identified herself, did not. The congealed white puddle dotted with butter and pepper repulsed her, and she pushed the plate away.

"I cannot eat this," she told Daddy.

"It's all right," he said, rubbing her shoulder. "You'll get used to the food here before you know it."

Grandma didn't seem to notice Yvonne's reluctance to eat grits, and Daddy used a biscuit to sop up the traces of food left on his plate.

Daddy told Yvonne that he would have to leave soon for the Port of New York, where he would board a ship and return, via stops along the West African coast, to South Africa. "Y'all are gonna stay here with my mama while I'm gone," he said.

Yvonne just nodded. It's not as if we have anywhere else to go, she said to herself.

"When will you be back?" Yvonne asked. "And when are we going to move into our own house?"

"Well, I should be back in a few months, and by then we can find a place of our own," he assured her.

Yvonne looked at Grandma, whose back was turned as she stooped over the sink washing dishes. They hadn't talked to each other very much; it was as if they were both just doing what Daddy expected of them. Yvonne didn't look too happy. She tried to smile, but as she looked at the tidy, worn floors of Grandma's kitchen, she kept thinking, I expected more than this, I deserve better than this. But she never said anything.

Grandma's house had two bedrooms, a large living room, a dining room, and a kitchen with a washer and dryer in the corner. Pictures of Jesus, Martin Luther King, and John F. Kennedy hung on the walls of the living room.

A hallway leading from Grandma's bedroom connected to the only bathroom, which was warmed by a small gas heater in the wintertime. Yvonne, Daddy, and I slept in the room next to the bathroom. Like Grandma's room, it contained a four-poster bed and two heavy dressers. Over one of the dressers was a poster-size, framed portrait of a woman who looked like Grandma—she had short hair and the same wide nose and full lips. The portrait looked really old, and the woman's eyes always seemed to follow me around the room.

Grandma's dining room was dominated by a table with a wood and glass top and the four chairs that were jammed around it. A corner cabinet held all of Grandma's fancy dishes and plates. On the other side of the table was a bureau adorned with an assortment of wooden and porcelain figures. Prominent among them was an intricately hand-carved wooden head of a man wearing what looked like an exotic African headdress. All around "the African head," as I came to call it, were wooden figurines of elephants, their tusks raised in battle; giraffes craning their necks toward some invisible tree; and tiny African warriors holding spears and shields. Daddy had stocked Grandma's mini-menagerie from his trips abroad to South Africa. Also in the dining room, a picture of Jesus and the twelve disciples perched on the wall above a large, white deep freezer.

The kitchen contained a green Formica table and three chairs, an electric stove, and an ancient refrigerator. A clock over the washer and dryer ticked off the time, and a calendar from Berry and Gardner Funeral Home counted the days and months. A kitchen window looked out into the backyard, where a gnarled apple tree stood in a field once used to grow collard greens, corn, tomatoes, and other vegetables. Grandma's chicken house was also in the backyard, and a few cats and dogs lolled around half-hidden in patches of grass.

Daddy began introducing Yvonne to people in Meridian. First he brought over Miss Inez, one of his long-time friends, who took Yvonne around the city and helped her meet other residents.

"You the first person I ever met from Africa," Miss Inez, a big, jolly woman who wore a permanent smile, confessed to Yvonne, after giving her a tour of downtown Meridian. "How you like it over here so far?"

"It will be better when Dave comes back," said Yvonne, as she stared at all the black people sitting on the street corners and walking around downtown.

By the time Daddy left for New York a couple of weeks later, Yvonne had managed to get a job as a nurse's assistant at Mattee Hersee Hospital. While she worked, I stayed with Grandma. For most of the day, I played in the front yard or sat with her on the front porch while she talked to neighbors who dropped by to visit. When Yvonne came home from the hospital, we ate the meals Grandma had prepared, and Yvonne often told Grandma stories about what had happened during her shift at the hospital.

"This old white man told the doctor today he don't want black nurses waiting on him," she told Grandma as they shared a cup of coffee at the kitchen table. They had eased into a more sociable relationship now that Daddy was gone.

Grandma snorted and said, "Honey, that don't surprise me none. These crackers in Meridian ain't never gonna change. What did the doctor say about it?"

"The doctor told the man that if he did not want black nurses to look after him, then he could get up and go someplace else," Yvonne reported with a laugh. "I never knew that kind of racism existed outside South Africa."

Grandma just shook her head and told her, "Chile, you ain't seen nothing yet. These white folks in Mississippi ain't got no use for black folks. I don't know how they act over there where y'all come from in South Africa, but over here they just plain low-down. You'll see what I'm talkin' 'bout fo' long."

Sure enough, while she was shopping at a downtown store, Yvonne encountered a white clerk who made her wait while she helped a white customer. Finally, the clerk, a pimply-faced girl, turned to Yvonne and demanded, "Well, what *you* want?"

Yvonne scowled at the girl and told her, "Not a damn thing!" before walking out of the store.

By the time Yvonne finished the nurse's training program at Mattee

Hersee, she had figured out how to get around on her own. Her next job was at Rush Foundation Hospital, one of four hospitals near downtown Meridian. Now she was making more money and was enrolled in the licensed practical nurse's training program at Meridian Junior College. Daddy wrote letters and sometimes called to make sure we were all right. Yvonne told him about her new job and her classes.

"When are you coming home, Dave?" she asked.

"Just hold on, it won't be long now," he promised. "We gonna get our own place as soon as I get back, so just hang in there now."

But Yvonne had already started looking for a new place to live. We moved out of Grandma's house after several months. Grandma didn't seem too happy when we left.

"What's the matter, ain't my house good enough for you?" Grandma demanded when Yvonne told her we were moving out.

"I just want to have my own house," Yvonne tried to explain, even though this was only partially true. Grandma's house had begun to feel like a prison to Yvonne: the house was too small, the bathroom was tiny, there were cracks in the wooden plank floor, and the little room where we slept was crammed with clothes and suitcases. And although she and Grandma tried to get along, their relationship was hopelessly strained. Yvonne was determined to stake out her independence and move toward her vision of the American Dream, while Grandma needed to demonstrate that she was the boss of her house. Deep down, they were strangers, approaching each other as foreigners in unknown territory, made familiar only by their mutual connection to Daddy.

We moved into a narrow two-bedroom house on Eleventh Street in an area of town called Red Line. The house was near an elementary school and kindergarten, where I was enrolled in nursery school while Yvonne worked in the daytime. She was going to school full time now as we settled into the tiny house, waiting for Daddy to come home. I missed running around Grandma's house and sitting with her on the porch, but I also liked having my own room at the new house.

When Daddy came home, we moved again, to a bigger place on Fifteenth Street, on the other side of Red Line. The new house had three bedrooms, a spacious dining room and den, and a big backyard next to a carport. We lived there for about six months, but we had to move out because Daddy's former wife Pearl went to court and claimed half of it. So Daddy sold the house and gave her half the money. We moved into a trailer outside Meridian, in a remote area of dirt roads and dense woods called Lost Gap, or "the country," as we came to call it.

Daddy had been married three times before he married Yvonne. All of the marriages ended in divorce. He had already fathered four children, two girls and two boys. One of the boys died as an infant and was said to be buried under the apple tree in Grandma's backyard. Daddy and his most recent ex-wife, Pearl, had two children, Alma Anita and Dave Jr., who lived with their maternal grandmother in Jackson. Daddy's other daughter, named Natalie, whom I met only once during my childhood, lived somewhere in New York.

✳

Daddy decided to retire from the merchant marines in 1968 because of high blood pressure and heart problems. He had been a chief steward for twenty years and had been to ports all over the world. Daddy had grown up in Meridian, but he left home at fourteen to join the navy; he told Grandma that he was "ready to get on the water." The navy found out how old he was and rejected him, so he waited until he was fifteen and somehow talked himself into the merchant marines.

Grandma was happy that he was coming home to Meridian. "My baby finally gonna get a chance to settle down," she told Yvonne when she found out about his retirement. Yvonne was also happy that Daddy was ending his career at sea because she was worried about his health. Daddy looked healthy—he was five feet nine inches tall, weighed about 180 pounds, and had never really been sick—but he smoked filterless Pall Mall cigarettes and could never sit still for very long. After we got settled in our trailer out in Lost Gap, Daddy got himself hired as Meridian's first black salesman for the Life Insurance Company of Georgia.

In March 1968, my brother Xavier was born. Daddy and Yvonne had never told me that I was going to have a little brother; I first found out about him when they brought him home from the hospital. But something was wrong: the doctors said that he was deformed; and, as he grew older, they were able to determine that he was retarded. Everyone thought that I was too young to understand his condition. I went into the bedroom to sneak a peek at him one day. He was so tiny and pale, with sandy brown hair. He didn't move around that much, and his hands were gnarled with cerebral palsy. Sometimes Daddy and Yvonne whispered to each other so that I couldn't hear them; all I could figure out was that Xavier was sick but that he was going to get better. As Yvonne began to work full time, and sometimes overtime, Grandma started taking care of Xavier.

The doctors in Meridian wanted to put Xavier in a special home for disabled children in Jackson because he had been diagnosed with severe mental retardation. Daddy and Yvonne took him to Jackson to be examined by a specialist, who also recommended placing him in an environment in which he could learn basic life skills and maybe improve his language capacity. But Grandma insisted that Xavier stay in Meridian.

"He belong with his family," she scolded Daddy. "It just ain't right to put that baby in some home where he gonna be surrounded by a bunch a doctors and strangers who don't really care nothin' about him."

Yvonne tried to convince Daddy that putting Xavier in the home was the best thing for him.

"Dave, we need to listen to the doctors in Jackson," she reasoned with him when they were alone.

"But he's our son. We cain't just turn our backs on him like that," said Daddy.

"We not leaving him. But he need to be in that school so they can help him," Yvonne explained.

For a while, Daddy seemed to consider the benefits of putting Xavier in the school; he and Yvonne made the ninety-mile trip to Jackson several times to talk to the doctors. But in the end, Grandma won him over, and Xavier stayed with her in Meridian while Daddy, Yvonne, and I lived in Lost Gap.

Now I saw Xavier only when Daddy dropped me off at Grandma's house or when I went there after school. I remember going into Grandma's bedroom one time and seeing Xavier stretched across the bed. I could tell there was something different about him; he just cried and cried. Grandma didn't know what was wrong with him, until one day she noticed that he had an angry, raw rash on the back of his legs. He screamed every time she tried to put lotion or Vaseline on it; even a special ointment that a doctor prescribed wasn't working. So Grandma stopped Mr. Jeff, a leathery, old bow-legged man who always wore knee-high boots and overalls, and asked for some of the axle grease from the wagon he steered through the neighborhood. He agreed, and she applied the thick, black grease to the rash on Xavier's legs. Within a few days, the rash was gone, and Xavier stopped crying and looked and acted just like a regular baby. Grandma believed that the Lord had given Xavier to her for safekeeping, and it was apparent that she would just as soon die as have Daddy or Yvonne put him away in some home in Jackson.

✳

We continued to live in the new trailer in Lost Gap. I started school at age six at St. Patrick's Catholic School near downtown Meridian. The school was a one-story brick building next door to St. Patrick's Catholic Church. Directly behind the school was a red brick apartment building where the nuns lived—a place where I spent many mornings being punished for some prank I pulled in school. Most of the time, I wound up in the principal's office, where I would receive my lashing and go back to the classroom and raise more hell.

One of my favorite places to go when Daddy picked me up from school and dropped me at Grandma's was to Miss Sis's house, just across the street. Miss Sis and most of her ten children lived in a three-room shack that seemed to bulge at the seams when everybody gathered inside. I loved to sit in the front room and watch television with her children. Three big couches and a big black-and-white television took up most of the room, and everybody huddled together to watch shows like *Bonanza, The Virginian,* and *Dark Shadows.* Even though Grandma had a snack waiting for me after school at her house, I knew I could always eat whatever Miss Sis was cooking.

I went there one day to play with two of her sons, Ernest James and Freelo (whose real name was Jerry), and ended up eating a piece of fried chicken fresh from the skillet and cracking jokes with everybody. Miss Sis was a stout woman with short hair, which she always kept wrapped in a scarf; her bottom lip invariably brimmed with chewing tobacco or snuff. Ernest James and I were in the kitchen getting our faces greasy on his mama's chicken when he asked me, "Man, what is you? Is you white or black?" Ernest James was skinny and chocolate-colored—in fact, most of the kids in the neighborhood were dark—and he said he had never seen somebody who looked like me before: high yellow with long, curly hair.

"I'm black, just like you," I told him, in between stuffing my mouth with the juicy chicken and bread. "What you doing calling me white?" I demanded. "I'm a-tell Miss Sis."

Ernest James just about died laughing while he picked away at a chicken wing, but I didn't think it was funny. Other children had started calling me names like "African blood and guts" and "white nigger," so it didn't seem like a joke to me.

I had first noticed the teasing and the taunts one afternoon when I was out playing with a group of kids from the block: Ernest James, Freelo, Bogie, Lester, Toby, and Leroy. We were full into a game of cowboys and Indians. Because we didn't have bikes or toy guns, we used what we could find: sticks and tree branches from a nearby field became our "horses."

"I got me a good one this time," hollered Freelo, dragging a branch out of the field.

"Yours ain't better than mine," Bogey challenged him, while the rest of us struggled to find the "horse" that would make us the leader of the posse. When everyone finished elbowing each other in search of their "horses," the wild steeds had to be groomed, so we stripped off all the leaves and thoroughly cleaned them. Finally, we had to properly bridle the "horses" by tying a piece of string around their heads to keep them under control.

All that was left to do was assign roles, a process that became heated at times. Most every boy wanted to be the Lone Ranger, the leader, with his trusty stallion, Silver. Nobody wanted to be Tonto, the Lone Ranger's sidekick, and certainly nobody wanted to be a lesser cowboy hero like Sheriff Matt Dillon from *Gunsmoke*. Once every boy had his cowboy hero role—I was Shiloh, and my "horse" was Ranger—the whole pack gathered to whip through the streets around Forty-sixth Avenue.

The sight of us riding those stick "horses" all around the neighborhood, kicking up dust and galloping to some urgent gunfight, must have appeared comical. But riding the "horses" was a mighty serious matter—and don't let somebody step on the tail of another cowboy hero's "horse"!

"Dog, l'il Dave, watch what you doing! You done stepped on my horse!" Ernest James howled. A fight was liable to break out, because every boy realized how much work had gone into finding and grooming that "horse."

Our posse had just tied up our prized colts at the corral near Miss Sis's front porch when Yvonne pulled up in Daddy's car.

"David, it's time to go home now," she called. "Tell your friends bye and let's go."

I was embarrassed and angry with Yvonne because the cowpokes were just getting ready for another sweep through the neighborhood. I could also see how the other boys stared at Yvonne and scrunched up their faces at the funny way she talked and the strangeness of her accent. I reluctantly said good-bye to the boys and turned over my "horse" Ranger to my buddy Ernest James.

As I got in the car beside Yvonne, one of the boys—Freelo, I think— yelled, "Hey, y'all, l'il Dave got a white mama!"

"I ain't never seen nobody look like her," another cowboy hollered out. I couldn't tell whether Yvonne had heard them. But I had, and I burned with humiliation and shame because everybody now thought that I had a white mama.

More and more, I began to realize that Yvonne and I were different— at least that's how the people in Grandma's neighborhood viewed us. Yvonne worked a lot, so she never made the effort to get to know people like Miss Sis or any of the other gossipy women in the neighborhood. Everybody knew we had come from overseas, so all ears and eyes were naturally attuned to what Yvonne was up to. By extension, I was painfully aware of all the things that made me stand out among the other boys: I was hopelessly pale, I had "good hair"—that is, jet black, curly locks— and Yvonne was zealously protective of me, limiting my play time with the other boys.

"You don't need to be spending a lot of time with those dirty little boys," she would say.

That afternoon began the pattern of being taunted because I didn't look like everybody else and because my mama looked like a white woman. It didn't help matters when I developed a severe stutter, and the kids ribbed me even more when I tried to defend Yvonne and myself.

"I'm g-g-gonna tell m-m-my Daddy if y'all keep b-b-bothering me," I sputtered.

Most of the boys just mimicked me and burst out laughing. But one of them, Toby, an older boy built like a beanpole, wanted to know why everybody called me "African blood and guts." At that point, all I knew was that Yvonne talked funny and looked different from all the other mothers. No one in the family had told me that we had come from Africa; I knew only that this was one of the rumors drifting around that dead-end neighborhood where everybody seemed to know everybody else's business.

If we were from Africa, Toby ventured, maybe there was a way to get back there; maybe if the kids in the neighborhood worked together, he insisted, we could find our way to Bassamakoula. Toby said he had seen a television program about a place in Africa called Bassamakoula, and maybe that's where I was from. I didn't know anything about Africa, much less some place called Bassamakoula, but I was willing to do anything to help Toby embark on his journey.

Toby figured that the best way to get to Bassamakoula was to build a raft and float there on the nearby Sowashee Creek. Along with four other boys—Ernest James, Bogie, Lester, and Darrell—we set out to build a raft out of discarded plywood and worn-out tires, assembling it under a bridge that spanned the Sowashee. We worked on the raft every opportunity we got: after school, on weekends, even late on week nights when I was staying over at Grandma's house. Sometimes we saw Mr. Jeff hauling buckets of slop over the railroad tracks to the pen where he kept his hogs. Occasionally a hobo glared at us from a boxcar as a train passed overhead. We worked hard to make sure our raft could make it safely to Bassamakoula. Surely such a place was a long way away, and navigating our raft among the sand drifts and the perilous piles of trash scattered along the creek would be only the first challenge before we reached the sea or the ocean, whichever would take us to the now-mythical land of Bassamakoula, and Africa.

Everyone was sworn to secrecy about our journey. I wasn't about to tell anyone, but I did look for Bassamakoula on a map and in the encyclopedia in the school library. Though I couldn't find any mention of the fabled country, I didn't lose my enthusiasm for our quest. Besides, Toby had seen a show about Bassamakoula on television, and I wanted more than anything to find out about this place called Africa that had given Yvonne her strange accent.

After two weeks of preparation, we all gathered around the raft on the shores of the creek. We chose to leave on a Saturday, figuring that we could reach our destination by Monday. The raft was built out of two sheets of plywood we'd found in an open field, about a dozen four-by-four planks, and two tires on either end to keep the thing afloat. An old bed sheet attached to a fishing pole lay furled on the raft; Toby said we would use it as a sail once we reached the open waters beyond the Sowashee. One by one, we boarded the raft, which creaked and groaned beneath the mounting weight, and pushed off into the churning creek waters.

"Y'all need to keep still," admonished Toby, as one of the tires split off from the raft and drifted ahead of us. Nobody seemed to worry at first when other pieces of the raft began to surrender to the weight and the water. Finally, Ernest James hollered out the unthinkable: "We gonna drown, y'all! Get me off this thang!"

We had floated only about thirty feet—we hadn't even cleared the other side of the bridge—and suddenly all the boys were abandoning the raft. I reluctantly jumped off the doomed craft and joined them on the creek bed, as we watched our dream of exploring the mysteries of Bassamakoula and Africa break up and get stuck in the pilings beneath the bridge. Since we had been denied our African adventure, we did the next best thing: we plunged buck-naked into a swimming hole in the creek and swam until our bellies ached with hunger.

From that day forward, I embraced my Africanness more readily and proudly. It didn't matter that my friends and I had failed to reach the shores of Bassamakoula, on that distant Dark Continent; it didn't matter that we were hopelessly ignorant about Africa. All that mattered to me was that I had been validated as a citizen of Africa—Toby and the other boys had not doubted the wisdom or possibility of our journey—and some of the glory of our aborted adventure clung to me. I was no longer just "l'il Dave" who had come from overseas with his white-looking mama. I had become, to my mind at least, royalty, the scion of a resplendent past, a past now mine to create, embellish, and embroider whenever I needed to feel special.

✳

A few weeks after the failed trip to Bassamakoula, infused with a new sense of entitlement and African noblesse oblige, I convinced Ernest James, Bogie, and his brother Lester to walk out to Lost Gap with me. I often bragged about what it was like to live there: I told all my friends that we had a swimming pool, a playground with all kinds of toys, and all the cake and ice cream and candy you could eat. In truth, Lost Gap was a lonely, hot place about twelve miles outside Meridian, but I couldn't disappoint my friends, who believed all the stories and, increasingly, the lies I told them about the treats in store for us. All we had to do was walk out there, and we could play and swim all day, I promised, and then we could sit around and watch television while feasting on unlimited quantities of goodies. Ernest James shared my love of adventure and readily accepted the challenge to walk out to Lost Gap.

Bogie, who was Ernest James's cousin, was a thickly built boy with a round face who played football and loved to wrestle. He wanted to come along too, but his brother Lester was scared.

"Bogie, how we gonna walk all the way out there?" he whimpered. Lester was scrawny and always wore a pained expression on his mousey face.

Though the sun had already begun to bake the streets, I reassured Lester and Bogie: "D-d-don't worry about nothin'. I t-t-told y'all that we got a swimming p-p-pool out there."

Ernest James, who was eager to get going, said, "Lester, l'il Dave gonna take us out to his house to have some fun. Now come on."

Lester seemed to take comfort in our confidence, and we started out from Grandma's front yard.

The first part of our journey was easy, and the four of us joked and laughed and talked about how great it would be to get in the pool and then gorge ourselves on ice cream. Nobody took notice of us as we walked up to Forty-ninth Avenue and cut over to Fifth Street, which would take us straight out to Lost Gap. The sun was now sitting high, almost as if it was focused on the four of us as we continued down the road, which suddenly seemed to be emptied of traffic. None of us had any money; we didn't need money, I had insisted, because we would be in Lost Gap in no time and all our dreams would be fulfilled. In my imagining of the merriment we were destined for, I hadn't considered what the boys would think when they discovered I had made it all up: that there was no pool, no playground with toys, no ice cream, and at best a pitcher of Kool-Aid in the refrigerator.

As we trudged on, the trip became less a quest to lead my friends to a wonderland of cool treats on a searingly hot day than a demonstration of my power over them—proof of my ability to shape them to my will and have them follow me without question. In my mind, I was African royalty—hadn't this been proved by our failed trip to Bassamakoula?—and they were my loyal subjects. I was puzzled, though, that all the pictures of Africa I came across at the library were of dark-skinned black people; I hadn't seen any pictures of yellow people with "good" hair.

We had been walking for about two hours, and at the rate we were going, I figured we'd be on the road for at least another hour, maybe longer. The sun hadn't let up, and I could see the heat rising from the road as a car occasionally whizzed past.

In an effort to rally the others—Lester was falling behind, and Ernest

James had stopped and taken off his sneakers—I joked, "Dog, y'all gonna m-m-mess around and it's g-g-gonna be t-t-too late for us to get in the p-p-pool. We need to g-g-get going."

I wasn't feeling tired at all. Eventually, we resumed our slow trek down the side of the road. Bogie hoisted Lester onto his back, and Ernest James removed his shirt.

"C-c-come on, y'all," I kept calling back to them. "We ain't got that m-m-much more t-t-to go."

But morale began to deteriorate when we rounded the bend where two cemeteries hugged the road. Lester began to cry and mewl that he was hungry and wanted to go home. Even Ernest James's fortitude began to wane.

"Damn, l'il Dave, how much more we got to walk to yo' house?" he panted.

"Yeah," Bogie chimed in, "my l'il brother is tired and hungry, and I'm startin' to get tired of this, too."

The situation was spiraling out of control, so I tried to reassure them. "Okay, we ain't g-g-got too much farther to go, y'all."

I herded the boys along toward the red dirt canyons that signaled we were about to cross the bridge over the interstate, finally closing in on Lost Gap. As we plodded along past the canyons and around a downhill bend, a solitary car—the first in a long time—breezed by. The car looked familiar, but I was so intent on shoring up morale among the boys—we were so close!—that I didn't pay much attention.

A few minutes later, just as we could see the bridge over the interstate— our halfway point—the car, a green Dodge Dart, came racing back down the road toward us. It was Daddy.

"What in the world are y'all doing out here in all this heat?" he called out. "Get on in this car, 'cause people are worried to death about y'all."

I sat in the front seat with Daddy and Ernest James; Lester and Bogie eagerly scrambled into the back seat. On the way to Grandma's house, Daddy just shook his head and kept asking me, "David, what done got into you, boy? Huh?" I just shrugged my shoulders and thought about how close we had gotten to reaching Lost Gap.

When we pulled up to Grandma's house, a lot of people were gathered in the front yard. A Mississippi State Patrol car was parked on the street, and an officer was talking to Grandma. Miss Sis rushed over and grabbed Ernest James when he got out of Daddy's car. Bogie and Lester's mother,

Nettie Pearl, jerked them across the yard and whisked them away in her car. I later heard that the boys had gotten severe whippings for leaving the neighborhood without telling anyone. But nothing happened to me. Daddy and Yvonne just scolded me and told me that I "better never do something like that again."

This incident helped to secure my reputation among parents as a "bad child, too smart for his own good," and among my friends as "a slick liar" who could get you into serious trouble. For me, however, the misadventure to Lost Gap fully revealed the power I had to concoct a myth of grandeur and purpose that soon overtook my search for identity—a myth that eventually morphed into a childhood of lies.

*

The only activity I enjoyed more than causing devilment in the streets around Grandma's house was hunting with Daddy in the woods around our trailer in Lost Gap. I begged Daddy to buy me a .22 caliber starter rifle for my seventh birthday. I felt useless on the many occasions when I tagged along through the woods as he and Dave Jr. and other men brought down squirrels and deer with their shotguns and high-caliber rifles. Daddy refused to buy me a .22—he said I was too small and couldn't handle it—but he promised to get me an air pump BB gun.

One Saturday, we drove down the road to a sporting goods store in Chunky, a town that consisted of a single strip of storefronts on the banks of the Chunky River. All sorts of weapons hung along the walls of the store: bows and arrows, pump shotguns, high-powered rifles, pistols of every caliber, hunting knives. I found the BB gun of my dreams beneath a shelf lined with rows of buckshot and other ammunition. It was a Daisy pump-action pellet gun—pellets were considered more powerful than the ordinary BBs—and its brown wooden veneer was just like that of the .22 caliber starter rifle I craved.

"You think you can handle that?" Daddy asked. "Un-huh," I mumbled, as I lifted the rifle to my shoulder, taking aim at all the imaginary squirrels and rabbits soon to incur my wrath in the woods of Lost Gap. Over the next few months, as autumn rolled around and the trees and bushes in Lost Gap braced themselves for the starkness of winter, I practiced with the BB gun: shooting cans, wild dogs that had the misfortune of straying onto our property, and any bird that dared to fly near our trailer.

One Saturday morning, before the sun made its appearance, Daddy roused me from bed and told me to get dressed because he was taking me hunting. Yvonne was still sleeping after an overnight shift at the hospital. I tumbled into the shower and then got dressed in the warmest pants and shirt I could find; winter mornings in Lost Gap were brutally cold. I brought my boots into the kitchen where Daddy and Dave Jr. were trying to figure out where we should begin our day in the woods. While I helped myself to oatmeal with maple syrup and a mug of orange juice, they weighed the merits of hunting in different sections of the vast forest that stretched downhill from the trailer.

"Well, John Taylor said he seen a buck by the lake last time we was down there," said Daddy.

"Then maybe we oughta start there and go on down past that old creek on the other side of the lake," Dave Jr. volunteered.

Daddy nodded and looked at me. "Boy, did you put on your long johns? 'Cause it's gonna be cold in them woods."

Dave Jr., who, unlike me, looked exactly like Daddy, with his round head, wide nostrils, and thin frame, had moved in with Grandma. He and Alma had left Jackson when their mother, Pearl, died in a car accident. At age fourteen, he was already using a .22 caliber rifle, and Daddy was teaching him everything about the timberlands around Lost Gap.

After retiring from the merchant marines, Daddy had bought a lot of land in Lost Gap; I never knew quite how much, but I knew that we could walk through the woods for a long time—descending into a valley lush with fir and pine trees and wildflowers; passing through a boundless field being readied for corn, tomatoes, and other crops; and rounding the banks of a lake brimming with fish—before we reached the limits of our property.

Once when Daddy and I were out driving wooden posts into the hard ground for stringing barbed wire, he told me, "All of this is ours, and there's enough room out here for all y'all—you and Dave Jr. and Alma."

"W-w-why we gotta live w-w-way out here?" I asked, trying to help steady the post for the fence that would keep in a herd of cows grazing nearby.

"Because this the only place where we gonna be able to have something we can call our own," he said, wiping the sleeve of his barn jacket across his forehead.

"Wherever you go, you know you always got somewhere to come back to. And don't you forget that, boy."

Daddy's dream was to transform the labyrinth of trees and trails and fields into a working farm, so he bought cattle, built hog pens, and cleared broad swaths of unruly bush and undergrowth around our trailer. In the early days, before Daddy started to claim the land, the trailer had looked like a rectangular dollhouse plopped down in the middle of a wilderness, accessible only by a dirt road that had been carved out of a stubborn red clay cliff. When he wasn't going door to door selling Life of Georgia insurance policies, Daddy was on his tractor, usually with a Pall Mall stuck in his mouth, firmly establishing our hold on the land in Lost Gap.

The morning of our hunting trip, we left the trailer and headed down a dirt road, where we met up with John Taylor, a big bear of a man who had served in the merchant marines with Daddy, and Gabby, one of Dave Jr.'s friends, who lived for hunting and fishing in the woods. The sun had just peeked over a hill, and the air was crisp and brittle. While the rest of the group checked and shouldered their rifles, I proudly pumped my Daisy BB gun and checked my supply of pellets; I was ready for action.

As we penetrated deeper into the cloak of trees, I had to get used to carrying a rifle while swatting away the ever-present gnats and chiggers and ducking hideously large spider webs. I had always been little more than a hunting mascot for Daddy and the others. Now I had to be extra careful about how I handled myself in the company of four deadly serious hunters.

A kind of decorum had to be observed when tracking wild game in the woods. No talking was allowed: we could use only hand signals and an occasional whisper. Everyone had to remain perfectly—often painfully—still if we stumbled on an unsuspecting deer or turkey. A sure way to get Daddy upset was to clumsily step on an old branch or log, whose dry crunch seemed to echo through the woods. The major breach of hunting etiquette was to fire your weapon without notifying the other members in your party; many people had been killed or gravely wounded in such accidents.

Up ahead of me, John Taylor abruptly stopped and slowly shouldered his rifle. Everyone in front of me—Daddy, Dave Jr., and Gabby—froze, but I was too busy choosing my steps and walked on before noticing that I had run afoul of hunting etiquette.

"Boy, be still," Daddy hissed in my direction.

For what seemed like forever, we stood in that opening in the woods until John Taylor gave up on his target—a squirrel perched high in a tree. On his signal, we plunged deeper into the netherworld of Lost Gap, stalking our prey, fending off mosquitoes and wasps, and watching out for snakes.

✳

Around the time I became a regular member of Daddy's hunting party, I started to have a recurring dream—at least I thought it was a dream. I couldn't be sure. In the dreamscape, which ran through my head like a 16mm film winding uncontrollably through my subconscious, Yvonne and Daddy were fighting. She wore a bathrobe that kept coming open and sliding off her shoulders, and he grasped at her with one hand and held a small pistol in the other. When Yvonne tried to escape through the trailer door, Daddy, his face contorted in anger, yelled something, grabbed her by the neck, and dragged her down to the yard while she screamed and tried to pull away. I stood by the door, clad in nothing but dirty underwear, crying and begging Daddy to stop beating on Yvonne. Amid all this confusion, Dave Jr. and Alma stood off to the side, laughing hysterically and urging Daddy to keep beating her.

The whole scene—like a silent movie—played over and over again in my head, popping up at the most unexpected times, edged by a haziness that made it difficult to tell whether it was indeed a nightmare or a painful memory. I had never seen Daddy and Yvonne fight, and I got along well with Dave Jr. and Alma. Though we had different mothers, I still considered them my siblings and didn't mind when they occasionally teased me about my stuttering. I never asked or told anyone about the dreamscape scene. It became the dark leitmotif of my childhood.

✳

Grandma, whose full name was Alma Mae Henderson, spent most of her life cooking in kitchens at hospitals, schools, churches, and private homes. She often took me along with her when she went to cook for Miss Patie, an elderly but spirited white lady who lived in the northern suburbs of Meridian. Miss Patie always gave me a dollar to clean her huge backyard. I would struggle behind one of those old push lawnmowers that required backbone and heft to power it along; Miss Patie apparently hadn't gotten around to buying a motorized lawnmower. While Grandma was inside, where she wore a white apron and thick-soled shoes as she commandeered Miss Patie's kitchen, I was outside huffing and puffing behind that rusty lawnmower, thinking about that dollar bill with my name on it and anticipating the familiar call to lunch.

I'd drop the lawnmower or the rake I used for gathering leaves and bound into the back entrance of the house, ravenous and ready to go home to spend my dollar on candy and cookies.

"Boy, go in there and wash your hands," Grandma would say.

When I returned, I'd find that she had arranged a nice spread of deviled eggs, ham sandwiches, 'Nilla wafers, pickles, and sweet iced tea on the little table in back of Miss Patie's sprawling brick house. Sometimes Miss Patie would come back there and ask how I was doing and whether I was doing a good job.

"Yes, ma'am, I'm taking g-g-good care of things b-b-back there," I'd manage to say while gorging on all the delicacies spread before me. Miss Patie and Grandma would just laugh and then go off to attend to some other housekeeping chore. At the end of the day, when Grandma and I packed up her car with all the leftovers and bags of clothes Miss Patie gave her, I would receive my dollar bill. Even though I had overindulged myself on Miss Patie's delicious food, I couldn't wait to get to the other side of town to spend my dollar at the curb market near Grandma's house.

Except for the weekends, I was spending more time at Grandma's house, and I came to love her even more. She was capable of great kindness and warmth—gathering me into her arms and ample bosom when I was sad—but she didn't hesitate to get out the thick black belt or venture outside to pick herself a switch, a long, sturdy vine torn from a tree or bush, if I misbehaved.

One day, Grandma sat me down at the table in her kitchen, which always smelled of her delicious pound cake, and taught me how to "tell the time." "You gettin' to be a big boy, so you need to know how to tell what time it is," she said. She patiently explained how the big hand and the little hand on the clock worked. I had no way of knowing then that Grandma could not read or write because she had been forced to drop out of school to care for her sick mother.

In between cooking for white folks and caring for her family, Grandma had also found time to devote to the civil rights movement in Meridian.

Long before Freedom Summer of 1964, Grandma was getting telephone calls from the local NAACP coordinator, Miss Witherspoon, urging her to come out to some church rally. "We need everybody to come out and help folks get registered to vote," she advised Grandma.

Grandma never talked about her work in the civil rights struggle, perhaps because she simply considered it part of her role as guardian and caretaker in the neighborhood. Much of what I know I learned later from others, such as my sister Alma and a neighborhood friend, Miss Bettye Holman.

Grandma was part of a clandestine network of unofficial support staff in the city, and her role in the movement intensified after the Freedom Riders triggered the cascade of hundreds of activists into Mississippi. She opened her home to them, feeding and protecting the serious young men and women whose cars and station wagons, with license plates from places like New York, Ohio, and Illinois, lined up outside on the street. Grandma also knew Mamie Chaney, the mother of James Chaney, who, along with Michael Schwerner and Andrew Goodman, would be murdered by the Klan in 1964.

When the mostly white civil rights workers from the North first arrived in Meridian, the local NAACP, in conjunction with CORE, arranged for them to live in a nondescript house on Forty-fourth Avenue, between Third and Hooper streets, near the railroad tracks and right around the corner from Grandma's house. The decision to place the civil rights workers in a predominantly black area was based on several considerations. Most white landlords in Meridian were reluctant to rent to anyone connected to the civil rights movement. The white man who did step forward to offer the workers shelter, a retired railroad engineer named Mr. Cunningham, owned what were called section houses, originally intended for railroad crews, in Grandma's neighborhood. In addition, Mamie Chaney, who often sheltered civil rights workers at her own house, had recommended placing them in this community to avoid detection by the Klan. No doubt she was sure, according to Miss Holman, that people such as Grandma would protect and care for the young men and women. (Mrs. Chaney had often helped to babysit Alma and Dave Jr. when they stayed with Grandma.)

Initially, people in the neighborhood were leery about having the whites in their midst, but the community soon warmed to them and made them feel welcome. More white volunteers arrived and stayed for a week or two, sometimes crowding the homes in the neighborhood, including

Grandma's. At first they were quiet, and those who lived in the house near the railroad tracks mostly kept to themselves. But soon they began to encourage the neighbors to get involved in voting rights activities. At that time, black citizens who tried to register to vote at the Lauderdale County Courthouse were forced to take a literacy test, in which they had to interpret a section of the Mississippi state constitution, and were then subject to a poll tax.

As the voter registration struggle expanded, the landlord who owned the section houses began receiving death threats from the Klan. Somehow, word had gotten out all over the city that he had provided housing for the activists. In an environment in which black churches were being bombed and lives threatened, the landlord began cautiously trying to find a way to remove the young people from his property. He didn't have to wait long or make any drastic moves, however, because on Sunday, June 21, 1964, with the disappearance of James Chaney, Michael Schwerner, and Andrew Goodman, the whites began to leave Grandma's neighborhood. As I learned later from Miss Holman, many people in the movement knew instinctively that the men had been murdered and that the FBI and the local police were unable or unwilling to protect them in Mississippi. With the Klan serving notice that it intended to eliminate all its opponents, both black and white, all the white students had left the neighborhood by the time the bodies of the three civil rights workers were found buried in an earthen dam forty-four days later.

✳

By the time the civil rights movement climaxed and waned with the death of the Rev. Martin Luther King Jr. and attention shifted from events around Meridian, Grandma had divorced my Granddaddy Frank. Most of her other relatives were dead, but she had tried to tell me as much as she could about my Mississippi ancestors. Frank had been born in Enterprise, Mississippi, just outside Meridian. His mother was a former slave, and his father, a white man, was the son of a former plantation owner. As a young man, Frank had passed for white to get a job on the railroads in Chicago. I used to think that he *was* a white man. When Daddy took me to visit him, I noticed that Frank's hair was straight and completely white, and the veins in his arms, hands, and neck beamed blue and green whenever he strained or stretched. He was a tall, gaunt-looking man—not skinny, just wiry and muscular after a life of working on the railroads.

Daddy and I often sat with him in the shade of his covered porch, cracking and shelling pecans, talking and listening to the radio. Grand-daddy Frank was a mystery to me, but I also felt a secret bond with him because we were both so pale. I took comfort in this, and I learned to steel myself against the taunts of neighborhood children who routinely called me such names as "white nigger."

I was less equipped to deal with the cries of "African blood and guts" that continued to pester me during my childhood. While I had a pretty good grasp of my Mississippi roots, nobody explained anything about Africa, that faraway place where I suspected I had been born. I was too scared to ask Daddy or Yvonne about Africa—they seemed preoccupied with Xavier—and Grandma seemed reluctant to tell me what she knew.

"You need to ask yo' mama about all that," she said, shaking her head and sucking her teeth. "It's a shame she won't tell you nothin' 'bout where you come from."

Of all the people in Grandma's neighborhood, no one knew more about other people's business than Ernest, affectionately called "Hog" be-cause of his squat, round body. Ernest, who was Miss Sis's brother, lived in the little hut in Grandma's front yard that she had once used as a snack stand. During tax season, people, black and white, came from all over Meridian to get him to file their income tax forms. He was a one-man clearinghouse for all the latest gossip in the neighborhood.

One day, I stopped by to see Ernest to ask him what he knew about me and Yvonne. He sat on a queen-size bed that, along with a small gas stove and a sink, took up almost the entire little hut. Old newspapers, maga-zines, and a collection of R&B albums were lined against the wall and scattered around the floor.

"Hey, Ernest, do you know where m-m-me and my m-m-mama c-c-come from?" I asked.

"The only thing I know, l'il Dave, is that y'all come from Africa," he answered. "I thank I heard yo' Grandma say somethin' about South Africa, but that's all I know."

"Well, how c-c-come I don't l-l-look like I c-c-come from Africa?" I persisted.

"What you mean?" Ernest said.

"Every time I see p-p-people from Africa on TV, they b-b-be all black," I told him. "And then when I look in the b-b-books at school, don't none of 'em b-b-be lookin' like me."

Ernest took a moment to shuffle some papers; he seemed to be trying to come up with the right answer—an answer that would satisfy me and certify his position as the smartest person in the neighborhood.

"But there's all kind of people in Africa, l'il Dave," he assured me. "And some of 'em is real black and some of 'em is white, but some is in between, too."

"W-w-what you m-m-mean, *in between?*" I shot back.

A look of strained patience now spread over Ernest's face; he sighed and said, "All I'm saying is there's lots of different people in Africa, that's all."

I had no concept of people being "in between," and I didn't think Ernest could admit that he had reached the limit of his knowledge about Africa. I just kept thinking that if I was from Africa, and I was what was called "in between," then what was Granddaddy? He was as pale and white-looking as I was, but as far as I knew, he wasn't from Africa. Were there "in between" people like me and Granddaddy in America, too?

Ernest and I quickly became friends. When I wasn't bugging him with more questions about Daddy and Yvonne and Grandma, he was introducing me to some of the characters and events that made the neighborhood a fun and, at times, quirky place to grow up. The cramped hut where he stayed was the center of activity in the streets around Grandma's house. Grown-ups and neighborhood kids flocked to Ernest's place to hear the latest R&B hit spinning on the record player. Some stopped by to get advice about dealing with a business or personal problem. Others sought out Ernest for small loans to get them through until the first or third of the month when the welfare and Social Security checks came. I saw my first "nasty books" at Ernest's place, glossy pornographic magazines he kept stuffed under his mattress. Sometimes he let his nephews from down the street at Miss Sis's house use his place to smoke reefer, listen to his records, and "do it" to girls.

✳

For most of my childhood, I was sheltered from the poison of racism. I got a whiff of it, however, when I was seven and Yvonne took me shopping at a downtown store. We walked into McRae's department store, and she planted me near a glass case while she browsed the jewelry and handbags.

While I stood there, fidgeting and wishing Yvonne would hurry up, an old white lady hobbled over to me and said, "Son, what's the matter? Did you lose yo' mama?"

I stared at the woman, about to explain that I was not lost, when I saw Yvonne look up from the jewelry case and start walking toward the woman, who was now stooped over me.

"What do you think you're doing?" Yvonne snarled at the lady.

The woman looked startled. "Well, this little boy is lost, and I'm just trying to help him find his mama."

"*I* am his mother," said Yvonne.

"But this is a white child," the woman insisted.

"No, this is *my* child," Yvonne seethed. "And he is *not* white."

She jerked me by the hand and pulled me toward the store entrance. People were staring in our direction, the old lady blanched in disbelief, and I felt my face growing red with embarrassment. Even at this young age, I knew that Yvonne would not hesitate to lash out at racist whites or ignorant blacks; I felt sorry for the old lady because she had simply seen a pale boy with straight hair who looked lost. Yvonne's reaction to the woman was unfathomable to me and made me suspect that she harbored a deep and smoldering resentment, a hatred, even, of white people.

I got a full dose of racism another time when I was knocking around the neighborhood with a group of boys that included a couple of poor whites who had moved into a house near Fifth Street, three blocks from Grandma's house. Sitting around on the street corner, someone suggested that we all go and get haircuts like the characters in *The Lords of Flatbush*, a movie about a gang of Brooklyn thugs who wore leather jackets and sported slicked-back, ducktail haircuts. There were no barbershops in the neighborhood; the nearest one was on Fifth Street, across Airport Boulevard. Completely oblivious to our lack of money, the six of us decided to go and get haircuts. We burst through the door of the Oakland Heights Barbershop, where the lone barber, a genial and kindly-looking white man, sat reading a newspaper.

"What y'all want?" the man drawled.

"We wanna g-g-get haircuts," I said.

"Well, I can give those two haircuts," he said, pointing to Jerry and

Michael, the two white boys. "But as for the rest of y'all, I'm sorry, but I don't cut nigger hair."

Those words—*nigger hair*—bounced around the chairs and razors and magazines in the barbershop, because my head, my mind, would not absorb them. Nobody had ever called me a nigger before, and I couldn't believe this man was including me in the group of boys whose hair he could not stomach to cut.

"Come on, y'all, let's get out of here," said Ernest James. "His old cracka ass probably cain't cut no hair no way."

Long after we left the barbershop, my mind kept returning to that word: "nigger." Was I really a nigger? The boys in the neighborhood called me "white nigger," but I had always identified with the "white" part of that insult. I never seriously considered that I might be the object of hatred and scorn by white people who apparently didn't care what color I appeared to be—pale, yellow, tan, or whatever. To them, I was just another nigger.

While the barbershop incident forced me to confront many of the issues of identity I had been able to avoid or shrug off, it also renewed my determination to find out all I could about myself and the African part of my family. I started rummaging through the heavy dresser drawers and bureaus in Grandma's house. I would wait for her to leave for prayer service at church and then began searching for anything that might shed light on exactly who I was. I had to work fast because I was sure to get a whipping if Grandma found me sneaking around in her house.

Mostly I found letters that Daddy had written to Grandma from South Africa, some postcards from New York, and boxes containing a collection of carved wooden giraffes and elephants. I kept digging until I came across a photograph of Yvonne sitting with two other women in the courtyard of a broken-down house. I could see pigs and chickens in the background of the photograph; Yvonne smiled and hugged one of the women. The house didn't look like any of those in Grandma's neighborhood, so I guessed it had been taken in Africa.

A sense of dread began to creep up on me, because I faced, for the first time, the possibility that the white man in the barbershop had been right, that maybe I *was* a nigger. After all, I reasoned, I had been to white homes and seen the way white people lived—their homes were clean and well built, and there were no animals running around outside—and now I had seen a photograph of Yvonne sitting outside a shack in what had to be

Africa. It was clear that I had come from nigger origins, so I must be a nigger.

Over the next few days, as I tried to reconcile myself to being a nigger, I resumed rummaging through Grandma's cabinets and trunks. The picture of Yvonne had fueled my curiosity. I dug up pictures of Daddy as a boy, flashing a gap-toothed grin; photos of Grandma holding Dave Jr. and Alma; and an old snapshot of three girls, dressed identically in gray dresses, bonnets, and black patent leather shoes. Something about the photograph of the girls made me turn it over, on the chance of finding some clue to their identity written there. On the back was an imprint that read: Crown Studios, Durban, 1965. Underneath the imprint were the names "Antoinette, Adrienne, and Geraldine." Beneath the names were the words "To mummy with love." When I asked Grandma whether she knew anything about these girls—without revealing that I had found the photograph—or whether she could tell me anything about where I had come from, she just sighed.

"All I know is that y'all come from South Africa," she said, adding a familiar refrain: "It's a shame that yo' mama don't tell you nothin' 'bout where you come from."

I kept the photograph of the girls. I sensed that it was yet another key that might help unlock the mysteries of my life.

✳

Daddy died of a heart attack on his forty-seventh birthday, when I was nine years old. I was the last person to see him alive—a fact that made me relive the details of our last night together again and again. On that evening, January 8, 1974, he came to pick me up at Grandma's house, where I always waited for him after school. As usual, he and Grandma sat around the living room or in the kitchen, drinking coffee and talking for a while. We then piled into his car and started out for Lost Gap. Daddy stopped by the Dixie Pak-a-Sak for gas and bought me a pack of grape-flavored Now-n-Later candy. "Don't eat those until we get home and you have your dinner," he said.

We pulled onto the highway and crossed the bridge leading to the interstate. The familiar sight of the cranes and piles of twisted metal of the Meridian Salvage Company appeared at the end of the bridge; Marvin

Gaye was singing on the radio, "And if you feel like I feel, baby, come on, oh, come on. . . . Let's get it on." We exited Interstate 20 West and turned left onto Meehan Road, riding past the closed gas station, the last outpost of civilization before we turned onto the hidden dirt road that led to the entrance to Lost Gap.

Once Daddy started driving up the steep road on the edge of Lost Gap, he slowed down to avoid hitting wild animals. Bucks and coyotes would sometimes suddenly spring onto the road from the dense woods, occasionally crashing into cars. The headlights of Daddy's car provided the only illumination for miles—there were no streetlights in Lost Gap—until we reached the bottom of the first of three steep inclines. The only other house near our section of Lost Gap sat at the bottom of the hill. The lights from its matchbox windows cast a slight glow onto the road as Daddy slowed down to cross a small bridge sitting astride a swampy creek; whenever it rained, the creek overflowed onto the road, and cars and trucks got stuck in the red muck.

On the final stretch of our journey home, the familiar copse of woods seemed to form an arch across the road—the moon and stars disappearing and reappearing as flecks through the tree branches. Every night when we drove through this stand of gigantic trees, I thought, inexplicably, about Vietnam. This must be what it was like in Vietnam, I thought. The woods were so dark and forbidding. I imagined that I was a soldier in Vietnam, trudging toward the enemy with my fellow scouts, fending off dangerous animals with yellow eyes, and swatting away hideous and alien insects. As Daddy pulled into the road that led to our trailer, the Vietnam soldiers disappeared into the woods.

Daddy and I had a routine when we got home, and that night was no exception. "Go on in there and get your shower," he said, heading to his room. Later, we reconvened in the kitchen. Yvonne was working the overnight shift and had left some steaks in the sink. Daddy had been a chief steward in the merchant marines and effortlessly prepared a dinner of steak, mashed potatoes, and corn for us.

"You got homework tonight?" he asked.

"Not too much," I answered. "Can I watch some TV when I get through?"

"First thing you need to do is finish all that food on that plate," he said, "and then do your homework."

"Yes, sir."

After dinner, I finished my homework and planted myself in front of the television in the living room. Daddy was wrestling with some paperwork and insurance policies spread over a couch and coffee table. I cast a mischievous look in his direction and dramatically released a thud of a fart into the living room; it soon became a pestilential fog that seemed to waft through most of the trailer. I smiled cannily at Daddy, trying to gauge his reaction to my stink bomb, but he acted as if nothing had happened. I turned again to the television, trying to think of some other way to get his attention. *The Dukes of Hazzard* had just gone off and a movie, *The Graduate,* was coming on when suddenly Daddy put down the document he was working on, lifted his right leg, and let out what must have been the granddaddy of all farts.

"O-o-oh, Daddy, you farted!" I said, pinching my nose.

"See, boy, that right there was a real fart," he said with an impish twinkle in his eye and returned to his work.

Just before ten o'clock, Daddy sent me to bed; I had to be ready for school in the morning, and he said that *The Graduate* wasn't a good movie for children to watch. I stumbled off to bed and drifted in and out of sleep, thinking about Daddy's birthday the next day. I had made him a birthday card out of blue construction paper, and I was sure there would be plenty of cake and ice cream at Grandma's house. Daddy had also promised to take me hunting on the weekend. I could hear him chuckling every now and then as he watched the movie in the living room.

About four hours later, I was roused from my sleep—someone was shaking me awake, saying, *David, get up. Come on, get up.* It was Grandma and Mr. Early, her new husband. They pulled me out of bed and gave me a coat to put on over my pajamas. I wiped my eyes and noticed a red light flickering off the wall of my room. What was going on? I wondered. The only explanation had to be that the Vietnam soldiers in the woods had finally attacked.

As we left the trailer, I saw men in white uniforms loading someone— I couldn't see who—into an ambulance. Grandma bundled me into the back of her car, and we pulled off from the trailer just as the ambulance tore out in front of us. Grandma and Mr. Early were both quiet on the fifteen-minute ride to her house; I drifted in and out of sleep in the back seat, convinced that I had been trapped in some strange dream.

When we pulled into Grandma's driveway, people were gathering in her yard and on the front porch. Grandma took me inside and put me in the bed at the back of the house. I could hear some of her friends—Miss Mary, Miss Louise, Miss Sis, and others I didn't recognize—make their way to the kitchen. Dave Jr. and Alma were visiting their grandmother in Jackson, and Xavier was at a babysitter's house.

Soon the smell of coffee and the sounds of people in the house aroused me from my sleep. I kicked the covers off the bed and fumbled with an old black-and-white television until I came across a Bugs Bunny cartoon. Every now and then, one of the old ladies craned her head through the bedroom door to check on me. "Don't worry, everythang gonna be all right, l'il Dave," she would assure me.

If everything was all right, I wondered, then where was Daddy? And who was that person the men put in the ambulance and took to the hospital? And where was Yvonne?

Others peeked in and delivered cryptic messages: "Now, you gonna have to be strong for your Grandma, okay?"

I got up from the bed and crept to the door to get a look at the activity in the living room. Grandma was sitting on an old green couch, hunched over the black rotary dial telephone, while two or three old ladies surrounded her, stroking her neck, whispering into her ear. A stream of traffic flowed through the living room: men brought in bags of groceries; more old ladies, some dressed in house robes, stopped by to offer words of support. Grandma was so bent over that she looked like she might disappear into herself. I thought about how often she had given comfort to people from the neighborhood, or shared a laugh or the latest gossip with them, in that living room.

Grandma's house served as a kind of way station for every person in need in that community. If you were hungry and didn't have money until the welfare and Social Security checks arrived, you went to Miss Alma's— Grandma was always cooking and shared all that she had. If your baby was crotchety or constipated and you didn't have aspirin or castor oil, Grandma's medicine cabinet surely had some tablet or salve to soothe the child. It was not uncommon to find one of Miss Sis's children, Nee Nee or Roy, bathing in Grandma's tub or the lady from up the street doing her laundry at Grandma's house.

I went back and stretched out on the bed and drifted off to sleep. I was sure that whatever was happening out there in the living room had nothing to do with me, that everything was going to be all right, and that all those people would soon go home.

I was awakened by the jangle of the telephone as it sliced through the hubbub in the living room. A moment in time registered and passed. Next came a low moan that quickly glided to a plaintive wail: "Oh, Lawd, dear God, why did you take my son!" It was Grandma, and now a chorus of the old ladies joined in her grief, sobbing in shock and disbelief that "Mr. Dave" had died.

I crawled out of bed and got to the door just in time to see a group of women shepherding Grandma to her room. A sense of unreality hung over the living room. Daddy had died of a massive heart attack in his sleep. Yvonne had finished her shift at the hospital earlier than usual and discovered that he wasn't breathing when she got into bed beside him. The doctors tried to save him, but the fifteen-mile trip from Lost Gap to the hospital in downtown Meridian diminished his chances of survival. Yvonne had gone to the hospital with him and had had to be sedated.

I turned back to the room and the television where Tom and Jerry were frolicking and slowly began rocking back and forth on my heels. Daddy was dead, and I was now supposed to cry, but I couldn't. I loved Daddy more than anything else, but I could not bring myself to cry; I could not shake the feeling that all of this was unreal and part of some cruel dream. I closed my eyes and prayed for tears, because I knew that it would not be good if someone were to come in and see me dry-eyed, like some heartless monster, right after Daddy had died.

I opened my eyes and saw John Taylor, Daddy's best friend, coming through the door. John Taylor was a huge man, and he had a kind face that made me feel secure. He squatted down next to me and said, "L'il Dave, I need to talk to you about something." This is it, I thought, he's going to tell me that there was some terrible mistake at the hospital, that Daddy was fine, and that everything was going to be all right.

"Son, your Daddy done passed away," said John Taylor. He reached out and pulled me into his massive arms, and I struggled to cry. I burrowed my head into his shoulder, praying that the pressure would force the tears to come. All at once, a shudder of shock coursed through my body—as I finally realized that I was wide awake, and not in some dream state, and that Daddy was really dead.

In the next few days, more people flooded Grandma's house: men and women hauling in bags filled with cakes, fried chicken, pans of corn bread, and pots of collard greens. The refrigerators and kitchen cabinets bulged with pecan pies, sweet potato pies, pound cake, and a bounty of other home-cooked goods that poured in from the community. I still hadn't seen Yvonne, and Grandma told me that she was staying with some friends until Daddy's funeral.

Miss Louise, a thin woman with graying hair and a pair of cat-eye eyeglasses perched on the bridge of her nose, took charge of coordinating Daddy's funeral service. She asked me whether I had any ideas for the eulogy, because she had heard that I was good with words and could read random selections from the encyclopedia and the dictionary. I told her that I would think about it, but I wasn't really interested. I still thought of death in the abstract, and even though I had cried on John Taylor's shoulder, I still hadn't fully absorbed the meaning of Daddy's death.

✳

Death didn't scare me because I had already seen it up close with my best friend, Darrell. Darrell lived across the road from the Enterprise Funeral Home, and he and I often wandered down into the basement of the building, where all the bodies were prepared for burial. We walked around looking at bodies stretched out on tables waiting to be embalmed. They were mostly old people, their skin slack and sallow, their arms or legs crooked into some unnatural position before they were made to fit into the casket. Sometimes we saw a young man or woman, a hapless victim of a car accident or a gunshot wound. The basement was usually deserted, but occasionally we ran into one of the embalming men, wearing a smock and heavy rubber gloves, who shooed us away and threatened to lock us in one of the dozens of caskets piled against the basement wall.

I was afraid to go upstairs to the viewing rooms; things just seemed so much creepier up there. Gloomy organ music seeped through the rooms, and a somber funeral attendant, a cadaverous old black man who seemed to live in the same shiny, dark three-piece suit, directed families to their loved ones. Three of the upstairs rooms contained bodies—fresh from the basement, their hair coifed and their faces burnished with rouge and powder—laid out in caskets for family viewing. Another room contained various models of caskets made of shiny mahogany and buffed chrome. Tiny price tags dangled from the caskets—some of them with names like "Peaceful Repose" and "Glorious Journey."

Daddy had been taken to Berry and Gardner Funeral Home, "the oldest funeral home in Mississippi, founded in 1882," and Miss Louise completed all the arrangements for his wake and burial. The only thing left to do was wait for the formal announcement of his funeral. And on the Thursday before the service, Miss Louise gathered all of us—me, Grandma, Mr. Early, Dave Jr., Alma, Xavier, and some people from the neighborhood—around the black-and-white television in the living room to watch *Potpourri,* a community affairs show broadcast on WTOK, Meridian's only television station. People tuned in to the show to find out what was going on in the city—births, anniversaries, graduations, reunions, and deaths.

The show's host, Don Cross, a dark-haired white man wearing a skinny tie and a pair of horn-rim glasses, began reading the schedule of events in Meridian and finally announced: "And the wake for Dave Houze Sr. will be held Friday from 5 to 7 P.M. at Berry and Gardner Funeral Home. Mr. Houze's burial service will take place on Saturday at noon at the Prospect United Methodist Church Cemetery in Savoy." A collective sigh issued through the room. A picture of Daddy stretched out on a table in the basement of Berry and Gardner Funeral Home flashed through my mind.

I finally saw Yvonne at the wake, but she hardly seemed to recognize me. She sat between her friends Miss Inez and Miss Taylor, shaking her head as tears streamed down her face. I went up to Daddy's casket and touched his cool face. Though his skin felt like plaster that might crack at the slightest touch, I leaned over and kissed him on the cheek and returned to my seat. The next day at the cemetery, Yvonne and Grandma and I sat together in the front row at the burial service. Yvonne wore dark glasses that seemed to cover her whole face. She appeared to be in a daze and didn't respond when I reached out to grab her hand.

In the months after Daddy's death, life in Meridian changed dramatically for Yvonne and me. She now had to handle all of Daddy's affairs. She made many mistakes—selling acres and acres of land, farm machinery, and cattle at rock-bottom prices—and angered Grandma and Dave Jr. and Alma, who accused her of profligacy. There were disputes over Daddy's will; Alma even wanted Grandma to exhume his body for an autopsy because she believed that Yvonne had poisoned him. Grandma refused because she understood that Daddy's death had devastated Yvonne, who retreated deeper into her work and spent more and more time with Miss Inez and other friends.

"Is your mama ever gonna come and see about Xavier?" Grandma asked me whenever I stayed with her. "Lord knows, I just don't understand how she can treat her own son like this."

"What is your Grandma talking about now?" Yvonne debriefed me in Lost Gap. "That woman never liked me from the minute your daddy brought us over here."

I was now forced to walk a tightrope between my life with Yvonne in Lost Gap and Grandma's house in Meridian.

✳

In the fall of 1975, at age ten, I started classes at Parkview Elementary School. Yvonne had taken me out of private school at St. Patrick's because she could no longer afford it after Daddy's death. I began making new friends at Parkview. Many of the children were white and lived in the northern suburbs of Meridian; there were a few other blacks, and we mostly stuck together.

But I needed something to establish my importance, something to make me feel unique among all the regular children. Since I hadn't found out anything else about Africa—I still hadn't identified the three girls in the photograph I had taken from Grandma's house—I took the liberty of inventing my past. Now, whenever someone asked me about my family and my background, I immediately launched into a full explanation of how Yvonne and I had come from South Africa and were of royal ancestry. Some of the kids wanted to know why I didn't have an accent. I told them that I had been raised by English nannies and that most people in South Africa spoke English anyway. The children appeared to accept my story, although a few teachers didn't seem to believe me. I enjoyed the way the girls at school looked at me and whispered among themselves while crowded around their lockers in the hall.

My desire to be special got a boost one day during music class, when the teacher taught us a new song, "Marching to Pretoria." The song was about men going into the mines in South Africa, swinging their pails and hard hats, looking forward to earning money to provide for their families. I couldn't believe my luck as I belted out the words, "We are marching to Pretoria, Pretoria. We are marching to Pretoria, Pretoria, here we come!" For days afterward, I heartily sang the upbeat song as if it had been sent especially to me to let me know that my life was not limited or determined by what happened in Meridian—that I was part of something much larger and more meaningful, reaching all the way across the ocean to Africa.

Not long after I enlisted "Marching to Pretoria" in my campaign to prove that I was special, the school hosted a showcase of different cultures and nations, preparing a program that would be presented to parents and other children. Each student chose a country to represent. One of my teachers, Miss Purcell, approached me in class and said, "David, since you're from South Africa, why don't you represent that country?"

"Okay, but what do I have to do?" I asked.

"Well, I'm sure you know one of the African languages, right?" she suggested, scanning my face for any sign of dishonesty. "We want each student to say something in his or her chosen country's language. Can you do that?"

"Yes, ma'am, I can say something in an African language," I assured her.

For weeks before the program, I weighed the wisdom of asking for Yvonne's help in preparing the greeting. Would she even know a tribal South African language? I wondered. She spoke with a heavy accent, but, as far as I knew, she spoke only English. Would she finally begin to break her silence and fill me in on her—our—roots in South Africa?

But I never did ask for help. On the night of the showcase—standing in a group of other students on a stage decorated with flags from around the world—I delivered the most outrageous string of gobbledygook I could summon to a mostly gullible and naïve audience.

"Boolaka manna toledada soamkani ganna bukalasa," I mumbled, surveying the audience to gauge reaction. I plunged ahead: "Dummiso boolaka kansanjani boolaki kunjani."

The majority of the parents and teachers appeared to buy the phony African greeting; I didn't want to look in Yvonne's direction because I was too embarrassed. On the way home after the showcase, Yvonne was silent. I sat beside her and fumbled with the car radio, knowing that I had made a complete fool of myself in the eyes of those few teachers and parents who were wise to my sham performance. I was well on the way to creating a glorious African past and culture for myself and my family—a past and culture held together by lies and thinly papered fantasies.

My brother Rasheid was born the next summer. I had been spending more time at Grandma's house—sometimes entire weeks—and had lost touch with Yvonne. She was still working at the hospital, but I knew little else. Now and then, Grandma told me that Yvonne was out of town with her friends or that she had been unable to contact her. One day, though, Grandma called me to the telephone to speak to Yvonne.

"David, yo' mama ain't doing too good right now," Grandma whispered. "You need to talk to her."

"What you m-m-mean? What's wrong with her?" I demanded.

I grabbed the telephone receiver and blurted out, "Yvonne, w-w-what's wrong? W-w-where you at?"

"I'm fine, David, everything is fine," she said in a calm voice.

"When you c-c-coming home?" I asked. "I ain't seen you in a long time."

"Don't worry, I'm coming home to see you real soon. Okay?" she said. "Don't worry. Now let me speak back to your Grandma."

Grandma got back on the phone. I went to play with Xavier, but I could hear Grandma yelling into the telephone.

When I next saw Yvonne, she was far into her pregnancy with Rasheid. When he was born, there was a lot of gossip about her. Many people in the neighborhood, including Grandma, thought that she was wrong to get pregnant by a married man, a preacher named James Cole, especially so soon after Daddy's death. I couldn't stand to know that people were saying mean things about Yvonne; I just wanted her to come back so that we could move back to Lost Gap.

But after Rasheid was born, Yvonne sold the trailer, and we moved into an apartment complex on the outskirts of Meridian. Once again, I was separated from Grandma and Xavier. Yvonne was always working, and sometimes, when she couldn't find a babysitter for Rasheid, I had to take care of him. When I began rebelling and demanding that she take me to see Grandma, she refused and threatened me with whippings and punishment.

"You are so damn selfish!" she screamed.

"I don't care 'c-c-cause I hate you!" I hollered back.

Eventually, she found a permanent babysitter for Rasheid and allowed me to go back to Grandma's house—and that's where I almost always stayed.

In those first months back at Grandma's house, I felt like a returning exile and basked in all the joys of the neighborhood. I hung out with my friends Ernest James, Freelo, Toby, and Lester and played hide-and-go-seek beneath the chinaberry trees. Groups of us walked across town to the

Village Square Mall to hang out at the Merry-Go-Round, the only really cool store in the otherwise boring shopping complex.

One day, Billy Holloway and I drank two bottles of Robitussin and danced to the jukebox at the Drive-In, a ramshackle club that had just opened around the corner from Grandma's house. Billy was a bug-eyed boy who had already started to sprout facial hair, and he loved getting into trouble as much as I did. We were too young to buy beer, so we scraped up enough change to get Robitussin cough syrup at Fred's Dollar Store. As soon as we left the store, we opened the bottles and drank the foul Robitussin and waited for the alcohol to kick in. A little while later, we were both stumbling around the neighborhood, recoiling slightly from the nasty cough medicine, but pleasantly tipsy.

On the weekends, I snuck out of the house and met up with other boys, and we made our way along Fifth Street to downtown. In contrast to other parts of Meridian, Fifth Street was run by black folks. A couple of downtown blocks featured a barbershop, a dentist's office, a drugstore, the Joe Louis Café, Henderson's Grill, several taxi stands, and other black-owned businesses. My friends and I usually wound up at the Magnolia Star Theater, the only place in town that presented the so-called blaxploitation films of the 1970s. While two or three of us distracted the ticket taker in the outside booth, the rest of us dashed up the steep stairs into the theater. Occasionally, we got caught and the manager dragged us out, but most of the time we scraped by and settled into the shabby purple seats to watch such movies as *Dolemite,* with Rudy Ray Moore; *Blacula; Cornbread, Earl, and Me; Superfly;* and *Sheba Baby,* starring Pam Grier. I always tried to sit near the back of the theater to avoid the inevitable commentary that broke out during the movie:

Man, you better get yo' ass outta there! Cain't you see that peckerwood got a gun?
O-o-oh, he is tearin' that pussy up, ain't he?
That sho' is one crazy nigga, I tell ya.

People smuggled bottles of liquor into the theater, and the smell of reefer sometimes drifted to the back, where I crouched. I feared that grown-ups from the neighborhood would see me and report back to Grandma that I had been at the Magnolia Star watching nasty movies. But Grandma never said anything, and I felt free to wander beyond the confines of the neighborhood, pedaling my white Evel Knievel bike all over Meridian.

I had just left the Village Square Mall one day when I noticed a group of people carrying signs outside a nearby Payless shoe store. They were mostly black people, with a couple of whites, and they carried signs that read, PRICE GO HOME, SAY NO TO RACISM, and DON'T HIRE MURDER-ERS. A patrolman from the Meridian Police Department sat passively in his car in the parking lot. I had never seen anything like this before, so I rode my bike over to see what all the fuss was about. A big black man with a beard noticed me on the sidelines and came over to me.

"W-w-what y'all doing up here at this store?" I asked him.

"This here is what's called a picket, little brother," the man said.

"W-w-what's wrong?"

"Well, you see that white man in there?" he said, pointing to a burly white security guard inside the shoe store.

I nodded yes, and he continued, "That white man right there was one of the people who helped kill them three civil rights workers down here a long time ago." The man looked to make sure I understood.

"You know what I'm talking about, right?" he prodded.

"Yeah, I think so," I said. I had heard something about how the three men—two white men and a black man from Meridian—had been killed by the Ku Klux Klan.

"See, that man—his name is Cecil Price—he ain't supposed to have no kind of job in Meridian after what he done," the man said. "So we here to make sure he get fired and don't never find no job in this city, ever."

I nodded my understanding of the situation and looked through the store window at the heavy-set white man wearing a cowboy hat. He didn't seem too concerned about the protesters. After the Payless shoe store picket, though, Cecil Price couldn't find a decent job anywhere in Meridian. For a time, he worked as a security guard in a rundown store, but the black folks in Meridian never forgot him and the role he played in the murders of the three civil rights workers.

The fun I had ripping and running through the streets of Meridian was balanced by the load of new chores Grandma piled on me. Alma and Dave Jr. now lived with Grandma, so I took turns with them washing dishes, sweeping, mopping the kitchen floor, and maintaining the yard. Chief among my other chores was looking after Xavier, who had begun to sneak out of the house and wander all over the neighborhood. I was charged with keeping up with him as he went from house to house and up and down the alleys and streets surrounding Grandma's house.

He was fascinated by trains and began to hang around the railroad tracks at the end of Forty-sixth Avenue. Grandma got calls from people who had seen Xavier trying to climb the gravel hill up to the railroad tracks, and she told me, "Go down there and get yo' brother before he gets hisself killed." Whenever I went looking for Xavier on the railroad tracks, I always thought about the danger he unwittingly faced. The massive freight trains were unforgiving as they barreled through the neighborhood. Stories abounded of people caught unawares and killed or injured on the tracks, including one man, Ronnie Charles, who had lost both legs when he tried to hop a train in a drunken stupor.

I was always able to head off Xavier before he got near the tracks, but I wasn't able to keep up with him at all times. He began to leave the neighborhood, and every now and then the police brought him home, laughing and drooling, in the back of a patrol car. Knowing that he was about to get a whipping, he ran to Grandma and hollered out, "Hey, Ma." Grandma said, "*Hey* nothin'. You know what I told you about leaving this house."

I loved Xavier, but I also felt ashamed of him sometimes, especially when other kids called him crazy or stupid. I didn't like being seen in public with him, and the back of my neck burned with humiliation when I scanned the faces of people who looked at him: his buck teeth, a constant string of drool hanging from his mouth, his labored attempts to speak. But what embarrassed me most were the times he messed his pants; Grandma had tried to toilet train him without success. When this happened, he had to be changed and washed, and this task invariably fell to me. After I took off his dirty underpants and threw them in the corner, I put Xavier in Grandma's tub and washed him all over before fitting him out in clean clothes and sending him back outside, where he was sure to mess his pants again. Grandma wouldn't allow the messy underwear to be put in her washer and dryer, so I had to wash it by hand with plenty of Mr. Clean and laundry detergent, in a basin of hot water or, occasionally, in the toilet. Living with Grandma had started to lose some of its charm.

✳

I got my first job the summer after I moved in with Grandma. I was happy to get out of most of my chores, including washing Xavier's shitty underwear. The Country Store had just opened up in a broken-down little building on the corner of Hooper Street and Forty-Sixth Avenue, around the corner from Grandma's house. A rickety tin shed supported by two paint-flecked poles sheltered the store. Neon Pabst Blue Ribbon and Coca-Cola signs hung in the plate glass windows of the store's brick front. A small house was connected to the store, and the owners, Shorty and his wife, Sharon, lived there. For the first time, people in the community had some place to buy a few staple food items and coal oil for kerosene lamps.

Every time I passed the Country Store, I noticed a big bike propped up against the wall. I went in one Friday and asked Miss Velma, a kind old black woman who had just been hired to help out in the store, if any other jobs were available. "Hold on for a minute," she told me and went to the back of the store. While she was gone, I looked around. A huge glass case, where all kinds of candies, cookies, and other sweets were neatly displayed, dominated the front of the store. Jars of dill pickles and pickled pigs' feet competed for space atop a massive meat case. Among the jumble of the store's wares were fly swatters, BC headache powders, bottles of castor oil, mousetraps, roach spray, and sundry other items behind the cash register.

As I was taking all this in, Miss Velma returned with the storeowner, Shorty Walker. "Just call me Shorty," the big, red-faced white man told me as he extended his hefty paw for me to shake. He took me outside, and we stood by the bike as he told me about the job.

"We need somebody to deliver groceries to people when they call in orders," Shorty explained. "You think you can handle that?"

"Yes, sir," I said.

"You also have to help Miss Velma behind the counter and help keep the store clean," he continued. I shook my head vigorously; I didn't care what I had to do—I wanted to work and make some money of my own.

"The job pays twenty-five dollars a week, and you work from nine-thirty to six, Monday through Saturday," Shorty said. "Are ya still interested?"

"Yes, sir," I answered.

"All right, come on back in here for a minute," he motioned, and I followed him back into the store while he went behind the counter and consulted with Miss Velma.

I could hear him whispering, "What you know about him?"

"Well, I know his grandmama, Miss Alma," she told him. "And he's lived here all his life. . . . "

Shorty seemed satisfied and came back around the counter. He extended his hand and said, "I'm gonna give you the job, so we'll see you on Monday."

I thanked him, and then I thanked Miss Velma for putting in a good word for me. I rushed home to tell Grandma, who told me, "I know, Miss Velma already done called me. You behave yourself up at that store, now."

I couldn't wait to get on that bike and start delivering groceries for the Country Store.

Since I knew the neighborhood so well, I had no problems during my first days on the job. When someone called in an order, I would scurry around the store finding and bagging the items and then dash out the front door and onto my bike. The bike was one of those huge clunky models— not nearly as nimble as my Evel Knievel bike—and I crashed a few times before I finally mastered it. But I soon began flying through the streets and alleys, with the groceries threatening to spill from the heavy wire basket attached to the handle bars. I became a familiar sight in the neighborhood, and the other kids whooped and hollered whenever I went barreling past them. When I wasn't delivering groceries, I cleaned and stocked the store shelves and helped Miss Velma behind the counter.

She was teaching me how to run the cash register one day when Shorty came over and told me, "Get a broom and clean up that rice that done spilled on the floor over by the door." I grabbed the broom and swept up the rice, but some of the stubborn grains kept getting caught in the cracks of the wooden plank floor. When I was satisfied that I had gotten up most of it, I returned behind the counter, where Miss Velma was waiting to teach me more about the cash register. I rang up my first purchase and was feeling pretty good when Shorty came back out front.

"I thought I told you to clean up that damn rice," he bellowed at me. "Dammit, you better get all that goddamn rice up now!"

I cringed at Shorty's cursing and looked to Miss Velma, but she turned away like she didn't want any part of the white man's wrath. I got the broom and returned to the spot in the floor where the rebel rice grains still refused to budge. I got on my knees as Shorty stood over me, watching as I used one of the broom's straw bristles to remove the individual rice grains. I cursed Shorty under my breath. I was beginning to think that he was just another racist white honky peckerwood.

Everything in the store seemed to run better when Shorty and Sharon, a short woman with a hornet's nest hairdo, steel-rim glasses, and bad teeth, weren't around. Miss Velma and I were a formidable team: I delivered the groceries and stocked the shelves, and we both ran the cash register and swept the floors. So I was secretly pleased when Shorty and Sharon took a vacation to Kentucky and left us in charge of the store.

While they were gone, I developed a reputation for generosity at the store—the kids and some adults called me "Mr. Givemore" when I waited on them behind the counter. If a kid came in with a dime for ten cookies, I waited until Miss Velma wasn't looking and stuffed twenty-five or thirty cookies into a small bag and thrust it across the counter. When Ernest came in the store wanting to buy fifty cents worth of bologna and some crackers, I cut him off a big hunk of the pink meat, wrapped it in a piece of white deli paper, and just gave it to him.

Word soon spread that "Mr. Givemore" would treat you right at the Country Store. Little kids stormed the store in packs to get free stuff. Whenever I was sure I could get away with it, I took their sticky pennies and let them walk with bags of chips, cookies, and other sweets. I walked around with a pocketful of candy and helped myself to Cokes, chips, sandwiches—anything I wanted to eat. As long as Shorty and Sharon were on vacation, I figured I was going to do whatever I wanted. More than anything, I hadn't forgotten about the spilled rice and how Shorty had talked down to me like I was nothing but a nigger. By the time he and Sharon returned from vacation, "Mr. Givemore" had made sure Shorty had paid for that insult.

✳

One day, while I was stocking some canned peas, Yvonne and a friend of hers from her nursing job came through the door of the store. I hadn't seen Yvonne in months, and I was surprised to see her in Grandma's neighborhood because they didn't get along. Grandma had never forgiven her for neglecting Xavier, even though Yvonne insisted that she and Daddy had tried to do right by wanting to place Xavier in the school in Jackson. I often had to endure Grandma's railings against Yvonne.

"Yo' mama wasn't nothing before yo' Daddy brought her over here," she said. "She didn't even know how to use a toilet when she got over here, 'cause all they had was a hole in the ground over there in Africa."

Other times, especially when she couldn't reach Yvonne on the phone, she said, "Dave wasn't really yo' daddy. Did yo' mama tell you that yo' daddy is some man still over in Africa?"

I tried not to listen to her when she had these fits of rancor, but it was hard not to let some of it sink in.

Yvonne hugged me and said, "David, come on outside so I can talk to you." She looked happy and healthy. I wondered what she was going to say.

"Rasheid and I are leaving Meridian," she began. "I'm starting a new job, and we're gonna leave pretty soon."

"W-w-where y'all moving t-t-to?" I said.

"We moving to Georgia 'cause I got a new job there," she explained.

"So w-w-when are y'all leaving?" I asked.

"We'll probably leave in about a week. So I need to know if you want to come with us now."

I hadn't expected this, so I said, "I don't w-w-wanna leave all my friends. Do I have t-t-to go?"

She looked disappointed. "Okay, you don't have to come right now. But I want you to think about it and let me know pretty soon."

"Okay, I will," I told her. She gave me another hug, and as she turned to go, she said, "I love you, David."

Then I watched her get into her friend's car, and they drove off. I stood outside the Country Store for a long time, looking at the car blend in with the road and then disappear into the distance, until Miss Velma called me back inside to get another order ready for a delivery.

Months passed before I heard from Yvonne again. I had just started classes at Kate Griffin Junior High School. I quit the job at the Country Store after Shorty grew suspicious of how generous I had been with his merchandise, and I was starting to rankle under Grandma's strict discipline. I risked whippings for staying out too late, and I still chafed at her suggestion that Daddy wasn't my daddy after all.

Besides, I was ready to get out of Meridian. I was afraid I would get trapped in the city and end up like the people roaming the streets around the neighborhood, looking for a job in some warehouse or factory or, worse, in the slaughterhouses. I knew that it didn't matter how smart or enterprising I was—in the end, I would be judged by the color of my skin in a small Mississippi town. And, deep down, I believed that I had been destined to discover a completely hidden part of myself and embark on an adventure of self-discovery that could begin only beyond the familiar but stifling confines of Meridian.

Grandma tried to convince me to stay, telling me that the only reason Yvonne wanted me to join her in Albany, Georgia, was so she could get my Social Security check, which she had stopped receiving now that I no longer lived with her. Nevertheless, even though I felt terrible about not staying with Xavier, I left Meridian in the spring of 1977. Over the next three years, Yvonne, Rasheid, and I lived in Albany, where we barely got by. Eventually, we moved to Detroit to be with Yvonne's boyfriend, who had gotten a job at one of the Chrysler auto plants. I fled Detroit in 1982, fed up with the snow and gritty depression of the city, and moved back to Georgia, this to time Atlanta, where I enrolled at Morehouse College.

I became a Morehouse Man, a member of the black elite, W. E. B. Du Bois's "talented tenth," but I still knew almost nothing about my past. What I did know had become a familiar dirge, which I could recite upon request. Yeah, I was born in South Africa, I would declaim weightily to any young Spelman College co-ed whose panties I was trying to raid. My mother and I escaped the evil apartheid regime, I would explain to a group of fellow Morehouse Men whose family escutcheons fairly groaned with privilege, while mine had to be fabricated.

After pledging Alpha Phi Alpha, I managed to get myself kicked out of college. Under the auspices of Morehouse, I participated in a summer fellowship program at Cornell, but I neglected my research, got entangled in campus anti-apartheid demonstrations, and hung out and drank beer with my fraternity brothers. My faculty adviser was not pleased and terminated my scholarship when I returned to Morehouse for the fall semester to begin my senior year.

For the next five years, 1985 to 1989, I cooked my way through quite a few Atlanta restaurants. I also managed to travel to all the places I had always wanted to see: New Orleans for Mardi Gras; New York City, to prowl through Times Square and along Forty-second Street; San Francisco, to ride the cable cars; and London, to hang out in Piccadilly Circus and the West End. When I found myself back in Atlanta delivering Domino's Pizza on a bike in 1989, I knew the time had come to complete my undergraduate degree.

I moved to Athens, Georgia, and enrolled at the University of Georgia, where I partied a little less and studied more. By the time I graduated in 1991, I sensed that the timing would soon be right to ask my mother again about South Africa—specifically, about the photograph of the three girls I had come across while rummaging through Grandma's house for clues to my identity.

Throughout all those years of moving from place to place, losing touch with Grandma and Xavier and Meridian, and living on the fringes of Atlanta, I never forgot that another world beckoned to me in South Africa— a world that would help me understand the trajectory my life had taken, a world that confirmed that my life in Meridian had been only the prologue to my story. Now, in my room at the Stratford Inn in Atlanta, as I looked at the time-worn black-and-white photograph of the three girls I knew to be my sisters, equipped with the name of the woman in South Africa who had taken care of them, I felt very close to entering and exploring that world.

2

Into the Breach

To know nothing about yourself is to be
constantly in danger of nothingness, those
voids of nonbeing over which a man walks
the tightrope of his life.

ATHOL FUGARD
Tsotsi

The American traveling to South Africa and
the South African visiting North America
share an experience that those who do not
make the diagonal journey across the Atlantic can never wholly comprehend. The
travelers pass through a kind of looking glass
and to one extent or another invariably find
themselves drawn to Carrollian imagery in
their attempts to understand and relate what
they have experienced.

RICHARD E. BISSELL
and CHESTER A. CROCKER, eds.
South Africa into the 1980s

I couldn't feel my legs anymore. It was a week before Christmas Eve of 1992, and I had endured eighteen hours of being scrunched into an economy-class airplane seat from Atlanta to Frankfurt, Germany, and now on to Johannesburg, South Africa. I had not been able to sleep, and my body had taken a real beating. My legs were numb with inactivity and exhaustion.

As I tentatively reached down to nudge my frozen legs back to life, the voice of a flight attendant came over the intercom: "Ladies and gentlemen, the captain has indicated that we are approximately forty-five minutes from Jan Smuts Airport in Johannesburg. Please do not block the aisles, and stay close to your seat, as we will be preparing for landing shortly."

All around the plane, people began stretching and yawning and moving into the aisles. Wide-eyed children stood up in their seats, and babies rediscovered their clamorous cries. Flight attendants, perfectly coifed and beaming, commandeered their food trolleys in preparation for serving breakfast.

Stumbling to my feet and motioning toward the aisle, I wedged my legs and torso past the disheveled man and woman seated next to me and made my way to join the line of people waiting to get into the lavatory. It seemed I had escaped my small, cramped room at the Stratford Inn in Atlanta only to find myself in another cramped space, on an airplane now hurtling toward a reunion that might not turn out as I'd planned.

✳

Getting out of the Stratford Inn had been the easy part. As soon as my mother told me about Auntie Bessie, I knew what to do: I waited for a couple of days and then snuck into the *Atlanta Journal-Constitution* building after hours and used international directory assistance to call South Africa from the foreign editor's desk. All around me, muted televisions with images of talking heads and the twenty-four-hour news cycle illuminated my furtive dialing. I prayed that the security guards in the lobby would stay away from the newsroom.

A sequence of whirring sounds and static briefly seized the telephone receiver before a woman's voice chirped, "Directory assistance. City and listing?" The woman's voice had the same lilting South African twang as my mother's.

"The city is Durban," I whispered. "Bessie Keachie on Mimosa Road, please."

After a brief pause, during which I pondered how incredibly expensive the call would be and whether I would be found out, the operator returned. She recited the phone number and then asked, "Shall I connect you?"

I looked around the newsroom. Not a soul here—might as well go for it, I thought.

The telephone ringing its unfamiliar double cadence seemed attuned to my every breath and echoed the incredible distance of the connection being made.

Suddenly, a woman answered the phone. " 'Allo?"

"Is this Auntie Bessie?" I blurted out. "Bessie Keachie?"

"Who's this?" the woman balked. "Do I know you?"

With my heart pounding, I told myself that now was not the time to stutter.

"Auntie Bessie, this is David," I rushed. "I'm Yvonne's son."

There was an audible gasp. "Oh, my Gahd! Is it really you, my baby!?" she shouted. "Is that David? Oh, I can hardly believe it!"

"Yes, it's me, I'm Yvonne's son," I kept repeating, amid her cries of disbelief and joy.

"David, oh, my baby, oh, my baby," she cooed. "How's Mummy?"

"Mummy?"

"Yes, your mother, Yvonne. We always called her Mummy," Auntie Bessie sniffled. "How is she?"

Over the next hour, Auntie Bessie and I talked, and she asked me countless questions, trying to bridge a gap of some twenty-five years: *Where was my mother? Was she still a nurse? Why hadn't she called? Why hadn't she written? Was I married?* Bessie and her husband had both retired—she from nursing and he from driving a taxi—and had reared two children of their own, Marcell and Xavier.

The girls, as she referred to my sisters, had all moved out long ago and started families of their own. Geraldine, the youngest, had become a teacher. She still lived in Durban, married to a man named Robbie Brooks, who owned a butcher shop. They had a daughter, Roberta. Adrienne, the middle sister, worked in the advertising department of a large chain store. She was newly divorced and lived in Johannesburg with her son, Angelo. Antoinette, the oldest, had become a bookkeeper. She lived in Johannesburg with a daughter named Kim and was also recently divorced. They were all leading perfectly normal and happy lives, according to Auntie Bessie.

"I need to get in touch with them, Auntie Bessie," I said. "Can you help me?"

"You want to call them?"

"Yes. I know it's been a long time, and they don't know me," I rambled, "and our mother left South Africa with me without taking them, but . . ."

"Oh, my baby, don't worry, don't worry. I'm going to give you Geraldine's number, since she's right here in Durban," Auntie Bessie said. "I see her every now and then, but not so much the other two since they live in Jo'burg.

"Oh, David, you were just a little boy when you and your mother left here," she continued. "When are you coming back to South Africa?"

"As soon as I can, Auntie Bessie," I said. "Just as soon as I can." I promised to stay in touch.

Not long after this—although I let some time elapse before sneaking back into the newsroom to use the foreign editor's telephone—I called Geraldine at her home in Sydenham, a suburb of Durban.

Disbelief tinged her voice in our first conversation.

"David, Auntie Bessie told me that she gave you my number," Geraldine said. "But I didn't really think you would call, after all these many years."

I didn't have a ready response and feared a turn for the worse in the conversation.

"Well," I said, searching for the right words, "I only found out about you guys a little while ago."

"You mean mother never talked about us or told you how to get in touch with us?"

"No, honestly," I stammered. "She told me about Auntie Bessie, and she told me that I had three sisters. . . . "

"David, I understand you didn't know about what happened, but . . . . I just don't know what to feel about you."

"Well, am I going to be able to see you when I come to South Africa?" I asked, almost pleading.

"We'll talk again before you come," she said. "Let's just see what happens."

Though my brief conversation with Geraldine should have given me pause in my determination to return to South Africa—for one reason or another, I never managed to talk to her again before I left—it instead only deepened my resolve to make everything right, to try to mend my fractured family.

✳

"Ladies and gentlemen, this is the captain speaking," the intercom crackled as I made my way back to my seat on the airplane. "We have entered South African airspace and will be arriving at Jan Smuts Airport in Johannesburg shortly."

A shiver ran down my spine as I looked outside the window and saw the first outlines of Jan Smuts Airport now materializing through the clouds. Named after a South African former prime minister and general, the hulking gray structure had until now been only an abstraction to me, symbolizing the sinister machinery of the white minority government. Since its opening in 1950, shortly after the ascendancy of the Nationalist Party and the entrenchment of apartheid, Jan Smuts Airport had been the country's only point of entry and exit, unless one was traveling by ship. And South Africa was the kind of place where entering and exiting was a big deal. In all the reading I'd done that cataloged the government's intimidation and brutalization of political dissidents, journalists, and ordinary people, Jan Smuts Airport had figured prominently in several of the accounts that had stayed with me.

Beginning with a gauntlet of uniformed and plainclothes police agents, travelers passing through the airport had faced intense scrutiny and coercion. Mark Mathabane, in his book *Kaffir Boy in America*, recounted some of the terror and humiliation associated with his departure from the country in 1978:

> Armed white policemen in neat uniforms and shiny boots stood at various locations inside the terminal. They stared at me as I made my way from the British Airways ticket counter to the international departure lounge. Except for the forlorn-faced men and women engaged in menial jobs, I was the only black in sight. I remained cool and occasionally stared back at an exasperated policeman. I relished the giddying and unbelievable prospect that in a few hours I would be beyond their reach, their persecution, their sadism, their vindictiveness, clean out of their house of bondage of which they were the guards.

Even after boarding the plane that would take him out of the country, Mathabane remained terrified of the South African police:

> I expected momentarily to be dragged off the plane by agents of BOSS (Bureau of State Security) and told that I was not leaving for America after all, that something was wrong with my papers. I had heard of black people at the last minute being hauled off planes and flung into detention to prevent their leaving South Africa and telling the world the truth about black life under apartheid. I began trembling uncontrollably and my clothes were drenched in cold sweat.

Mathabane remained jittery until his plane left South African airspace, beginning his journey to an American college, where he would pursue a tennis scholarship. Others trying to leave the country hadn't been so lucky.

Breyten Breytenbach, a dissident Afrikaner poet, was arrested at Jan Smuts Airport for traveling on a false passport on his way back to France in August 1975. The apartheid government had targeted Breytenbach for his attempts to recruit members for a group called Okhela, which was composed of non-Communist South African exiles aligned with the outlawed African National Congress (ANC). The government seemed particularly appalled that the poet was a native son who had strayed from the Afrikaner *laager* by marrying a Vietnamese woman and settling in Paris after leaving South Africa in 1960.

As Breytenbach's literary fame grew in Europe and South Africa, he applied for a visa to return home with his wife in 1964. When her visa application was denied because the government deemed their interracial marriage illegal, Breytenbach became enraged and vented his anger through progressively more strident poetry and prose directed at the South African regime. In his book *The True Confessions of an Albino Terrorist,* Breytenbach captured some of the paranoia and dread associated with attempting to negotiate the security blockade the government had thrown up around the airport to rein in and quash its perceived enemies:

> I had arrived earlier that evening at Jan Smuts Airport on my way back to France. I had known even as I arrived earlier that evening that I was blown, that they knew about me and rather in the fashion of a small child closing its eyes hoping that in doing so the hideousness will go away, I'd hoped against hope that I'd be able to slip through the net which had been closing around me for some time.

Despite his realization that the security police were on to him—he was wanted for engaging in subversive activities as proscribed under the Terrorism Act—Breytenbach proceeded to check in for his flight, fully aware that he might be detained.

> In the departure hall, I became intensely aware of several men sitting there, moving around, watching me. One is never so oblivious as when you're trying to integrate with your surroundings. In fact, I became so paranoid that I went downstairs to the gents' toilets with one of them dogging my footsteps, and there, unzipping my pants, hunching my shoulders, I managed to swallow a few lines of paper with names on it. Not everything, unfortunately, could be disposed of in that way.

After his attempt to dispose of incriminating documents, "Monsieur Christian Galaska," the identity Breytenbach had assumed, was summoned over the public address system to the South African Airways desk. There he was accosted by undercover security police and taken to a room to be strip-searched and interrogated before being transferred to the state security offices in Pretoria. "Just so one is delivered into the hands of one's enemies," Breytenbach wrote. He was subsequently charged and jailed for seven years under the Terrorism Act for his active opposition to the apartheid regime.

Because Jan Smuts Airport substantially controlled the movement of people into and out of the country, I suspected that the security police regulated its operations—and used its unseen warrens and underground rooms for interrogation and staging areas for launching attacks against enemies of the state. Exiled South Africans in Atlanta had shared stories with me of the government's attempts to kill the Rev. Frank Chikane, an ANC member and an outspoken critic of the regime, whom the security police had tried to poison on two occasions: once while he was driving from South Africa to Namibia, and again when he departed from Jan Smuts Airport for a church conference in the United States. I had also been told that a special police unit in the basement of the airport had assembled the parcel bombs that killed Ruth First, an exiled anti-apartheid activist, as well as Jeanette and Katryn Schoon, the wife and daughter of ANC operative Marius Schoon.

True, it was 1992 now, and the country seemed to have stepped back from the brink of terror and insanity. But it was only then, as the plane touched down, that I had any serious misgivings about the situation in which I found myself: essentially alone in a strange country, hoping against hope that somebody would be on hand at the airport to fetch me and transport me to safety.

By the time I reached the Immigration and Customs Hall, some of my initial apprehensions had abated. Looking around the cavernous hall, I didn't see any machine gun–toting guards or soldiers; in fact, besides the immigration clerks, I observed no other official South African presence. When it was my turn to approach one of the immigration checkpoints, I quickly checked to make sure my passport was in order.

"Good day, sir," the red-faced clerk chirped while swiping the passport and entering information into a computer. "Business or holiday, Mr. Houze?"

"Uh, holiday," I hesitated, as the clerk gave me a hard glance and scrutinized my passport photo. Somewhere in the line behind me, a baby's scream emerged from the crowd of anxious travelers.

"Enjoy your stay in South Africa, Mr. Houze," the clerk said, stamping and handing back my passport.

I thanked him, let out a sigh of relief, and stepped through the Immigration Hall to claim my baggage. Unbeknownst to either my mother or Auntie Bessie, I had packed everything I owned into two large black duffel bags on wheels and two smaller bags that contained a desktop Apple computer and various South Africa–related books and articles. As far as I was concerned, I had no plans to leave South Africa at the end of my three-month tourist visa. I had about two hundred dollars and a pack of cigarettes in my pocket.

Auntie Bessie was the only person who knew when I'd be arriving at Jan Smuts; I hadn't been able to reach my sisters. A week before I left Atlanta, Auntie Bessie had assured me that someone would be at the airport; after all, both Adrienne and Antoinette lived in Johannesburg.

After getting my bags, I began pushing the cart toward the arrival hall like a homeless person looking for shelter. As the doors slid open, I began searching through the faces in the crowd, watching people beckon to their loved ones. Inching my overburdened baggage cart through the throng, I became acutely aware of several people staring and pointing toward me. My heart fluttered with the possibility that someone—anyone!—would emerge to greet me. But as the crowd slowly dissolved around the other arriving passengers, and I was left standing alone in the middle of the concourse, I finally understood that there would be no one to meet me.

Shaking off the shock of anonymity, I began pushing the cart aimlessly while all around me people dashed off to other parts of the vast airport. There were still no signs of security or military police or any of the other terrifying things I'd read about; perhaps the scariest sight was that of a grizzled old African man whose earlobes dangled down to his shoulders. His cheeks and forehead were also deeply scarred. I was at once repulsed and fascinated. Must be a tribal thing, I thought. Meanwhile, black men and women were doing all sorts of jobs in the terminal: emptying garbage cans, selling food at kiosks, assisting mostly white passengers with their luggage. Streams of white passengers filtered through the airport; every once in a while, I saw an Indian or African rushing to catch a flight.

The beauty of the women also caught my attention. They must be feeding the girls in South Africa some serious food, I mused, because nearly every woman I saw had a robust body, with nicely formed buttocks. It was summertime in South Africa, and most of the women were dressed for the weather. Even as I stared at the white women—leered, really—I had to catch myself: I mean, this was South Africa, after all, and I thought about the fate of poor Emmett Till, who had supposedly gotten fresh with a white woman in Mississippi. With that sobering, slightly paranoid, thought, I pushed my cart outside to get some air, smoke a cigarette, and figure out what to do next.

✳

All eyes were on South Africa at the moment as the country struggled with the birth pangs of democracy. Most countries had lifted sanctions against South Africa after the dismantling of the major pillars of the apartheid state, including the Population Registration Act, which had required all South Africans to register an assigned racial classification; the Group Areas Act, which had assigned ownership and occupation of land according to race; and the Land Act, which had ensured that the white minority would own 87 percent of the country's most desirable land, setting aside the remainder for the black majority and other nonwhites. Increasingly, South Africa was also being welcomed back into the community of African countries, and many speculated that the United Nations would consider removing sanctions as an inducement to further political and economic change. Informal negotiations on a new constitution had actually begun in December 1991 under the auspices of the Convention for a Democratic South Africa (CODESA), even though not all elements of the ruling National Party had bought into the idea of radical governmental change, echoing the fears of some white South Africans.

In March 1992, President F. W. de Klerk had taken the unprecedented step of calling for an all-white referendum to gauge support for euthanizing the apartheid state. Nearly 70 percent of white voters affirmed their willingness to continue negotiations toward a new, democratic constitution. In effect, the majority of whites signaled their belief that the government had no choice but to consult with its erstwhile enemies, even if it meant negotiating itself out of existence. As usual, right-wing elements of the white population predicted an apocalypse and vowed to fight to the bitter end against any constitutional accommodations with the ANC and other negotiating parties in CODESA.

But CODESA itself was rent by controversy and caught up in a spiral of escalating violence as the year wore on. Tensions between the predominantly Zulu Inkatha Freedom Party (IFP) and the ANC erupted amid accusations of police brutality and allegations that the government was covertly supporting the IFP's leader, Chief Mangosuthu Buthelezi. This internecine struggle over territory and influence reached a crisis in June 1992, when IFP supporters attacked and massacred nearly fifty ANC loyalists in the township of Boipatong, near Johannesburg. Under the illogic of apartheid, African workers who had been transplanted to Johannesburg and surrounding areas were housed in dreary hostels according to tribal affiliation. In this case, Zulu hostel dwellers, who were invariably IFP supporters, sought revenge for purported attacks by rival ANC members.

The Boipatong massacre occurred just as the international community had begun to recognize the South African government and CODESA as valid and effective negotiating partners. ANC supporters claimed that the apartheid government had supported the slaughter in Boipatong by deploying a shadowy "third force" of police and military personnel to create further dissension in CODESA and strengthen the government's hand in the constitutional negotiations. F. W. de Klerk and Nelson Mandela agreed to a Record of Understanding that promised police protection for ANC hostel dwellers and laid the foundation for the Goldstone Commission, which eventually revealed that a "dirty tricks campaign" against the ANC had indeed been authorized by the top echelons of the South African military establishment.

Meanwhile, Buthelezi had become increasingly critical of CODESA because of the ANC's strong presence and role. His organization, the IFP, was essentially an ethno/geographic political party dominated by Zulus from the Kwa-Zulu Natal region of eastern South Africa. Buthelezi and the IFP took great issue with the idea of a unitary state as envisioned by CODESA; taking a page from the apartheid handbook, the IFP advocated a federal state wherein ethnic minorities like the Zulus and the whites of British origin, historically predominant in Natal, could maintain their autonomy. As I finished off my cigarette, the Concerned South Africans Group (COSAG), spearheaded by Buthelezi and the IFP to look after minority interests, was locked in a stalemate with CODESA at the World Trade Centre in Kempton Park, only minutes from the airport.

✳

My most pressing task at the moment, however, was letting somebody know that I had arrived in the country. So I wheeled my cart back through the airport doors to find a phone to call Auntie Bessie. When I reached her, she immediately said, "Where are you? Everybody's been looking for you."

This took me aback, because I'd made sure to tell her my travel plans, but I just let her continue talking. Everybody—all the girls and their families—had converged in Durban for the Christmas and New Year's holidays. There would be no one to pick me up at the airport in Johannesburg.

"Well," I asked her, "what am I supposed to do?" I didn't have a lot of money—at least not enough to get a flight to Durban. I hadn't even met these people yet, and I was already starting to feel like a burden.

"Look, David," said Auntie Bessie, "just hang on there, and we'll figure something out and call you back."

"But I'm on a pay phone," I whined.

"Just give me a chance to call Geraldine. You stay right there in the airport," she directed. As I got ready to hang up, she offered a warning: "David, watch out for the *skollies*, man—don't let them steal your things."

Skollies were hoodlums who preyed on naïve tourists like me. They usually hung out at airports, bus stations, and other tourist centers looking for suckers to rob or swindle, or worse.

Only after I replaced the telephone receiver did I become more aware of my immediate surroundings. I could see certain idle teenagers lounging around my baggage. A couple of them, both in ill-fitting clothes and scuffed shoes, stared at me, trying to catch a whiff of fear or desperation. I had to suppress a chortle at the thought of these young skollies casing the bags that contained my clothes and antique computer. They'd probably be doing me a favor to take this junk off my hands, I thought.

I decided to keep moving until I found a seat near a coffee shop, where there were lots of people and plenty of activity. I was hungry and really wanted a cup of coffee, but I was so paranoid about leaving my crummy bags unattended—even for a few minutes—that I resigned myself to waiting to be rescued. The effects of a now-gnawing hunger, deep exhaustion, and escalating paranoia were enough to send me into a meditative funk.

After all, what was I doing here in South Africa? I moped. What did I expect to accomplish? Did I really believe that I could reunite with the three sisters—half-sisters, really, because we had different fathers—and everyone would get on as if a twenty-five-year separation had been just an inconvenient hiccup in our lives? Maybe they knew I was coming and decided not to show up just to send me a message. Or maybe they blamed me for taking their mother away. Maybe my presence here was an uncomfortable reminder of growing up without a mother, never having someone to talk to or run to or—

My last punishing thought was suddenly interrupted: "South African Airways is paging Mr. Houze. Mr. David Houze, please check in for a message at the nearest South African Airways ticket counter." I regained my composure and set off to find the ticket counter.

"I'm David Houze," I announced to a hapless customer service agent. "I believe you have a message for me."

"Ah, yes, Mr. Houze, we have a message from your sister Geraldine. She has arranged a flight for you to Durban. Your flight leaves in thirty minutes."

The agent slid the ticket across the counter and checked my bags. It took nearly everything I had to suppress the urge to jump up and down with happiness. Auntie Bessie and Geraldine had come through for me, I thought, as I ran to find the gate for the hour-long trip to Durban.

On the plane, I discovered that I was the only passenger of color. Everywhere I looked, people flashed fake smiles at me. When I asked one of the flight attendants for some water, revealing my American accent, one of the passengers, an older man in a brown leisure suit carefully preserved from the 1970s, leaned over from his aisle seat and said, "You're from America, aren't you?"

I nodded yes, hoping to avoid obligatory small talk. Unfortunately, the man, who resembled the country singer Kenny Rogers, just felt like yapping.

"So, what brings you to Sef Efrika?"

Since it was apparent that the man would persist in his questioning, I launched into the spiel that explained my presence in South Africa.

"Well, I was actually born in Durban," I said, "but I left for the United States with my mother when I was a child. I'm on my way to meet my three sisters for the first time since leaving South Africa twenty-five years ago."

"Well, that is a great story," Kenny Rogers said. "Here's my card. Give me a call while you're in Durban, and I'll give you a tour of the place."

I took his card, knowing full well that I would do nothing of the kind. The last thing I needed was to meet up with some white liberal—as amiable as he was—looking to atone for his apartheid guilt. Mercifully, the flight attendants began serving dinner, and I escaped further conversation.

When the plane landed in Durban, I tried to get myself together by straightening my shirt and pants and adjusting my baseball cap to effect a certain devil-may-care attitude. I waited until everyone around me had exited the plane before I gathered my belongings and stepped outside into the darkness to descend the steps to the tarmac. I couldn't see anyone through the airport's observation windows, and no one elsewhere seemed to be waving or beckoning toward me. I pulled my cap down around my eyes to stem the fear and humiliation I felt surging from my belly to my brain.

Unlike Jan Smuts Airport, Louis Botha Airport was relatively small and sedate. Moments after I had claimed my bags and maneuvered my luggage onto a cart, I heard someone shouting in my direction. As I turned to investigate, two women, one carrying a child, came into view and approached me.

"David, is that you?" the woman with the child asked. I ran over and hugged them. It was Geraldine and her daughter, Roberta, who looked like a little blonde doll with green eyes. The other woman was Antoinette, and she joined the three of us in an embrace. For a few minutes, we just stood there, hugging each other, until Antoinette pulled me away and said, "David, I can't believe you finally made it here. What happened to you?"

Before I could answer, Geraldine interjected, "Why don't we go to the bar for a drink? I also need to change Roberta's diaper."

"David, you certainly have a lot of baggage, man," Antoinette remarked as we made our way to a table in the airport lounge. "By the way, just call me Nettie. Now, how long are you planning to stay in South Africa?"

Her question took me by surprise, so I lied and told her, "Well, my visa is only good for three months, and then I have to go back to the States."

She scrutinized my face thoroughly. I met her eyes and studied her face as well. She resembled my mother in many ways: Nettie had shoulder-length brown hair, high cheekbones, and olive skin tinged by moles and a few freckles. When Geraldine returned with Roberta, I could see my mother in her as well. Curiously, she had a brown complexion, darker than Nettie's and Roberta's. Geraldine's jet-black hair was pulled back into a ponytail. She shared my mother's pointed chin, angular face, and high forehead. Roberta had obviously inherited her father's eyes, hair, and skin color; she could easily have been mistaken for a white child.

Though the conversation was somewhat stilted—I busied myself with a gin and tonic—we managed to bridge the quarter-century gulf that separated us. Adrienne hadn't been able to come, Geraldine and Nettie said, because of some emergency. Both of them smoked cigarette after cigarette, and I recounted my journey from Atlanta through Europe to South Africa. So when Nettie stopped and just stared at me as if I were some kind of laboratory experiment, I shifted uncontrollably in my chair.

"Geraldine," Nettie whispered conspiratorially, "look at his ears—he's got ears just like our father."

Geraldine reached across the table and turned my head toward her to inspect my ears. "Yes, he does have ears like Daddy, you're right," she agreed.

At this point, my head was spinning. I had a slight buzz going from the drinks I'd consumed, but I was also trying to follow this new turn in the conversation. I didn't know how to respond to their insistence that I had ears like their father, so I just smiled like an idiot and gulped my drink as a way to get through what was becoming an increasingly awkward situation. Geraldine and Nettie kept drinking and smoking and discussing how I looked like their father, Nick. I preoccupied myself by playing with Roberta and pretending to be completely comfortable.

As we were preparing to leave the airport, Nettie said, almost offhandedly, "You know, David, I'm glad we now know that you're our real brother, and that we have the same father. Otherwise, I really don't know how I would have felt about you."

That last sentence seemed to reverberate all around me. I smiled weakly and braced myself for a world of revelations I had not anticipated and was not sure I could reconcile with the story of my life as I knew it.

I was so distressed and perturbed by Nettie's validation of me as her *real* brother that I barely noticed anything on the ride north to Geraldine's house in Sydenham. On the few occasions when I managed to skirt my growing depression and look out into the darkness, I could make out neighborhoods and houses that could have been found in practically any suburb of Atlanta (except for the abundance of palm trees). The streets contained rows of ranch-style houses and driveways filled with jeeps and foreign sedans. This was far from the black townships that had become synonymous with South Africa, I thought; in fact, Sydenham was populated mainly by coloureds, or mixed-race people, and Indians.

We pulled into the driveway at Geraldine's house, which was just off Sparks Road, not far from the Main Road in upper Sydenham. As the garage door closed behind us, Geraldine got out to reactivate the security system. The garage opened onto an enclosed yard overflowing with plants and flowers of all varieties, with lemon and mango trees tucked in the back. The house itself was divided into two sections, separated by a small patio: Geraldine and Robbie and Roberta lived in the back, and Robbie's mother occupied the front.

"Come, David," said Geraldine, motioning toward my bags. "Robbie isn't here, so you'll have to bring them in on your own."

The back part of the house was surprisingly small. Beyond the front hall, a narrow passage led to a living and dining area, with a kitchen to the left. Two bedrooms, one for Robbie and Geraldine and the other for Roberta, along with a bathroom, took up the right side of the suite. Flowers and plants seemed to inhabit every available corner.

"Just leave your bags near the door, and we'll sort them out tomorrow," Geraldine said. "Come sit down at the table, and I'll warm some food for you." Nettie took Roberta to prepare her for bed.

Just as Geraldine started bringing dishes of chicken and potatoes and salad to the table, I heard keys turning in the door. Robbie called out, "Howzit, guys?" and walked over to shake my hand. He was a sinewy man with fair skin, green eyes, and a short curly Afro. He wore expensive running shoes, a t-shirt, and shorts.

"Ah, Dave, so you finally made it, hey?" he said. "*Ja*, we were worried you'd missed your connection in Frankfurt to Jo'burg."

At this point, I didn't feel like rehashing the logistics of my trip, so I just nodded and tried to be as affable as possible.

"Can I get you something to drink? Whiskey? Beer?" he offered. As if on cue, Geraldine brought out a bottle of brandy, some beers, and some canned Cokes. Nettie joined us at the table, lit a cigarette, and poured herself a brandy. I helped myself to a beer and some chicken.

Robbie got up and turned on the radio, and the four of us made small talk about my trip, the weather in South Africa compared with Atlanta, and sports. No one asked about my mother; the conversation seemed calibrated to avoid any discussion of her. It was almost as if broaching the issue of our mother on my first night in South Africa was considered to be in bad taste. I sensed that both girls wanted to ask about her but wouldn't; the nonchalance and randomness of our conversation seemed too calculated.

After a while, Geraldine and Nettie announced that they were headed off to bed and said good night. Robbie pulled the brandy bottle closer and offered to pour me a drink.

"Dave, you must try this, man," he said. "You will soon discover that brandy and Coke is the unofficial national drink of South Africa—everybody drinks the stuff."

Soon I was guzzling brandy and Coke. I helped myself to Robbie's cigarettes, and we began talking about the things he was interested in: American movies, television, music and women, cycling and running, and politics. Robbie owned a butcher shop in the community, so he knew everybody and was involved in practically every local organization.

Leaning closer to me, he said, "I'm ANC, but don't tell anybody because this is not the place to be ANC."

Durban was in the grip of a low-grade civil war. An estimated ten thousand people had died in fighting between the ANC and the Zulu-dominated IFP since the ban on opposition political parties had been lifted in 1990. The clash between the ANC's commitment to a unitary government and the IFP's push for a federal system that would allow it to leverage its traditional dominance of the Durban/Natal area had helped to deadlock the constitutional negotiations in Johannesburg—and scores of people were dying weekly in Durban/Natal from the political fallout.

The ANC had been able to recruit in every part of the country except Durban/Natal and the Western Cape, the traditional stronghold of the Nationalists and their coloured allies. IFP members staged daily attacks against proclaimed or suspected ANC members in Durban. Robbie protected himself and his family by operating as an undercover ANC supporter and never revealing the extent of his involvement or his party activities. He might have felt safe talking to me because he figured that I was too uninformed about the country's politics to cause any concern.

Truthfully, while I was deeply interested in the political dynamics of the country and the blow-by-blow accounts of the grassroots struggle in Durban, I was slowly succumbing to the liquor and the rigors of travel. I told Robbie that I really needed to get some sleep.

"Okay, mate. We're going to have to put you on the couch for tonight and figure out something for tomorrow. Is that all right?" he said.

I nodded yes. I had already begun to remove my shoes, and I moved to the couch while he retrieved some blankets and a pillow from a closet. I thanked him and sank into the couch, grateful to be home in South Africa and blissfully unconcerned with what the coming days would bring.

＊

I awoke the next morning to the sound of someone moving around in the kitchen. It took me a few minutes to remember where I was. I wasn't ready to get up and face my new situation, so I burrowed deeper into the couch and drifted off to sleep. A little while later, I heard a woman's voice calling out from far away: "Good morning, would master like coffee or tea?" Again the voice drifted in: "Sir, would master like some coffee or tea?" I raised my head in the direction of the kitchen, wondering whether I was still dreaming—and whether the woman realized I was still sleeping. Only when I saw a black woman in a peach pastel dress standing in the doorway did I realize that she was directly addressing me.

"Sorry, master, can I make you something to drink?" she repeated in a timid voice. I realized that the shy woman must be the maid, so I answered, "Yes, okay, I'll have some coffee, please." I was still stunned that the woman had called me "master" and that, according to my watch, she was in the kitchen at the insane hour of 7 A.M. No one else seemed to be up. A bird outside the living room window ululated as the sun crept into the room.

When she brought the coffee to the dining room table, I thanked her and asked her name. "Thoko," she said quietly, with her head staring down at her bare feet. In addition to her brightly colored dress, she wore a black head rag and a white apron. She must have been in her late teens or early twenties, but she carried herself as if she were much older, a woman with many obligations to unseen family members, perhaps her own children, in some place well outside Sydenham. African women like Thoko had few options other than working as a domestic, primarily for whites but also for coloureds or Indians who could afford such a luxury. I wondered whether there were coloured and Indian maids in South Africa; I was sure there were no white maids.

But what both repulsed and fascinated me was that the woman had called me "master." Here I was, a parasite, a loser from the lower rung of American society, I reflected, and overnight I had assumed the mantle of "master" in South Africa.

Growing up in Mississippi, I had learned to take solace in being light-skinned and having "good hair," and this obsession had fed directly into the sense of privilege I carried into my adulthood. Because the truth was, while I had eventually come to identify with black people politically, in opposition to white supremacy, at times I chose not to consider myself authentically black—a conceit betrayed by my contempt for the dysfunctions of black American culture, including its anti-intellectualism, mindless materialism, and contempt for light-skinned "sellouts" like me. In a warped sense, I could understand how poor white South Africans and poor whites in the American South had taken comfort in knowing that there was always someone inferior to them, that no matter what happened, they weren't black and thus among the *truly* unlucky and dispossessed.

Eager to establish my liberal bona fides, I was about to engage the woman in conversation when I heard a truck pull up outside and Robbie walked through the door.

"Howzit, David?" he greeted me, seating himself across the table from me. The woman wasted no time in bringing him a cup of coffee while he lit a cigarette.

I kept staring at her as she bent over the sink, scrubbing pots, while Robbie talked about getting up at 6 A.M. to get to his shop to receive a shipment of lamb shanks and spices.

"Listen, why don't you come with me to run some errands? I can show you a bit of Durban," he said.

While he drank more coffee and plowed through a pack of cigarettes, I showered and changed into fresh clothes, the first I'd worn in two days. We left the house in Robbie's *bakkie,* his pickup truck, just as Geraldine was getting up to help the maid prepare breakfast for Roberta and Nettie.

Our first stop was Robbie's butcher shop, about two blocks from the house. A gray cinderblock building with a single plate glass window, the shop reminded me of stores in Mississippi. Inside was a counter for the cash register, a large refrigerated case containing various cuts of meat and a few vegetables, and a large walk-in freezer. Two men in blood-stained coveralls assisted a steady stream of customers.

Outside, the neighborhood had come to life. Minivans blaring loud music sped up and down the roads, stopping occasionally to take on and disgorge passengers. Men on bicycles competed with the few cars racing toward the main artery into Durban. Children in school uniforms gathered in groups along the road, seemingly reluctant to start the day. Christmas was only a few days away, and I was getting my first experience of the humidity and heat of Durban in summer.

After Robbie completed some paperwork in his little office in the back room of the store, we hopped into his truck and headed downtown. I glanced over and saw him take something from under the truck seat as we got on the highway. It was a silver 9mm pistol. He caught my eye as I stared at the weapon, now resting on the floor of the truck between us.

"What's that for?" I asked.

"Oh, that's just for our protection, man," he replied. "Durban can be a dangerous place these days."

As Durban's modern skyline came into view, Robbie gave me a quick tutorial on personal safety in the city. The possibility of becoming a crime victim, a statistic, was ever present, so weapons were a necessity, he asserted. He was especially concerned about a wave of robberies at shops in Sydenham—the gunmen had taken to killing everyone at the scene. Since carjackings had increased, motorists rarely stopped at the traffic lights (called robots) that controlled the city's intersections. Muggings and attacks in the city's crowded streets had become so commonplace that most people carried their own weapons. As we parked his truck and got out to explore the city, Robbie stuffed his revolver in the small of his back and covered it with his shirt.

The sidewalks along West Street, in the main business district, were filled with Christmas shoppers. Hawkers occupied almost every inch of the pavement, selling everything from bananas to clothing to live chickens in wire cages. Cars, buses, and minivans, known as *combis,* were crammed with people and choked the roadway. A man in a Father Christmas costume rang a bell to attract people into a clothing store; his face gleamed with perspiration in the steadily rising heat. The sounds of "Silent Night" and "Jingle Bells" competed with Whitney Houston's "I Will Always Love You." The combination of Durban's subtropical weather, the hordes of people and vendors clogging the sidewalks, and a bearded, fully outfitted Father Christmas made for a truly surreal street scene.

Durban was known for its substantial Indian population, and we gradually entered this world as we walked west of downtown past the Grey Street Mosque and toward the Victoria Street Market. Men and women in traditional Indian dress were everywhere, and the smell of curry wafted through the air. Indian merchants sold everything from expensive American stereo equipment to spices and exotic foodstuffs. Indians, for the most part, had managed to maintain their cultural traditions and ties to India in a country that had not exactly welcomed them with open arms.

✳

Indians had initially poured into Durban in 1860 to work on the fledgling British colony's sugarcane plantations. The indigenous Zulu population was unwilling to do the backbreaking work required for harvesting sugarcane. The British, who recognized the potential of this industry, decided to import laborers, pejoratively known as coolies, to work the fields, offering them free passage and the opportunity to own land after their period of indenture ended. As historian Mabel Palmer pointed out, however, "the coming of the Indians to Natal was no spontaneous uncontrolled movement of adventurous individuals seeking a better livelihood than their home country gave them. It was part of an elaborate system organized and controlled by the governments of Great Britain and India."

After completing a five-year indenture and remaining in the country for a total of ten years, the laborers could either return to India or claim a parcel of land in the colony. Many of them chose to stay on in Durban rather than return to India to face an uncertain future and comparatively limited prospects.

Over time, the Indians in Durban became a prosperous community, constituting the bulk of the merchant class and speculating in real estate (although their property rights and freedom of movement were later curtailed). As the Indians climbed the socioeconomic ladder, forming the largest concentration of Indians outside India and Pakistan, they became the targets of whites and Africans, who bitterly resented their success. This animosity became even more pronounced when the Afrikaner Nationalists came to power in 1948 and set about entrenching white supremacy and legislating complete racial segregation, mainly through the Group Areas Act. Apartheid ideologues began devising a way to rid the country of Indians by deporting them to India. The Indians responded by appealing to the United Nations for support.

Most Indians, who had been radicalized by the example of Mohandas K. Gandhi during his twenty-two-year fight for Indian rights in South Africa, shared the sentiments of Palmer, who argued: "In the first place, the European community and the government must face the fact that the Indian is a permanent element in South African life and cannot be got rid of. . . . The fact that something like 90 percent of the existing Indian population were born in South Africa and are by international law South African nationals makes this practically impossible."

As each successive wave of Indian workers elevated themselves from the sugarcane plantations, adapting to Western material standards and achieving commercial success, Africans were further displaced to the periphery of the labor market. Indian shopkeepers developed a reputation for being brusque and condescending in their treatment of Africans, who were classified at the bottom of the South African racial hierarchy. The fact that Indians, like whites, were a minority particularly galled the African majority. Africans' antipathy to what they perceived as the superior socioeconomic status of Indians came to a head in the Durban riots of 1949.

The Durban riots were sparked by an incident involving an Indian shopkeeper and an African boy on Friday, January 14, 1949. The African boy reportedly argued with and then struck an Indian boy who was minding the shop. The shopkeeper came to the aid of his young assistant and confronted the African boy. In the encounter, the boy was injured when his head was pushed through a window. Passersby took note and began spreading the rumor that an Indian merchant had killed an African boy. The details of this incident were soon exaggerated and amplified throughout African neighborhoods. In a matter of hours, mobs of Africans began assaulting Indians and burning stores and houses.

According to *The Forum,* an Indian magazine, "the forces of law and order stood, almost helplessly it seemed, as the Africans swept forward in their savage march, and the terror immediately spread to the peri-urban areas where the outburst of the previous evening became an orgy of murder, arson, rape and looting which did not seem altogether without aim, purpose and direction. The storm burst with unbridled fury on people who, in the main, lived almost under the same conditions as the Africans who attacked them."

By the time the riots ended the next day, 142 people had died (87 Africans, 50 Indians, 1 white, and 4 of undetermined race), and 1,087 had been injured, 58 of whom later died. Hundreds of stores, as well as more than a thousand homes, were destroyed. The authorities, for the most part, had simply ignored the riots, viewed by many whites as comeuppance for the upwardly mobile Indian population.

In the aftermath of the riots, Indians reflected on their future in South Africa. Although some community leaders called for mass repatriation to India, the predominant sentiment was reflected in a symposium on the riots sponsored by the South African Institute of Race Relations several years later. That meeting concluded: "Though they are a tiny minority, Indians have not feared their neighbors on the grounds of religion, race, culture or numbers. Nor are they intolerant of other people's customs and manners. Left alone they are sure of achieving a higher synthesis of living in this plural society." Over the years, the Indians in Durban continued to prosper and cemented their rights to South African citizenship. Not only did they make common cause with Africans, coloureds, and liberal whites in the anti-apartheid struggle, but they also made lasting artistic and social contributions to the cultural mélange of the country.

Their contributions were evident in Durban's Victoria Market, where Robbie and I decided to stop for lunch. Over the din of music, hawkers, and barely controlled pandemonium, I heard Robbie say, "How about a nice hot curry, hey, David?" I nodded in his direction and followed him to a tiny restaurant tucked away in a corner just outside the market. Before we sat down, Robbie removed his pistol and handed it to the hostess at the door. She gave him a claim check for the gun, and we sat down to a satisfying lunch of chicken curry and mince and potato samoosas.

✳

Adrienne showed up at Geraldine's house the next afternoon. My three sisters and I sat around the dining room table and made small talk—small talk that danced around the conversation we knew we must have sooner or later. Adrienne looked like a clone of my mother, from her facial structure and hair to her mannerisms. She had the same reddish brown hair, high cheekbones, cleft chin, and fair skin. And I could tell that she had inherited Yvonne's bluntness.

"So, David, how is Mummy?" she asked.

I wasn't prepared for the question, but I was relieved that someone had finally mentioned our mother.

"She's fine," I answered, trying not to sound curt but feeling skittish about where this discussion might go.

Geraldine's maid, Thoko, brought out a platter of tea and biscuits from the kitchen and placed it on the table. She quickly left the room and went to check on Roberta, who was waking up from a nap.

"Does she know you're here?" asked Nettie, who efficiently stirred milk and sugar into her cup of tea and reached for one of the biscuits.

"Yes, I told her I was coming here." I was not accustomed to drinking tea in the afternoon, but I was enjoying the ritual as a diversion from the discussion the four of us were creeping around.

"Did she tell you about us, David?" Geraldine inquired. She wasn't bothering with tea or biscuits; she sat with her hands clasped on the table in front of her.

"Well, she did, but Auntie Bessie told me how to contact you." I was trying to keep our discourse lighthearted and pleasant.

"You know, David," Nettie remarked, "I was never sure what happened with you and Mummy. I mean, no one ever explained to me what happened. Not even our father." She had poured a second cup of tea, which she stirred mechanically while analyzing me.

"Uh, I guess it has been a long time," I babbled, "so that's understandable." If I can just stick to one-sentence answers like this, I thought, everything will be all right: Robbie will come home for his lunch, or the maid will bring in Roberta and the conversation will naturally turn to baby talk. I had had enough of grown-up talk—and grown-up questions—for the day.

But the questioning had become relentless now: *Where was Mummy living? Where did she work? Did she live alone? When was she coming back to South Africa? Why hadn't I brought her with me?*

And then came the question that could no longer be put off.

"David, did Mummy ever tell you why she just up and left us here in South Africa?" blurted out Nettie. "That's what I want to know!"

It took me a second to absorb Nettie's outburst. Then I said, almost ashamedly, "I'm sorry. She's never told me."

Once again, just as the awkwardness of our situation threatened to overtake us, Robbie pulled into the garage and bounded into the house for lunch.

"Howzit, everybody?" he called out. The talk I so desperately dreaded yet craved was for the moment averted, lost in the shop talk Robbie brought home with him. But I knew that the time for truth telling was closing in fast.

＊

After lunch, I was relieved when Robbie suggested taking a ride over to the shop so that he could show me something. Not only was my curiosity piqued, but I was also grateful to be rescued from having to deal with my sisters. I also hadn't come to South Africa to be cooped up in a house; I wanted to get out and meet people and see everything I could.

Robbie backed his truck to the rear of his shop, and a couple of his assistants loaded several huge plastic bags into the flatbed. Robbie got out to supervise the men, and I joined him to get a better look at the contents of the load. The bags contained mounds of bones—chicken bones, lamb bones, other bones I didn't recognize, and gobs and gobs of gristle that had been pared from various cuts of meat and carcasses. This was the dark side of owning a butcher shop, I mused, because the only fit place for this offal was a dumpster, where I guessed we were heading.

After securing the load, we headed down Sparks Road, past blocks and blocks of ranch-style houses, some with swimming pools visible from the road. Robbie pointed out the wide boulevards and the palm trees and lush greenery that separated some of the houses. What I saw as precious green space, he explained, was actually a series of buffer zones, emblematic of the checkerboard segregation of residential areas. White spots alternated with coloured and Indian spots along the stretch of Sparks Road we traveled.

As we neared the Botanic Gardens, the terrain grew stark, and fewer houses appeared on the side of the road. Up ahead, I could see the road morphing into a major highway system; I still had no idea where we were going. Suddenly, Robbie jerked the truck off the road, and we were dodging branches and vines while rolling into a mesh of greenery and darkness. Before I could turn and ask where the hell we were, the truck penetrated through the woods into a vast canyonlike opening.

It took a moment for my eyes to adjust. We entered a makeshift road that wound up the side of the valley below, fronted by a cliff that seemed to be shifting in front of us. As we climbed higher, people began emerging from the canopy of trees—women and children carried buckets of water, men dragged pieces of wood and plastic sheeting to some unseen location, emaciated dogs lazed about in an open field. Nearing the top of the road, I could see that people living in makeshift hovels and lean-tos populated the entire face of the cliff, from the apex to the valley floor. The structures and their inhabitants resembled a huge labyrinth of humanity, planted precariously on the side of the cliff. Everywhere I looked among the improvised shacks, I could just make out squirms of bodies. People trudged up and down the cliff wall, some carrying bundles of wood, others building or adding onto their homes. Fires dotted the encampment, and a pall of smoke gave an ominous cast to the otherwise sun-lit landscape.

Robbie stopped the truck and looked over at me. "This, my brother, is what's known as a squatter camp," he stated.

I had figured that out, and I nodded to him to convey my understanding of the situation. I nervously looked around, hoping that I wouldn't have to get out of the truck. We just sat there for a few minutes, looking over the camp.

Soon, several people approached the truck. One man wearing a baseball cap, torn jeans, a faded rugby shirt, and sandals came up to the driver's side and began speaking Zulu to Robbie. From their banter, it was obvious that they knew each other. Robbie got out and took the man around to the back of the truck, to the bags from the butcher shop.

"David, come on out here, man," he motioned to me.

By now, a group of children had gathered as the man and a few ragged boys began unloading the bags with great enthusiasm and joy. At that moment, I realized that what I considered smelly waste was destined to become food for these people. As the men removed all the bags, Robbie explained that the bones and other scraps would be used to make soup and whatever else could be concocted from the fly-specked ingredients. Robbie brought the leftovers from his shop every week to help sustain this settlement hidden away off the busy roads of Durban.

Camps like this existed in and around all of South Africa's major metropolitan areas, including Durban, Cape Town, Johannesburg, and Pretoria. The tide of African humanity had begun breaching the formerly white cities with the repeal of the Pass Laws in 1986, although these restrictions on the movement of Africans in urban areas had in fact started to crumble in the early 1980s, when the government's crackdown on labor unrest became untenable in the wake of increased industrialization and a shrinking pool of white labor.

Unlike the black townships, some of which had running water and electricity, the squatter camps were slums where people drifting in from rural areas made their homes while searching for work in the cities. Hundreds of thousands of people crammed into such places, with no jobs, little potable water, and no access to health clinics or schools for the children. Tuberculosis and other respiratory illnesses as well as nutritional ailments were rampant. There were camps like this all over Durban, Robbie told me. They were filled with people anticipating the demise of apartheid and the promise of a better life.

When we were back on the road, Robbie put in a Lionel Richie tape—he was crazy about Lionel Richie, he said—opened a fresh pack of cigarettes, and headed south toward the Durban beachfront area. I helped myself to a smoke and marveled at the incongruity of the secret world of squalor we had just left and the sight of hotels and modern apartment buildings in the distance. Robbie mentioned that he wanted me to meet some people he knew, and I was looking forward to seeing more of the city, especially the beaches.

From the Botanic Gardens area, we sped back toward the Victoria Market and got onto West Street, which was a straight shot to North Beach. Now we were back in the traffic and congestion of Durban's commercial district, where hordes of people of all colors scrambled to get ready for Christmas, only a few days away. The streets seemed to vibrate with nervous energy, trebled by the fact that the country's fate was being determined elsewhere while hundreds of people were being killed in political violence each week.

As we neared the beach, the landscape became increasingly cluttered with ramshackle hotels and shops catering to tourists with signs that exclaimed, SEAFOOD BUFFET, CASTLE LAGER ON TAP R10 ALL DAY! and GUEST ROOMS BY THE DAY OR HOUR. Suddenly I started to notice little groups of women wearing skimpy dresses and garish makeup hanging out on the street corners. Seagulls dive-bombed for discarded chicken bones that were strewn across the sidewalks. We were getting closer to Durban's "Golden Mile," the main attraction of a thirty-mile stretch of coastline unmatched in the country.

In fact, most South Africans had taken to vacationing, or going on holiday, in Durban. The view up the Marine Parade revealed a spectacle of hotels, restaurants, holiday flats, outdoor carnivals, flea markets, and bathing pools. The mighty Indian Ocean buffeted the coastline, to the immense pleasure of a few surfers straddling its waves. Several ships waiting for permission to enter Durban Harbor sat off shore like so many toy pieces.

Zulu rickshaw men dressed in colorful outfits ferried passengers up and down the oceanfront in the rising humidity. The view from the beach inland was equally majestic. Robbie pulled the truck over to point out an area called the Bluff, a range of emerald hills separating the Indian Ocean from Durban Bay, and Berea, a summit of hills that encircled the city center. I was remarking to Robbie about the number of bronzed, bikini-clad women strolling nearby when his cell phone rang. It was Geraldine, who wanted to know where we were, what we were doing, and when we'd be returning home.

Robbie skillfully told her that we had another stop to make before heading back. He looked at me when he said this; I think he knew that I wasn't in a big hurry to continue the inquisition from my sisters that he had interrupted earlier that day. I just wasn't ready to deal with all their questions yet, mainly because I didn't have any answers. It was a miracle that I had even gotten this far in my journey, I thought, as I reached for another of Robbie's cigarettes to numb a feeling of doubt, fear, and uncertainty growing in my belly.

We stopped at a beachside food stand for a couple of Cokes and samoosas before heading back down Snell Parade to meet Robbie's friends. Up ahead rose Addington Hospital, the facility for coloureds, where I'd been born. The huge L-shaped building was situated, appropriately enough, on Addington Beach. Robbie told me that the hospital was thoroughly integrated these days, even though people in Durban still thought of it as "the coloured hospital."

The towering derricks and cranes of Durban Harbor now came into view as we entered an industrial area lined with warehouses and loading docks. Durban was the busiest port in the country, and all these businesses obviously depended on the harbor for commercial survival. Robbie turned down a road away from the oceanfront and pulled up to what appeared to be a junkyard: an imposing fence topped with barbed wire sheltered the carcasses of cars and trucks scattered across the enclosed compound. A couple of fierce Alsatians ran yelping at full throttle toward the fence. The beach suddenly seemed far away.

Robbie blew the truck's horn. A few minutes later, a white man emerged from a building that looked like a garage and came to the gate. He carried the largest shotgun I had ever seen, in addition to a pistol he wore in a shoulder holster. He calmed the dogs and shooed them away. Robbie and the man greeted each other in Afrikaans while we waited for the gate to the compound to swing open. I remembered that Robbie's gun was tucked just underneath his seat.

After he pulled the truck into the compound, Robbie motioned for me to get out with him as he retrieved his pistol and, this time, stuffed it in the front of his pants. The big grizzled man came over to greet us, and Robbie made the introductions.

"Christo, I want you to meet David, my brother-in-law from the States, you know, the one I was telling you about."

"Howzit, David?" Christo said, grabbing me by the forearm and shaking my hand. "Welcome to Durban, man. Is this your first time in South Africa?"

Before I could answer, Robbie spoke up. "No, man, David was born right here in Durban, *ja.*"

Christo looked at me and said, "So you're a goddamn South African, man. How about that? Come on up to meet the other guys."

As we walked up to the garage, Robbie and Christo spoke in Afrikaans as I tried to figure out Christo's ethnicity. Though he spoke Afrikaans, I knew that historically Durban had been settled by the British and that many of their descendants still predominated in the province, whereas the Boer, or Afrikaner, farmers had trekked to northern provinces such as the Orange Free State and the Transvaal, away from the intrusive and dreaded racial liberalism of the British in the Western Cape and Natal. I hadn't counted on meeting any decent white people in South Africa, I thought, as we entered the garage, but Christo and Robbie were obviously good friends.

In the corner of the garage, a bare-chested Indian man was welding parts onto a car engine. A rubber visor shielded his face from the sparks of the acetylene torch, but I could tell his ethnicity from the mass of straight black hair atop his head. He wore a pair of shorts and boots and what looked to be a .357 Magnum revolver in a waist holster. What appeared to be an AK-47 leaned against the wall of a dimly lit office in the corner of the garage. A tiny brown man came out to meet us; he, too, wore a pistol. The man waved to Robbie and squinted over at me.

"Hey, Joseph," Christo called out to him, "I want you to meet Robbie's brother-in-law, David. He's from the States."

Joseph extended his hand and just smiled, revealing several missing teeth. I took his calloused hand and said hello, and the little man just laughed.

The Indian man with the welding torch had taken a break and came over to greet us. His name was Vikram, and he was immediately interested in talking to me about "the States."

Joseph pulled several chairs from the office, and Christo produced some glasses, a bottle of brandy, and a few bottles of beer. Everybody fired up cigarettes. I had to bum one from Robbie, who, I sensed, was wondering why I hadn't bought my own.

Christo was the first to start asking questions: *What did I think of South Africa? What was I doing in the country? Did I have any hundred-dollar bills I needed to exchange on the black market?* ("I can get you a good deal on rands," he insisted.) *Could I get my hands on any CB radios, which were hard as hell to come by in South Africa?*

The others listened intently while I told Christo that I was a journalist just trying to reconnect with my family and that I probably wouldn't need to do any black market currency exchanges, since the little money I had would have to last until I got a job—if I ever got a job. And, no, I told him, I had no way of procuring CB radios.

Christo looked at me with what seemed like displeasure, gulped his drink, and joined in a conversation the others were having about the recent wave of violence spreading through Durban.

"*Ja,* this chap I knew," Joseph was saying, "was closing his shop one night—just last week!—and the bladdy keffirs came in, robbed him, and shot him dead. Dead, man!"

Robbie jumped in: "Well, in Sydenham, we've had two butcheries hit in the last month. It's fuckin' out of control—and the cops do nothing. They can't be found."

By now, the bottle of brandy had made its way around the group again. The burnt orange of the sun could be seen through the two windows high above the garage door. I was grateful that the arc of the conversation had been deflected from me.

"Let me tell you something," said Joseph in a surprisingly methodical and menacing tone, "if I ever see one of these blek bastards coming in here, I'm gonna blow their keffir arses to bladdy hell! I'm not pissing around with these blek cunts. I say we kill them fuckin' all, the *skellum!*"

Joseph paused to take a drag of his cigarette, and Vikram started in.

"Man, I tell you, before all this constitution shit, we never had any trouble out of the bleks. We always had an understanding with them: you work, we pay you. Everything is fair. But now the only language the blek buggers understand is this," he said, pointing to his obscenely huge gun, "and I will *moord* [murder] any blek bastard who tries to rob this place."

Robbie just sat with his drink and cigarette; he was mostly silent and his face was inscrutable.

Christo chimed in, "You see, David"—as if he felt it necessary to add an explanatory note to the torrent of racist vitriol just unleashed in the room—"South Africa is still very much a dangerous place, and we must protect ourselves because nobody knows what the fuck's gonna happen in this country, man. Nobody knows shit, so we must just arm and protect ourselves, *ja*."

But what I wanted to tell Christo and the others was that I *did* understand their anger and fear and uncertainty. I understood that through its twisted social engineering, South Africa had destroyed the lives of countless people, forcing them to commit unspeakable acts of violence and hatred against one another. I could understand their instinct for self-preservation and protection against people who had nothing to lose through robbery, murder, and mayhem. As Peter Lambley observed in his book *The Psychology of Apartheid,* South Africa had long been a deeply troubled and psychotic society—a society in which "you were expected to express your hurt, anger, dismay or whatever by one of the many institutionalized rituals available—'drink yourself mindless, drive and cheat recklessly, bunk school or work, fuck indiscriminately, beat someone up . . . anything but show the proper emotions, the proper shock, or recognize the ungodly mess that you live in in the first place.'"

What truly disturbed me, though, was the intensity of racism expressed by the men sitting around in the garage. Vikram and Joseph especially surprised me because they were the darkest people in the room; under apartheid, Vikram, an Indian, and Joseph, a black or coloured—I couldn't tell which—were both relegated to the racial rubbish heap. Admittedly, my disgust was tempered by the reality that at one time or another I had expressed similar racist views, either in the company of friends from college who had slipped the noose of low expectations for black students and entered the middle and upper-middle classes of the American establishment or as I fulminated in private against the "ghetto niggas" who made it hard for me to puncture and defy white stereotypes.

I was equally likely, however, to rail against "stupid racist white crackers" whenever I felt slighted by whites—yet another symptom of the schizophrenia on matters of race and identity that I had grappled with over the years. Now all my notions of interracial solidarity, of people of color sticking together to battle white supremacy, and racial chauvinism in general, were skewered by the realities on the ground in a country careening toward anarchy. And as I looked around the group, nothing seemed out of the ordinary: Joseph fetched a fresh bottle of brandy, and somebody started talking about the Kaiser Chiefs, a South African soccer team.

✳

The morning of Christmas Eve in Durban augured an unusually hot and humid day. When I woke up in the stuffy living room, kicking off the blanket twisted around me on the couch, Nettie and Adrienne were already in the kitchen preparing breakfast. Geraldine was feeding Roberta at the dining room table. The maid, Thoko, had been given two days off to spend with her family. Robbie and I had gotten in late the previous evening after leaving his friends at the garage. He was nowhere to be found; probably at the butcher shop, I thought, leaving me to deal with the three women. My head hurt slightly from the endless rounds of brandy punctuated by beers with the men at the garage. I dragged myself off the couch, grabbed some fresh clothes from a duffel bag, and went into the bathroom to have a cool, soothing shower.

After dressing and cleaning up after myself—I was paranoid about leaving the shower or bathroom dirty and calling attention to myself—I took a deep breath and stepped outside into the living room to start the day.

"Good morning, David," said Geraldine from the living room table while feeding Roberta. "Are you having coffee and breakfast this morning?"

I said, "Yes, please," and sat down at the table. Adrienne came out of the kitchen wearing an apron over a pair of shorts. I couldn't help staring at her because she looked so much like our mother.

"Hi, David," she said. "Shall I make you some eggs and bacon and toast?"

"Yes, I'd like that very much."

"Are you okay this morning?" she asked. "You and Robbie were out partying last night, hey? Nettie, come look: David is *ibabhalazi. Ag,* shame."

Nettie came out of the kitchen to have a look at me. "Are you *ibabhalazi,* David?"

I guessed that *ibabhalazi* meant hung over, so I smiled sheepishly, and they all burst out laughing—even Roberta let out a high-pitched giggle. Their warm-hearted teasing and laughing about my hangover created a sense of fun and harmony among the four of us. I sensed that I had been granted a respite, albeit temporarily, from all the weighty issues we still needed to discuss. Adrienne brought me a plate of food and a cup of coffee, and I felt my spirits—and the deadening thud in my skull—now lifting. After all, it was Christmas Eve, and I was in South Africa of all places—far from the dreariness of the Stratford Inn in Atlanta.

Eventually, Adrienne and Nettie joined Geraldine, Roberta, and me at the living room table. Right away, the talk turned to last-minute shopping and preparations for Christmas dinner. Geraldine handed Roberta to me and took out a list of shopping and chores. First, she said, she needed to go to Musgrave Center, a shopping mall not far from Sydenham, to pick up some specialty grocery items. She also wanted to visit a shop in Overport City, another mall in Durban's northern suburbs. And she wanted to stop by a friend's house to drop off a present. She went on checking off her list while Roberta jumped and squirmed in my lap.

"Well, the only thing I want to make sure we do is get to the bottle store before it closes," said Nettie with a whoop that made us all laugh in approval.

"I know that's right," I attested. From my reading and research, I knew that drinking was a ritual in South Africa—and a highly politicized one, at that. Every meal and any conversation seemed to be accompanied by some form of alcohol, whether brandy, scotch, beer, or wine. Although the Christmas holidays provided a convenient rationalization for overindulgence, I believed that it was symptomatic of a more intrinsic societal disease that pushed people to drink indiscriminately without regard to health or decorum. South Africans drank to excess to escape the ravages of apartheid, plain and simple, I theorized. This was a society hooked on booze to deaden the painful reality of a country mired in social dysfunction and human suffering.

Roberta began exploring my face with her pudgy fingers as Adrienne and Nettie cleared the table. I felt a perverse pride in the toddler's green eyes and silky blonde hair.

Geraldine put down her list and looked at me playing with Roberta.

"David," she said, "do you think Roberta looks more like me or Robbie?"

I was a bit startled by the question. "What do you mean? She looks like both of you."

"Look," she said, pointing at her arm, "I have brown skin, and Robbie's skin is fair. And she also has Robbie's eyes and hair. I mean, she looks like a little white child, not my child. A few weeks ago, I was out shopping with Roberta, and this white lady comes over to me and says, 'O-oh, what a cute little baby. Are you keeping her for your madam?' I just looked at her and walked away. I was so disgusted. That's what I mean: it seems like every time I go out with Roberta, people just assume that I'm her nanny, and not her mother. It makes me so mad."

Roberta began kicking and crying on my lap, and I handed her back to Geraldine, which was perfect timing because I had no idea how to respond to her story. I recalled being in McRae's department store with my mother in Meridian when an old white lady mistook me for a little white boy. Then, as now, color consciousness had intruded on my family's life, I reflected.

"Shall we get going then?" said Adrienne, coming back into the living room. "We need to get back before it gets too late." Adrienne's ex-husband was dropping off their son, Angelo, at Geraldine's house for Christmas. Nettie's boyfriend was also driving her daughter, Kim, from Johannesburg to be with everyone at Geraldine's place for the holidays. So we packed up and piled into Geraldine's car for the trip to Musgrave Center.

The huge mall and its neighborhood of Berea, in the northwest part of Durban, felt like another planet. I had never seen such a bubble of white affluence. Immaculately manicured lawns sprawled across gated communities. Range Rovers, BMWs, and Mercedes-Benzes competed for space on the clean and beautifully maintained streets. Young whites walked dogs and jogged and loafed about on the avenues. Specialty shops and boutiques offered everything from gourmet coffee to women's fashions. I had to look hard to see black people—the women dressed in the perennial pastel dresses, the men in blue or green coveralls—on the periphery of this opulent vision. But there they were, performing their muted roles in maintaining the illusion of happiness and beatific calm in an otherwise turbulent society.

The atmosphere at the mall was that of a service economy tightly tailored around blacks being at the beck and call of whites. Blacks, for the most part, were not at Musgrave Center as customers; rather, they were cashiers or baggers, custodians or security officers. Most of these people lived miles away in the townships of Kwa Mashu or Umlazi—if they were fortunate enough to live in a township rather than a squatter camp. The whole scene felt like a relic of some discredited, soon-to-be-dismantled civilization hanging on to the last gasp of white privilege. I was happy to get back to Sydenham and the reality of a multiracial, multicultural South Africa, confirmed by the sight of a man maneuvering a donkey-drawn wagon on the main road.

A few blocks from Geraldine's house, we stopped at the bottle store. The place was jammed with people, so only Nettie and I went inside. I instinctively offered her money, but she refused and proceeded to order five cases of assorted beers—Castle and Lion lagers and Hunter's Gold— as well as two cases of brandy, a case of wine, several bottles of scotch and gin, and a case of champagne. As a clerk packed the boxes of liquor and beer into the trunk of Geraldine's car, a gnarled old black woman came up to Nettie. Pointing toward me, she said something in what I guessed was Zulu and started snickering. When I asked Nettie what the woman had said, she replied, "She said you and I look alike, that you must be my brother." Of course, this gave me a tremendous boost of self-confidence and helped allay some of the fears and doubts I had about fitting in with my sisters.

Robbie was home when we returned, and he and I unloaded the groceries and alcohol from Geraldine's car. We were just about to hop into his truck and head over to the garage to visit his friends when Geraldine called out, "David, I need you to stick around because our father is coming over tonight and wants to meet you."

My only visible reaction to this news was to smile weakly and fold my body into a nearby chair. But the gnawing feeling in my belly had returned, and I proceeded to douse it with as much liquor as possible in preparation for meeting "our father."

✳

The first thing I noticed about Nick when he came through the door later that night was how much he looked like my father—that is, the father I knew from Mississippi. He had Dave's slim build, complexion, and facial features; in fact, they could have been brothers. Nick, I had learned, was a welder who traveled up and down the South African coast to work in shipyards.

All the children had been coaxed to bed, and the rest of us were sitting around the living room table drinking, smoking, and listening to music.

The scene had an element of the unreal and seemed to unfold in some far-off place.

Geraldine introduced me to Nick, and he grabbed me in a bear hug that lasted for several moments. "David, man, I am so happy to see you," he said with a wide smile, revealing several gold teeth.

I thought momentarily about all the people with bad teeth and the prevalence of gold teeth among the South Africans I'd met so far; I could definitely relate to this because my mouth was riddled with dormant cavities.

Nettie and Geraldine brought out some food and a glass of ice for Nick for the first of many drinks, and we settled in with occasional small talk. But Nick ate his food without talking, his eyes never leaving my face. Geraldine, however, was all business and seemed determined to get everything out in the open.

"So, Daddy, can you tell us what happened between you and Mummy when we were all children?" she demanded.

Nick pushed his plate aside and reached for his cigarettes before answering. "Well, what do you want to know? That was so long ago."

"Well," Nettie spoke up, "why did Mummy leave us? And is David really our brother?"

Robbie shifted in his seat, probably wishing he could be elsewhere.

Realizing that he had everyone's attention, Nick leaned back in his chair and began telling the story of his marriage to Yvonne and how he had tried to keep her from leaving South Africa and taking me to live with the American seaman named Dave in the United States. All he could remember, Nick told us, was that there had been a big fight when he showed up to stop Yvonne from going. Although he had begged and pleaded with her, Yvonne had been determined to leave South Africa and move to the United States with the American. He had fought in vain to have me remain with him, he said, and he described how devastated he had been.

In all those years, he exclaimed, with a dramatic flourish of his arms, he had not heard from Yvonne and had no way of contacting us. But he had never stopped thinking about me, he asserted, looking at me intensely, and had always known that I was his son.

As if for emphasis, Nettie said, "So, you're saying David is really your son after all?"

"Of course, he is my son," Nick retorted. "I fought with your mother to keep him here in South Africa. He is my son."

At this point, my head was reeling. No one uttered a word. Only the sound of a jazz quartet on the radio rushed headlong into the silence that descended upon the room. Suddenly, I knew what I had to do.

I stood up and cried out: "Why didn't anybody ever tell me this?! Why didn't anybody ever tell me this?! Why didn't I know?!"

I was fine-tuning my histrionics as I collapsed onto the floor, flailing my arms and legs and maniacally repeating: "Why didn't anybody tell me? Why didn't anybody tell me? Why didn't anybody tell me?!" Robbie dashed around the table to lift me from the floor, and the others stood up from the table, unsure of how to act or what to think.

I remained on the floor, kicking and crying, until Geraldine threw a blanket on me. Nick and Robbie urged me onto the couch, where I continued to sob and moan in fake agony, until I drifted off into a self-induced stupor. Of course, the breakdown was all an act, a ruse to dodge the issue of Nick being my real father and, through this irrational outburst, to somehow make it a foregone conclusion. I had to appear as distraught as possible to escape the fact that my entire life story in Mississippi was now being called into question and dismissed as a fabrication perpetrated by my mother. I also recognized the opportunity to completely ingratiate myself with Geraldine, Nettie, and Adrienne. Now there could be no doubt that I was their real brother, and not just some freeloading, half-blood stranger looking to run a game on them.

Robbie nudged me awake early the next morning. "David," he whispered, "I need you to help me with something, man. Come on." I pulled on some jeans and stumbled out of the house and into his truck.

He offered me a cigarette and asked, "Are you okay? I know that was a lot for you to deal with last night."

My whole shameful performance came back to me, and I simply said, "Yeah. I guess I just got carried away by the situation." We didn't speak of it again as we pulled up to his shop, got out, and went in through the back entrance.

Ostensibly, Robbie had recruited me to help with some last-minute preparations for Christmas dinner. We began loading boxes of food into his truck and rearranging huge packages and slabs of meat in the walk-in freezer. Soon enough, though, he produced a bottle of brandy and a couple of glasses and suggested that we take a break. I looked at my watch and saw that it was eight-thirty—it seemed early to start drinking on a day sure to be filled with more alcohol.

Handing me another cigarette, Robbie began: "You know, David, I wanted to talk to you about Geraldine. I think that after what we all went through last night, I can share some stuff with you." I pulled up a chair as he began telling me his concerns about Geraldine's drinking and the marital problems they'd been having.

Robbie confided that he and Geraldine had had several confrontations, some of them physical, over what he perceived as the proper duties of a wife and mother—having dinner ready for him when he got home, cutting short the time she spent with her rowdy friends in the neighborhood, and spending more time with Roberta rather than foisting her off on the maid. While I had noticed that Geraldine tended to drink throughout the day—a habit indistinguishable from that of others—I hadn't seen any evidence that she neglected Roberta. I suspected, though I didn't dare mention it to him, that Robbie had a problem with Geraldine having a successful teaching career and making time to visit with several friends who lived nearby.

Overall, South Africa was a rigidly patriarchal society, and I interpreted his complaints about Geraldine in that light. During the short time I'd been in Durban, I had observed that Robbie treated Geraldine condescendingly—telling her to shut up at times and demanding that she stay at home more—rather than according her the respect typically given to a career woman. But at this point, I didn't want to get drawn into any conflict, so I just nodded my head in understanding, if not agreement. Robbie stared at me as if to reassure himself that I was his ally.

"So you see what I'm dealing with here, right, David?" he said.

I just smiled diffidently and reached for the brandy. We drank half the bottle, packed up the remaining supplies, and headed back to the house.

✳

The heat of the Durban sun bore down on my shoulders as I helped unload the boxes of groceries. If not for the brightly colored presents and the children running about playing with toys, we could have been preparing for a picnic on a hot summer day. Most South Africans didn't bother with Christmas trees or lights, instead focusing on the exchange of presents and the huge family gathering and meal. Geraldine and Nettie were in the kitchen, busy with the cooking, while everyone else gathered in the tiny living room and dining room. Robbie's mother had come to share in the meal and was holding Roberta. Adrienne had been put in charge of arranging the table and festive decorations around the room. Robbie's brief was to sort out the bar and beverage arrangements. He and I naturally helped ourselves to a couple of beers while packing several coolers with ice and more booze than I had ever seen for one dinner.

Nick came over, and we both acted as if the previous evening's performance had been slightly embarrassing. "Still," he said, out of everyone else's earshot, "David, we must strike while the iron is hot. I want to take you around Durban when we can find the time." I sensed that he wanted to make up for lost time or perhaps was struggling to reach out to me. I still wasn't totally convinced that he was my father. I was in fact quite ambivalent about the notion, but I agreed to go with him and decided to give him the benefit of the doubt.

When everyone gathered around the table, I was astonished at the amount and variety of food: turkey, smoked ham, roast lamb, curried lamb and chicken, *boerewors* (farmer's sausage), steamed mussels, some kind of fish I didn't recognize, about a half-dozen different salads, vegetables, and rolls, not to mention an incredible array of desserts, including bread pudding, milk tart custard, and several cakes.

"Before we begin," Geraldine announced, "I want to welcome my brother, David, from the States to South Africa to be with us for Christmas."

Nick, who was sitting next to me, squeezed my hand. Geraldine then blessed the food and thus began one of my most memorable Christmas dinners. The children began pulling crackers, colorful little cardboard tubes containing twists of papers that created a small pop when pulled at both ends. Crackers had come over with the British in the 1800s and endured in the Christmas traditions of Durban. Adrienne's son, Angelo, laughed and asked, "Don't you have crackers in America, Uncle David?" Yes, I told him, we certainly did have crackers in America, though not the kind he and the other children used to celebrate Christmas.

As the meal wound down, the children began exchanging gifts. Kim came over to me with a brightly wrapped present, saying, "Uncle David, this is for you." I was embarrassed because I hadn't even thought about Christmas gifts for anyone, partly because my money situation was so tight. Anyway, Geraldine and Robbie had refused to accept any money from me, warning that I would need it while I looked for work. In fact, nobody seemed to be paying me much attention; this was, after all, a day for the children, and they were all—including little Roberta—fiddling with gifts and gadgets at the table and around the living room. Robbie had begun bar service, and I signaled him for a stiff whiskey and water. I hadn't felt such contentment and such a sense of family in a long time.

One of Robbie's friends, an African guy named Derek, came over after dinner. Geraldine offered him some food, but he simply asked for a beer and drifted into the living room to listen to the radio.

Adrienne was starting to clear food from the table and called out jokingly to Derek, "*Ag,* man, it's okay if you come to the table and sit with the coloureds!"

Everybody burst out laughing, and Derek just lifted his beer and toasted us all from his chair in the living room.

"Don't worry," he said derisively, "I'll just get madam to give me a plate to take back with me to the township."

Even more laughter erupted at this because, as Robbie told me later, Derek lived in a new brick house in an affluent part of Durban and was a computer engineer for a major corporation. According to Robbie, in the newly emerging South Africa, Derek was not typical: he was highly educated, employed, and mixed well with other racial groups, particularly people of so-called coloured origins. Robbie later explained to me that Durban had been the birthplace of the Black Consciousness Movement, a campaign spearheaded by the martyred Steve Biko that emphasized the commonality of the struggles of people of color against white supremacy. At the height of apartheid, when the government banned all opposition groups, Durban had given birth to the multiracial United Democratic Front (UDF).

We joined Derek in the living room and talked about current events and sports and listened to Kim play Whitney Houston's "I Will Always Love You" over and over again. Yet I couldn't help thinking about the coloured versus African issue we had joked about. Like the coloureds in South Africa among their fellow Africans, I had always seen myself as different from—and, shamefully, sometimes better than—the black people I had grown up around in Mississippi. My interactions with the black people in America's permanent underclass, whose boardinghouses and drug hangouts I had frequented into adulthood, had, perhaps unfairly, cemented in my mind an image of an essentially impoverished and dissolute population: roguish, promiscuous, shortsighted, prone to violent outbursts, and deeply suspicious of anyone among them who tried to talk or act "white."

Even when I spent time with the kids in my grandmother's neighborhood, we approached each other as "the other"—I was separated by my love of reading and curiosity about the wider world, inevitably defined in terms of whiteness. Self-hatred was fundamental to the boundaries and contours of my childhood in Mississippi, and this toxin had shaped my development and interaction with my black "brothers and sisters." I sensed that beneath the laughter and teasing about Derek the African failing to qualify for the privilege of being coloured lay issues that South Africans hadn't yet begun—or weren't ready—to face.

✳

Since arriving in Durban, I'd been so caught up with seeing the city and hanging out with Robbie that I'd forgotten all about Auntie Bessie. So when she called to check up on me, she brought me back to the reality of why I'd come to South Africa. I cradled the telephone receiver and shifted uncomfortably from foot to foot as she scolded me for not calling. "Shame, David, you didn't even contact us here to say 'Merry Christmas' or anything," she complained. "Are we going to see you while you're here in Durban?" I can be seriously absentminded sometimes, especially when drinking alcohol from dusk to dawn every day, so I felt extremely guilty and promised Auntie Bessie that I'd be over as soon as possible.

Geraldine drove Adrienne, Nettie, Roberta, and me to Auntie Bessie's house in Greenwood Park, on Mimosa Road in the northeast section of Durban. Even though we were traveling through the affluent northern suburbs, evidence of the city's immense poverty and social inequality was everywhere I looked. At all the intersections, small boys and old men hustled everything from newspapers to bananas, oranges, and litchis. A young coloured woman shuffled along the side of the road with a pack of bedraggled children. A huge black security guard cradling a shotgun stood outside the only door of a busy supermarket. A teenage Indian boy sped past us in a souped-up Volkswagen Golf, leaving strains of Tupac Shakur's music in his wake. Geraldine turned onto Mimosa Road and began the climb to Auntie Bessie's house, past a 1960s-era hospital where dozens of people milled about, apparently waiting to be seen by doctors.

"That's a hospital for bleks," Nettie pointed out.

At one time, Auntie Bessie's house must have been notable in the community, but it now seemed a faded replica of itself. Emerald green walls had lost their luster, and the cracks in the exterior of the house signaled either decrepitude or old-world charm. As we came to a stop in the yard, a tall, fair-skinned woman with her dark hair pinned back into a bun came out of the house and waved. Across from the door was what could only have been the servants' or maids' quarters. We all got out of the car, and Auntie Bessie came up and gave me a great hug.

"Oh, my Gahd, David, look at you!" she exclaimed. "You were just a child, crawling and walking around here, when you left, and now look at you!"

She continued hugging me as the others looked on and began drifting into the house. Out of the corner of my eye, I saw someone—an old woman, maybe—peeking intently out the door of the servants' cottage.

We went into the kitchen, which led into the living room and then to a porch fronting a yard that bristled with plants, lemon and mango trees, and ducks and chickens. Three bedrooms and a bathroom sat off the kitchen. Auntie Bessie's husband, Raymond, and her son Xavier were not home. While she was urging the others to get settled in the living room, my eyes were drawn to the ceiling of the house. Sections of the ceiling were missing; great, gaping holes yawned over the living room and the kitchen. I quickly looked away, not wanting to let on that I had noticed the obvious: the house had definitely seen better days.

"Come, David, sit down and tell me about your trip, eh? Let me get us something to snack on, shall I?" Auntie Bessie offered.

She went to the kitchen door and called out to the cottage, "Tombe! Come here, girl!" A few minutes later, a small, elderly African woman came in and began bowing toward all of us. She had a slight stoop but seemed resilient and sturdy from a life of waiting on other people. She looked at me and flashed a broad smile. "Tombe, please bring out some snacks and cool drinks for us, thank you," ordered Auntie Bessie.

Nettie and Adrienne looked bored, and Geraldine had her hands full with Roberta, as Auntie Bessie asked me about my trip and Mummy. I was able to discern that she and my mother had grown up together and had been close, especially since she had cared for Geraldine, Adrienne, and Nettie. I wasn't sure, though, whether they were actually related.

"So, is your mother still in nursing, David?" she asked. "I haven't talked to her since a couple of years after you and she left here, way back when."

I brought her up to speed on my mother's situation and assured her that she was still in good health and working as a nurse practically every day.

"Well, what about your brothers Xavier and Rasheid? How are they?" she delved.

I explained that Xavier had been placed in an institution in Mississippi, where he was receiving care for his mental retardation, and that Rasheid was in a Michigan prison serving a five-year sentence for possession of crack cocaine. At my mention of Xavier and Rasheid, Geraldine, Adrienne, and Nettie looked up from the photo albums they'd been browsing. The four of us had already discussed "Mummy's other children" during the first couple of days after my arrival in Durban. It was a subject fraught with awkwardness and tension, however, and we had tacitly agreed not to explore it any further. Now that I had revealed more about my brothers—who were, I suddenly realized, their brothers, too—they seemed to move beyond a mere perfunctory interest. I didn't want to talk about Rasheid or Xavier anymore, though, because I sensed that their circumstances—both, in a manner, institutionalized—solidified my sisters' grievances against a mother who had abandoned not only them but, seemingly, her other children as well.

"Ah, I see," said Auntie Bessie, as the maid brought bowls of chips and a pitcher of punch to the coffee table. As I scooped up a handful of the stale chips and tried to wash them down, I noticed the old black woman staring at me with intense, almost abnormal, interest.

Auntie Bessie must have noticed, too. "David, I bet you don't know who this is," she said, pointing to the maid. Of course I don't know who it is, I thought, almost choking on the dry chips, while passively shaking my head no.

"This is Tombe. She used to take care of you when you were just a little boy," Auntie Bessie explained. "*Ja,* Tombe used to keep you when your mother was away at work."

The old woman had backed into the kitchen, smiling and bowing. I began to feel a strong sense of connection to her and Auntie Bessie's house. I stood up and went over to the woman and introduced myself before hugging her. She felt so slight and fragile in my arms, as if she had weathered many years of abuse and mistreatment while caring for other people and their children. I could tell that she and Auntie Bessie had a good relationship and had grown closer over the years, but I couldn't help wondering what Tombe had given up or what family she had forsaken in some godawful township or squatter camp to care for me, my sisters, and Auntie Bessie's two boys.

"*Nkosi* Malan?" the woman said through a toothless grin. "*Nkosi* Malan."

I asked Auntie Bessie what she was saying.

"That was her name for you when you were a baby, *Nkosi* Malan," said Auntie Bessie. "She said you were the chief, named after Malan, the state president."

I excused myself to go to the toilet because I was suddenly overcome with the feeling of a powerful bond with the stooped-over black woman.

After regaining my composure, I looked into one of the bedrooms, where I could see photographs of Adrienne, Geraldine, and Nettie. I stepped into the room and looked at the huge metal bed and the tiny window. This must have been their room, I thought; this must have been the room where all the girls stayed while at Auntie Bessie's house. I tried to imagine what it must have been like for them, together, in that room. I had been able to find out only the sketchiest details about their lives in South Africa after my mother and I left.

Adrienne, who had turned out to be the easiest to talk to, had told me how Nettie had clashed with Auntie Bessie and then moved to Johannesburg to begin a career in accounting while she was in her late teens. She got married in Johannesburg, had a child, and then divorced. Geraldine had remained in Durban, married Robbie at an early age, and become a teacher before having Roberta. Adrienne herself had left Durban to be with Nettie in Johannesburg. She married, had a child, and then divorced before finding a job as a clerk in a department store. I had pressed Adrienne for more details of their lives under apartheid. But all she would say was, "Life was not that bad for us in South Africa. Yes, we suffered like everybody else, but what we really missed was having a mother."

I was thinking about how I could get my sisters to open up to me more. As I reentered the living room, I was surprised to find that Nick had arrived. He motioned to me across the room, and I said hello and sat down to play with Roberta.

"So, David, Nick tells me he is your father," said Auntie Bessie, rather abruptly. "What do you think about that? What about your father Dave in the States? You don't believe *he* was your father?"

Geraldine, Adrienne, and Nettie definitely took notice of this line of questioning. Nick wrapped himself in a haze of cigarette smoke on a couch in a corner of the room. Tombe lingered awhile and then returned to her cottage. Auntie Bessie stared at me, waiting for an answer.

"Well," I ventured, "I've always kind of wondered about Dave, because I remember my grandmother saying something about him not being my real father."

"So . . . you mean your grandmother, Dave's mother, said he wasn't your father?" Auntie Bessie interjected.

I couldn't tell whether I was now well into a full-blown lie, because I really did remember Grandma saying something like that, or whether I was performing for the benefit of Nick and my sisters.

"I just think there's a lot that I haven't been told . . ." I advanced hesitantly.

"Look, the boy is my son!" Nick cried out across the room to Bessie. "I already told him and the girls what happened and how I tried to stop Yvonne from taking him to the States with Dave. I don't care what anybody says: David is my son."

Auntie Bessie got up to get ashtrays for Nettie and Geraldine; Adrienne was changing Roberta's diaper and was apparently unfazed—bored, even—by the whole exchange. As if to conclude the discussion, Auntie Bessie stated, "Dave was a good man, and we were very sorry to hear that he had passed away. He stayed here in this house many times when he was in South Africa. He was a fine man. In fact, he left something here for you."

She went over to a cabinet in the corner and pulled out a plate with the words "Farrell Lines" emblazoned in silver gilt script. She handed it to me. I registered some faint recognition of the ship's name. "This was Dave's ship," she told me. "There's a whole set of dishes and glassware, and he made me promise that I'd give it to you one day when you returned here. You see, he knew you would come back here one day."

Yeah, I thought to myself, but did he know that I would be renouncing him as my father, in order to be fully accepted by three sisters, who sat across from me scanning my face for every possible reaction or evidence of fraud?

Tombe came back into the kitchen and made sandwiches—not a moment too soon, because I was starting to suffocate under the weight of my own duplicity and the others' expectations. I nervously looked around the kitchen and living room for a drink, but there was only the cloying punch.

Nick apparently noticed my fidgeting and suggested that we take a trip over to Gogo Katie's house. Gogo Katie was Auntie Bessie's mother, who ran a *shebeen* out of her house a few miles away. Shebeens were usually illegal or unlicensed places in the neighborhood where you could get a drink and listen to music or have a meal. My sisters and I decided to drive over together; Nick said that he would meet us there. Auntie Bessie declined to join us.

Gogo Katie was a big woman with a ready smile. Auntie Bessie was the product of an interracial alliance, I surmised, because her mother was quite dark. Gogo Katie was busy with a customer, so she told us to help ourselves to whatever we wanted. I walked through the house, which was split between the shebeen in the front and the living quarters in the back. A pot of some kind of stew meat was simmering on the stove, and flies rested on seemingly every piece of bread, fruit, and other uncovered food in sight. I decided to concentrate on the shebeen's liquid menu and walked over to a huge deep freezer in the corner of the kitchen. Inside were bottles and bottles of Castle lager. Gogo Katie's place reminded me of Della's Café in Meridian, where people always showed up for a cold beer or a stiff drink and a once-over of the jukebox. I grabbed a couple of beers and took them to the back porch, where Nick had kicked off his shoes and sat smoking a cigarette.

Nick took a long swig of his beer and said, "*Ja,* David, we must strike while the iron is hot."

I nodded toward him while upturning my beer. I didn't know that would be the last time I'd ever see him.

✳

New Year's Day, in the British tradition, is known as Boxing Day in South Africa. Unlike Christmas Day, it is usually celebrated by families flocking to the country's beaches. This year, though, most of the coloured, white, and Indian families were staying home because the Africans had taken over the beaches.

South African television was broadcasting images of busloads of black people flooding in from the townships and elsewhere to enjoy Durban's North and South beaches. Adrienne, Nettie, and I watched as video from a news helicopter panned across the stretch of the city's beachfront, where thousands of black people were frolicking in the white sand and water. Beach apartheid, it seemed, was dead.

"My God, the bleks are just taking over," said Nettie. "The next thing you know, they'll be building squatter camps right on the beach."

"*Ja,* I wouldn't be surprised to see them slaughtering goats right on the sand," scoffed Adrienne. "Look, I don't have a problem with them using the beach, but they're such unclean people."

I listened to their reactions with a mixture of amusement and disgust. Apartheid's engineers had legislated separation and inequality into every aspect of South African life: from the home to the workplace, the lunch counter to the toilet, the school to the hospital, the bathhouse to the beach, the cradle to the grave.

Anthony Heard, a journalist who had grown up in Durban, described the scene at the beaches in earlier years: " 'Non-whites' were banned from the main beaches in Durban, except to work for whites. Indian waiters in high-necked white tunics padded on the hot sand offering refreshments. Zulus did heavier work, carrying loads of umbrellas and deck chairs and preparing them for sunbathers. Apart from the massed armies of black labour in evidence, whites had the beach and surf to themselves."

Like other coastal South African cities, Durban had beaches for each population group under apartheid—whites, Indians, coloureds, and blacks. Of course, whites enjoyed the favorably located North and South beaches, while coloureds and Indians swam and bathed on Addington Beach and at other less favorable locations, and Africans were relegated to the still less desirable areas of the coastline. "The only amenity the African beach has," wrote E. J. Khan in *The Separated People,* "is a single water tap at the edge of the road that leads to it. The other non-white beaches are a little better, but not much."

Now, as the legal edifice of apartheid crumbled—the Group Areas Act had been repealed in 1991—the African majority experimented with its freedom of mobility and began streaming into the country's urban areas without hindrance or harassment. The sight of so many Africans flocking to Durban's beaches certainly debunked the myth that black people feared and loathed water.

"I want to go to the beach!" I announced as Geraldine and Robbie entered the living room. Adrienne and Nettie looked at each other and burst out laughing as I ran over to my bags to fish out my swim trunks. Geraldine packed a picnic basket of fruit, beer, and cold chicken; and the six of us, including Roberta in her tiny pink bathing suit, were off to the beach to be with our South African brothers and sisters.

After finding a parking spot a couple of blocks from the Marine Parade off North Beach, we ventured out to survey the scene. Buses, taxis, and cars filled with Africans continued to clog the beachfront. The air was filled with the cacophony of shouts, car horns, exhaust fumes, and the faint smell of *dagga* (marijuana). Overhead, a South African Police Service helicopter skimmed the horizon, apparently assisting the few police personnel on the ground with crowd control.

Negotiating our way through packs of people who were rushing to the water, we managed to find a tiny patch of sand where we could hunker down and observe the human drama unfolding before us. From our position on North Beach to Addington Beach, nearly two miles away, stretched a dark sea of humanity that virtually blotted out the beaches' golden sand. I craned my neck to take it all in.

Children—a few of them naked—ran up and down the beachfront. Women in traditional Zulu dress of hand bands and beads carried little bundles of babies on their backs and brightly colored towels over their shoulders en route to the surf's edge. Hordes of people lined up at food stands and waited in line for toilets.

We unpacked our picnic basket and broke out the chicken and beers. After our lunch, Geraldine and Roberta napped, while Adrienne and Nettie worked on their tans.

"Hey, David, look at that," Robbie said, nudging me and pointing toward a woman whose exceedingly large breasts—the biggest I'd ever seen—forlornly threatened to break through a ragged t-shirt.

"Nice set of lungs, hey?" he cackled.

While I laughed with him at the woman's protruding bosom, I was also becoming deeply embarrassed because other people had come to the beach in similar inappropriate attire, such as torn t-shirts and ripped shorts.

I decided to have a swim and wound up beside an Indian man and his son. I hadn't seen any whites on the beach, only a few Indians and fewer still coloureds. The water was warm and salty. The smell of the ocean and the sight of so many people gamboling in the surf made me forget about all the crudities of apartheid-era beach etiquette. I could see Addington Hospital where I'd been born.

A wave crashed into me and the Indian boy and his father. "O-o-oh, *lekker* wave, Daddy!" the boy shrieked, a terrific wave.

"*Ja, lekker* wave," the father answered.

Since Durban was not only a surfer's paradise but also a shark's potential feasting ground, lifeguards in speedboats skimmed over the beachfront and near the shark nets, which were about a hundred yards from the shore.

Every now and then, the boats pushed back crowds of people, preventing them from approaching the shark net barriers.

"Do not breach the shark nets!" one of the orange-clad men in the boats shouted into a megaphone. "This is for your safety!"

When I returned to shore, Geraldine and Robbie were packing up, and Adrienne was folding a towel and knocking the sand from her feet. "We've had enough, David," said Nettie, who was wrapping Roberta in a towel. I shrugged, pulled on my shorts over my swimming trunks, grabbed a beer and a piece of chicken from the basket before Geraldine could pack it all away, and straggled behind them—as Robbie led the way with the familiar bulge of his 9mm pistol in the back of his shirt. On the way out, I could have sworn that I saw a man dragging a stubborn goat to the beachfront.

✳

Later that evening, Robbie, Nettie, and I attended a Boxing Day party at a club near Durban Harbor. Adrienne wasn't feeling well and decided to stay home with Geraldine and Roberta. I relished the chance to get out and meet some girls, so I searched through my duffel bag and found an old rep-stripe tie, a white button-down shirt, and a pair of khakis.

"*Ag,* can you look any more American?" scoffed Robbie, as he poured a round of pre-party whiskies. He and Nettie were dressed casually and continued to tease me about my white-bread attire. I didn't care, though. I was determined to hook up with a nice coloured girl, no matter what happened or how I was dressed.

Earlier that day, Geraldine and I had gone to the local pharmacy, where she saw a couple of her girlfriends. After Geraldine introduced me to the women—both of them stunningly beautiful—they each kissed me on the lips and said, "Compliments of the season." I was dumbstruck and more than a little turned on by this until Geraldine explained that they had simply extended a traditional Boxing Day greeting to me. Whatever the backstory was, I was looking forward to mingling with other women who observed this tradition.

The nightclub was impressive. A fortress of sandstone walls encircled a courtyard of perfectly landscaped trees and gardens. A circular driveway led to the club's columned entrance, where valets dispatched cars and people mingled. Robbie decided against valet service and parked on the side of the building.

The parking lot was packed with expensive cars, and the people sparkled as well as we neared the entrance. Robbie dragged a cooler containing beer and assorted liquor up to the ticket taker, and we emerged into a peculiar world possible only, I thought, in South Africa. "Oh, David, by the way," whispered Nettie, "this is strictly a coloured party."

Rows and rows of tables framed a huge parquet dance floor. As we made our way to our table, we crossed paths with some of the most striking and exotic-looking people I'd ever seen: olive-skinned women with blonde hair and blue eyes; men with reddish brown skin and mops of dark, curly hair; girls with alabaster skin, aquiline noses, full lips, and gray-blue eyes; boys with the swarthy complexion of Italians and straight, sandy brown hair. Even after we situated ourselves—and our liquor—at the table, my gaze remained fixated on the people dancing and drinking to excess all around the room.

I had no problem wrapping my mind around the concept of colouredness, since I considered it part of my heritage. But these were the uber-coloureds, it seemed. Whereas my coloured lineage had been diluted—or so I had been led to believe—by a black American father, these were the pure coloureds, as it were, the "real deal" South African half-breeds. Compared to them, I was just a run-of-the-mill light-skinned American black. I didn't know whether to be sickened or depressed by this train of thought, so I sat down and prepared myself a nice stiff whiskey with a beer chaser.

Nettie dug out some sausages, chicken, and salad from the cooler, while Robbie went back to the car to retrieve a satchel containing plates and utensils. This was my first South African party, and I soon realized that there was no bar or buffet. Everyone had simply purchased a table in the club, bringing their own food and alcohol. The dimly lit room contained dozens of round tables sporting candles, individual liquor displays, and containers of every imaginable South African delicacy.

The sounds of big band music shot through with occasional American pop and rap hits—a concession to the young people, I guessed—pulsated through the cavernous room. Smartly dressed men and women mobbed the dance floor and assailed the DJ with requests for songs. Since none of the men wore ties, I ripped mine off, stuffed it in my pants pocket, and settled in for a long night of drinking, gluttony, and, I hoped, debauchery.

While Robbie and Nettie drifted off to talk to people at other tables, I immediately surveyed the room for women, most of whom seemed to have dates. I was drinking at a marathon pace now and feeling a surge of confidence. To the left of my table, I noticed a group of guys drinking and smoking with a lone girl. She was beautiful, with shoulder-length black hair, almond-shaped eyes, and luscious tan skin. I couldn't figure out the dynamics of the group: Was her boyfriend among the guys? I wondered. Did she even have a date?

My courting strategy consisted of staring at her until I finally caught her eye. She smiled at me and turned back toward the boys and their shenanigans. In the next instant, she was on the dance floor with one of the boys, a tall fellow with a ducktail haircut. I continued to stalk her with my eyes. When they passed me on the way back to their table, I practically bucked my eyes at her and managed to elicit a look of either concern or interest from her. By now, I was emboldened, and besotted besides, so when the DJ put on a Shaba Ranks song, I knew that destiny called. I finished off my drink, girded myself, and stepped over to the girl's table. One of the guys was apparently in the middle of a story or a joke, so no one noticed me at first.

"Hello," I croaked, sidling up to the girl. "Excuse me, but would you like to dance?"

She turned toward me, starting a ripple effect among the boys.

Then, in the most beautifully lilting South African accent I'd heard, she said, "Oh, no, thank you. I'm fine for now."

Just like that. Shaba Ranks was thumping his reggae beats in the background, but everything suddenly slowed down to the speed of a warped 78-rpm record. The girl's last utterance—"I'm fine for now"—seemed to dribble out of her mouth like cold molasses, and the boys' mouths and eyes seemed poised to heap scorn and derision on my now ungirded body. Grinning like an imbecile, I nodded my head and backed toward my seat at the table where Robbie and Nettie were refreshing their drinks. I couldn't tell whether the girl and her cronies were laughing at me, because I had erased them from my reality; they simply didn't exist for me anymore. Only my drink glass did, which Robbie graciously filled with a double shot of whiskey, this time with no water, thank you.

"Everything all right, David?" he asked. "Oh, yeah," I assured him, before bumming one of his cigarettes and heading outside for some air.

People trickled in and out of the party, while some stood around talking and smoking. The night was warm, stirred by a gentle breeze coming off the unseen ocean. So much for that, I thought, cursing myself for risking rejection by approaching the beautiful girl. I mean, who was I kidding anyway? When it came right down to it, I wasn't much of a catch: my breath probably reeked of untreated cavities, I had bad skin, I was dressed like a nerd, I was almost broke and pretty much living off my newly discovered sisters and brother-in-law, and my whole concept of myself had been thrown into doubt by meeting Nick, who swore that he was my real father. I was preparing for more self-flagellation when a guy came up to me.

"Pardon me, but do you have a light?" he asked, dangling a cigarette from his mouth.

"Sure," I said, offering him a book of matches. "Can I bum one of your cigarettes?"

He extended his pack, and I sized him up. He was probably in his early twenties and had the rakish air of a playboy. His pale skin and brown curly hair reminded me of my brother Xavier.

Neither of us spoke for a while, until he said, "Say, you're American, aren't you?"

I nodded yes, while wondering if my attire or my accent had given me away.

He paused again and then inquired, "How are the niggers there?"

For a moment, I thought I'd misunderstood him, so I replied, "What? What did you say?"

"How are the niggers?" he repeated. "You know, the black Americans."

While my instinct was to condemn his racial insensitivity, I was also intrigued by his question. It pinpointed an issue that had been just on the periphery of my awareness since I had arrived in South Africa and encountered the subtle and sometimes not so subtle racism of coloured people. What I really wanted to do was to sarcastically turn the question back on him and ask, How are the coloureds? What's up with the coloureds in South Africa? Because though coloureds intrigued me, they struck me more and more as some seriously screwed-up people.

✳

Drawing from my obsession with South African history, I knew that coloureds were the only South African population group whose identity had always been disputed and debated. Africans could call on a proud, rich, and stable cultural history. Indians were able to insulate themselves from the vagaries of South African life by relying on the cultural traditions of their homeland. Coloureds, by contrast, were maligned as hotnots, bushmen, "God's stepchildren," "brown Afrikaners," half-castes, misfits, leftovers, tainted people, residuals, nonpersons, nowhere people, quislings, a miserable, sad, and tragic people, and a host of other pejoratives denoting impurity or shame. Often overlooked, however, was the role that coloureds had played in South Africa's history.

When the powerful Dutch East Indies Company dispatched Jan van Riebeeck in the mid-seventeenth century to set up a station at the Cape of Good Hope, in what is present-day Cape Town, his assignment was supposed to be temporary. Instead, the Dutch built a fort and gardens at the Cape to feed and refresh sailors on passing ships, and Cape Town eventually became known as the "tavern of the seas."

Keeping an eye on the Dutch activity at the Cape were the aboriginal San and Khoikhoi peoples, who collectively composed the Khoisan. The San and the Khoikhoi were also referred to as Bushmen or Hottentots, respectively.

The San/Bushmen were described as "slight of build and yellow skinned; the only feature they have in common with their large-boned, darker-skinned neighbors, the Negro or Bantu tribes living at the edge of the Bushmen's territory, is their peppercorn curly hair. Otherwise, Bushmen are very like the Asian peoples, often having Mongolian eyefolds and rather broad, flat faces with almost no noses at all." According to scholars Richard Lee and Irene DeVore, "the San have lived in southern Africa for at least 11,000 years." Some researchers have speculated that the San once lived all over southern Africa "as a separate genetic development from the black-skinned peoples of Africa." Notably, Lee and DeVore also observed that "peoples of San origin who have completely lost their language and culture now form a significant proportion of the 'coloured' population of the Republic of South Africa."

The Khoikhoi/Hottentots also had been in southern Africa for thousands of years and probably had the same ancestors as the San/Bushmen. Unlike the San/Bushmen, however, who were hunter-gatherers, the Hottentots (a Bantu word for "stutterers," referring to the group's unusual speech patterns) were cattle herders.

Despite a few skirmishes with these small yellow and brown people on the slopes of Table Bay, van Riebeeck and his fellow whites (a group that included few women) soon began intermingling with the natives and incorporating them, invariably by force, into their community at the Cape. Al J. Venter argued, however, that "there is evidence of sexual contact between early travelers who passed around the Cape and local tribespeople even *before* van Riebeeck landed. Though these additions of extraneous blood could hardly have any marked influence on the racial patterns which were to evolve later, it is noteworthy that contact did take place. Academically speaking, therefore, the history of the Coloured people as we know them today goes back to the years before 1652."

Over a period of some two hundred years, the white settlers and the indigenes at the Cape mixed uneasily as the frontier station became more established. Newly arriving Dutch whites—"free burghers," as some of them were called—began pushing farther and farther north of the Table Bay fortress in search of more land for grazing and agricultural development. During this process, some of the Khoikhoi/Hottentots and San/Bushmen fled into the Northern Cape beyond the Orange River, while others crossed the border into modern-day Zimbabwe to escape enslavement by the whites. As *The Oxford History of South Africa* detailed: "During the process of the displacement and destruction of the indigenous societies, many Khoikhoi and some San were incorporated into the new society as servile dependents of white farmers, working for barely more than their keep as herdsmen, domestic servants, or agricultural labourers." The indigenous population was also decimated by smallpox and other epidemics brought ashore by the marauding Europeans. And, eventually, the remnants of the Khoikhoi who had escaped white hegemony at the Cape withered away as their livelihood—cattle herding—came under increasing attack by the settlers.

By the early nineteenth century, the whites had conscripted and indentured most of the remaining indigenous population into the service of the Cape Colony, which was the first formal European settlement in South Africa. They had also imported slaves from West Africa and the east, mostly Malaysia and Madagascar. Gradually, cohabitation and miscegenation among the aborigines, the slaves, the whites, and the Bantu-speaking peoples of South Africa began to break down the barriers between the groups, producing a new group distinguished by its mixed-race heritage. Increasingly, the Cape became a place where people of disparate ethnicity, including visiting sailors, made sexual contact and produced offspring who in turn contributed to an ever-lightening slave and serf population. Whites at the Cape became increasingly reliant on this group of slaves and indentured workers, while growing distant from their European roots. The stage was set for the British occupation of the Cape in 1806.

Initially, the British seemed to have no plan for exploiting the potential of South Africa; they were more interested in the strategic value of the twin harbors of the Cape, which provided a crucial link to the East Indies trade route. The industrious Dutch farmers, known as Boers, who had ventured away from van Riebeeck's outpost at Table Bay were left to their own devices on the Cape frontiers, free to eke out a living from the land and dispense rough justice toward the aborigines as they saw fit. Contrary to the myth promulgated by the architects of apartheid that the interior of South Africa was mostly uninhabited when the Boers arrived, roving bands of Khoikhoi and Xhosa/Bantu tribes occupied land on the northern and eastern frontiers—the areas where the Boer settlers, with their retinues of slaves and coloured servants, staked their claims and established huge farms. When the Boers were joined by an influx of English settlers, beginning in 1820, the British authorities began to heed calls from settlers and the mainland for the establishment of law and order and greater colonial regulation, drawing the British occupiers more and more into the socioeconomic life of the Cape Colony.

As the Cape Colony grew in importance and attracted more investment and more British citizens looking for opportunity, some religious leaders in England began calling attention to the issue of slavery in the British West Indies and, increasingly, in South Africa. On the strength of social reforms ushered in by the Industrial Revolution, the British parliament abolished slavery throughout the British Empire in 1834. Scholars George Golding and Franklin Joshua observed: "After the abolition of slavery of 1834 and at the elections of the Municipality of Cape Town, Coloured persons enjoyed the vote on the same basis as White persons. In the Cape there were no changes in the political status, and there as in Natal they enjoyed the franchise, whereas in the Transvaal and the Orange Free State it was withheld from them."

The British abolition of slavery had a tremendous impact at the Cape and reverberated throughout the frontier settlements, where British and Boer settlers signaled their intention to ignore or flout the new legislation. Unlike the more liberal Cape Colony, the scattered settlers, in constant conflict with marauding Xhosa tribes on the eastern frontier, considered themselves to be in a battle for survival against an inferior race of heathens.

Meanwhile, the Cape Colony had established a bicameral parliament, which was, of course, entirely beholden to the British Crown. It was, however, empowered to extend the franchise to all adult males, regardless of race, although the stipulation of property ownership effectively denied the vote to the majority of former slaves and Khoikhoi servants. With emancipation, this group of former slaves and Khoikhoi became known as the Cape Coloured People.

The white Boers, or Afrikaners, considered themselves a divine people, entrusted by God with the stewardship of the lesser races. In reaction to the abolition of slavery at the Cape, which was perceived as a challenge to Afrikaner notions of white supremacy, thousands of Afrikaner men and women, and their coloured servants, fled to the northeast frontier from 1836 to 1854 in protest against British hegemony, an event memorialized as the Great Trek. By the late 1850s, coloureds were free in name only, as the Afrikaners, the Europeans most closely related to the coloureds, ousted them from their churches and schools. The liberalism of the British at the Cape gave way to the realization that coloureds, like all the former slaves, were still viewed as inferior savages, especially by the settlers in the hinterland.

Coloureds occupied an uneasy position in South African society throughout the events leading up to the South African War (also known as the Anglo-Boer War), which was fought from 1899 to 1902 between the Afrikaner settlers, in the northern colonies of the Orange Free State and the Transvaal, and the British, now intent on exploiting the mineral resources of the fledgling and fragmented country. Since emancipation, most coloureds had remained in the Cape Colony, with the exception of those who had accompanied the Afrikaners on the Great Trek and those who had established settlements in the Northern Cape. They had become a diverse group, including Christians and Muslims, and excelled as artisans and craft workers. Given their intermediate status in the emerging South African society, coloureds began to consolidate and form a sense of identity and kinship. According to Ian Goldin:

At the turn of the century Coloured people were exempted from the pass laws and from the health and housing ordinances which in the Western

Cape had been used to regiment African people into segregated townships. As the position of Africans rapidly deteriorated, the relative position of Coloured men and women improved and the assertion of Coloured identity became a means to escape pass and other laws. Coloured political identity did not, however, necessarily signify a deep rooted commitment to it; whenever possible Coloured people who were able to pass for White were keen to assert a White identity.

The British forces defeated the Afrikaners in the South African War and then proceeded to annex the two Boer republics, the Orange Free State and the Transvaal. The British, who already occupied the Cape Colony and had annexed Natal, now effectively controlled the whole of South Africa. The Union of South Africa was formed in 1910. But the troubles of the country's coloured, African, and Indian people were only just beginning.

As part of the postwar treaty between the British and the Afrikaners, known as the Treaty of Vereeniging, black Africans were formally disfranchised in all parts of South Africa except the Cape. Though some in the Cape Colony objected, the Boer republics refused to consider granting blacks the right to vote or the right of parliamentary representation in their areas. As a concession to the British, however, the two republics agreed to postpone the matter until they achieved self-government. Eager to move forward with the uninterrupted exploitation of the country's nascent gold and diamond industries, the British agreed to another implicit condition: coloureds would retain the franchise in the Cape Colony and could not be removed from the common voters' roll without a two-thirds majority of parliament when the Boer republics became self-governing.

In 1909, a draft constitution was negotiated that established a unitary state with parliamentary oversight and three branches of government. Also included was a provision granting each of the four colonies the right to institute its own franchise laws, although the voting rights of coloureds and other nonwhites in the Cape Colony were protected. In another provision, the votes of rural citizens were given greater weight than the votes of urban dwellers. Dutch and English were designated the official languages.

Coloureds who lived in the former Boer republics felt betrayed by the British concession: they had expected the franchise to be extended to all the colonies. The British responded that the franchise could not be extended to coloureds until the Orange Free State and the Transvaal became self-governing. But, as R. H. Du Pre pointed out, "when [the Orange Free State and the Transvaal] were granted responsible government in 1906 and 1907, respectively, the British reneged on their promise, ignored reminders of their commitment to equal rights, allowed the Boers in the north to retain their all-white franchise, and callously tossed aside the claims of the Coloured people to a say in the affairs of the provinces of their birth."

The British attempted to salvage their liberal bona fides by negotiating and settling for the coloured franchise in the Cape Colony. They came up with what became known as the "entrenched clause," which guaranteed voting rights for coloureds in the Cape and which could be amended only by a two-thirds majority of both houses of the Cape parliament. (The entrenched clause would eventually place the status of coloureds at the center of a constitutional showdown between the future apartheid government and the courts.) The implementation of the draft constitution was known as the South Africa Act; it was the last gesture of good intentions toward the nonwhite people of South Africa for the next half-century or so.

When the Act of Union was declared in 1910, effectively welding together the components of the modern South African state, the stage was set for the material and economic advancement of the country. Still under British control, South Africa further exploited its mineral resources and expanded its manufacturing base; indeed, the country became even more of a magnet for foreign investment.

While the issue of the rights of nonwhites was shunted to the side, Afrikaners began asserting more and more control in the country's social, economic, and political affairs. Rural Afrikaners, so-called poor whites, began moving to the urban areas, bringing with them the Afrikaans language and the racial ethos that had characterized the policies of the former Boer republics. These new arrivals from the countryside also began to compete with blacks and other nonwhites for jobs. Afrikaners, who constituted more than half of the ruling white population, pushed to establish a large-scale "affirmative action" program ensuring that poor whites would be favored to get jobs on the railroads and in the manufacturing sector and the civil service. Increasingly, black workers had been sucked into the vortex of the urban manufacturing and industrial sectors, but they now found themselves replaced by whites.

In the context of this consolidation of white power, the African National Congress was founded in 1912 to advance and protect the interests of blacks. The South African government could not ignore the overwhelming number of Africans and their importance in the mining and manufacturing sectors of the economy; even after the sop of patronage had been extended to poor whites, there was no denying that the country depended primarily on cheap, regulated black labor for its survival.

Eventually, this inconvenient fact, coupled with the British-dominated government's decision to enter the two world wars on the side of the Allies, proved to be decisive in splitting whites along ethnic lines: Afrikaners against Britons. The position of black workers as cogs in the industrial machine that had become South Africa was now taken for granted by both sides; blacks were easily dealt with by a brutal, militaristic state, despite the rumblings of discontent that had been heard as far back as the founding of the South African Native National Congress, the forerunner of the ANC, in 1909. Rather, whites were fighting among themselves for control of South Africa. The British tended to care more about wringing as much capital as possible out of the fledgling industrial state, whereas the ascendant Afrikaners focused on staking out and consolidating their positions in the cultural and political realms.

These same Afrikaners soon began to agitate for independence from the British Crown. They were emboldened in their efforts by successive political victories and by splits among the British along class lines. The Afrikaners, in contrast, fed off a mythology that heralded them as a people of divine provenance, the *volk*. Equally important was the demographic predominance of the Afrikaners and the provision in the constitution that accorded more weight to rural Afrikaner voters. This provision would have far-reaching consequences for the country's political future.

Against this backdrop of white domination and the emergence of Afrikaner nationalism, coloureds became part of the restricted, landless peasantry and worked on honing their identity. "The reconstitution of Coloured identity at the turn of the century," Goldin observed, "provided the bedrock on which the future generations would build separate coloured organizations."

The most obvious manifestation of the coloureds' new preoccupation with identity was political, legitimized mainly by the activism of the African Political Organization. This organization, Goldin asserted, "aimed to extend Coloured education and wealth in order that the 'civilised

Coloured' population would increase its numerical significance and that the Coloured share of the franchise would accordingly be increased."

The APO's founder, Dr. Abdullah Abdurahman, began casting about for ways to mobilize the coloured vote. Initially, his idea was to join forces with African activists, but it quickly became clear that these two groups had little in common except their status as victims of a racist state. Sociologist S. P. Cilliers commented:

> Living as they did, as part of the developing White-dominated South African society, but in a subordinate position to the Whites, it was to be expected that the Coloureds would gradually internalize the dominant white values. Whites in earlier years generally believed that cultural retardation and skin pigmentation stood in direct causal relation to each other. This led to status being ascribed to a person on the basis of his color. The belief in the inherent inferiority of all men with dark skins came to be accepted and shared by the Coloureds themselves.

This ethnic cleavage between coloureds and Africans was not unexpected; after all, coloureds had more in common with whites than with Africans when it came to language, customs, and culture. Coloureds had no tribe to provide support or validation (though many claimed kinship to the Griquas of the Eastern Cape). Coloureds could not deny their white provenance, nor could they ignore all the disparate elements that had contributed to their ethnic makeup. As Goldin noted, "the growing preference shown towards Coloured men and women in the Western Cape served to heighten further the ethnic identification of Coloured and African people and to increase the significance of the racial divide. Perhaps most important in this respect was the continued exemption of Coloureds from influx control and residential segregation. These regulations caused immense hardship for people defined as African. Simultaneously, the assertion of Coloured identity provided a means to escape the obnoxious laws."

For their part, Africans harbored resentment toward coloureds because of the perceived preferential treatment accorded to coloureds by whites when it came to voting rights and job opportunities. Eugene Dvorin wrote that "the Coloreds are regarded by the Bantu as socially apart and are likewise excluded from Native social functions unless they are willing to consider themselves as Natives without qualifications. This, of course, few of them are willing to do, and, as a result, they are caught in a social pincers between two blood-proud and numerically superior groups, each of which regards the Coloreds 'as something apart.'"

Nonetheless, ideologues within the Afrikaner-dominated Nationalist Party (NP) had become concerned about the possibility of a coloured-African alliance that could potentially swamp the numerically inferior white population. The Nationalists cynically went about ingratiating themselves with the coloureds as part of their plan to remove Africans from the voters' roll in the Cape Colony and consolidate their power throughout the country. Despite moves by the NP to court the coloured vote, designed to undercut the British-backed South African Party (SAP), coloureds in the end remained powerless in all the Union's colonies except the Cape Colony, where they enjoyed only a limited franchise that allowed them to elect a white representative to parliament. As Du Pre maintained:

> The NP had never really intended elevating Coloureds to a position of equality with Whites. It had not been very serious about a "new deal" for Coloureds. Its promises of voting rights for Coloureds in the north, economic protection against Africans, and political and economic separation between Coloured and African had merely been empty words. The NP had all along wanted the Coloured vote in order to strengthen its parliamentary power so as to implement its race laws.

With each election, the NP, under the leadership of Barry Hertzog, consolidated more and more power, while increasingly dismissing the coloured vote after it had outlived its usefulness. As Du Pre emphasized:

> Hertzog and the National Party between 1924 and 1934 were not concerned about the Coloured man's dignity or citizenship, nor about humanitarian and moral considerations and a Christian conscience. All they were after was the Coloured man's vote. That vote was needed to defeat the SAP and remain in power; that vote was needed to implement the NP's race policies (of which, ironically, the Coloured people themselves would be the target). When that had been achieved, the Coloured vote and the Coloured people were no longer needed. They were expendable.

When African voters were finally removed from the common voters' roll in 1936, the leaders of the opposition United Party, mainly the

Afrikaner general Jan Christian Smuts, promised to safeguard the coloured franchise. But, through a series of political compromises among the major white parties—namely, the Nationalists and the United Party—the coloureds became the target of efforts to segregate them and remove them from the common voters' roll. Coloured citizens mobilized opposition parties to resist encroachment on their rights. But world events intervened and played a decisive role in determining the dynamics of South African society.

When World War II erupted, the governing United Party, led by Smuts and based predominantly among the British, took the country into the war on the side of the Allies, causing an irreparable rift with the Afrikaner whites, who rallied to the side of the Germans. The racist and eugenicist ideas pouring out of Dutch and German universities and the Nazi propaganda machine appealed to Afrikaner leaders who had studied abroad. Many had adopted notions heralding a *volksgroep,* a divinely ordained race of people meant to rule over the weak and inferior nonwhite population of South Africa. The National Party became a haven for these disaffected and fanatical Afrikaners, who set about stripping the United Party of power. The Afrikaners, who had suffered defeat and humiliation at the hands of the British in the South African War, were now poised to seize complete political power.

Their opportunity came in the election of 1948. Afrikaner intellectuals, farmers, and business people, the majority of whom belonged to the Broederbond, the super-secretive Afrikaner self-help organization, consolidated power among their rural and urban followers and pushed for a government premised on complete racial separation. Blacks were to be strictly limited in competing with whites for jobs; Indians were to be shipped back to India; and coloureds were to be completely disfranchised and removed from all affiliation with whites at all levels of society. Coloureds, by their very existence, were an insult to the Afrikaner mythology of racial purity. As Alex La Guma summarized it, "the advent of the National Party Government in 1948 and its policy of apartheid soon revealed to the non-white population as a whole the true nature of white supremacy."

Once the National Party assumed power after the gerrymandered election of 1948 (the Afrikaners had craftily relied on the constitutional provision established by the Treaty of Vereneeging that accorded more weight to rural voters and thus rallied their constituents), the Afrikaners set about removing all nonwhite participation in the governance of South Africa. Coloureds were eventually placed on a separate voters' roll and then were completely disfranchised in 1956 through a series of legal maneuvers that resulted in the removal of their only safeguard, the entrenched clause, from the constitution. The National Party became a self-help organization for Afrikaners: they controlled the entire civil service and every state institution, while the British whites, along with non-whites, were marginalized in the zeal to apply apartheid to every facet of South African society. "Apartheid, then," wrote Du Pre, "was devised as a means of ensuring, forever, that non-Whites would never be able to become equal with Whites. Thus every apartheid law passed after 1948 had that in mind."

While Africans were to be sealed off in reserves, from which their labor could be siphoned off and exploited by the South African industrial complex, coloureds were to be completely disinherited and abandoned in separate areas with their own deficient social services; it was imperative to whites that a clear line be drawn between them and their coloured "stepchildren." Coloureds gave the lie to the purity of the Afrikaner volk. Indeed, Christian Ziervogel reasoned, "it would be difficult to find a line of demarcation dividing the peoples of South Africa into white and coloured. To trace back the descent of every individual would be a well-nigh impossible task, and would not be pleasant for a good many people, whose descent had best remain in obscurity." Something had to be done, then, to erase the noxious coloured presence from South African society. This whitewashing came in the form of several pieces of repressive legislation that were to have a profound impact on generations of coloureds specifically, but also on Africans and the Indian population.

The most significant was the Population Registration Act, which divided South Africans into four categories: white, black (African), coloured, and Indian. Douglas Brown described this as "apartheid at its most inhuman—worse, in its way, than Hitler's Nuremberg Laws. Its victims are seized in a double trap. In a country where a fair skin seems the only passport to happiness, their own fair skins avail them nothing. Henceforth they belong nowhere and, for some, suicide has been the only recourse." Equally opprobrious were the Prohibition of Mixed Marriages Act, which outlawed marriages between whites and nonwhites; the Group Areas Act, which prescribed residential locations for each racial group; the Immorality Act, which forbade sexual relations between whites and nonwhites; and the Reservation of Separate Amenities Act, which segregated all public facilities.

These laws were primarily aimed at definitively putting coloureds, who were viewed as embarrassments, in their place and safeguarding the purity of the Afrikaner race. As Sheila Patterson concluded, "The African living in his tribal culture and environment is in his proper place, the detribalized African has strayed from his proper place, but may be reclaimed by implementing the policy of apartheid; but the Cape Coloured, that member of a 'marooned community,' is doubly in error, for he has lost any vestiges of culture other than the European and is also a racial hybrid."

Even though apartheid now dominated South African society, Africans had begun organizing and surreptitiously agitating for liberation. Coloureds, however, while pressing for political change, still remained an ambivalent group, unsure about throwing their support behind the non-racial anti-apartheid movement. For the vast majority of coloureds, Peter Lambley theorized, "the Afrikaner was an immovable presence firmly imposed on the present and future of South Africa. They were the framework around which the Coloured person had to build his life. And, not surprisingly, the Afrikaners were seen as the focus, obsessively so, of Coloured life and activity."

Ralph Bunche, the African American diplomat who traveled extensively through South Africa in 1937–1938, found many parallels between coloureds and American blacks and was particularly fascinated by the interaction of Africans and coloureds in response to white supremacy. "From time to time," he wrote, "some Coloureds and Africans found common cause politically, but middle class Coloureds were divided over whether they should accommodate themselves to whites." Despite, or perhaps because of, their ambiguous societal position, coloureds went about consolidating a cultural profile characterized by accommodation with and occasional defiance of the apartheid status quo.

Thus, coloureds were set adrift in the political wilderness. Because they had received slightly better treatment from the Afrikaners in the past, they were in many respects isolated from Africans and Indians. Even after being disfranchised, some coloureds still cherished the notion of joining white society, with which, after all, they shared a common language and culture. This frustration led to many painful contortions in the coloured psyche. Most notably, many coloureds sought escape from their existential circumstances by passing for white—and, in fact, many succeeded. Coloureds, and some blacks and Indians, attempted to escape into the white population by contesting their official racial status in an application to the government's Kafkaesque Race Classification Board.

The apartheid reclassification bureaucrats had developed a basic test to determine a coloured person's suitability for reclassification as white: known as the pencil test, it consisted of passing a pencil through the applicant's hair. If the pencil stuck, the person was judged to be black; but if the pencil easily fell out of the applicant's hair, they were reclassified as white. This test, coupled with analysis of a person's family lineage and community perceptions of that person's race, trumped skin color, in a sense, because there were a great many people with fair skin and frizzy or kinky hair. The bureaucrats reasoned that the combination of straight hair and fair skin corroborated whiteness.

The whole phenomenon of racial classification—and the seriousness with which coloureds, especially, pursued it—added up to a sad and tragic episode in the history of the coloured people. Entire families were destroyed, ripped apart when, say, a son or daughter was deemed coloured while the parents were seen as white. Children were disinherited, marriages were dissolved, and communities were upended as a result of the apartheid obsession with color.

As the racial boundaries in South African society became even more impermeable, something resembling coloured culture began to emerge. This culture was formed, in part, from the perceptions held both by whites and by the other nonwhite groups, the Africans and the Indians. Increasingly, coloureds were thought to be under the control of whites, which explained their preoccupation with passing. John Western enumerated some of the negative traits that were attributed to coloureds, including bastardy and the perception that coloureds were "impure, immoral creatures."

They were also seen as a musical people, blithely unaware of or unconcerned with politics or serious reflection on their social status. This image coincided with that of Coloureds as powerless and discountable, that is, people who are negligible, inconsequential and ignorant, which implied immaturity and weakness. Since Coloured frustration with their lot in life was well known, the image of them as criminals, prone to violent behavior, was perpetrated as crucial to understanding them. Finally, since Coloureds were of mixed-race origins, they came to be seen as a lascivious and "sexually profligate" people, essentially depraved and opportunistic sexual predators unfazed by, and in fact creations of, amoralism.

Politically aware coloured intellectuals and artisans resented and rejected these stereotypes and sought to make common cause with the burgeoning African National Congress and other anti-apartheid groups. La Guma observed, "The struggles against the destruction of the franchise, against Group areas, against poverty and cultural and educational discrimination, as well as support for the Freedom Charter of the Congress movement, a National Convention and the like—all have registered the Coloured community's rejection of the generations-old system of racism in South Africa."

More than any other South African group, coloureds had been fractured by the dictates of class. Whites, who benefited from an extensive affirmative action program courtesy of the apartheid state, constituted a united front; there was perfunctory dissent from the British whites, but by and large they shared in the spoils of repression. Africans were compelled to join forces regardless of class to challenge apartheid, while Indians rallied to maintain their precarious position in South Africa itself. But coloureds continued to grapple with their confused and equivocal status in South African society, reflected in the class divisions described by Cilliers:

> In general, three distinct social classes, differing also on "racial" or physical basis, could be distinguished. The upper social class were those who resembled the Whites most clearly in appearance. Middle class people were those who had so-called "trappies haar," a kind of frizzy hair midway between pepper-corn and straight hair. The lower classes were those with "short" hair, i.e., pepper-corn. Special derogatory terms applied to these people and were in common use amongst Coloureds themselves.

This class consciousness had produced a special breed of self-hatred and self-loathing mixed with feelings of superiority over Africans, Indians, and, curiously, the so-called niggers of America. This was the particular strain of contempt and scorn I had heard in the question posed by the young coloured man at the party that night—*How are the niggers?*—which disgusted me.

Since I had run out of cigarettes, I walked back through the crowd of partygoers and returned to our table, where Robbie poured me a nice stiff whiskey to help assuage my still raw feelings of rejection. Mercifully, the girl I had approached had left with her friends. Meanwhile, the tempo of activity accelerated around the room: more bottles of liquor were added to the tables, larger pots of food made the rounds of revelers—and the good coloured people of Durban jammed the dance floor until nearly daybreak.

✳

Once the holiday euphoria wore off, I sensed that it was time for me to choose whether to move on from Sydenham—to Auntie Bessie's house in Greenwood Park, maybe?—or to remain with Robbie and Geraldine. Nettie confirmed that feeling when she approached me with a proposition.

"David, why don't you come to live in Jo'burg with Kim and me?" she offered. "I have quite a large house, and there's plenty of room there for you. Plus, there's just so much more going on in Johannesburg compared to Durban."

I had known that sooner or later the issue would arise. I was sleeping on the couch in the living room, and my money was dwindling—I was down to about three hundred rand, which worked out to roughly a hundred dollars.

Besides, there had been a palpable shift in the atmosphere of the house now that all the merry-making had been replaced by the routine of everyday life with Robbie and Geraldine. Adrienne and Angelo were making plans to return by Greyhound bus to Johannesburg. Robbie was clearly preoccupied with running his shop, and Geraldine was preparing to return to her teaching job. I accepted Nettie's offer with a mixture of apprehension—she and I hadn't exactly hit it off—and relief.

I was also relieved to be rescued from the tensions and unpleasantness that had begun to bubble to the surface of Robbie and Geraldine's marriage. One night in particular stuck in my mind. A few nights after the party at the coloured nightclub, Geraldine, Roberta, and I went to visit one of her friends, a woman Geraldine had known since childhood. What was intended as a short courtesy call turned into an hours-long drinking and smoking session, or *joll,* a party. The woman, impressed to have an American in her house and eager to demonstrate her hospitality, began pulling out bottles of liquor and beer and even coaxed her husband into starting a *braii,* a South African–style barbecue.

Geraldine was at first reluctant to stay because she knew that Robbie would be coming home and expecting his dinner. But her friend was persuasive, saying, "*Ag,* man, you mustn't let a man run your life. Come, David, have another drink, and we'll have some *lekker* food here soon, and everything will be fine. Don't worry, Geraldine."

Amid all the drinking and eating and partying, I managed to pull Geraldine aside to voice my concern. But by then she had begun her steady regimen of brandy and Cokes, and there was no reasoning with her. By the time we left for home, around midnight, Roberta was sound asleep, and I was uneasy about the kind of reception we'd get from Robbie. I pictured him sitting at the dining room table in a funk of cigarette smoke and whiskey fumes. Geraldine seemed not to have a care in the world.

As soon as we walked in the door, Robbie was on top of us.

"Geraldine!" he screamed. "Do you know what time it is? Where in the hell have you been?"

Geraldine didn't answer and just went about tucking Roberta into bed, leaving Robbie to grow increasingly enraged. He ignored me as I sat on the couch, wondering where Nettie, Adrienne, and the others were. I wished that I were somewhere else at the moment. When Geraldine returned to the living room, Robbie got up in her face and continued his rant.

"Dammit, I want to know where you've been. Do you know what time it is? Huh?" He had cornered Geraldine against the wall by their bedroom and was jabbing his finger in her face.

"I don't have to report to you on where I go all the time!" she screamed in matching rage. "Why don't you just *voetsek* [fuck off], man!"

Robbie was practically sputtering with anger now, his face reddening by the moment; it was clear that they were both intoxicated. Suddenly, he pushed Geraldine up against the wall, and that's when I instinctively jumped up to intervene.

But before I could get across the room, Robbie turned to me and growled menacingly, "You better just sit your big lips down, hey? This is none of your business."

I was doubly stung by the threat and the insult. I had grown up with kids teasing me about having big lips; it was just one of the trivial insults that had damaged my already fragile self-esteem. Equally troubling to me was the familiarity of this kind of domestic abuse: I had come to the defense of my mother over the years when she had been threatened or assaulted by several of her good-for-nothing boyfriends. I knew at that moment that I couldn't stay with Robbie and Geraldine. They were obviously having problems—as he had tried to explain to me on a couple of occasions, I now recalled—and I was just another problem they couldn't bear.

Geraldine turned to me and said, "Don't worry, David. Just sit down and don't worry about it."

Robbie glared at me and taunted, "Yeah, that's right. I know your big lips don't want any of this. Hey?"

Mercifully, at that very moment, when I felt compelled to rescue my sister from her position under Robbie's elbow up against the wall, Roberta began wailing in her room. There was a pause in the hostility while Geraldine looked at Robbie, and Robbie looked at me, before he released her and she fled into the room to look after the baby. I left the room and went to sit on the patio in the coolness of the night. Eventually, the lights in the house began going out. Only the light in the living room remained on. I just continued to sit outside, weighing my slim options, wondering what in the hell I was going to do in this wretched country.

So I was eager to accept Nettie's offer. I would be leaving the next day, she told me, with her boyfriend, Cedric, who was driving back to Johannesburg. She and Kim planned to take the bus with Adrienne and Angelo in a couple of days. I was ready to leave Durban. Not only was I eager to escape the fallout of Geraldine and Robbie's tumultuous marriage, but I was also ready to establish some independence from my sisters and the overprotectiveness that had prevented me from looking for a job, preferably in journalism. At least that's what I told myself the night before I left Durban. Robbie made a braii in the backyard and, as usual, we all had plenty to drink and eat. Everyone acted as if we were just one big happy family. It was my initiation into the schizophrenia of South African society.

*

The next morning, I was packing my bags when Cedric showed up to fetch me. He was a slim African man with a round, jovial face and a missing tooth that filtered his sly smile. The house was silent; I hadn't slept well and hadn't heard Adrienne or Nettie come in. I grabbed my bags and went out to meet Cedric, who helped me load them in the trunk of his car. Bob Marley was on the radio crooning, " . . .every little ting gonna be alright. . . ," as we left Sydenham and got on the nearby N3 Highway for what would be a six-hour trip to Johannesburg.

"So how do you like South Africa so far, Dave?" asked Cedric, as Durban's skyline disappeared beyond the horizon. I really hadn't seen South Africa, I acknowledged, since I had been sheltered and chaperoned throughout my stay with Robbie and Geraldine. I told Cedric that I was looking forward to exploring Johannesburg and getting out on my own.

"Is it?" he asked, with a hint of incredulity in his voice. "And what will you do, hey?"

I dutifully told him that I was a freelance writer working for the *Atlanta Journal-Constitution*. This wasn't a complete lie because I had made an arrangement with the paper's foreign editor to pitch some story ideas while in South Africa. I was also planning to visit the paper's correspondent, who lived in Park Town, a suburb of Johannesburg.

With the formalities out of the way, I settled back in my seat and watched the scenery fly by. We were leaving the Lowveld, the narrow coastal strip of Durban, and climbing through a landscape of gentle, rolling hills and valleys toward the Great Escarpment, a buffer of mountains, on the way to the Highveld, where Johannesburg sits. In the distance, flocks of brown sheep appeared in a field on a valley slope; tendrils of smoke filtered out of distinctive Zulu *rondavels,* beehive-shaped, thatched huts plopped down in the middle of the vast platteland.

As Cedric drove through the hills on the outskirts of Durban, I noticed people on the side of the dusty two-lane highway: women walking with parcels balanced on their heads; men peddling bicycles to some unknown destination; and small children—in the middle of nowhere, I mused— selling bags of oranges and bunches of bananas. None of the cars and trucks thronging the highway seemed to slow down in their relentless push to the Highveld.

Cedric seemed to pick up on my thoughts. "*Ja,* it's beautiful country, hey?" he said. I nodded in agreement, fascinated by thoughts of the many battles that had taken place against the backdrop of the ancient landscape rolling by. Perhaps the most devastating attack against British forces, who were intent on invading land claimed by King Cetshwayo and the Zulus, occurred during the Battle of Isandhlwana in 1879. "The African societies of Southern Africa experienced intensified pressures after 1870," historian Leonard Thompson recounted. "Although they differed in many other respects, white farmers and businesspeople, traders and missionaries, and government officials had a common interest in subjecting the Africans, appropriating their land, harnessing their labor, dominating their markets, and winning their hearts and minds." On the morning of January 11, 1879, nearly twenty thousand Zulu warriors overran a British force of seven thousand at Isandhlwana, killing nearly all of the British troops. Despite this rout, the Zulus were eventually defeated, and the whole of Natal fell under white rule.

The mountains of the Great Escarpment came into view dramatically. All the reading I had done about the Drakensberg Mountains could not do justice to the panoramic spectacle of this magnificent range now looming to the west of the highway. This is sacred land, I thought, as the mountain's soaring peaks and precipitous valleys stretched across the horizon, seemingly endless. Thousands of years ago, the San people, considered the original inhabitants of South Africa and the ancestors of the coloured people, had occupied the caves and valleys of the Drakensberg. They had left rock art and other evidence of their society scattered among the rocks and on the sheer cliff faces of the mountain range. Cedric was talking on his cell phone, no doubt inured to the sight of the mountains after many years of commuting between Johannesburg and Durban. But I could not take my eyes off the colossal range and was in awe of how the sun cast deep shadows across its peaks and deep valleys. For the first time, I was overcome with pride and awe at my connection to this place, to South Africa.

On the outskirts of Harrismith, the midway point in our journey, Cedric pulled into a Caltex gas station. Pump attendants dressed in red and blue coveralls and red baseball caps immediately assailed us; the smiling African men seemed perfectly matched to the sleek, ultramodern gas station. "Come on, let's take a break," said Cedric, giving the car keys to one of the attendants. The young African boy smiled and bowed to us before fueling and servicing the car with an efficiency that might have been a vestige of 1950s American culture.

Cedric went into the store, and I went to the toilet. I'd never seen such a clean restroom at a gas station, especially one out in the countryside. A young boy emerged from a utility closet in the restroom. He was dressed in the same coveralls as the pump attendants and carried a mop. Weirdly, a Phil Collins tune played over a loudspeaker. As I was leaving, the boy rushed over to turn on a faucet in one of the many sinks lining the bathroom wall. Normally, I would have shied away from accepting such courtesy—I hated feeling obligated to bathroom attendants at clubs back in Atlanta—but I was extremely impressed with the boy's professionalism and enthusiasm. I noticed a saucer on the edge of one of the sinks that contained a few forlorn coins. The whole situation seemed so sad, yet hopeful. I turned to the boy and gave him a five-rand coin, which he accepted with both hands extended and a slight bow.

"*Dankie, baas,*" he said.

I left the restroom feeling embarrassed for both of us and went to find Cedric, who was waiting for me in the car. As we pulled out of the gas station and back onto the N3 for the last stretch to Johannesburg, I realized that I was slowly being seduced by the dystopian amenities of South African society.

I must have dozed off for awhile, because when I awoke the landscape had dramatically changed. The vast brown fields had given way to the savannahs of the Highveld. Low shrubs and acacia trees dotted the cracked and dry land. Cedric mentioned something about the country's low rainfall and the intermittent droughts that plagued farmers and the agricultural industry. The traffic on the highway picked up. More trucks appeared, and vans stuffed with people sped by. The foot traffic increased, too. Men dressed in dusty, dingy brown suits and broken shoes trudged alongside the road. A few people seemed to be waiting for a bus or taxi.

In the distance, out of a sheen of dust blowing across the land, I could begin to make out their destination, and mine: Jozi, Egoli, the City of Gold, Johannesburg. The city's skyline looked like a mirage in the middle of the brown vastness of the Highveld. For many, Johannesburg was the "emerald city," a place of wealth, jobs, excitement, and opportunity. And in that sense, I was really not too different from all the others making this pilgrimage.

As we drew closer, Cedric pointed out the huge dune-shaped mounds of dirt on the outskirts of the city. The mounds represented the residue of years of intensive gold mining, for which Johannesburg had become famous. To my mind, they were the visible by-products of all the economic and social forces that had given life to the South African state. In another sense, they embodied my conception of the coloured people—

they were the residuals, the leftovers that nobody quite knew what to do with but kept around just in case they might prove useful in the future.

Then we were in the city, headed to Nettie's house in the suburb of Malvern. It was a late Sunday afternoon, and the streets were mostly quiet. A few taxi drivers were washing their vans on the side of the road. I rolled down my window to let the sounds and smells of the sprawling metropolis float over me. As we approached a section of town called Hillbrow, Cedric barked over at me: "Dave, you must put up your window and lock your door, man. This place is not so safe." There were more people on the sidewalks now. Women stood outside seedy hotels. Groups of boys loitered in front of abandoned storefronts. These were all black people; I strained to spot a single white person in the crowds of shoppers and hawkers jamming the streets of Hillbrow. Up ahead, I could see the Hillbrow Tower, an impressively tall structure that seemed to puncture the skies above the city.

Just over the hill from Hillbrow, we took Jules Street to Malvern. Cedric pulled into an unimpressive side street and parked in front of a tiny, whitewashed duplex with a wrought-iron fence.

"This is it," he said. "You're home."

The street was a dead-end, and there was no one out and about. Cedric helped me with my bags, and we entered the house. I had been expecting a larger house, especially after Nettie insisted that she could better accommodate me. I felt a pang of disappointment as I surveyed the house. The entrance served as a sun porch and led into the living room and dining area. A master bedroom sat off the living room, and another bedroom was located down a narrow hallway leading to the kitchen. Across from this bedroom was a bathroom with a tub, but no shower. Off the kitchen was what appeared to be a utility room or laundry room containing some boxes and odd pieces of furniture. I had a feeling that this would be my room.

A lean-to that seemed to be occupied squatted in the backyard of the house. A small garden had been planted outside, and clothes were hung out to dry on a clothesline. A wall separated Nettie's house from the other half of the duplex. The place was eerily quiet, but I felt the sensation of being watched. Cedric brought in a bag I'd left in the car and bade me farewell.

"*Ja*, I've got to run a few errands and get ready for work tomorrow," he said. "But I'll see you again, probably next weekend. Keep well, Dave."

After he left, I sat on the couch in the living room, tinkering with the television, filled with alternating anticipation and dread at the prospect of living with Nettie and exploring Johannesburg.

✳

The next morning, the sounds of someone moving around the house jolted me awake. Despite my initial apprehension at being in a strange house in a strange neighborhood, I had eventually crashed on the couch fully dressed. The sounds were insistent, so I got up to investigate. I remembered my first encounter with Thoko, Geraldine's maid, on the morning after my arrival in Durban. And, sure enough, I found a black woman in the kitchen, bent over a sink washing dishes. She was dressed in a green housecoat, wore a scarf over her head, and was barefoot. She apparently hadn't heard me enter the kitchen, so I called out, "Hello."

The woman kept right on scrubbing.

I tried again. "Hello. Excuse me."

This time, she turned her head toward me with what looked like anger; her stolid face bore a look of permanent cynicism and indifference. I waved to her. She turned back to her dishes and effectively dismissed me. I returned to the couch and fell into a deep sleep.

When I roused myself about an hour later, Nettie and Kim were coming through the door. I helped them get settled, and then we all sat down at the living room table.

"Paulina, get us some tea, please," Nettie requested. "Have you met Paulina, David?"

I shook my head, and she summoned the woman to the living room.

"Paulina, this is my brother, David, and he'll be staying with us." Paulina's head was turned downward toward her bare feet. She briefly looked up and nodded in my direction and dutifully returned to the kitchen.

"She comes in three days a week. Just let her know if you need laundry or anything else done, and she'll do it," Nettie told me. "She's really quite good but doesn't talk much."

Kim had drifted into her room, and, of course, the sounds of Whitney Houston singing "I Will Always Love You" wafted into the living room. Nettie wasted no time in explaining the rules of the house. She and Kim were usually out of the house by seven o'clock each morning for work and school. Paulina usually arrived at eight and stayed until three or four in the afternoon. All the doors and windows were to be locked at all times; a couple of houses on the block had been burglarized in the past few months, so precautions had to be taken. For everyone's safety and peace of mind, Nettie suggested, I should be home before nightfall, except, of course, when accompanied by someone who knew the city. For the time being, she explained, I would have to sleep on the couch until she could get a bed for the room near the kitchen. Finally, she informed me that Johannesburg was a very dangerous place—lots of muggings, robberies, and murders.

"You must always watch your back here, David. This is not like Durban; you can't just walk around by yourself."

I nodded my head politely in understanding, although I didn't intend to be deterred from exploring Johannesburg by talk of crime and danger. Paulina brought our tea, and Nettie droned on about the necessity for safety and the importance of watching out for skellums and other riff-raff wandering the streets around Malvern.

The next day, after Nettie and Kim left, I stuffed some books and a Walkman into my book bag and ventured up to Jules Street, the main drag in Malvern, to catch the bus into downtown Johannesburg. "Do be careful, hey, David?" Nettie had urged when I asked her about the public transportation system and getting around the city. This place can't be any worse than New York or Detroit, I thought, as I looked around and up and down the street.

Jules Street was pockmarked with all kinds of shops: a Portuguese bakery, a dry cleaner, several fast food stands, a couple of banks, a hardware store, and a plethora of curio shops run by Muslims and Indians, who sat outside waiting for customers. The two-way traffic on the wide street was relentless. Combis careened from stop to stop picking up passengers headed downtown. Those who couldn't afford either the bus or a combi trudged along on the sidewalks and on both sides of the road toward the city.

I reached down to check my pocket for change as the double-decker bus pulled to the curb. The bus driver, an Indian man enclosed in a wire cage, beckoned to me, "Hurry up, man. We must go."

I vaulted up the stairs and plopped down a one-rand coin. The bus lurched forward down Jules Street. Most of the riders were schoolchildren in plaid uniforms and old people, mostly whites. I had noticed that many of the blacks opted to take the combis into town. I settled into my seat and watched the panorama of furniture stores, auto repair shops, and beauty salons roll by. I did a double-take when we passed by a street corner where a white man was assaulting a black man, chasing the cowering man down the street while pummeling him with a stick. Off in the distance, I could see the needlelike Hillbrow Tower and the circular Ponte Hotel, both of which I could identify from my reading about Johannesburg. My obsession with all things South African was paying off as we rolled into the central bus depot downtown.

Stepping off the bus was a little like stumbling on a honeycomb of bees. Dozens of buses clogged the depot, picking up or depositing hundreds of people. Nearby, cars, delivery trucks, and taxis competed for dominance on the pulsating streets. The combis rushed maniacally from street to street in search of passengers, spewing loud reggae and rap music and leaving in their wake a general impression of mayhem. Overhead, skyscrapers held court over the ceaseless pursuit of wealth upon which Johannesburg had been built. "Jo'burg, Johannesburg," the poet Mongane Wally Serote had written:

> Listen when I tell you,
> There is no fun, nothing in it,
> When you leave the women and men with such frozen expressions,
> Expressions that have tears like furrows of soil erosion,
> Jo'burg City, you are dry like death,
> Jo'burg City, Johannesburg, Jo'burg City.

Martin Flavin, a writer traveling through South Africa in the mid-twentieth century, described Johannesburg as "an urban island in the midst of nowhere, a pin point in the vast, sad wilderness of Africa," a city "about half of which is black and lives on the wrong side of the tracks—really outside the town in sordid Jim Crow areas to which it is restricted."

Modern, restless Johannesburg had sprung from a rough-and-tumble mining town that had been hastily erected to exploit the vast gold deposits discovered on the Witwatersrand (White Waters Ridge), a place on the flat veld originally valued for its abundance of flora and fauna and grazing land. After the discovery of gold in 1867, the dusty shanty towns attracted speculators and fortune seekers from around the world overnight, all of them eager to cash in on some of the richest deposits of gold ever unearthed. Significantly, the British also took notice and decided to take over the burgeoning and potentially hugely profitable mining economy in the Transvaal, where they clashed with the Boers who had trekked there from Cape Town and Natal to escape what they perceived as British liberalism and hegemony. This clash of ideologies and economics laid the groundwork for the South African War of 1899–1902.

At the conclusion of the war, the British, eager to consolidate power over Johannesburg's gold fields and stabilize the country, acceded to the Afrikaners' demand that nonwhites be disfranchised in the Transvaal. The Afrikaners, with the tacit approval of the British, set up the framework of what later became a segregated city, built on the cheap labor of black workers, who were increasingly shunted to the outskirts of Johannesburg, in the South Western Townships (Soweto) and Alexandria. Flavin emphasized the key role of these black workers: "The wealth of South Africa is gold, but the statement should be carried a step further: the real wealth of the country is cheap labor, deprived of which the Union would be bankrupt overnight. Without ruthless exploitation, and suppression, of a vast, subsistence-level labor pool, the economy of the country would be incapable of functioning."

Once I recovered from the initial shock of being in the city, I took a deep breath and plunged into exploring its streets. The first thing I noticed was that almost every person I encountered on the sidewalks carried a gun. Men in reflective sunglasses and sidearms darted in and out of buildings. A couple of men carrying automatic weapons were stationed outside what looked like a bank. I even saw a little old white lady with a pistol strapped to her shoulder. The streets were awash in guns, though I saw only an occasional group of heavily armed police officers walking about. The police, I later learned from the newspaper, had become targets in the chaos of the country's political transition: more than thirty officers were killed in the opening months of 1993.

The pavements were teeming with vendors, adding to the deafening noise of the city. Most were black, and they were selling everything from roasted mealies (corn), *boerewors* (sausage links), peanuts, fruit, samoosas, and chicken curry to sweaters, baseball caps, coats, handbags, wallets, cigarettes, candies, and shoes. On Commissioner Street, where many banks and other buildings of Edwardian and Victorian architecture figured prominently, a man was getting a haircut at an open-air barbershop, where the barber powered his clippers with a car battery. A couple of teenagers checked out the barber's array of styles from a poster board featuring color photos of apparently satisfied customers. Only a few paces from the al

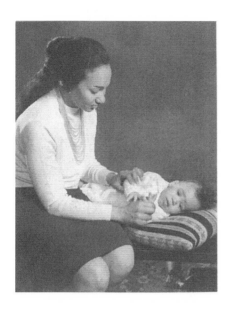

The author at the age of six months
with his mother, Yvonne Houze,
in Durban, South Africa, in 1965.

Yvonne at age twenty-seven,
two years before leaving
South Africa.

Yvonne (far right) and unidentified
friends on Durban's South Beach,
ca. 1960.

One of several ships on which the author's father, Dave Houze Sr., worked as a merchant seaman. The ships typically originated in New York City and made stops along the West African coast en route to South Africa. Photo courtesy of Alma A. Houze.

Dave Houze Sr. (1927–1974), in his early thirties. He left Meridian at age fifteen, determined to begin a career at sea. Photo courtesy of Alma A. Houze.

The author at age six, around the time he began to explore his family's history. Photo courtesy of Alma A. Houze.

The author's sister Alma Anita, age twelve.

The author's brother Dave Jr., age eleven.

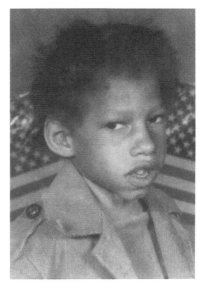

The author's brother Xavier, age five. Photo courtesy of Alma A. Houze.

Auntie Bessie and her husband, Raymond, surrounded by their children, Xavier and Marcell, and, in plaid dresses, from left to right, the author's sisters Geraldine, Adrienne, and Antoinette. Auntie Bessie cared for the girls after their mother left South Africa in 1966.

The author's grandmother, Alma Mae Henderson Houze (1920–1997), pictured fourth from the right, spent most of her life cooking in school cafeterias and cleaning the homes of whites in Meridian and elsewhere. Photo courtesy of Alma A. Houze.

Yvonne, shortly after arriving in Meridian, in 1966. One of the first things she did was cut her hair to signal the start of her new life in America. Photo courtesy of Alma A. Houze.

Two of the author's childhood friends, from left to right, Freelo and Nee Nee, who were Miss Sis's children. Miss Sis lived across the street from the author's grandmother. Photo courtesy of Alma A. Houze.

Ernest Bronson, Miss Sis's brother, lived in a small hut in the author's grandmother's front yard. He was the local expert on the neighborhood and was widely sought out for advice by people, black and white, all over Meridian, especially during income tax filing season. Photo courtesy of Alma A. Houze.

The author at the Carlton Hotel, in 1994, with Joe Slovo, former commander of the ANC's military wing, Umkhonto we Sizwe (Spear of the Nation), and a stalwart of the anti-apartheid struggle, on the evening of the historic South African election. Slovo and others had gathered to celebrate the election of Nelson Mandela as the country's first black and democratically elected president.

From left to right, Geraldine, Adrienne, and Antoinette, 1964. Photo courtesy of Antoinette Cockman.

Adrienne and the author's niece
Roberta, in Durban, ca. 1998.

Yvonne in front of city hall in Kokstad,
the South African town where she
grew up. This visit in 2004 was her
first trip back there in fifty years.

Yvonne and Xavier at Boswell Regional Center in Sanatorium, Mississippi, in 2004.
Yvonne was seeing her son for the first time in thirty years.

fresco barbershop was a beauty salon of sorts, where a large African woman was braiding a young girl's hair and pointing out hair weaves to a couple of onlookers.

Mesmerized by the incessant drone of traffic and the sheer hubbub of hawkers and pedestrians, white and black, racing through the city, I stumbled to Eloff Street, where more vendors, an open-air bazaar, and ragtag shops beckoned. Skinny black boys sold copies of the *Sowetan* and the *Star* on every street corner I passed: Diagonal Street, with its Indian market and butcher shops and Chinese delicatessens; Jeppe Street, where the main train depot was located and where most black commuters entered the city. Though no one seemed to notice me, I instinctively checked over my shoulder every couple of blocks. I knew enough about Johannesburg to guard against pickpockets and muggers.

Like Atlanta and other American cities I'd visited, Johannesburg had fried chicken places on almost every corner. Crowds of people mobbed these places, leaving a trail of chicken bones scattered on the pavement. Here and there, I came across the smell of urine from the alleys beside grimy buildings with peeling paint. At storefronts, people sat on the curbs, staring straight ahead, waiting for something or someone. A few black men dressed in blue coveralls, obviously on their lunch breaks, sat on the curb of Wanderer's Street, eating great gobs of bread and gulping down containers of milk.

Bree Street offered more fast food restaurants advertising Castle lager, Peter Stuyvesant cigarettes, and Nestlé condensed milk. The scene on Fox Street, which led into the city's financial district, featured a phalanx of bicycle messengers and motorcycle couriers, some rushing out with packages and others taking smoke breaks. Large trucks drove through the area, bearing produce, equipment, or coal and, invariably, a contingent of black men in soiled coveralls. The city reeked of decay and faded glory, worsened by violence, crime, and economic inequality—all overshadowed by an indomitable and chaotic thirst for wealth.

I decided to head over to the Carlton Centre, a large shopping and office complex in the center of the city that housed the exclusive Carlton Hotel. The complex also contained a mall and several travel agencies and other shops that catered to its mostly tourist clientele. Here I began to see more white people, some apparently well-off blacks, and a few Indians and coloureds. Security guards at the doors scrutinized the people who flocked through the complex.

The place seemed a little threadbare, another victim, I guessed, of the deterioration of downtown Johannesburg. The shop owners here, offering the latest in Nike and Adidas running shoes and an array of highly prized American jeans, seemed desperate, standing outside their shops pleading with the few passersby to check out their merchandise. "We give you good deal," one Indian man shouted to me. Most of the merchandise cost hundreds, even thousands, of rand, an absurd amount for the average South African.

I was down to my last two hundred rand. I needed to be frugal, but I was also hungry. I went to the food court at the bottom of the Carlton Centre and found a coffee shop, where I ordered a cappuccino and a toasted ham and tomato sandwich. The few patrons in the restaurant were mostly white, and the staff was, of course, all black. A few customers were hunched over newspapers; one woman talked on a cell phone; another man tapped away on a laptop computer. A relentlessly cheery selection of American pop music pulsed through the coffee shop. But for the unruly city just outside the sanctuary of the Carlton Centre, I could have been in almost any American mall.

✳

Later that evening, Nettie asked me, "So, David, how was your day in Jo'burg? Are you looking for a job yet?" I sensed that this issue of finding a job could end up causing friction between us. After all, she was buying all the groceries and going off to work every day, while I puttered around with my books and assorted notes and journals. So the next morning I went to the corner store, bought a newspaper, and began searching the classifieds for work.

Most of the jobs required Afrikaans speakers or individuals with technical experience, although there were a few listings for domestics and laborers. When I did find something like an ad for a clerical position that looked appealing, I'd be defeated by my American accent; most of the people at the places I called simply hung up on me as soon as I opened my mouth. I also noticed that quite a few ads called for "affirmative action" candidates, which, I learned later from Nettie, now meant blacks, rarely coloureds or Indians. Rather than sit around the house and watch the Larry King show, the only decent news show I found amid the wasteland of South African television, I grabbed my bag and headed off to downtown.

This time I decided to take one of the combis cruising Jules Street. I hailed one of the white vans, the driver stopped, and I climbed in. The cramped van was filled to capacity with African men and women, some of whom glared at me. The driver shouted, "It's fifty cents," and I passed the coins up to him. The radio was blasting reggae music, and the driver kept veering to the side of the road to pick up passengers along the three-mile stretch to downtown.

I was jammed in the back seat next to an old woman and a teenage girl. They were speaking what I guessed was Xhosa. I wondered if they were talking about me. Any apprehension I felt was stripped away, however, when the young girl turned to me and smiled. As we were deposited in the center of town next to the Carlton Centre, I decided to take the combis to get around for as long as my money lasted.

Having been disabused of any notion of getting a job right away, I was determined to check out a couple of places in Johannesburg that dramatized the history of South Africa's ongoing struggle for democracy over the years. Dodging pedestrians and weaving in and out of the hawkers along the street, I headed west, to the corner of Bree and Wolhuter streets.

One of the ways I had connected with South Africa was through its arts and culture scene, so the Market Theater was first on my list. Arguably, no other institution had played such a subversive and humanizing role in the anti-apartheid struggle. The theater's commitment to nonracialism had attracted actors and playwrights such as Zakes Mokae and Athol Fugard, both of whom had garnered international acclaim for their perseverance against apartheid laws that mandated segregated audiences at performances.

When I came upon the theater complex in Newtown, I was immediately struck by how much it resembled a huge warehouse. In fact, the area had once been the scene of a produce market. Several street artists were displaying their wares outside the theater. A couple of posters advertising upcoming shows hung outside the main entrance, with its three cathedral-like windows and a couple of domes on either side. The current director of the complex was Barney Simon, a writer and director who, along with producer Mannie Manim, had founded the Market Theater in the early

1970s—not the most auspicious time to establish a theater committed to nonracialism in South Africa.

From its inception, the Market challenged the apartheid regime's Group Areas Act, which mandated that white actors could perform only for white audiences and blacks could perform only for blacks. Before long, South African actors, playwrights, and other theater artists were flocking to the Market for the opportunity to nurture their craft in a liberating atmosphere while engaging in a theater of subversion. Some of Athol Fugard's most controversial plays found a home at the Market Theater. Fugard, considered South Africa's foremost playwright, opened a channel of anti-apartheid dialogue with plays such as *Master Harold . . . and the Boys*, which brought worldwide attention to the debilitating effects of apartheid on human relationships; *My Children! My Africa!*, a play that illustrated the pernicious influence of apartheid policies on South Africa's educational system; and *Sizwe Banzi Is Dead*, a scathing indictment of the Population Registration Act.

Fugard was by no means alone in his artistic rebellion against the apartheid state: Barney Simon, John Kani, Adam Small, Winston Ntshona, Zakes Mda, Pieter Dirk Uys, and a host of other artists used the Market to call international attention to the worsening crisis in South Africa. Historian Anne Fuchs described the significance of the Market Theater: "The many voices of the New South Africa together with those of the old were present within its walls, the African majority were on the move and their particular voices were not only to be heard interpreting and reciting roles written for them by whites, but they had begun to speak for themselves."

After walking around the complex for a while, peering though a window to get a better look inside, I ducked into a little bar on the corner of Bree Street. The place was deserted, so I pulled a chair up to the bar, ordered a Castle lager, and dug into my jean jacket for a cigarette. The bar's stereo system was pounding out a lively stream of what sounded like rap, only with a South African flavor.

"Hey," I asked the dreadlocked bartender, "what kind of music is that?"

"It's *kwaito*," he said with a big grin. "*Ja*, it comes from the townships—Soweto and Alex and so forth."

I downed my beer and ordered another; at this point, I had quit worrying about my dwindling money supply.

"So, where you from?" asked the bartender, placing the fresh beer in front of me.

"The U.S., but I was born here in South Africa." I felt it necessary to add the last part in order to justify my existence in the country.

"Oh, how interesting," he said. "Where were you born? And when did you go to the U.S.?" I responded with the standard stump speech.

"So you're really American, then. I mean, this is your first time back in South Africa, right? I bet it's hard to convince someone that you're South African, hey?"

"Well—" I began, but the man was called away by a ringing telephone. I was glad, because I was irked by his insinuation that I was just a run-of-the-mill American, with no right to claim my South African roots. I looked around the bar, wishing that someone else would come in.

By the time he returned, I had taken out a ten-rand bill and placed it on the bar.

"So, as I was saying, you're really only half South African—are you done already? What's the big hurry, man? Your story is very interesting."

"No," I insisted, "I've really got to get going. But could you tell me how to get to John Vorster Square from here?"

The man's smile drooped. "John Vorster Square? Why on earth would you want to go there?"

"I'm a journalist," I lied, "and I might want to write a story about it."

His smile returned. "Ah, a journalist. Why didn't you say so at the beginning?"

With that, he explained how to get to the infamous police station. As I got up to leave, he called out, "Hey, my name is Bheki. Feel free to come around anytime so we can talk more."

I waved back to the man and made a mental note to avoid that particular bar for the duration of my stay in Johannesburg.

✳

Whereas the Market Theater represented the heroic struggle of South African artists to defy the tragic lunacies of apartheid, John Vorster Square, now looming ahead of me on Commissioner Street, beneath the busy M2 Freeway, epitomized the regime's ruthless determination to crush its foes. The police station was named after a former prime minister and state president, John Balthazar Vorster, who had assumed office in 1966 after the assassination of Prime Minister Hendrik Frensch Verwoerd, the chief theorist and architect of apartheid. When Verwoerd was felled by a dagger to the heart at the hands of a deranged messenger, Demetrio Tsafendas, the regime intensified its repression of dissidents. Vorster wasted no time in implementing Verwoerd's vision of "grand apartheid," which entailed complete territorial separation for blacks and other nonwhites and complete police repression. John Vorster Square was opened in 1974, and its reputation for the atrocities perpetrated behind its walls soon assumed mythic proportions.

At first glance, the twelve-story building looked quite drab, except for its partially blue façade, perhaps a minor concession thrown in to project some semblance of decorum or temperance. Police personnel and other bureaucrats streamed in and out of the main entrance. A few shabbily dressed men and women sat on a nearby curb; some looked dazed or lost, while others seemed to be waiting for someone to emerge from the building. Police vans with wire cages, known as *kwela kwelas*, rushed back and forth along Commissioner Street, some of them transporting human cargo. "Kwela kwela" is a Zulu phrase translated as "climb up, climb up, hurry," which is what the South African police barked at prisoners as they bundled them into the vans and hauled them off to jail. Most of the pedestrians I encountered went about their business, some of them perhaps willfully clueless about what the police station represented.

I knew from my reading that the place had been—and probably still was—the scene of torture, murder, and other human rights abuses. One case in particular, that of labor activist and medical doctor Neil Aggett, had stayed in my mind. Aggett was taken into custody on November 27, 1981, for his trade union activities with the African Food and Canning Workers Union; any trade union at the time was considered a direct challenge to the regime. On February 5, 1982, Aggett was found hanging in his cell; he was twenty-eight years old and became the first white person to die in the custody of the South African security police. Despite international condemnation and widespread protests after his death, an official presiding over an inquest absolved the police of all blame, ruling that Aggett had died of suicide by hanging.

Many other activists, the majority of them black, had also "committed suicide" on the tenth floor of John Vorster Square, which housed the interrogation rooms for the sadistic Special Branch. Some people mysteriously slipped on pieces of soap and fell out of windows to their death. A few people reportedly fell in the shower and broke their necks. Some activists told of being tortured into false confessions. All this had been done out of the Afrikaners' fanatical determination to root out a perceived *swart gevaar*—the black menace—sometimes coupled with warnings of a Communist onslaught.

Among others killed at John Vorster Square were Ernest Moabi Dipale, a twenty-one-year-old activist found hanging in his cell; Matthews Mabelane, a twenty-three-year-old student activist from Soweto, who "fell" from the tenth floor of the police station; Aaron Khoza, whose death was ruled a suicide by hanging; Ahmed Timol, age thirty, who supposedly jumped to his death from the tenth floor of the jail; and Wellington Mlungisi Tshazibane, a thirty-year-old activist, who seemed to have hanged himself from the bars of his cell, according to the South African Security Services.

Why was I so fixated on John Vorster Square, especially when there were so many deaths in detention—some never fully investigated—all over South Africa? I was equally concerned about all the other faceless and famous people caught up in the carnage and blood sport of apartheid. Steve Biko's death in detention in a filthy cell in Port Elizabeth particularly haunted me every time I heard the opening lyrics of "Biko," Peter Gabriel's moving tribute to the Black Consciousness leader: "September '77, Port Elizabeth, weather fine, it was business as usual, in police room 619 . . . "

But two issues stuck in my craw when it came to John Vorster Square. First, the place and all the evil perpetrated there—right there in the middle of Johannesburg—made me think of the tragedy of Emmett Till in Mississippi, ripped from his family and murdered because of a dare, his killers later exonerated by an all-white jury. And it made me think of Mack Charles Parker, another black man murdered in 1959 in Mississippi for allegedly raping a white woman, taken from his jail cell by a white mob, shot several times at close range, and strung up on a bridge over the Pearl River. Indeed, NAACP stalwart Roy Wilkins had recognized the link between the two slayings, observing, "No clearer examples of the advantages to the ruling white clique of racial disfranchisement on the local level can be found than the Till killing and the Parker lynching, but the ramifications extend beyond county lines and help to erect protective ramparts for segregation far from the Pearl and Tallahatchie rivers."

Though it had once seemed a stretch to connect John Vorster Square and Jim Crow Mississippi, I now understood the similarities of these two abominations: both systems had, in a ruthless and calculated manner, expunged any and all threats, real or imagined, to the mantle of white supremacy. That's what it was all about, I finally realized. Both these institutions, officially and unofficially, overtly and covertly, served the purpose of protecting white nationalism—and, in the case of Mississippi, especially, the sanctity of white womanhood—against the specter of the dark bogeyman, the swart gevaar, the taint of race impurity.

The second thing that bugged me about John Vorster Square was its damned normalcy—its utter sense of just-going-about-the-business-of-law-and-order. As I turned to leave, I couldn't help thinking about Hannah Arendt's well-known formulation of "the banality of evil." So many people had been killed, so much indecency foisted upon the human spirit at this one place. Yet everything was so proper, and people just walked around like the fucking world went on despite the bloodshed and the tortured screams that were forever a part of this John Vorster Square.

I'd had enough and turned to go when I inadvertently stepped on a ragged and dirty boy sitting on the curb.

"Please, *meneer,* money for food," he moaned.

I reached into my pants pocket, hurriedly threw a few coins on the ground, and made haste for the comfort of the Carlton Centre, the one place where there was no unpleasantness, where the studiously groomed black security guards filtered all the ugly reality of the city from the food court's sterile atmosphere, accented with American pop music. By the time I reached the Carlton Centre, though, I realized that I needed to conserve what little money I had left instead of blowing it on fast food. I had also resolved to do more walking, both out of frugality and a sense of adventure, so I set out to find Jules Street, which would take me straight to Malvern.

Nettie and Kim would be home by now, I guessed, as I trudged past garages and auto repair shops. Johannesburg stretched its industrial tentacles throughout its periphery, and all kinds of businesses had sprung up to fill the city's voracious appetite for labor and resources. Warehouses occupied virtually every corner I passed. Every street featured a machine shop, often with a lone welder who seemed intent on some urgent job. Several take-away restaurants and corner stores catered to the now familiar sight of men in greasy blue and green coveralls queuing for loaves of bread, tins of sardines, chunks of *polony* (bologna), and giant bottles of green and blue cool drinks. Trucks hauling men and produce and machine parts constantly rattled up and down the street.

About halfway to Malvern, the sky suddenly darkened. Johannesburg, Cedric had told me, was notoriously prone to sudden rainstorms in the summer. The first raindrops came softly and then became more insistent. I noticed a beer hall off the next street and considered ducking inside to wait out the rain. When I looked in, though, I saw that the place was indeed an authentic beer hall. Lots of African men sat around nursing vats of homemade beer and talking in Xhosa and other languages I didn't recognize. None of the crude signs pasted on the walls were in English. I spotted a bus shelter down the street and darted inside to escape the now pelting rain.

Just as I stumbled into the shelter, an African man with his wife and child entered on the other side. They were shabbily but respectably dressed. The woman held the little girl to her hip and shushed her when the lightning cracked. The man took off his jacket and gave it to his wife and daughter. The four of us cowered at separate ends of the shelter while the rain soaked the unquenchably dry South African earth. I turned to make contact with the man—a gesture of goodwill meant to acknowledge being stranded in the same situation—but he never looked my way.

✳

One thing I had learned so far was that South Africans loved nothing more than a good joll, especially after working so hard to survive in a city as grim as Johannesburg. At the end of my first week at Nettie's, Adrienne showed up in Malvern, ready to hit the streets. Kim had gone with her father for the weekend; I wondered about Angelo, Adrienne's son.

Nettie was in rare form when she got home from work. She immediately changed into a crisp pair of blue jeans and a sparkly blouse.

"Dammit, I work hard and I play hard," she proclaimed, holding aloft an unopened bottle of KWV brandy. Adrienne, who also wore stylish American designer jeans, ran to the kitchen to fetch glasses and ice. I settled in for a long night of intense and varied drinking.

"How do you say in the States, David—TGIF—hey?" Nettie cackled.

"TGIF, indeed," I said, lighting a cigarette and looking forward to some excitement and carousing in the clubs of Johannesburg. Adrienne turned on the radio, and the three of us drank and bobbed our heads to the music before heading out into the electric night in Nettie's clunker of a car.

Though Johannesburg offered an endless variety of party spots in neighborhoods such as Yeoville, Berea, and Braamfontein, the only real destination for nightlife was Hillbrow. Since Adrienne lived in this densely populated area not far from downtown, we headed to her building across the street from Hillbrow Hospital, where Nettie parked the car. Row after row of huge apartment blocks flanked the street. Crowds of people were out and about, some of them sitting on benches outside the buildings, talking to friends, and drinking from bottles in brown paper bags. Other people milled around the liquor store and supermarket down the block. As we exited the car, the sounds of laughter and the unmistakable smell of dagga floated through the air.

Nettie locked the car and activated its alarm, which I found amusing because her car was a real piece of crap: the paint was fighting a losing battle with rust patches; the windscreen was cracked; and something—the muffler maybe?—hung from the car's underbelly. The three of us started walking past the barbed-wire compound of Hillbrow Hospital toward the nightclub district. Nettie briefed me as if we were about to enter a combat zone.

"Now, David, we're going to have a good time, but you must always be on your Ps and Qs. Hillbrow is a very dangerous place."

Adrienne chimed in, "*Ja,* David, just mind your own business, stick with us, and you should be fine."

"And another thing," Nettie added, "don't ever come here by yourself, especially at night, because the bleks will just tear you apart. They're really starting to take over. Shame."

We walked past people lurking in the shadows—some of them street kids sleeping in the gutters or prostitutes selling their wares—until we got to Pretoria Street. Here were the familiar sights of street vendors and stores. More people mobbed the streets and sidewalks as we arrived in the center of Hillbrow amid a huge complex of shops, restaurants, and bars.

"This way," Adrienne motioned, and we slipped inside a dark, nondescript club where the music was thumping. A long bar took up one side of the club, and a few people sat around tables or on benches in the dim room. A tall, lanky man got up and approached us.

"Hi, Tommy!" said Adrienne, embracing him. "I want you to meet my brother, David, and you know Nettie, right?"

Tommy and I shook hands, and he waved to Nettie.

"So what are you guys drinking?" he asked when we settled at a table in the corner.

"David, what are you having?" asked Nettie. I couldn't tell whether she was trying to supervise me or probing to see if I could buy my own drinks.

"I'll just have a beer for now," I said. "What would you two like?"

Nettie look astonished when I returned with the drinks; I guess my offering to buy a round of drinks didn't jibe with her newly forming image of me as a freeloader. It was true that I was down to my last hundred rand, but I just didn't care anymore. Something had to come through for me in Johannesburg, I reasoned, because one thing was for sure: I had nothing to go back to in Atlanta—no job, no apartment, no car, nothing. But I didn't want to think about any of that as I chugged beer after beer and, later, cocktail after cocktail to the accompaniment of tunes like "Baby Got Back" by the rapper Sir Mix-A-Lot, Kris Kross's "Jump," and "Rump Shaker" by Wreckx-N-Effect.

When Nettie pulled Tommy to the dance floor, Adrienne slid her chair closer to mine.

"So, David, how do you like living with Nettie?" she asked. "She can be a real bitch, can't she?"

I wanted to be diplomatic, in case Adrienne was setting a trap for me, so I just smiled and said blandly, "It's definitely been interesting."

"Oh, come on, I know her," she insisted. "I grew up with her. She can be a bitch sometimes."

I nervously looked over at Nettie and Tommy on the crowded dance floor.

"It's all right, David," Adrienne assured me. "Look, I really wanted you to come and stay at my place, but I only have a flat, and it's so small. But I really feel for you because I know what you have to put up with. Hey, David?"

Of course, Adrienne was right. Nettie was clearly losing patience with me. I hadn't found a job, even though I'd been in Johannesburg only a week. I didn't want to give Nettie the satisfaction of confirming her suspicions that I was a freeloader, the ne'er-do-well brother from the States. But I also didn't feel comfortable sharing my anxiety with Adrienne, so I changed the subject.

"What was it like for you guys growing up?" I asked her. She took a moment to drain her drink before refocusing her attention on me.

"Well, things were really hard for us here in South Africa, David," she began.

"How so?" I pressed, hoping to get as much information as possible from her before Nettie returned to the table.

"Growing up in Durban with Auntie Bessie was tough because our father was never there and we never really knew our mother. The three of us just had to depend on each other. I mean, it was just really hard."

Just as I was getting ready to push Adrienne beyond these platitudes, Nettie and Tommy returned from the dance floor. "Hey guys, let's go to another place down the street," said Nettie. "Tommy says there's a really good band playing there tonight."

The little hole I had opened into my sisters' lives under apartheid snapped shut, and we piled out of the club and back into the chaos of Hillbrow on a Friday night.

The next club turned out to be a more upscale affair. Valets dashed around the parking lot, and a crowd waited to get inside, held at bay by two armed security guards at the door. As we approached the place, Tommy turned and told us to wait. He walked around the crowd to speak with one of the guards, and a few minutes later we were at the bar in the club.

"Tommy, you deserve a drink for that," Nettie declared. He flashed a big smile, and we all laughed about the people still waiting to get inside. Adrienne's cell phone rang, and she drifted off to take the call. I fired up a cigarette, and we began another rotation of heavy drinking. The club was packed with lots of smartly dressed people, but it reeked of smoke, cheap perfume, and perspiration. The music pumped, the dance floor swelled, and the room seemed to vibrate with a sense of giddiness and expectation. After all, official apartheid had been scrapped, and the National Party government, the ANC, and other groups had resumed multiparty negotiations after a spate of political violence and the breakdown in the CODESA proceedings. Talk of an interim constitution and the country's first election was in the air, and the possibilities of freedom seemed endless. What would have been just another Friday night at the club was now fraught with new meaning and a new sense of celebration and triumph.

Adrienne returned and whispered something into Nettie's ear. Tommy had disappeared. I stepped outside to get some air. It was nearly 3 A.M., and the parking lot was starting to empty, though people continued to flock to the club. I sat on a ledge on the side of the building and lit a cigarette. As soon as I took my first toke, a guard, a black man dressed in army fatigues, came over and stood in front of me.

"You can't sit here," he announced. "No loitering."

The man held a *sjambok* in one hand, a nasty little whip made out of rhinoceros hide, which South African police were notorious for wielding against civilians. I stood up and flicked out the cigarette. I wasn't looking at the man so much as I was eyeing the sjambok.

"You must leave this area," he said, tapping the whip against his side as a not-so-subtle hint of impending violence.

Instead of backing down, I reached into my pocket and pulled out my passport, which I always carried.

"Look at this!" I shouted at the man. "Do you know what this is? Huh? This is an American passport. I am an American citizen, and if you touch me with that damn thing, I will report you to the U.S. Embassy. Do you understand?"

My whole body stiffened, not knowing whether the gambit had worked or whether to expect a bruising blow at any moment.

But the man stepped back. "Okay, okay," he said. "It's no problem. No problem, *meneer.*"

I was ready to leave the club and went back to get the others. But just as I reached the door, Adrienne ran out, followed by Nettie and Tommy.

"What's wrong?" I asked, as Adrienne ran off down the street.

"She's upset because she was supposed to meet someone, and he stood her up," Nettie sighed. "Maybe we should all just leave now."

"I'm gonna try to catch up with her," I said.

"Okay, David. I'll stay with Nettie, but be careful, man," Tommy warned.

"Yes, David, please be careful," said Nettie, as I dashed after Adrienne. I could just make out her outline about a block ahead.

When I finally caught up to her, she was wiping tears from her face. I put my arms around her. "It's okay. Don't worry about it. You'll meet someone else. Don't let it upset you," I tried to soothe her. She nodded and sniffled a few times. Doubtless, we had all had too much to drink, and emotions and alcohol never mix well.

We returned to her building and took the clanging elevator up to her twelfth-floor flat, which was indeed small: it was one large room, with a closet-size kitchen, a compact bathroom, a queen bed, and a twin bed for

Angelo. Adrienne had obviously tried to fix up the place by putting in a dining room table, which almost blocked the front entrance. The only other furniture in the flat consisted of a couple of chairs, a dresser, and a television set. A clothesline decked with drying clothes stretched from the bathroom to a hook on the wall. The only redeeming feature of the place was the balcony, overlooking the concrete canyons of Hillbrow.

By now, Adrienne had recovered and was busy securing the four or five locks on the front door. "You can sleep in Angelo's bed," she said.

I took off my shoes and flopped on the little bed, whose sheets bore tiny imprints of racecars and motorcycles. I thought I heard Adrienne say, "Thank you, David," before I drifted off into a deep, inebriated sleep.

✳

Adrienne shook me awake the next morning. "Come on, David. Nettie called, and she wants us to come over to her house for brunch."

I went to the bathroom and threw some cold water on my face; I was surprised not to have a hangover. Adrienne grabbed her bag, and we took the elevator down to the street, which had already begun to fill with people and cars. On our way to find a taxi to Malvern, we passed a man and a woman folding a couple of large cardboard boxes and storing them on the side of a building. Their day, I thought, would most likely be consumed by the search for food and a few cents here and there on the streets of Hillbrow.

When we got to Malvern, Nettie was in the back of the house, shouting orders to a couple of workmen: "See here, can't you fit them here in this corner?" Only when I drew closer and looked in the little room next to the kitchen did I realize that the men were wrestling with a mattress and box spring.

"You have a bed now, David," Nettie announced, "and your own room as well."

I thanked her, though I wasn't looking forward to sleeping in the claustrophobic little room. For the time being, however, I was at her mercy.

While Nettie and Adrienne finished cooking, I made myself a potent mimosa and greeted Tommy and a couple more of Nettie's friends, whom she had invited over for brunch. Nettie was an excellent cook, and I was famished from all the drinking and smoking of the previous night. I went out back to help Tommy with the braii; mostly, I watched while he prepared and stoked the fire. Soon the smell of grilled steak, sausage, and chicken blanketed the backyard, and everyone wound up out back with drinks and conversation.

When the time was right, I piled my plate high with generous portions of salads, beans, pumpkin, chicken, sausage, and steak. At that moment, all was right with the world—until I bit down on a chunk of steak and was rudely greeted by an old friend: a back tooth whose filling had threatened to come out several times since my arrival in South Africa. The jolt of pain was excruciating. I had to put down the plate and nurse my jaw. Nettie and the others were busy eating and laughing. I ran to the bathroom and tried to blunt the pain with a wad of toilet paper; the filling had definitely come out this time, although I couldn't find it. Until now, I had managed to get by with having a mouthful of crappy teeth, but my luck had run out. I needed to get to a dentist as soon as possible.

I waited until Nettie came into the kitchen.

"Nettie, I'm having some serious dental problems," I moaned. "I need to get to a dentist."

She looked at me in complete bewilderment. "What do you mean? How could you let this happen? I don't understand."

"Well, it just happened," I explained. "I didn't think the filling would come out."

"So didn't you think about this before coming to South Africa?" she said. "I mean, I don't understand how you could not take care of yourself and get into this situation."

It was obvious that my pain wasn't registering with her. Like so many other times in my life, I was just fucked and on my own.

I turned to walk toward the living room, and she came after me.

"What do you want me to do, David?" she said, her voice practically dripping with exasperation.

"I need to get to a dentist," I mumbled. "But don't worry about it. I'll be okay."

In truth, I had no money and had no clue about how medical care worked in South Africa.

"David, it's Saturday, man, and nothing's open. Can't you wait until Monday, and we can try and get you into a dentist's office somewhere?"

"Don't worry about it," I repeated. I went to the sun porch and lit a cigarette, hoping to deaden the pain with nicotine—a trick that had seemed to work during previous bouts of dental agony. Nettie rejoined the others in the backyard, and a sense of normalcy returned to the tiny house in Malvern.

*

The next day, the pain in my mouth had deadened sufficiently for me to resume my exploration of Johannesburg. This time, I decided to walk over to Hillbrow, since I had only glimpsed the outlines of the area while hanging out the previous Friday. By now, I was down to about twenty rand and a few coins, so I took a combi to downtown Johannesburg and asked a street vendor for directions to Hillbrow. According to the withered old African woman, Hillbrow was less than a mile northeast. I bought a bunch of grapes and a banana and took off walking up Smith Street.

Like the Market Theater, Hillbrow had spoiled the fantasy of the apartheid theorists and their visions of a strictly segregated society. Though the neighborhood had been classified as a white area under the Group Areas Act of 1950, segregation began crumbling by the 1970s. As the apartheid edifice disintegrated in the 1980s, Indians, coloureds, and increasing numbers of blacks flocked to Hillbrow to be close to Johannesburg. In fact, the area, which had a reputation for violence, had been nicknamed the "Manhattan of South Africa." Another nickname for Hillbrow was "Soweto of the Sky," because of the huge number of people who lived on the neighborhood's rooftops. Including those who resided in the ubiquitous flats, the street people, and the roof dwellers, the population of Hillbrow was about thirty thousand people, in an area less than a mile in circumference.

Two of Hillbrow's most prominent landmarks came into view as I approached the center of the neighborhood: the ninety-story J. G. Strijdom Tower, also known as the Hillbrow Tower, supposedly one of the tallest structures erected in Africa; and the fifty-four-story Ponte Hotel, a cylindrical structure built in 1975, now reportedly infested with drug dealers and in a state of disrepair.

When I arrived at Highpoint, a shopping and residential plaza in the center of Hillbrow, I got a panoramic look at the life of the neighborhood and its considerable concentration of fast food shops, laundromats, travel agencies, and cell phone shops. Building after building of overcrowded flats, seedy hotels, and bars stretched along the main thoroughfares of Pretoria and Kotze streets. High-rise apartments crowded the horizon, with clothes and people draped over balconies. People of all colors lived next to one another, and cultures mingled. This element of hybridity contributed to the sense of excitement and danger in the neighborhood. I didn't see many white people, though, and only an occasional group of police, who invariably carried shotguns and AK-47s.

The streets were packed with people from the townships of South Africa as well as from cities of other African states. South Africans called these foreigners the *amakwere-kwere,* a disparaging term for outsiders. These people came to Hillbrow in search of fortune and jobs and brought drug trafficking and high levels of crime with them.

Hillbrow was a petri dish of social dysfunction. Along with its bustling commerce and its thousands of apartment dwellers, it was also home to AIDS-infected prostitutes and vicious pimps, glue-sniffing street children, drug dealers, homeless people, and petty thieves. Many of the side streets featured sleazy strip joints and sex shops, including those that catered to transvestites and the gay population. Sex workers stood in front of buildings, openly soliciting pedestrians. For the more discreet customer, the neighborhood contained a number of escort agencies and massage parlors. Hillbrow, it seemed, offered something for every appetite.

Ominously, the specter of AIDS was only slowly beginning to be recognized in Hillbrow. HIV/AIDS would have enormous implications for South Africa's future: an estimated 1 percent of the population was already infected with the virus at this point. A study conducted by the University of the Witwatersrand in Johannesburg in 1991 had concluded that "the HIV epidemic will cause the sickness and death of many young adults . . . [and] could significantly reduce the rate of population growth by the year 2005." Later, as South Africa entered the twenty-first century, researchers estimated the number of AIDS orphans at 660,000, a number that was expected to more than triple to 2 million by 2010. In a study of the demographic and economic impact of AIDS in South Africa, economist Jeffrey D. Lewis noted: "Since the onset of the AIDS epidemic, estimates are that more than 1 million South Africans have died of AIDS-related causes. By 2010, this number is projected to grow to more than 6 million deaths."

Somewhere a Hillbrow bar was pumping out West African *zook* music, and the smell of dagga was thick in the air. Up ahead, I spotted a *biltong* stand and decided to have some lunch before venturing any farther. Biltong is a uniquely spiced South African version of beef jerky, which comes in many versions other than beef, such as springbok, porcupine, and ostrich. My favorite was the peri-peri spiced beef, a kind of Portuguese version of the national staple. I bought a candy bar and a Coke to wash it all down—taking great pains to chew on the right side of my mouth, away from the bad tooth—and resumed my slow, cautious walk through the center of Hillbrow.

A couple of blocks from Highpoint Plaza, near a Shoprite Checkers supermarket, a street kid ran up to me.

"Hello, *meneer*," the boy pleaded, "can you help me, sir?"

He looked to be in his early teens. He stuck out his filthy hands, and his dirt-encrusted fingernails repulsed me. My first instinct was to clutch my book bag closer to my chest and stop in the middle of the sidewalk.

The boy continued to beg for money. "Please, sir, I am very hungry. Can't you please help me get food?"

I looked around to make sure there were people nearby in case I needed to call for help, but most of the pedestrians just continued to stream by with stony, indifferent expressions.

"What do you want?" I asked dumbly. "I don't have any money to give you."

"Yes, you do, mister," the boy insisted. "You are eating food. Please, please, sir, I just want to have some food."

I offered the boy a stick of biltong. He took it and greedily crammed it into his mouth. I gave him the rest of my Coke and the candy bar, hoping this would appease him. But it didn't.

"I am still very hungry, *meneer*. Would you take me to get a pie?" he asked, pointing to a corner store. I fished out a five-rand coin, went in and bought a curry chicken pie and an orange soda, and brought the food out to him.

The boy flopped down on a nearby stairwell and began tearing into the food. He was no longer a little boy but a famished animal in the wilds of Hillbrow. He wore tattered pants, and his toes poked through a pair of laceless and dingy tennis shoes. I watched with fascination as the pie disappeared into the maw of his emaciated frame, his chin and fingers glistening with the juices and crumbs of the food.

Some researchers at the time estimated that thousands of street children, who were often runaways or orphans from the surrounding black townships, called Hillbrow home. They were referred to in Afrikaans as *skadukinders,* or twilight children; in Zulu, they were known as *malunde,* or those of the street. For the most part, they hung out in groups and slept on cardboard boxes in street gutters or in abandoned buildings. Many street children survived by begging or, for a few cents, guarding parked cars in Hillbrow's shopping districts. A great number of them, however, prostituted themselves to eat and maintain their corrosive drug habits— mainly sniffing glue and smoking dagga mixed with mandrax, a dangerous synthetic drug similar in its effects to methamphetamine.

I wanted to know more about this boy, who now pulled a grubby cigarette butt from his back pocket and was beckoning for a light. I pulled out my pack and gave him a fresh cigarette.

"So, what's your name, and where do you live?" I asked, extending my lighter to him.

The boy told me that his name was Daniel, that he was twelve years old, and that he mostly lived in any abandoned building he could find in the neighborhood. He was from Soweto, he said, and had come here after his mother died. As far as he knew, he had no other relatives. He said that he had been living alone in Hillbrow for about six months.

"Well," I asked naïvely, "what happens when it rains, or when it gets cold? Where do you go when you can't find a building?"

Daniel took a long drag on the cigarette and exhaled through his nose. "*Ja,* that's easy," he answered, a sly smile creasing the corners of his mouth. "Sometimes we go to the shelter. They have food there, but too many rules. I don't like to stay there."

On an impulse, I said, "Where is the shelter? Would you take me there?"

Ever the opportunist, Daniel replied, "I'll take you there for two rand, but I won't go in. I will only take you there."

The Twilight Shelter sat just off the main strip of Hillbrow, a couple of blocks north of the Highpoint shopping plaza. Daniel walked a little ahead of me, pointing the way. A few people shot quizzical looks in our direction, perhaps wondering whether I realized the gravity of getting involved with a street child. At the end of the sidewalk, we turned right onto a narrow strip of pavement. Here, there were many other street children, some of them laid out on the pavement, others crouched with their heads between their knees.

"That is the shelter." Daniel pointed to a blue, three-story building ahead. He stretched out his hand, and I gave him the two-rand coin. Before I could thank him and wish him well, he dashed off with the money. I guessed he was trying to protect the precious money from the other children, some of whom had taken notice of me and began to accost me before I could slip into the shelter door.

A countertop and a desk in the corner took up the front room of the shelter. The walls were painted light blue. Photographs, one of the musician Paul Simon and the others, I assumed, of the shelter staff and street kids, hung on one wall. A poster underneath the photographs read: "Give a man a fish and you will feed him for a day. Teach a man to fish and you will feed him for a lifetime." An old white lady came out of a small office in the corner of the room and asked if she could help me.

"Um, yes," I stammered, trying to come up with a good cover story. "I am a journalist from the U.S. I was thinking about doing a story about the Twilight Shelter, and I just wanted to get some more information."

The woman stepped quickly to the counter. "Oh, my, that is wonderful," she said. She asked my name, and I told her. "Well, David, you can just call me Gogo; that's what all the children call me. It's Xhosa for grandmother."

I described my encounter with Daniel and how surprised I was to find out about the shelters in Hillbrow. "Why don't more children come to the shelters?" I asked.

"Oh, it's very complicated. Won't you come in, and I'll give you a tour?" she offered, ushering me into a corridor off the main reception area. "You know, we had some Americans come in last week. You see, we are trying to raise money for the shelter. We get nearly nothing from the government."

I nodded and answered in the appropriate places. I felt terrible because I had lied to the lady about being a journalist; I felt especially bad because I was beginning to recognize that the shelter and its plight presented a good story for a legitimate journalist.

"Maybe you can write a story about us here and help us get money from the States, hey?" suggested Gogo.

"Yes, I think so," I lied.

Gogo told me that the shelter had a staff of about fifteen people, who took care of some seventy boys ages eight to sixteen. The boys were runaways or orphans and either walked in off the streets or were brought in by the police or concerned citizens. The shelter had strict rules: no drugs, no fighting, and no cursing, and every boy had to attend school. The staff hoped to eventually reunite boys with their families, when it was possible, according to Gogo.

She showed me the main floor, with a kitchen, a dining hall, and a large room where the children ate and played games. "*Ja*, every day is a struggle," she intoned. The back of the shelter served as a playground for the children. The boys lived on the upper floors, which had bunk beds and communal bathrooms.

Offering to let me meet some of the boys, Gogo took me into one of the rooms, which was stuffed with four bunk beds. Two or three boys were cleaning the room and putting clothes away.

"Boys," she called out. "This is Mr. David. He is from America. He is going to write a story about us and help us get some money for the shelter."

The boys pounced on me with yelps of laughter and excitement. I shook their hands and patted them playfully on the back. Gogo turned to a boy who had just entered the room.

"David, this is Joseph. He has a job as a messenger in an office downtown. Say hello to Mr. David, Joseph."

The boy smiled shyly and said hello. Joseph had been in the shelter for a year, Gogo said, and had managed to find a job as a messenger and tea-boy in the office of an advertising agency. He had already finished his matric, the South African equivalent of graduating from high school.

Gogo looked expectantly at me, and I asked, "So, how do you like the shelter, Joseph?"

"It is good here," he replied. "Everyone is very nice to me here. And the other children are safe and go to school."

The other boys gathered around us, and I couldn't figure out what to say next.

Stupidly, all I could come up with was, "Well, keep up the good work, Joseph—and everybody else, too." Then I turned to signal to Gogo that it was time for me to go.

"Thank you, sir," said Joseph as I began descending the stairs.

"Please, you must write about us here so we can get some money from the States," Gogo urged as we stood at the front door of the shelter.

I turned to her, took her hand, and promised that I would. And for a brief, shining moment, as I began the journey back to Malvern, I almost fooled myself into believing that I would keep my promise to Gogo.

✳

I had now reached the point I had been dreading—and had tried to avoid—since arriving in South Africa: I was down to my last five rand. I had become increasingly despondent about ever finding a job, and, of course, there had been no let-up in the frequency with which Nettie asked me, every day, "What did you do today, David? Any luck finding a job?"

It was clear that I needed to summon all my dwindling resources to stay afloat in Johannesburg. I emptied the contents of my book bag and rifled through them until I found the phone number of the *Atlanta Journal-Constitution*'s special correspondent in Johannesburg. The foreign editor had given me the man's number before I left Atlanta. I had taken the number out of courtesy, much as one accepts a fruitcake as a Christmas present. I admired the correspondent's work, but I never thought that I'd actually have to call on him in desperation.

When I phoned him, though, his enthusiasm gave me a glimmer of hope that maybe, just maybe, he could pull some strings and help me get a journalism-related job in Johannesburg.

"How long have you been in the country?" he asked.

I began the now familiar, and unprovoked, recitation about my birth, the reunion with my sisters, and my desire to discover my roots. I also mentioned that I had been in the country for just over a month. The man went on to ask about people at the *AJC* and about news from Atlanta, where he had lived for a time. He seemed incredibly eager to talk and suggested that I visit him at his house in the northern suburb of Parktown.

"Are you working?" he asked.

"No," I answered, "that's kinda what I wanted to talk to you about."

"The market is pretty tight all over, especially here in Johannesburg," he said noncommittally. "But, hey, we'll talk and see what we can do."

When I told Nettie about my conversation with the correspondent, she seemed uninterested. All she said was, "Parktown is a very nice area, lots of whites. But you'll have to take a bus from downtown to get there because I can't take you. I must work."

The main bus depot in downtown Johannesburg was a chaotic and confusing place. Rows and rows of double-decker buses chuffed in and out, filled with people headed to all corners of the city. Nettie had given me directions, as best she could muster, of where and how to catch the Parktown bus. But now, caught up in the whirlpool of people, traffic, and dozens of buses, I was hopelessly confused. I had arranged to meet the correspondent at three in the afternoon. It was a few minutes after two, and I started frantically running from bus to bus, trying to discern each one's destination from its window placard. I looked around for help, but no one—neither the black men and women rushing to catch buses nor the few whites hurrying along the sidewalk—seemed eager to muck around with an obvious foreigner.

Finally, I ran up to a stalled bus, ducked inside, and asked the driver, a round black man, "Excuse me, is this the bus to Parktown?"

The man looked at me and curled his bottom lip in palpable distaste. His eyes narrowed with what looked like hatred. In that moment, all I could guess was that he disliked me because I was a foreigner and because of the complexion of my skin. I had encountered this same overt hostility while riding in the combis, with their mostly African clientele. It had puzzled me until I remembered that both whites and blacks historically saw coloureds, whom I claimed as my people, as impure, immoral creatures.

At the moment, though, I needed to get to Parktown. So I asked the bus driver again, hoping that he simply hadn't understood me.

"Please, sir, I need to go to Parktown. Is this the bus for Parktown?"

He continued to glower and then abruptly turned away from me to adjust the side mirror on the bus. Clearly, this man hates me, I thought.

I had just turned to go when one of the passengers yelled out, "Yes, this is the bus to Parktown. You are on the right bus."

A white man, perhaps in his early twenties, got out of his seat and advanced to the front of the bus, where I was standing. He walked with some difficulty. When he drew closer, I noticed that his head shook occasionally and that a slow trickle of drool was inching down his chin. My immediate thought was that he suffered from some form of cerebral palsy; I had seen the same symptoms in my brother Xavier.

All the other passengers seemed to cower in their seats as the young man bore down on the bus driver.

"You could have told him that this bus is going to Parktown," he thundered. "You are a public servant. I will report you."

He seemed genuinely upset. Turning to me, he said, "My name is Brent. I want to apologize for the behavior of people in this country. There is no excuse for such rudeness. I am sick of it!"

Brent swept a mop of brown hair from his forehead. He wore shorts, a t-shirt, and tennis shoes. Except for his tremors, he was unremarkable in appearance.

Surprisingly, the bus driver appeared chastised. He turned to me and said softly, "Yes, this bus is Parktown." Then he closed the door and abruptly wheeled the bus out of the depot and into traffic.

The bus was silent for a few blocks until Brent inquired, "You are from America, hey?"

I said that I was and told him my name.

"And what do you think about our great South Africa, David?" he asked, with a trace of mockery in his voice. We were now seated opposite each other in the front of the bus near the driver. I told him that I didn't really know what to think since I had seen only parts of Durban, downtown Johannesburg, and Hillbrow.

"I live in Parktown," he said. "So, why are you going there?"

I told him about the correspondent and my search for work. Another thin line of drool hung at the edge of his mouth; I wondered whether he knew it was there and whether he owned a handkerchief.

What fascinated me about Brent was how he had spoken up for me and reprimanded the surly bus driver. The exchange between an angry white man and a sullen black functionary could easily have been viewed through the prism of apartheid: the *baas* putting the boy in his place. Or the same scene could have been interpreted simply as the result of a bus patron's impatience with an indifferent public servant. Regardless of interpretation, the bus driver's behavior intimated that the day might soon arrive when he would not feel compelled to cringe at the threats of a white man.

We were now entering the leafy streets of Parktown. Unlike the industrial drabness of downtown Johannesburg, the vista here featured magnificent houses, constructed mostly of stone, with nineteenth-century architectural features. Stunningly colorful gardens brimmed with lavender, rosemary, hibiscus, and hydrangeas. Tall jacaranda trees, fruit orchards, and carefully manicured shrubs framed and accentuated these bucolic scenes. Without exception, all the houses were enclosed by impressively tall fences, many of them garlanded with barbed wire or spikes. Every house was marked by signs that announced PASSOP VIR DIE HOND (BEWARE OF THE DOG) and warned of rapid response paramilitary protection from companies such as CHUBB and ADT. Now and then, I caught a glimpse of swimming pools and rock gardens, rolling emerald lawns and sparkling ponds.

But there was real fear here. I could see it in the faces of the blacks who were sitting on the curbs, waiting for a bus or combi to get back to the townships. I could sense the tension in the bodies of the men watering the grass and washing the expensive cars in the driveways of the barricaded mansions. Most tellingly, I could sense white fear and uncertainty in the mere fact that I never saw a single white person walking along the streets of Parktown.

The bus driver announced the stop, and Brent and I got off the bus in front of a colonnaded and fenced sandstone mansion.

"Do you know where you're going?" he asked.

I had to admit that I didn't—I had misplaced the correspondent's address—so Brent suggested that we walk to a nearby mall and call him from there.

"You do have the number, right?" he asked, with a hint of humor.

"Yep," I replied.

"Good, then you won't mind if I come along, hey?"

Actually, I was ready to be rid of him by now, but, of course, I said, "No problem. You've been really helpful."

As Brent promised, we came upon an ultramodern mall a couple of streets over from the bus stop. The parking lot was filled with expensive cars. Like Musgrave Center, which I had visited before Christmas with my sisters, this mall was a vision of sleekness, luxury, and conspicuous consumption, populated by a mostly white clientele, with black workers cleaning, serving, and guarding the entrances.

Brent took me to a pay phone, and I called the correspondent. His house was only a couple of blocks from the mall—an easy walk, he said.

Two huge German shepherds greeted us when we arrived at the gate of his house. I rang the intercom and announced our arrival, and a couple of minutes later, the correspondent calmed the dogs and came out to fetch us.

"Good to finally meet you," he said, pulling us into the front yard of the massive house.

I shook the man's hand and introduced him to Brent. "Ah, good, I see you've made a friend," he said. "You two must come in." Brent and I followed him up the stone path to the house.

The correspondent looked Spanish—Cuban, maybe—and was tall and thin with a full head of black curly hair. He was probably in his early to mid-forties. He ushered us into a cavernous room that led to a patio and a nearby swimming pool. A little boy was doing belly dives in the pool, calling out, "Daddy, Daddy, look here!"

The correspondent motioned for us to sit down on a couple of over-stuffed couches and offered us a drink. I requested a beer, and Brent settled for a Coke.

"Not a drinking man, Brent?" the correspondent gently chided.

"No, I have to go home soon, and my mother doesn't like me to drink," he answered self-consciously.

"So, you live in this neighborhood?" the correspondent said, returning with the drinks.

"Yes, my house is about three or four blocks from here. Not far at all," Brent told him.

The correspondent turned to fiddle with an expensive stereo system, and the sounds of John Coltrane flooded the room. "You like Coltrane?" he asked me.

"Sure," I replied, though I was more interested in hearing whether he'd be able to help me find a job.

The correspondent went outside to check on the boy and brought him back in to meet us. "Christopher, this is Mr. David and Mr. Brent. Mr. David is from America, the same as Daddy."

The boy was trembling and dripping water as his father struggled to dry him with a towel. "Daddy," he whined, "I want to go for another swim. Please, Daddy."

"All right," the correspondent sighed, and the boy raced back outside and did a belly flop in the pool.

"You guys look like you need more to drink," he observed and headed off to the kitchen. When he returned, he began, mercifully, talking about his experiences in South Africa. He had been the special correspondent for the *AJC* for the past three years; before that, he had worked as a freelancer in Atlanta and the southeastern United States. He had met a lot of people while in South Africa—other writers, actors, politicians, musicians. In fact, he noted as a kind of hint, he was scheduled to attend a party at trumpeter Hugh Masekela's house that very night.

But he was getting frustrated lately, he said, because of the shocking crime rate in the country. Almost all of his friends had been touched by the violence: his best friend, a fellow writer, had come home to find his wife raped and murdered; another colleague had been robbed at gunpoint and his car hijacked. Although he was excited about the current constitutional negotiations in preparation for a national one-person, one-vote election, the correspondent admitted that he feared for the safety of his family—his wife, a fellow journalist off on assignment in Zimbabwe; and his six-year-old son, blithely splashing away in the pool.

"Too many people are dying every day in South Africa," he said, "and I'm just tired of living like this."

Finally, the issue of my job search arose. "So, what have you been doing? Who've you been talking to?" he asked.

I told him about my rather limited experience mining the want ads of the newspapers, mentioning the negative reactions of the people I called about jobs. Brent had dozed off in a chair across the room.

"Yes, it can be very frustrating, but you mustn't give up," the correspondent counseled. "Unfortunately, I don't know of anyone at the moment looking to hire journalists. Do you want another beer?"

I shrugged.

When he returned from the kitchen, he asked, "So, you can't speak Afrikaans, huh?"

I shook my head.

"I ask because I just thought about a friend who runs a radio station. They need a radio guy, but you've gotta speak Afrikaans."

I shook my head again and took a good long swig of the beer. Might as well catch a buzz before I go, I thought, because I sure as hell wasn't even close to getting a job through this guy.

The boy came running back in screaming, "Daddy, I'm hungry! When are we going to the party?"

Brent was now awake, and I figured that it was time for us to be moving on. The correspondent was quite blunt. "Listen, guys, we've gotta get a move on for the party. And I've gotta get him ready. So . . . "

"Oh, no problem," I piped up. "We'll just be on our way. I enjoyed meeting you."

"Sure thing, David," said the correspondent. "Don't hesitate to call me if I can be of any further help. And just hang in there, and I'm sure something'll turn up."

He shook Brent's hand and said, "Brent, you take care now. It was good meeting you, too."

Brent started to mumble something, but I just pulled him out the door and through the gate. I couldn't bear any more of the correspondent's platitudes. I just wanted to get back to Malvern.

The only problem, as Brent soon informed me, was that the buses had stopped running; even the taxis dried up after around six in the evening, he said. Instantly, my old familiar companions—dread and fear—returned. How was I going to get home? I knew that there was no chance of Nettie coming to get me. I doubted that her car could even make it to Parktown. I took off my book bag and flopped down on the curb.

"Do you need a ride home?" asked Brent. I nodded miserably.

"My dad will give you a ride," he said. "Just come over to my house."

I shouldered my book bag and followed Brent through the strangely deserted streets of Parktown. Brent also lived in an enormous house, hidden behind a security fence. After we entered through the gate and climbed a steep driveway, he showed me into the three-story house.

"Mom! Dad!" he shouted. We walked down a hallway lined with books and entered a kitchen. A white-haired woman was gingerly removing pieces of fried fish from a pan on the stove. Off the kitchen was a den, where a teenage boy lounged in front of a television.

"Hey, mom!" Brent announced, "this is my friend David. He's from America." The woman turned to me and greeted me with a wide and genuine smile.

"Hey, Jamie," Brent cried out to the boy glued to the television. "Come meet my friend David." The boy uncurled from his position on the couch and slunk into the kitchen. He was unusually thin, and his face was acne-scarred but friendly.

"David needs a ride home, mom," Brent hollered. "He lives in Malvern. Do you think Dad can take him home?"

"I'm sure it won't be a problem, Brent," she said soothingly. "David, why don't you have some dinner with us while you're here?"

I declined, even though I was rather hungry.

I couldn't help noting the contrasts between how these people lived and how we were living in Malvern. The kitchen contained all the latest appliances and gadgets, the house was huge, and it exuded a sense of being protected from the hardscrabble fight for survival endured by the majority of people in South Africa.

Brent and Jamie were playing a video game when their father appeared. He was a short, thin wisp of a man with gray hair, dressed casually in slacks and a sweater.

"Dad," shouted Brent. "This is my friend David. He's from America, and he needs a ride home."

Brent's father shook my hand. "Hello, David, welcome to our home. Would you like some food?" he offered, as his wife began spreading platters of fish and chips on the kitchen table.

"Sure," I said, with a change of heart, not wanting to offend him or his wife. The five of us gathered around the table, a bit awkwardly at first, but eventually finding harmony in hunger.

The meal was delicious. Brent picked at his food, while his father recounted the history of his family. His ancestors had come over from England, he said, and settled in Johannesburg. Most of them had worked in the mining industry, but he had become an architect—the lone rebel of the family, he was proud to say. He was eager to express his anti-apartheid views, pointing to his hiring of black drivers and laborers for his architectural practice. Also, he hastened to tell me, he and his wife had a few Indian and coloured friends that they saw occasionally. Things were changing in this country, he insisted. Brent and Jamie had returned to the video game; and his wife, who had been mostly silent throughout the meal, started gathering the dirty dishes.

British South Africans, I knew, had held a conflicted position in South Africa, although, essentially, they had differed with Afrikaners only on the details of apartheid. Furthermore, some theorists argued that the British had laid the groundwork for apartheid through the segregationist practices and customs of the original Cape Colony in the eighteenth century. Afrikaners had disdainfully referred to the British with the phrase *sout piels,* which meant salt penis—the idea being that the British historically found themselves straddled between two countries, South Africa and Britain, with their, uh, appendages dangling in the ocean.

I wasn't so sure how Brent's father would feel about this little analogy, so I tried to think of something intelligent to say about architecture. That lasted all of fifteen minutes, and then I looked at my watch. It was almost eight o'clock, and I needed to get going.

He apparently picked up on my gesture and said, "So, you say you live in Malvern? I haven't been to that part of town in years. Come, David, let's go before it gets too late."

I said good-bye to Brent and his brother. Brent wrote down his telephone number and gave it to me.

I promised Brent that I would indeed contact him, and for a moment I was almost convinced that I would do so. After all, the guy had been so nice and helpful. I said good-bye to Brent's mom, thanking her for the hospitality. Then her husband and I got into the largest Mercedes-Benz sedan I had ever seen, which rode so smoothly that we practically floated to Malvern.

✳

Over the next several weeks, my life in Johannesburg settled into a depressing routine. A typical day started out with me waiting for Nettie and Kim to leave the house. Then I'd get up and have a cup of tea and toast, or whatever else I could dig up in the kitchen. Paulina, the maid, came in Wednesday through Friday. I was usually on my second cup of tea by the time she walked in, barefoot and stony-faced, and headed for the kitchen. I tried to make sure that I completed my morning ablutions before she arrived so that I wouldn't be in her way. Every gesture I made toward her—offering to tip her a rand or two for washing my clothes, trying to engage her in small talk—had failed; she went about washing, sweeping, mopping, and scrubbing as if I weren't there.

Most mornings, I sat around fidgeting with the television in the living room, trying to find newscasts in English and waiting for the Larry King show on CNN. Most of Larry's show featured day-old news or interviews with flaky, fading celebrities; I didn't mind, though, because South African television was pretty worthless, littered with cheesy American sitcoms from the 1980s or earlier.

Sometimes, just to get out of the house, I'd walk up to the corner store to buy a newspaper with a few coins I managed to cadge from Nettie's dresser drawer. South Africa's economy was deeply mired in recession, yet I continued looking through the Help Wanted section of the newspaper. And, of course, it was always the same story when I made a few perfunctory calls: successful applicants must speak Afrikaans, Xhosa, or Zulu; must belong to a population eligible for affirmative action (meaning that coloureds and Indians need not apply); and must be eligible to work in South Africa. I hadn't heard anything about a job from the correspondent in Parktown, and I didn't want to be a nuisance by calling him again.

Usually I'd grab my bag, walk downtown, and skulk around the Carlton Centre and the central business district. Or maybe I'd go over to the Johannesburg Public Library and poke around the stacks. I sometimes ventured over to Magistrate's Court to get a glimpse of what passed for South African justice. On the weekends, I busied myself by checking out the flea market outside the Market Theater. Most days, however, I'd go over to Joubert Park to watch chess players maneuver four-foot chess pieces across a giant outdoor board. I found it particularly fascinating when white men lugged their white pawns, rooks, knights, bishops, kings, and queens into place against black men and their black chess pieces. A crowd would gather and watch the duel between white and black, each player matching and using strategy to dominate the board. These games mirrored the very real struggle then playing out between the apartheid government and the African National Congress over the future governance of the country.

✳

Shortly after June 1992, the CODESA talks had broken down over the issues of violence and minority rights in a new constitution. Although multiparty negotiations had now resumed, the National Party government, the African National Congress, the Inkatha Freedom Party, the Afrikaners' Freedom Front, and a coalition of other slates remained deadlocked over the composition of a transitional government. While attempts were being made to put apartheid out of its misery, South Africa was still being torn apart along ethnic lines. Many issues complicated any potential agreement between the parties, and political violence continued to flare up throughout the country.

Politicians such as Zulu leader Mangosuthu Buthelezi and General Constand Viljoen of the Freedom Alliance, a white right-wing group, fought to consolidate their influence in a power-sharing arrangement brokered by the NP and the ANC. The Pan Africanist Congress (PAC) threatened to boycott the constitutional talks, portraying the ANC negotiators as sell-outs. The puppet leaders of the former black homelands, or bantustans—the Ciskei, Bophuthatswana, the Transkei, and Venda— were resisting reincorporation into a newly formed South African government. Further, Indians and coloureds began to mobilize to look after their own prospects in post-apartheid South Africa.

A glance through the newspaper highlighted a season of political jockeying in a country teetering on a knife's edge between chaos and calm. The NP, according to the *Weekly Mail,* sought "to convey the image that it is non-racial, in touch with ordinary people, and that it best represents the aspirations of moderate South Africans of all colours" and to demonstrate "that this is a new NP, a fundamentally changed party, and one that has adapted to the future."

The ANC had its own public relations problems. Winnie Mandela, who in 1991 had been found guilty of kidnapping and assault, had taken to the hustings to criticize the ANC leadership and its tendency toward elitism at the expense of the majority of black South Africans. Coloureds were threatening to sever ties with the ANC over the party's perceived failure to address coloured concerns in the Western Cape province. "We are unhappy about both the national and regional leadership's attitude to the coloured people," said one activist, quoted in the *Weekly Mail.* "Coloureds are noticing that they are not being spoken of in national politics. There is a great sense of insecurity and they are beginning to feel their minority status."

Indian students at the University of Durban-Westville (UDW) were protesting the traditionally Indian university's affirmative action plan, which was designed to admit more black students. With a reference to former prime minister Verwoerd, the architect of apartheid, a columnist in the *Weekly Mail* railed at the hypocrisy of the new policy: "Shorn of all the double-speak, it seems that UDW intends to continue Dr. Verwoerd's practice of racism, but of a somewhat inverted kind." The apartheid government had erected and maintained nineteen different education departments for each race, in each province, and for each of the four nominally independent black homelands. The white universities were better funded and better equipped; the government had built a few so-called bush colleges for blacks and the University of the Western Cape especially for the coloureds.

As if the country's political and social problems weren't burdensome enough, the taxi industry was threatening to implode. The government was pushing for greater regulation of the industry. Taxi drivers complained that traffic police dealt with them rudely and manufactured excuses to issue tickets. "Until they learn to smile and shed their bias toward us," taxi driver Ray Nxumalo told the *Weekly Mail,* "the us-and-them mentality will not stop and the enmity between us . . . will continue." Police countered that the drivers were mostly unlicensed and operated dangerously overcrowded vehicles. The government declared a state of emergency. Thousands of commuters were stranded, and police and taxi drivers engaged in running gun battles in downtown Johannesburg.

Meanwhile, anarchy and continued bloodshed provided the backdrop for the constitutional negotiations. Durban/Natal was still embroiled in murderous fighting between followers of the ANC and Buthelezi's IFP, which, in turn, according to the findings of the Goldstone Commission, was receiving arms and assistance from the government's Orwellian-named Internal Stability Unit. At stake for both parties were potential votes in the country's first democratic election, the plans for which were being hammered out by government, ANC, and opposition party negotiators at the World Trade Centre in Johannesburg.

In what political journalist Phillip Van Niekerk called "probably one of the most dramatic developments since the release of Nelson Mandela and the unbanning of political organizations," the government and the ANC finally reached consensus in February 1993—but not before F. W. de Klerk had tried, unsuccessfully, to mandate white veto power and power-sharing in the interim constitution. In addition to creating an interim constitution, the negotiators acceded to a five-year period of power-sharing in the new government and agreed to set up a "sunset clause" that protected the jobs of white civil servants. Elections were scheduled for April 27, 1994, to be orchestrated by an Independent Electoral Commission. The situation on the ground remained tense, however: the IFP and the PAC voiced dissatisfaction with the settlement and continued to stoke the fires of political violence in the country.

✳

After a while, I stopped going downtown altogether. I was officially broke; and I had pretty much rifled through all of Nettie's and Kim's things looking for money, to no avail. My daily routine now consisted of sitting around the house all day waiting for the abbreviated CNN newscast or the Larry King show. Alternatively, I often sat on the sun porch reading the books and notes I had brought along. Around noon or so, I'd shuffle into the kitchen to look for some lunch. Nettie cooked most days or stopped at the supermarket to pick up some roast chicken or pizza on her way home. Kim didn't eat much, so there were always leftovers. I'd make a sandwich or finish off the leftovers and return to the porch and my reading.

Of course, the first thing Nettie asked when she got home was a loaded question: "What did you do today, David?"

Oh, not much, just zipped downtown, did some shopping, you know, and picked up some gifts, is what I wanted to say, until I thought better of it. She had to know that I was broke. She'd go to the kitchen next and start sifting through the refrigerator and mumbling under her breath. Sitting in the other room, I could hear snatches of her comments: I gathered that she wasn't too happy with me eating the leftovers, especially since I wasn't contributing to the household. Over the past month, this had become a problem, I could tell. She never came right out and said anything, but I picked up hints here and there that she was fed up with my free-loadin' ass.

A funny but sad incident occurred one day when Nettie was looking through the kitchen cabinets for a jar of mayonnaise.

"I know I just bought mayonnaise," she said in exasperation, to no one in particular.

Turning to Paulina, who, as usual, was washing or scrubbing something, she asked, "Paulina, have you seen the jar of mayonnaise, hey?"

"No, madam," Paulina replied, assuming her customary pose of looking down at her bare feet. I was sitting in my room near the kitchen.

"David, have you seen a jar of mayonnaise?" said Nettie. "It was a brand-new jar!"

I shook my head no. She harrumphed and stormed out of the kitchen. I suspected that Paulina had taken the mayonnaise home with her, although I never said anything.

But any doubt I might have had about Nettie's growing resentment of me was confirmed a few days after the missing mayonnaise incident. Around midnight, when Nettie and Kim were already in bed, I was ensconced in my little room next to the kitchen, feeling hungry for some ice cream. I got up and crept into the kitchen. To avoid detection, I didn't turn on the light. I had hit the bucket of ice cream pretty hard already, and I hoped that some was left. I reached into the freezer to dig out the container, opened the lid, and saw what looked like a slip of paper inside. Strange, I thought.

On closer inspection, I discovered a note that read: DON'T BE A PIG. SAVE SOME FOR OTHERS. I instantly closed the container, stuck it back in the freezer, and fled to my room, where I resolved to remain until I could figure out how to get the hell out of Nettie's house—and out of South Africa.

※

From that point on, I stayed in my room whenever Nettie and Kim were home. I knew what time they usually got home, and I'd disappear into my room when they came through the front door. I could hear them in the kitchen, but I never came out. I'd wait until they went to bed to creep out and pilfer a piece of bread and a hunk of cheese or meat. I stuck to my routine of watching CNN and Larry King during the day. Paulina and I had never talked, so there was no awkwardness between us. The weekends, however, were rough, because Nettie and Kim usually stayed in the house for most of the day before going out to shop or visit friends. I'd just curl up on my little bed and wonder about Adrienne—whether she would call and ask for me or come over and rescue me from my cell. She never came.

Naturally, I started looking for a way out. I checked my ticket: it was restricted, unchangeable. I couldn't leave the country sooner than March 15. It was now February 16, and the days were getting longer.

During this period of self-imposed isolation, I countered my hunger and loneliness the only way I knew how. I read my books, particularly a novel I had discovered several years earlier when I was first enraptured with all things South African. André Brink's *Looking on Darkness* was, depending on your perspective, either an illuminating depiction of the social/psychological impact of South Africa's Immorality Act or a depressing and morose meditation on death. For me, the book encapsulated everything that repelled and fascinated me about South Africa, namely, its combination of the heroic and the profane. Brink evocatively intertwined the coarseness and tragedies of South African history with stunning descriptions of the country's beauty. Fundamentally, the book, which had been censored by the apartheid government when it was first published in 1975, portrayed the complexity of human relationships in a country plunged into the darkness of a racial nightmare.

Simply told, the story opens with its narrator, Joseph Malan, a coloured actor, on death row for murdering his white lover. Interracial intimacy has been banned under the Immorality Act. Joseph is no ordinary killer, however. He aims to take the reader on a journey to explain how he wound up in Pretoria Central Prison, in the shadow of the gallows:

> Truth is not a collection of facts which can be narrated, but a landscape through which one travels in the dark. And my particular journey has its origins far beyond Bain's Kloof, beyond Jessica, immediately far beyond myself. I am really an almost incidental moment in a pattern fulfilling itself over generations and centuries and in infinite space.

In his darkest hours, Joseph traces the history of his slave ancestors back to the Dutch occupation of the Cape, the missionary settlements of the frontier districts of the Eastern Cape, the streets and alleys of Cape Town, the wilds of Graaf-Reinet, the coast of Port Elizabeth, on to Grahamstown, northeastward to Natal, west across the Little Karoo, and back to Cape Town. He is the offspring of slaves, he tells us, all of whom were eventually crushed in horrible ways by their life circumstances. Therefore, it is his destiny to suffer as a slave, a coloured, just as his ancestors did.

Joseph is seemingly saved from his fate, however, when his white baas, the owner of the farm on which he and his mother work and live, sees potential in him and sends him to school. The boy is drawn to classics such as Defoe's *Robinson Crusoe,* Shakespeare's plays and sonnets, and poems such as "The Rime of the Ancient Mariner" and "The Raven." He takes great pleasure in reciting Shakespeare and resolves to become an actor. He organizes and acts in plays with the white and black children on the farm and at school. After a performance of *The Tempest,* in which he plays the role of Prospero, Joseph tells his aging mother that he plans to become an actor. He recalls his mother's reaction to the news:

Her rich voice came back to me like a bell tolling in the dark, the one sentence I'd heard so often in my life: "You Coloured, Joseph."

"The Whites also applauded me tonight."

"So what? Tonight they clep hen's fo you, en tomorrow they kick you unne yo' arse." We walked on. "Remem'er yo' fa'rer's hist'ry," she said quietly. "Remem'er what happen to Braam. The Lawd shell visit the iniquity of the far'ers upon the third enne forth generashun."

"I'm not trying to play for white, Ma. I only want to be an actor. I don't care about the rest."

"You think you don' care. A Coloured care fo' everything, you'll fine out."

"I thought you wanted to help me. Is this help, standing in my way like this?"

"I want to help you so you don' get hurt. You got hurt in yo' blood en' I don' wan' to see as how it get too much fo' you."

"How can I get hurt when I'm acting? I'm not in anybody's way."

"You trying to get into the light, thet's what. En' we people mus' stay out, it's not our place. The Lawd made us fo' his shadows, we his night people."

The rest of Joseph's life is consumed with trying to prove his mother wrong. Eventually, he runs up against the strictures of apartheid and accepts an opportunity to study theater in London. While there, he contacts the community of exiled South Africans, some of whom are happy to be free of the country, although others are tortured by their decision to leave and are dying of homesickness. One such person is Simon, a black poet who married a white woman and therefore could never return to South Africa. Simon tries to soothe the pain of being unable to return home by drinking heavily, and he sinks into depression. He tries to convince Joseph to return to South Africa, arguing that he mustn't run away from the struggle against the apartheid state.

Joseph refuses and continues to tramp through Europe, soaking up its culture and exulting in the variety of theatrical productions in which he performs. Eventually, however, he realizes that he does not belong in Europe, that he is an outsider. He discovers that he belongs back in South Africa, where he was born.

> I had thought I could escape. Now I had to return to pick up the link with my prehistory again. The years on the farm had been a prologue to the Cape, and the Cape a prologue to London, and my years in London a prologue— to what? That was what I had to find out, and more than that, on the basis of everything which had already happened, I had to create a future for myself.
>
> I was thirty years old. Young enough to have faith and to work; but old enough to be tired of a continuing process of preparation which never reached fulfillment.
>
> And so I went back.
>
> Home.

Joseph sails to South Africa and is immediately confronted with the indignities of apartheid when he arrives at the port in Cape Town and is faced with signs announcing SLEGS BLANKES—WHITES ONLY. Nevertheless, he throws himself into the local theater scene and eventually forms a company of his own. Using theater to subvert the ideology of apartheid, Joseph has some initial success in reaching eager audiences in Cape Town and in towns all over the Western Cape. Soon, however, the security police target Joseph and his company for intimidation and harassment. As the political situation in the country worsens, some of his friends are murdered while in police custody. He faces a crisis over whether the theater can ever be truly effective in the struggle for human rights in a totalitarian society.

While brooding over his predicament, Joseph meets Jessica, a white Englishwoman from an affluent family. She has been traveling through Africa and seems as untethered as Joseph. He falls in love with her. But they must hide their relationship lest they come under police scrutiny for contravening the Immorality Act. Tensions mount, and their affair is revealed, leaving both of them vulnerable to prosecution and possible imprisonment. Even as his romantic life is becoming unbearable, Joseph's acting career is crumbling, and the members of his troupe cave in to police intimidation.

The couple's only escape is to leave the country and return to England to be married. But Joseph, mindful of his friend Simon, realizes that he could never move to England and marry Jessica—because he would never be allowed to return to South Africa. So they are caught in a double bind: they cannot be together in South Africa; and they cannot leave the country without destroying Joseph and his connection to his homeland.

Finally, when all seems lost, they make a suicide pact and resolve to end their lives by inhaling carbon monoxide in Joseph's car; they reason that it is better to escape the world together than to suffer apart. At the last moment, however, Joseph backs out of the pact, leaving Jessica to die alone. He reasons that he is bound by fate to his ancestors, that he too must face a cruel demise at the hands of others rather than take his own life. He resolves to submit himself to the authorities for the inevitable torture and beatings—and eventual death sentence—he will receive for killing a white woman. As he awaits his execution, he ponders his history and the meaning of his existence. His fate, like that of his ancestors, is sealed.

> And yet, I look upon the same darkness which the blind do see and find meaning and beauty in it. The night is a great redeemer. No, not happiness: all I wish is to remain open: aware, to the end, of what is happening, denying nothing, excluding nothing.

I kept coming back to *Looking on Darkness* for many reasons. But what was most significant to me was that the book featured a coloured antihero. André Brink had delved into the history of coloureds and their experiences in colonial and apartheid South Africa—topics I found revelatory. I also found similarities between myself and the character Joseph: we were both wanderers looking for some purpose in our lives, ultimately finding it in ourselves; we both longed for home, for South Africa, even if we felt unwelcome here; and we both had acclimated ourselves to loneliness and solitude. I would return again and again to this haunting book as I counted the days until my departure from South Africa.

✳

Around the second week of my self-imposed seclusion, Adrienne showed up outside my room and insisted that I come out.

"David," she called through the door, "open up so I can talk to you."

I hadn't seen or talked to Adrienne since we'd hung out in Hillbrow. I guessed that Nettie had called her out of desperation because I had stubbornly refused to come out of the room. Truth was, I was bored out of my mind and felt like a trapped animal. I got up to open the door. Adrienne stood there, beer in hand, with a look of concern on her face.

"Are you all right? What's been going on here?" she asked. I could hear Nettie talking and a voice I didn't recognize in the front room.

Adrienne thrust the beer into my hand and pulled me out of the room and into the kitchen.

"Well?" she demanded. "What's gotten into you two over here, not talking and all? Hey?"

I didn't have a coherent answer, so I just upended the beer bottle and avoided her questions. She pulled me into the front room. Nettie and Cedric were sitting at the dining room table, a bottle of brandy between them.

Cedric greeted me, "Howzit, Dave! It's been a long time, man."

I smiled and nodded toward him. I was more interested in how Nettie would react to me being out of my cell. She didn't exactly look at me, but I could tell she was trying to be civil.

"Dave, sit and have a drink with us, man," said Cedric, obviously trying to lighten the tension in the room. "We were just talking about taking a trip for the weekend. Tell him about it, Nettie."

Adrienne looked at her intently, as if telegraphing a previously agreed-upon directive to be nice to me.

"Yes," Nettie said, still not looking at me, "our Uncle Henry has invited us to his place in Secunda. I told him you were here, and he wants to meet you."

By now, I had poured myself a nice stiff shot of the brandy and helped myself to one of Nettie's cigarettes. She didn't seem to mind and went on to tell me that Henry was the older of Nick's two brothers; the younger one, Frankie, lived in Cape Town. Henry worked for SASOL, a petrochemical company, and lived with his family in Secunda.

"Henry is very interested in meeting you," she commented, "because he said he had never known that Nick had a son."

Nettie's seemingly innocent statement held, I thought, some element of accusation and innuendo, some doubt that Nick was my father after all. Ever since I'd arrived in South Africa, she had treated me with suspicion, as if it was incumbent on me to prove that I was really her brother. But this no longer bothered me as much as it had. Now I was just looking forward to getting out of Johannesburg and seeing more of the country, even if only for a weekend.

Secunda, about fifty miles southeast of Johannesburg, is the home of the huge SASOL petrochemical plants that primarily convert coal to oil and supply fuel for cars and planes. Like other South African parastatals—ARMSCOR and ISCOR, which manufactured weapons and steel, respectively—SASOL had been founded in 1950 by the newly entrenched white minority government to reduce its dependence on the outside world for fuel. Further industrial innovation occurred at SASOL during the 1970s and 1980s, when South Africa became a pariah state and was squeezed by an international divestment campaign. The company, which had been privatized in the 1970s, employed thousands in its mines and engineering labs and, ironically, had become an industrial powerhouse whose innovations were welcomed throughout sub-Saharan Africa and even in some European countries.

Our two-car convoy—Nettie, Adrienne, and Kim in one car and Cedric, Angelo, and I in another—arrived in Secunda on a Friday afternoon. Secunda is the quintessential company town. Miles of identical houses stretched across the flat land for as far as I could see. Very little vegetation lined the roads. The place had the feel of a stripped-down, well-run machine: every building, every house, every road was in perfect synchronicity with the needs of the towering SASOL plant looming on the horizon. I remembered reading somewhere that the ANC had attacked the SASOL plants in the 1980s as part of its plan to sabotage and cripple the apartheid government.

We turned off the main road and entered a neighborhood of ranch-style houses: small lawns, narrow driveways, one-car garages, all painted in slightly different shades of brown. Up ahead of us, Nettie pulled into the driveway of one of the modular units. Just as we all began spilling out of the cars, a woman came to the front door of the house and greeted us.

"How you?" she called to Nettie and Adrienne. The women exchanged hugs and made small talk.

"David, this is Henry's wife, your aunt," said Nettie. The woman smiled and embraced me.

"Hi, David. It's so nice to meet you. All the way from America. You call me Aunt Polly, hey?"

Okay, I nodded my head, genuinely happy to meet the short, jovial woman. She made her way around the group, greeting Kim, Angelo, and Cedric. Aunt Polly and Uncle Henry had two children who were in their early twenties, Serena and Henry Jr., but they were nowhere to be seen.

"Henry's just gotten home, and he's expecting you," said Aunt Polly. We stepped inside from the dry heat rising from the flatlands of Secunda.

She urged us to make ourselves comfortable around the small living room. The house was immaculate and tastefully furnished, although it seemed to have been hastily constructed. A television announcer was providing play-by-play analysis of a rugby match in the next room. Aunt Polly brought out some glasses, a pitcher of lemonade, and a tray of cookies. I was aching for a beer right about then, but I got the impression from a couple of religious icons scattered around the living room that Aunt Polly and Uncle Henry didn't indulge.

Nettie and Adrienne were talking with Aunt Polly and the rest of us were chomping on the snacks when Uncle Henry finally appeared.

"Howzit, everyone!" He went around the room hugging and greeting everyone until he got to me.

"So, this is David." He gave my hand a firm squeeze and embraced me. "Welcome to South Africa, and welcome to the family."

He and Nick had the same slim, agile physique and carved facial features; both men exuded a sense of having worked for many years at backbreaking jobs with little complaint. Cedric excused himself, promising to return later in the evening; Angelo and Kim set about looking for Serena and Henry Jr.

The rest of us sat around the living room making small talk. Uncle Henry wanted to know all about my trip to South Africa, so I recounted my journey and my decision to return. He asked about my mother.

"I knew Yvonne when she and Nick dated in Durban," he recalled, with something akin to wonder in his voice. "Then they moved to Cape Town and lived there for a while . . . *Strues'* God, it's been a long time!"

I nodded like an idiot, not really knowing what to say in this situation, with everybody looking at me, scrutinizing me, even. Fortunately, Nettie asked Uncle Henry about Serena's impending graduation from a local technical school. This proved a distraction for a while—the girl was mulling moving to Johannesburg to pursue a career in public relations—but throughout the conversation Uncle Henry kept his eyes on me.

I sensed that he wanted to say something to me. Mercifully, he finally came out with it.

"You know, David," he said haltingly, "Nick never told me anything about having a son. I mean, all these years, and he never said a word. I dunno know, it's just . . . strange, is all."

What was I supposed to say to that? I wondered. Oh, don't mind me, Uncle Henry, I'm just the bastard son who's wandered in from the wilderness? It seemed that the question of my legitimacy just wouldn't go away, despite my best efforts to reassure the naysayers in my own family.

"How about some lunch?" Aunt Polly interjected. "I've got some nice chicken curry, and I made a lovely salad. Do you like curry, David?"

"Sure," I said, already wishing to be out of Secunda.

We stayed overnight with Uncle Henry and Aunt Polly. But I was far removed from everyone now, even as I accompanied Adrienne and Nettie while they visited friends and showed me around the nondescript little community with its one church, bottle store, supermarket, and rugby field.

✳

Although the trip to Secunda ended my self-imposed isolation, it did nothing to alter my daily routine. Nettie and I had reached a kind of tacit rapprochement in our daily interactions: she stopped badgering me about finding a job, and I tried to help out more around the house, even though Paulina didn't take too kindly to me intruding on her housecleaning. The critical new factor in the household dynamic was that everyone knew my days in South Africa were limited.

I had decided to return to America for a number of reasons: I didn't feel welcome, I was broke, and I feared for the future of South Africa.

More than anything, however, I missed the United States, mainly its laissez-faire culture and the relative possibility of upward mobility regardless of race or background. South Africa was clearly a country of the white haves and the black have-nots, whereas in America a college-educated person had more options and opportunities to slip the chains of ancestry.

My decision to return to the United States was also influenced by a couple of news stories. On February 26, the Friday we had traveled to Secunda, the World Trade Center in New York was bombed; I had heard about the attack on a frustratingly terse South African radio news bulletin. I had since learned from CNN, the BBC, and Larry King that police suspected that a car bomb had been detonated beneath the World Trade Center. At least five people had been killed and many others injured. According to the BBC, an eyewitness to the explosion reported, "It felt like an airplane hit the building." Watching footage of bloodied and bruised people escaping the World Trade Center, I felt an unaccountable urge to return to America as soon as possible.

Whether this urge sprang from a genuine concern for the country or whether I was thinking more about my mother and brothers Xavier and Rasheid, I wasn't sure. But I was even more transfixed by events in America when David Koresh, the leader of an obscure cult called the Branch Davidians, began a bloody standoff with police on February 28 in Waco, Texas. Four federal agents were killed in an assault on the Branch Davidian compound, and the world watched as government negotiators tried to end the siege without further bloodshed. Events in South Africa—the debate over the shape of a post-apartheid state, the internecine violence—suddenly seemed tangential.

A couple of nights later, the phone rang. As usual, Nettie answered it. After speaking in hushed tones for a few moments, she called me to the phone.

"Who is it?" I asked as she passed me the receiver.

"It's mother," she said and deliberately left the room.

Before leaving for South Africa, I had given my mother Auntie Bessie's phone number in Durban in case she needed to reach me. But I hadn't expected her to call in light of all the tension surrounding my visit.

"Hello, Ma. How are you?"

"David," she said with obvious concern, "are you all right? Why haven't you called?"

I told her that I'd been traveling and had been distracted. Of course, that answer proved unsatisfactory.

"Listen, David. When are you coming back home? These people don't want you there, can't you see that? You need to get on back here just as soon as you can. They are not your family; they don't want you there."

I knew that she was right: I hadn't been welcomed to South Africa with unconditionally open arms, and I had had to pretend to be my sisters' full-blooded brother to gain their complete acceptance.

"Ma, I'll be leaving here for Atlanta on March 15," I tried to reassure her. "Don't worry, I'm all right, and I'll call you when I get back to Atlanta."

We talked awhile longer, but I finally urged her to hang up because I knew the call was costing her a fortune. Nettie and I didn't talk about the call from our mother when I hung up the phone. The trip to Secunda had helped to ease some of the tension in the house, but a palpable sense of brooding anxiety lingered for the remaining days of my stay.

On the day of my departure from South Africa, I packed all my junk and tidied my room. My flight wasn't leaving until later that evening, but I wanted to be ready. Geraldine called from Durban to say good-bye.

"I guess we won't see you again for another ten years, hey?" she said.

I couldn't tell whether she was being sarcastic or genuinely sad about my return to the United States. I promised to stay in touch with her and vowed to return to South Africa at the earliest opportunity. "We'll see, David," she remarked.

I hadn't talked to Auntie Bessie or Nick because I didn't want to answer any other uncomfortable questions about why I was leaving.

Nettie, Adrienne, and their children, Kim and Angelo, accompanied me to the airport that evening. We all piled into Nettie's jalopy and made our way through driving rain to make my British Airways flight to Atlanta via London. After I checked in, we stood around the entrance to the departure lounge; because of security measures, I would have to proceed alone to the gate.

Adrienne was the first to hug me and say good-bye. "You must keep in touch with us, David. Please don't lose touch again, okay?"

Kim and Angelo came forward and embraced me. Finally, Nettie approached me with a stiff hug and said, "David, you must write or call us here in South Africa. Don't be a stranger, hey?"

For a brief moment, I felt the bond that must exist between brother and sister. I was filled with a sense of regret and loss, wishing that I had tried to reach out more to Nettie, Adrienne, Geraldine, and everyone else I had come across in South Africa. I'll do better next time, I thought, as I waved good-bye to them and made my way through Immigration. My happiness in leaving South Africa was tempered by the realization that I was returning to Atlanta without a job, a place to stay, or a dime in my pocket. I adjusted my book bag, stowed my passport, and braced myself for the long journey home.

3

Truth and Reconciliation

Voyagers discover that the world can never
be larger than the person that is in the world;
but it is impossible to foresee this, it is impossible to be warned.

JAMES BALDWIN
The Price of the Ticket

Just a few blocks beyond the hotels and resorts of Durban's South Beach, the landscape suddenly gives way to the harbor and the port city's industrial and manufacturing district. As we look out the window of a Greyhound bus, the view from the N2 Highway reveals warehouses, wharves, and piers and offers just a glimpse of the perpetual motion of workers, ships, derricks, and supply trucks in South Africa's busiest port. As we travel toward the outskirts of the city, my mother, Yvonne, who is seated next to me, recognizes a building where she once lived. Even from the road, the place looks dilapidated, with peeling paint and clothes slovenly draped over its balconies. My mother clucks her tongue and shakes her head.

"What a shame," she sighs. "That place used to be so nice."

It is July 2004, and we are on a bus headed to Kokstad, a town in the Eastern Cape region of South Africa, about 160 miles south of Durban. Although my mother grew up in Kokstad, she has not been there in nearly fifty years. She left the tiny hamlet at the age of sixteen and moved to Durban with relatives. For years, she tells me, she's thought about her childhood in Kokstad—going for walks in the nearby mountains, venturing into the center of the dusty town to buy sweets at its decrepit shops, running down to the train station to wave to the passengers headed for Durban or Pietermaritzburg. This return is a trip she never expected to make, she says. In so many words, she makes it clear that life has been hard since my father died in 1974—and that a trip to a remote part of South Africa stands out as an extravagance in the challenges of daily survival in Detroit.

For myself, this is a trip that I'd dreamed about as a teenager in Mississippi, ever since stumbling upon pieces of Yvonne's mysterious history. We are not only going back to the beginning of her story in Kokstad, I think; we are also tracing the journey that took her to Durban. Now we will see how the plot line of her story led her to leave three daughters in South Africa and start a new life in America.

My own history of involvement with South Africa had produced its own plot line. After returning to Atlanta in early 1993 from my first trip to South Africa and my first meeting with my sisters, I dangled on the edge of homelessness for about a month, crashing on a friend's couch before hitting rock bottom and checking into a Salvation Army shelter. I desperately needed a job, so I called a couple of editors at the *Atlanta Journal-Constitution* and begged for work, but they didn't need any clerks, only writers, I was told. So I did what I could to survive: I went out every morning with other hapless men trapped at the shelter to labor pools scattered around Atlanta and surrounding areas. One day I might be cleaning a warehouse downtown; the next I could be planting tree pods in the backyard of a mansion in Buckhead. I was resigned to do whatever it took to collect my wage of twenty-five dollars a day, minus bus fare, and survive in the precarious environment of the shelter. At night, when the lights were turned off at curfew time, and I lay in one of several rows of bunk beds amid the swirl of hacking coughs and putrid odors, I wondered what would become of me.

Eventually, I managed to escape the shelter and move into another single room occupancy hotel, the Welcome House, conveniently located on Memorial Drive across the street from Atlanta's Pretrial Detention Center. Like the Stratford Inn, this place had just been built and was designed to accommodate recovering addicts, alcoholics, and people similarly down on their luck. I fit right in and quickly acclimated myself to the small but clean room and communal bathrooms. I also managed to work my way out of the labor pools and returned to cooking, this time at the downtown Hard Rock Café. Around this time, whether out of depression or an impulse toward self-destruction, I resumed hanging out in crack houses—buying and smoking crack—in the sketchy neighborhoods around Atlanta's baseball stadium.

What began as a night or two out with my fellow cooks from the Hard Rock Café, where drug use was rampant among the workers, devolved into my total immersion in the drug culture mostly inhabited by restaurant and bar employees. One particular night during my slide into nihilism and dissatisfaction stands out in my memory. We had just shut down the kitchen when T, one of my co-workers, suggested that we go around the corner to a bar in Peachtree Center for a beer. On the way there, he fired up a joint. We took furtive tokes and talked shit about the night's work—problems with the wait staff, special orders from customers, and the million other annoying things about cooking in a high-volume restaurant.

Sitting at the bar, T asked me, "So, you ever hit that shit?"

"What?" I asked coyly.

"The pipe, man," he said. "You know, crack."

I looked around the noisy, crowded bar to see who might be listening. No one was. I told him that I'd done crack before but had had a pretty messed-up experience. He took a deep toke on his cigarette and exhaled the smoke across the bar.

"You down to party tonight?" he said. "Coupla bitches gonna be there."

For months, I had been trying to fool myself into thinking that this whole experience—living in a shitty little room in a fancy flophouse and sweating over a hot grill or a deep fryer every night—was some anthropological exercise à la Margaret Mead. But that night, I had to face reality. I was a bottom-dweller, just like all the bottom-dwellers at the shelter and the Welcome House. I was no different, I understood.

In addition, I was still tormented by Nick's claims that he was my father, claims that had thrown the story of my life as I knew it into a tailspin. I had confronted my mother with his claim, which she flatly denied, but I was still plagued by lingering doubt. The warped syllogism that constantly ran through my head went something like this: If Nick were my father, then my whole life had been a lie. And if my whole life had been a lie, then only my mother was to blame. Therefore, my identity depended on whether I trusted Nick, whom I had only recently met, or my mother, who hadn't exactly gone out of her way to explain my family history over the years. My usual reaction to such dread and unease was to escape into the mindlessness of drugs. So I accompanied my friend T to the crack house to smoke crack, or geek joints, and party until the early hours of the morning.

The turning point for me came in November 1993, when I ran into one of the staff writers I'd befriended at the *Atlanta Journal-Constitution*. After the man got past his shock at seeing me in a food-smeared chef's coat on a downtown street corner, we talked about the goings-on at the newspaper. Everybody I had known from my earlier employment was still there, he told me, including my former editor, who was in fact looking for someone to fill a part-time slot staffing the phones on the city desk. I begged the writer to put in a good word for me, and I subsequently called my old boss.

"Sure, kid, we got an opening," the old editor growled. "Are you interested?"

Before I could answer, he barked, "Listen, I gotta go, but why don't you come in tomorrow and we'll talk?"

After explaining why I had "just up and left" the previous year to go to South Africa, I managed to satisfy the editor that I was serious about the job and would stick around for awhile. I went back to my previous schedule of working part time at the newspaper and cooking full time at the Hard Rock Café.

But just as soon as I'd promised to sit tight and try to build a career at the newspaper, I found myself looking for a way to get back to South Africa. I had been watching events there closely, especially as the date of the country's first all-race election, April 27, 1994, drew near. There was no way I could miss that. I volunteered to return as an election monitor under the auspices of the Lawyers' Committee for Civil Rights Under Law and the American Friends Service Committee, which was headed locally by Tandi Gcabashe Luthuli, daughter of the legendary Chief Albert Luthuli, president-general of the African National Congress and a Nobel Peace Prize Laureate. As a student at Morehouse, I had met Tandi during one of her many anti-apartheid programs on campus, and she remained one of my key connections to South Africa over the years.

My situation became more complicated, however, when I managed to score a full-time job in the newspaper research library. I was able to quit my cooking job, but I had been at the newspaper for only four months, and a leave of absence was out of the question—or so I thought. The paper's head librarian agreed to give me the time off to travel to South Africa to monitor the election on the condition that I document the experience and present my findings when I returned. I left Atlanta with a group of other volunteers in mid-March 1994.

We arrived in Johannesburg in the midst of a tense situation. Buthelezi's Inkatha Freedom Party and other factions were continuing their threats to boycott the election. The country was still reeling from political unrest and several high-profile assassinations, including the murder of ANC leader Chris Hani, who had been gunned down in his driveway in suburban Johannesburg on Easter morning in 1993. The streets of downtown

Johannesburg were garlanded with concertina wire, machine gun–toting soldiers and police camped out on every corner, and armored cars and tanks hugged the road outside stores and along major intersections.

Our group was but one of hundreds from around the world converging on South Africa to observe the election. Thousands of volunteers of all colors and nationalities swarmed the Great Hall of the University of the Witwatersrand, where the Independent Electoral Commission (IEC), the organization charged with orchestrating the election, provided orientation and conducted training sessions on everything from setting up polling stations to dealing with bomb threats. From Johannesburg, volunteers would be dispatched to the far-flung corners of the country.

Meanwhile, the right-wing Afrikaner Weerstandbewiging (AWB, the Afrikaner Resistance Movement) was threatening a race war; although the majority of white South Africans were committed to governmental change, the far right continued to demand a white homeland and attempted to hinder the political transition. The Zulus, the most populous group in South Africa, were threatening to secede, taking Natal province with them. And a high-level delegation of Western diplomats, including Henry Kissinger, had just left the country, having failed to broker an agreement between all of South Africa's parties to proceed with the already-scheduled election.

Fortuitously, my team wound up in Cape Town, where we settled into our headquarters at the Arthur's Seat Hotel in Sea Point. I had never been to Cape Town, and I was mesmerized by the beauty of the place. The slopes of Table Mountain provided a stunning backdrop for the nearby beaches and the roiling waves of the Atlantic. Though Sea Point was a bit seedy, with its blocks of take-away stands, bars, and aggressive streetwalkers, the presence of the ocean and the towering mountains more than compensated.

We dug in and began to organize our headquarters for the upcoming election, in which, thankfully, Buthelezi and the IFP finally agreed to participate. After conducting an abortive bombing campaign, the white right wing seemed placated by the prospect of holding a referendum on a *volkstad,* the quixotic and risible concept of an all-white, self-governing entity located somewhere within the perimeter of South Africa where there were no black people.

I had intended to try to contact Geraldine in Durban or Nettie and Adrienne in Johannesburg, but I became distracted by touring Cape

Town, hanging out at the massive Victoria and Albert mall at the city's waterfront, and following the political situation. I felt guilty because I hadn't kept in touch with them as I'd promised.

As observers, we attended political rallies all over Cape Town during the run-up to the election. The ANC and the National Party were competing for the coloured vote in the Western Cape, with each side predicting that the country would go to hell if its party lost. Pamphlets began appearing around town warning coloureds about a swart gevaar, a threat that blacks would swamp and annihilate coloured culture under the presidency of Nelson Mandela. To counter this hysteria, a group called ERASE (End Racism and Sexism through Education) distributed flyers urging people of all races, coloureds mainly, to disregard the National Party's attempts at pandering to racial fears. "Down with false racial divisions! Down with racism!" the flyers declared. According to ERASE, coloureds had to realize that there were "not many 'races' in South Africa, but one human race. No 'Africans,' 'Coloureds,' 'Indians.'"

Many coloureds were indeed terrified at the prospect of an ANC government; they trusted the white government to care for them, and they feared that blacks would seek retaliation against coloureds because of their somewhat favored status during the apartheid years. I had a chance to witness this paranoia firsthand a week before the election and found it deeply troubling.

The National Party had scheduled a rally at the Good Hope Centre near downtown Cape Town, where President F. W. de Klerk and Hernus Kriel, the candidate for the premiership of the Western Cape province, were scheduled to appear to rally thousands of coloured supporters. The atmosphere at the site was tense: police barricades separated ANC supporters from the phalanx of coloureds pouring into the rally; a small pack of right-wing AWB thugs was on hand to stir up trouble; and a huge contingent of journalists from around the world jostled for position. Meanwhile, buses and taxis filled with coloured National Party supporters kept arriving.

Inside, rows of coloured people held National Party banners and sang "Die Stem," the Afrikaans national anthem. Occasionally, an area of the crowded hall broke out into a chant praising de Klerk; almost everyone wore t-shirts and hats emblazoned with the National Party logo. When de Klerk took the stage, the place erupted into a deafening roar that lasted for at least ten minutes. Music flooded the auditorium, old women wept, and young girls danced in jubilation, as de Klerk and his cronies on stage savored the euphoria of the moment and let it run its frenetic, slightly manic, course. I couldn't help thinking of Leni Riefenstahl's *Triumph of the Will:* the experience of seeing so many ardent—fanatical, even—supporters of the party that had institutionalized apartheid was both tragic and sad.

When de Klerk was finally able to speak, mostly in Afrikaans, the audience went dramatically quiet. Since most of the foreign journalists, and many of the international observers, including me, couldn't understand Afrikaans, de Klerk's address seemed calculated to cater exclusively to the coloureds in attendance. I was sure that whatever de Klerk was telling these people was intended to subtly manipulate their most backward prejudices—the same prejudices nurtured and codified by the National Party in the apartheid years.

At one point, a scuffle erupted in the balcony. A black man—apparently an ANC infiltrator—yelled out something in English, but he was immediately subdued, to the applause and cheering of the party faithful. De Klerk, trying to appear reasonable and conciliatory, called from the podium, "No, do not harm him. We must have a country where everyone can speak their mind. South Africa must be a democracy." He waited for the man to be brusquely dispatched before continuing his speech. I left the campaign rally seriously confused and disturbed that coloured people planned to vote for a party that had historically been responsible for their oppression and exploitation.

✳

On the day of the election, our team set out to open and operate polling sites around Cape Town on behalf of the IEC. I was partnered with a young dreadlocked woman from Cameroon, and we were dispatched to the townships of Khayelitsha and Guguletu. The trunk of our car contained the most serious and extensive first aid kit I'd ever seen, including materiel for treating gunshot wounds, bomb blast injuries, stab wounds, and any other injuries potentially incurred in the course of our election monitoring duties.

When we entered the massive acreage of shacks that is Khayelitsha, we seemed to be the only vehicle on the road. Then, up ahead, we spotted a Red Cross vehicle slowly treading along the entrance to the township.

One of the car's passengers, wearing a t-shirt with the familiar Red Cross sign, was hanging out the window waving a huge white flag. The townships, it was feared, could become flash points of political violence; religious leaders such as Alan Boesak were calling for calm and urging patience and cooperation at the polling places in and around Cape Town.

We made our way to Matthew Goniwe High School, where we were to help set up a polling station. A depressing number of shacks and shanties crowded the road to the school. Here and there, people turned to stare and point at us. Old men with bicycles stood on the side of the road, perhaps unaccustomed to seeing a car in their midst.

A crowd had gathered outside the school. As we approached the entrance, we came upon a small man who was beginning to get really worked up about something—it took a moment to decipher his shouting.

"Where is the IEC?" he cried. "I want to know why there is no one here from the IEC." He was dressed in a black overcoat and a wool cap, and his narrow brown face seemed to tighten with his every gesticulation.

"The IEC has abandoned us here! They do not care about our vote here in the townships!" he screamed. "This is the white man's vote! The IEC is not here because it is the tool of the white man."

The crowd was tightening around the man, and I looked to my colleague for guidance. On the day of the country's first nonracial election, the drama of his political speech was magnified.

"We are from the IEC," my colleague called out, while pulling me forward with her toward the center of the crowd. "What is the problem?"

All eyes—some hostile, some curious—suddenly shifted toward us. I immediately, and stupidly, became conscious of my light skin, here in one of South Africa's dumping grounds for people deemed inferior because of their dark skins. Apart from a few stares, however, most of the people were watching my colleague, who was questioning the man and had ascertained the source of his anger. The polling station, as he understood it, had been scheduled to open earlier in the morning, not in the early afternoon when people would be forced to stand in line in the withering heat. And, the man complained, no one had shown up with ballots and the other necessary materials.

My colleague let the man wind down. Then she told him, "Look, we have come here to set up this polling center. We are from the IEC, and this is our job."

"But you people should have been here long ago," the man persisted. "There is no one here, nothing is here. . . . "

I had managed to subdue my irrational fear of being attacked, and I stepped forward.

"We will call the IEC right now and make sure that the polling place is up and running in an hour, I assure you," I promised the man, hoping that the crowd would also hear the promise and begin to disperse. "We're really sorry, and we plan to do whatever it takes to make things right and let the people vote."

The man looked at me for what seemed like a long time before his strained face loosened into a smile and he extended his hand to me and my colleague.

As people began drifting away, she pulled me to the side and exclaimed, "My God, man, are you all right?"

"What do you mean?" I asked.

"Well, you seem like you're scared of your own people," she charged. "Don't you get it? You're a South African, David—*these* are your people, too."

Instead of responding to her—we had already had several passionate arguments about African identity since becoming partners—I took out my cell phone and called the IEC headquarters for urgent assistance in opening up the polling place at the school.

After we set up the voting booths and arranged for local volunteers to supervise the voting, my partner and I moved on to Guguletu to repeat the same process, minus the drama. On the way to the community center being used as a polling place, we passed the corner where the American student Amy Biehl had been killed some years before. Biehl, a Fulbright scholar from California, was working on women's issues and voting rights in the township at the time of her death. Sadly, she was killed by a group of students returning from a Pan Africanist Congress rally, where their rage had been stoked by the group's slogan "one settler, one bullet." Biehl had just dropped off a friend in Guguletu when she encountered the students. They saw her as just another white face—the enemy—and pulled her from her car, stoning and stabbing her to death. I saw that someone had erected a makeshift memorial to the young woman, and I thought of her sacrifice in the historic journey the country was only just beginning.

A few days later, I found myself back in Johannesburg, in the main ball-room of the Carlton Hotel. Nelson Mandela had just been declared the new president of South Africa, and the hotel and the streets were bustling with merrymakers, some of whom burned effigies of de Klerk. I was awestruck at being in the same room with some of the people I recognized at the celebration: Albertina Sisulu, wife of former ANC secretary-general Walter Sisulu and a legendary freedom fighter in her own right; former Zambian president Kenneth Kaunda; renowned journalist Charlayne Hunter-Gault; Coretta Scott King. I even introduced myself to and had a beer with Joe Slovo, former commander of the ANC's military wing, known as Umkhonto we Sizwe (Spear of the Nation), and long one of my heroes in the anti-apartheid struggle.

But when Nelson Mandela, impeccably dressed and ramrod straight, entered the room to thunderous applause, I felt a surge of electricity. I knew at that moment that I would one day return to South Africa, because I belonged here. This was my home, I exulted, while watching Mandela, Slovo, and other ANC stalwarts break into celebratory dances on the ballroom stage.

✳

The next day, I called Adrienne. We arranged to meet at her job, at Woolworth's department store in downtown Johannesburg. We embraced for a long time and talked about her son, Angelo, and about Geraldine, Roberta, Nettie, and Kim.

"Look here," she said, "I brought some photos of our dad for you to see."

For a moment, I was confused, but then I realized that she was talking about Nick—*our dad*. The photo showed Nick sitting with friends at a table littered with beer and brandy bottles. He wore a baseball cap and flashed a broad smile.

When Adrienne and I parted ways, I promised to contact her and put her in touch with our mother, who had peppered me with questions about the country, mainly Durban, and my observations of the girls when I met them for the first time. Through all her questions and conjecture about their lives, it was obvious that she was looking for a way to reconnect with her daughters. When I realized that I could facilitate their reunion, I left South Africa even more invigorated and optimistic: I had played a small part in the country's history, and this time—unlike my first disastrous trip to the country—I was going back to a job and an apartment.

A few months after I returned to Atlanta, I called my mother with a proposition.

"How'd you like to go back to South Africa?" I asked.

She didn't hesitate. "Oh, David, yes, I would love to go back."

My experiences during my two trips seemed to fire my mother's own enthusiasm for revisiting the past, regardless of the uncertainties and the unanswered questions she might face from her daughters. Although I wanted to travel with her to witness their reunion, I knew this was impossible; I couldn't just up and leave Atlanta again—there were bills to pay and a job to consider. So I bought my mother a ticket in October 1994, and she left for South Africa, her first visit in twenty-five years, at the age of fifty-six.

I didn't hear from her for awhile. Then I received a postcard that read, "Everything has changed so much here. Thank you so much. I love you. Mother." But things weren't going too well with her daughters, which I discovered when I called Geraldine in Durban to get an update on how the trip was going.

"David, she is such an awful person," Geraldine whimpered.

From what I could gather, my mother had gotten along well with Adrienne but had quarreled with Geraldine and Nettie, although I could never get a complete understanding of their conflict.

Geraldine just kept repeating, "She's just an awful person, that's all."

When my mother returned, she would not talk about the trip or go into detail about her encounter with Geraldine and Nettie. All she would say was, "They have to realize that I am the mother and that they can't just talk to me any old way. I won't accept it." In less guarded moments, she told me that she felt mistreated by the three girls because they blamed her for having left them in South Africa. She was also disappointed because the trip had ended in acrimony before she could see her old school in Durban and the neighborhood where she had lived. More than anything else, she admitted, she had wanted to visit the place where she had grown up, Kokstad. Now, ten years later, as the bus hurtled along Natal's south coast, I was happy to give her that opportunity.

✳

Looking out the bus window at the South African countryside, I thought about how the country was sometimes seen as a mix of the First World and the Third World. Skyscrapers and modern buildings dominated the cities. But here majestic hills rose with sturdy, prosperous homes on the upper ridges and scattered shacks at the bottom; spectacular views of the Indian Ocean intruded intermittently, flanked by colorful cabana houses; an occasional rondavel bobbed up in a herd of cows; and the smell of bush fires, evidence of the drought afflicting the country, suffused the bus as we neared Craigehorn. Now there were hills of tall grasses, people standing on the roadside hawking bags of oranges, and fishermen standing in the surf on a distant beach.

We passed through Umzumbe, rumbled past Banana Beach and Club Tropicana, and headed to Port Shepstone, the main city on this stretch of the south coast. Port Shepstone was a city of stark contrasts. As the bus pulled into a gas station to pick up passengers headed for Cape Town, I noticed a Mercedes-Benz dealership, where a line of bedraggled people clutching bags and boxes sat in full view of the latest Mercedes-Benz SUV. I wondered where these people were headed and whether they would ever get there. After Port Shepstone, the N2 turned, and we began heading into the interior of the Eastern Cape, past Marburg and the township of Boboyi, where an old woman assiduously swept the dirt yard outside her shack.

The ocean receded, and we were back in the South Africa of breathtaking hills and valleys; men urinating on the roadside; wild goats straddling the highway; and a poster of President Thabo Mbeki, an ANC stalwart, stapled to a pole in what was traditionally Zulu and Inkatha territory—a sign of the journey the country had taken in reconciling its various political factions in the far-flung territories outside the major cities.

A cloudless sky accentuated the majesty of Mount Currie and heralded our arrival in Kokstad. At first, I couldn't make out the town as the bus pulled off the highway and into a rest stop. Yvonne sensed my confusion and said, "There . . . there is Kokstad," pointing toward the mountain and the town splayed along its flanks.

Here and there, wisps of smoke drifted upward from among the houses of the densely packed town, which more closely resembled a military base: spare, functional, and unassuming. Kokstad was the largest town in East Griqualand, and somewhere up in the little town, in the shadow of the mountain, lay the remnants of my mother's past—and what I hoped would be the beginning of my understanding of her and of my place in the land of my birth.

The bus dropped us off in town in the parking lot of a Shoprite Checkers shopping center. I had neglected to book accommodations before leaving Atlanta, so now we stood with our bags, unsure of what to do. A group of men sat across the parking lot drinking and talking. There were no signs of taxis or public transport, and I could feel Yvonne getting angry as she stood beside me.

"Do you know where we're going?" she asked.

I told her that I hoped we could check into a hotel or bed and breakfast somewhere in town. Her silence confirmed her displeasure. I was just starting to gather the bags into a defensive posture to fend off potential attackers when a couple of guys—they looked like coloureds—loped by.

"Ask them for help," said my mother. I could tell that she was tired, and I had also noticed that she wasn't able to walk very far without resting.

"Excuse me," I called after the men. "Can you help us?"

They turned and walked back toward us. They both had ruddy yellow complexions and black curly hair.

I explained our situation, and they immediately volunteered to help us.

"*Ja,* we're from Durban. I'm Goodwin, and this is Stan," the taller of the men said, while grabbing some of our bags and beckoning to his partner to get the others.

"We just came from Durban," I explained, pointing to Yvonne, who was now smiling, no doubt relieved to be getting help. "We need to get to a hotel or bed and breakfast. Do you know of any around here?"

"Right on the main road, I believe there's a place, hey?" Stan offered.

"*Ja,* we'll go there," Goodwin agreed, and we set off into the center of Kokstad.

While Goodwin and Stan made small talk with Yvonne, I took in the sights of the town. African women carried perfectly balanced boxes and parcels on their heads. Men in black gumboots pushed carts loaded with bricks and pieces of wood toward a construction site. An occasional truck or car stirred up the dust, but cars were few, in contrast to South Africa's major cities. The sounds of some sort of tribal music blared from a loudspeaker. Sidewalk vendors offered vegetables, fruits, live chickens, clothing, and a seemingly endless assortment of shiny and useless merchandise.

All the buildings seemed ancient, from another era, a stark reminder of the South African frontier.

We arrived at a storefront that advertised a bed and breakfast.

"We can go here," Goodwin said, pointing to the building. He beckoned me inside while Yvonne and Stan waited.

The lobby was dreary and dank; I was already apprehensive. A young girl sat at a window enclosed by steel bars. She used a nail file to pick at her fingers, which seemed to be encrusted in some sort of revolting black gunk.

She just kept picking away at the hideous nails until Goodwin spoke up. "Do you have any vacancies for the night?"

The girl looked up with a dull stare and said, to my great relief, "No, there is nothing. Try around the corner."

This place around the corner, the Kokstad Guest House, on Barker Street, turned out to be marginally better. We entered a small courtyard containing three or four whitewashed buildings. A sign in front of the office read, NO PROSTITUTES ALLOWED. The place seemed deserted until a woman—a maid, perhaps—sauntered out of one of the buildings.

"Hello, we want to get a room," Goodwin called.

The woman seemed not to understand English but nodded her head and walked off. A few minutes later, a young man with a serious look emerged and greeted us. He took me into the cramped office, where a photo of Nelson Mandela beamed from the wall. A single room was one hundred twenty rand for the night, he informed me. And there was water only from 9 A.M. till 4 P.M.; the town had imposed water restrictions because of the drought. Goodwin and Stan helped us to our rooms, which were surprisingly clean if not entirely comfortable. All the other rooms in the place seemed to be empty. I thanked the men for helping us get situated and tipped them ten rand each.

"We can come back later and give you a tour of the place, if you'd like," Goodwin offered helpfully. I told him that we'd consider it but that we'd take some time to settle in before exploring Kokstad. We had to be back on the bus to Durban the next day, and we had a lot of ground to cover.

✳

Kokstad's founder, Adam Kok III, envisioned the town as a kind of coloured homeland, making it unique in the history of South Africa. Kok was the leader of the Griquas, a mixed-race people descended from the interactions of Boers, the Khoisan people, escaped slaves, and other African tribespeople. They had originally lived at the Cape, but as the vise of European settlement tightened there, they were forced to flee into the area of the Northern Cape, past the Orange River, and eventually to the northeastern part of the country.

These mixed-race people were sometimes referred to as Hottentots because of their Khoikhoi ancestry. The Dutch colonialists at the Cape called them Bastards, or Basters, because of their non-Christian origins and the affront they presented to the rigid Dutch attitudes toward race and miscegenation. In 1815, a missionary with the London Missionary Society urged them to adopt the name of a Khoikhoi group called the Chariguriqua, and they became known as the Griquas. According to historian Robert Ross, the Griquas "formed a community which attempted to discover what their role in South Africa was, or if there was none, to create one for themselves."

The Griquas settled at Philippolis in the early 1800s and laid the foundations for a culture that stressed independence, religious dedication, and entrepreneurial thrift. The Kok family took the lead in organizing the rapidly expanding settlement and its considerable herds of cattle. The area of Philippolis, in the southern Orange Free State, was rather underdeveloped and deserted, except for the presence of a few African tribes to the north. Here, in what came to be called West Griqualand, the Griquas set about establishing political and social institutions to guide the young community—all the while casting a wary eye toward the frontier for signs of others who might claim dominance over the land.

Unfortunately, events in South Africa were to propel the Griquas into contact and then conflict with a rapidly expanding Boer population. When the Boers decided to leave the Cape en masse in 1836, in the Great Trek, they had to grapple with the challenges of grazing their cattle and sustaining their families on inhospitable land. As their numbers expanded, they eventually crossed over into Griqua territory. Since the British Crown claimed the land, there was initially no dispute between the Griquas and the Boers; the two groups existed in an uneasy rapprochement for some time. But resentment grew among the Boers: "All felt bitter toward the Griquas, who had unrestricted access to the land and grazing which they coveted, and whose cattle . . . could be sold in the colonial markets where, fattened on the northern grasslands, they fetched higher prices than did those of the Boers."

Like everything on the Cape frontier, the truce between the Griquas and the Boers played out in the context of larger historical processes. The British parliament had only half-heartedly agreed to become involved in the interior of South Africa; the economic prospects were limited, and the British feared further entanglement. The strategic value of the Cape, however, soon trumped Westminster's queasiness about deeper involvement. Invigorated British participation in the affairs of the young country fundamentally changed the dynamic of race relations. "Consistently," argued Ross, "the British supported the colonists in their disputes with Africans and 'coloureds' for land. The process of law and the naked exercise of force were used, perhaps unwittingly, to establish *baaskaap* [white man's rule] throughout southern Africa." Although the Griquas, under the principled leadership of their spiritual father, Adam Kok III, strongly resisted, the debilitating effects of colonialism made their position untenable, and they were forced to leave Philippolis in 1861.

Thus began the great Griqua trek eastward over the ridge of the Drakensberg Mountains, down into an area called Nomansland. Kok and his followers, estimated at around two thousand people, endured an arduous journey, herding cattle and pushing wagons and oxcarts through treacherous terrain as well as fending off assaults from African tribes and isolated bands of San hunter-gatherers. There was no existing path over the mountain range, so the Griquas had to cut and clear the way across to Nomansland. The trek, which took two years, caused much suffering, physically, spiritually, and economically.

Kok and his people settled into mud huts on the slopes of Mount Currie, where they lived for ten years before moving five miles south to found Kokstad. In their new homeland—land still claimed by the British—they set about trying to resurrect the economy, their social support network, and the sense of identity they had originated and nurtured in Philippolis. The British authorities forced Kok to agree to supervise and control the African tribes in parts of Nomansland.

Again, the Griquas became bit players in an overarching colonial drama. The British, who wanted to annex all the land between Natal and Cape Town and fill it with white settlers, formalized sovereignty over East Griqualand, including Kokstad, in 1874, two years after the founding of the town. The nascent parameters of modern South Africa's preoccupation with race intruded on the Griquas' vision of coexisting as an independent, Christian, and industrious people in a once thinly populated

South Africa. "Where there had been a certain degree of fluidity," Ross wrote, "by the late nineteenth century the colour line was hardening, even if it took until the mid-twentieth century before the poor whites were fully absorbed into the ruling class. But in the new scheme of things there was no place for such as the Griquas."

Griqua identity and pride were further shaken with the death of the Griqua patriarch, Adam Kok III, in 1875. Kok had embodied the somewhat quixotic hopes and aspirations of his people; more important, he had shown that mixed-race people could not be expected to simply pay allegiance to a "coloured" worldview and cosmology, which increasingly portrayed coloureds as a drunken, dissolute people created by and dependent on whites. Kokstad had been founded on the belief that the Griquas possessed a culture and heritage inherited from the Khoisan people, the indigenes of South Africa.

Despite an abortive rebellion against British forces in 1878, the Griquas were effectively finished as an organized and mobilized community. Their story encapsulated the travails of a people caught up in historical forces that ultimately swept them away. As Ross noted, however, "it could be argued that the Griquas' rejection of the Africans among whom they lived contributed to their downfall. . . . Although they were prepared to admit Africans into their community it was always on the Griquas' own terms. . . . Because they had attempted to dominate, they could not have allies." The remaining Griquas, dispossessed of their land, drifted across the country; some ended up near Plettenberg Bay in the Eastern Cape. They were eventually subsumed into the rest of the coloured population of South Africa.

Ironically, a woman named Sarah Baartman (she was later renamed Saartjie, under Dutch rule), who lived more than a half century before the founding of Kokstad, would later become important in a modern movement to revitalize Griqua identity and pride. Baartman was born in the Gamtoos River Valley in approximately 1788. She was from the Quena clan of Hottentots, who later became part of the Griquas. Baartman had quite pronounced steatopygia (enlarged buttocks) and elongated labia. After moving to Cape Town, she came under the sway of a British naval doctor, who convinced her that she could capitalize on her unusual physiognomy in Europe.

Baartman left Cape Town with the doctor in 1810 for London, where she was variously displayed as a circus freak and kept naked in a cage to the jeering of morbidly curious crowds in Piccadilly Square and Haymarket. Described as the "Hottentot Venus," she was paraded through London and Paris for the next four years, from the ballrooms of high society to the indignities of a traveling circus. Europeans were both repelled and intrigued by Baartman. Eugenics and phrenology were infant pseudosciences at the time, and white supremacists sought validation for their racist theories about the inferiority and lasciviousness of the dark savages of Africa.

Baartman died in 1815, possibly of syphilis. She had worked as a prostitute in Paris and reportedly drank to excess to handle the shame and degradation of her existence. After her death, a Parisian anthropologist dissected her body, removing her brain and genital organs and preserving them in bottles. The body parts were displayed at Paris's Musée de l'Homme for more than 150 years before researchers called attention to this travesty. Griqua activists and South African government officials led the movement to demand that her remains be returned to South Africa.

In January 2002, the remains of Saartjie Baartman came home to South Africa from Paris; she had emerged from the twilight of her freak show existence to claim the dignity she was denied during her short life. In an emotional ceremony attended by dignitaries and a contingent of Griquas, Baartman's remains were placed in a coffin and transported to Hankey in the Gamtoos River Valley in the Eastern Cape for burial.

Mansell Upham, who was one of the researchers responsible for calling attention to the tragedy of Saartjie Baartman in 1995, explained the significance of her return: "The Quena are the ancestors of a lot of people in this country, some of them marginal people out there who don't exist in the eyes of anybody. Bringing back her remains can help to address this and stimulate a debate about aboriginal groups—like the 'bushmen,' Griquas and coloureds—who have been neglected in the reductionist black and white versions of our history." Upham's emphasis on the importance of reclaiming aboriginal history presaged a public discussion in South Africa that grappled with the need to see the post-apartheid landscape as more than just a struggle between black and white polities—many still straddled the netherworld of indeterminate, mixed-race heritage; many still lurked in the shadows of South African society.

The new national conversation spurred the resurgence of the Griquas, among other groups in South Africa. Increasingly, the Khoisan people, the ancestors of the Griqua, were seen as the aboriginal people of South

Africa. Even the ANC government, which argued with the Griquas over the disposition of Saartjie Baartman's remains, came to acknowledge the Khoisan people as "the first indigenous people of our country," according to Deputy President Jacob Zuma at the opening ceremony of the National Khoisan Consultative Conference in 2001. Zuma went on to say that "we, as a nation, are successfully moving away from the darkness of the past into the brightness of the future. It is a future that seeks to achieve a living African Renaissance, where the dignity of all our citizens is respected, and where all communities are free to explore, explain, reflect and rejoice in that which makes them unique." The stories of the Griquas and Saartjie Baartman had melded and reinforced each other; and both had finally found honor and dignity in their homeland.

Before embarking on the trip with my mother, I had pressed her for more information about her birthplace. I wanted to know whether she identified with a particular tribe or group of people. "I was born over there in East Griqualand," she said. "You know where Nelson Mandela was born, near Umtata? That's where my people came from. We were the coloured people."

✳

That day in Kokstad, my mother and I faced the challenge of finding the place where she had grown up. We had both freshened up from the bus trip, and now we stood outside the guest house on the cracked and dusty road. She looked toward Mount Currie and said, pointing to the left, "There, I think I know how to find it."

We started off slowly down the road. Groups of African women walked by, some of them staring at us, most of them ignoring us. Now and then, a truck sped by toward the center of Kokstad. The houses we passed were either boarded up or in various states of disrepair. We arrived at the bottom of a hill and paused.

"There used to be a rugby field here," my mother said, gesturing to a patch of ground clogged with weeds and bushes. "And this street here leads up to the church and the hospital."

I followed her gaze to the church spire and the outline of the hospital, with the mountain in the background.

We crossed over into an area of modest houses, sheltered behind security fences and protected by German shepherds. "This must be where the whites live," my mother remarked. I nodded, guessing that she was right but still surprised that we hadn't seen any signs of life other than the few African women and men we encountered on the road. Most of the houses and other structures were ramshackle and seemed hastily built, perhaps merely improvements on what had once been huts or simple shacks. Trash filled the ditches on the side of the road. The brownness of the winter landscape added to the sense of devastation and desuetude.

We walked on, climbing a hill that offered a more panoramic view of the mountain, before stopping before the Kokstad Development Centre. A sign perched atop a crumbling fence outside the tiny complex advertised business training classes, credit counseling, and courses on various topics, including bread baking and, amusingly, fence making.

"I think the place is right around the corner," my mother said, "because I remember this road."

She removed her coat and leaned against the fence for a moment. The air was still and had grown increasingly hot since we began our slow journey through the sloping streets. I was worried about her because she was walking slowly and sweating profusely. But I was anxious to move on so that we could get back to the guest house before sunset.

Around the bend from the Kokstad Development Centre, we came upon a small warehouse district.

"Oh, my God, this used to be all houses up and down here," my mother exclaimed. "Our house was down at the end of this road, down by that tree. Do you see where I'm talkin' about?"

I could see the tree towering over a rusting corrugated steel shed. A few panel trucks were parked nearby, and a concrete fence circled the whole complex. We walked uncertainly toward the tree and stopped.

"My house used to be right here. I didn't think it would be here after all these years, but there ain't no more houses here anymore. We used to have people living all up and down here. I ran up and down this neighborhood when I was a little girl, playing with my friends."

She pointed out the rusted railroad tracks on the other side of the tree and the ruins of the train station just down the street.

"We would run down to the tracks and wave to the people. I don't know why we did it—I suppose it was silly—but we used to have so much fun running around here."

The train station had long been abandoned and taken over by weeds and a few squatters. I tried to imagine the area as a vibrant community.

By all appearances, though, the neighborhood had been wiped clean of any signs of its former inhabitants.

"What do you think happened to the people?" I asked her.

"Well, you know, a lot of people moved to Durban and Cape Town, 'cause ain't nothing really here in Kokstad," she replied.

That there was nothing left of my mother's home drained the occasion of any drama I had expected. But for her, simply returning to the site of her childhood home seemed worthwhile, especially after an absence of nearly fifty years.

We drifted back into the center of Kokstad to have dinner at a Kentucky Fried Chicken shop, which was mobbed with people. Outside the shop, the sidewalks bustled with even more people, some selling vegetables and fruit, others pushing wheelbarrows of grain and millet, still others lugging bags of ice or firewood. Everyone seemed to be moving purposefully toward some inscrutable goal in downtown Kokstad. Quite a few men and women were dressed in suits and business clothes; a few teenagers sported t-shirts and jerseys emblazoned with the Nike logo or the names of American colleges and universities.

This scene made me think about a passage from Paul Theroux's *Dark Star Safari,* one of several books I had brought along on this trip. While traveling through Tanzania, Theroux comes across Mbeya, a sprawling town in the south of the country. "I began to fantasize that the Africa I traveled through was often like a parallel universe," he wrote, "the dark star image in my mind, in which everyone existed as a sort of shadow counterpart of someone in the brighter world. . . . I saw Africans wearing T-shirts saying Springfield Little League and St. Mary's Youth Services and Gonzaga and Jackman Auto Co. and Notre Dame College Summer Hockey, Wilcox, Sask, and I imagined the wearers to be the doppelgangers of the folks in that other world." I wondered about these people's lives and how they survived in this desolate town.

Meanwhile, my mother and I were proving to be quite a novelty at the restaurant. Africans, most of them wondering what to make us, occupied all the tables around us. Two women sat nearby and carried on an excited conversation, occasionally staring over at us.

"They say we are Malays," my mother reported, with a chuckle. "And that we must be from Cape Town."

I was intrigued that my mother still understood Xhosa, Zulu, and, apparently, Afrikaans after all these years. This knowledge made her more of a mystery to me—and reinforced my belief that she had her own story to tell.

Suddenly, she asked, "So, have you talked with Adrienne or anybody?"

I told her that I planned to contact Geraldine when we returned to Durban the following evening. I wanted to call Adrienne in Johannesburg, too, but I had pretty much abandoned any intention of calling Nettie. Although Adrienne and I had communicated sporadically by e-mail over the past couple of years, I hadn't talked to either Geraldine or Nettie in several years because I felt such an overwhelming sense of guilt and regret at having been a lousy brother. I was sure that Nettie hated me: after all, my stay at her house had been disastrous, and I was sure that she had influenced the other girls' opinions of me. Though I was none too eager to call them, I knew that sooner or later we would have to meet and reconcile as a family—at least, that's what I hoped would happen.

"Well, all I got to say," my mother sighed, "is that I'm not gonna beat up on myself no more."

"What do you mean by that?" I asked.

She looked around the restaurant and said, "Wait until we get back to the place, and I'll tell you."

Before we returned to the guest house, we walked around downtown a little while longer. We visited the old Griqua church, and my mother reminisced about attending services there as a young girl. We also passed the Kokstad town hall and the small public library next door. I had read somewhere about a memorial to Adam Kok III in the town.

I stopped a police officer on the sidewalk and asked, "Do you know where Adam Kok is buried?" The man grimaced at me and shook his head in confusion. "Adam Kok?" I repeated dumbly. I wished we had more time to explore the town's history.

The wind had picked up, and the temperature was dropping with the ebbing daylight. Inside a shop window, the headline from the *East Griqualand Herald* announced, "Brutal Home Murder Shocks Kokstad."

"Let's get on back before it gets too dark out here," said my mother.

She and I seemed to be the only visitors at the guest house; the other buildings were all dark when we entered the courtyard. The place made me nervous. I made sure my mother got into her room.

"I'm gonna go turn on the heat so I won't be too cold later on tonight," I told her, "and then come back to your room."

I waited until she locked her door before entering my room. The bed was hard, and the tiny heater in the corner was laughable in the frigid space. I turned on the television and checked the window for burglar bars. I was eager to get back to Durban and the comforts of a decent hotel. I returned to my mother's room, where she had wrapped herself in a blanket and turned on the television.

"This place is something else, isn't it?" she laughed.

"It sure is," I agreed, before shifting awkwardly back to the conversation we had begun over dinner. "Now, what were you saying about you're not gonna beat yourself up anymore? What was that about?"

"Oh, yeah," she said. And for the next hour or so, I did not interrupt as she launched into an extemporaneous, sometimes meandering, explanation of many of the unanswered questions and issues that we had come to South Africa to confront and, with any luck, resolve.

✳

"I'm not beatin' up on myself no more," she began, "because all them years, you know, I had been beatin' up on myself. Feeling guilty and all that, and it wasn't my fault. It was his fault—it was Nick's fault. Him and his mother and Bessie and Esme, who was my best friend. And with Bessie, I don't really care if I see her or not, you know? Because she tried to hurt me too many times.

"My childhood, oh, boy, it was rough. I had a rough time. Like I said, we stayed here in Kokstad for awhile. Now, I was born in Umtata. We moved from there when I was really little. I remember when we lived up here, my adopted mother worked for these white folks, and she had quarters away from their house, where she kept me. Servants' quarters. But I think they didn't really want me over there, so I stayed with her son, who I called my uncle. I was just a little girl.

"Now, my adopted mother. . . I was her husband's granddaughter's child. So that's how she adopted me. But a couple of years after she adopted me, her husband—my great-grandfather, I guess—he died. After he died, we moved to Durban. I believe we stayed here until I was maybe twelve or thirteen, and then we moved to Durban. But I would come down here every summer. My foster mother would send me down here. Her name was Mary Winlock.

"Then, I believe, my real mother had another child, and his grandmother, his father's mother, adopted him. I didn't know my mother until

I was grown. I was about eighteen or nineteen years old, and that's when I found out that she was my mother. A friend of hers told me. Her name was Mavis Simpson; that was my mother's name. But I didn't find out really in depth until I got ready to come to the United States, and I had to have a visa and passport. I had to get a birth certificate. I had to write to the Census Bureau in Umtata, and that's how I got a birth certificate—to find out who she was.

"My foster mother . . . I guess she tried her best, but I didn't have shoes, I didn't have nothing for a child growing up. She had to put me in an orphanage for awhile, you know, 'cause she didn't have a place to stay herself, and she didn't have a place for me. 'Cause she was working for white people all the time. She had a place on the white people's property, but, like I said, most of the time they didn't want you there. So my foster mother put me in an orphanage—it was called St. Philomena's—for maybe four or five years. My mother was still alive, but she didn't claim me. Why she didn't, I don't know. I never tried to find out. I never tried to find out who my father was, either, or nothing like that.

"The orphanage was horrible. Older children would take care of the younger ones. And there was this girl . . . she was really mean to me, really mean. I think that's how I got claustrophobia—because she would lock me in this bathroom and had the water on and made me stay in there. To this day, I think that's how I got claustrophobia. I still won't ride an elevator by myself; for the longest, I wouldn't ride it at all. I couldn't stand no closed places. That's why when I'm on the plane, I have to see out the window. It's gotten a little better over the years.

"I had long hair, and the girl would pull my hair and actually beat me up. But there was nobody I could tell.

"At the orphanage, you had a certain place that you had to clean up. We used to make brooms out of sticks, and me and another girl had an assignment where we had to sweep the front of the school. It wasn't nothing but dirt, but we couldn't have no leaves out there.

"And then we would get tapioca pudding and a thick slice of bread, and that was our meal, that was our food. When you prayed, you had to put your hand on that piece of bread, otherwise somebody would steal it.

"We slept in iron beds in a dormitory, and we used to have a big old bucket that we had to use at night for going to the bathroom. Then you get a turn, and you and somebody had to carry that bucket and go and throw it out.

"When I got out of the orphanage, I went back to my foster mother's house. I know she was doing her best, but by then I was a teenager, and we just had one room. One room. Then a friend of my foster mother's got sick, and she moved her in there. That's when I moved out and went to stay with Bessie's mother in Durban.

"I think I was around eighteen when I met Nick in Durban. And what I was thinking was that getting married was getting away from all this other crap, you know? I met Nick through Esme and Bessie, who were my best friends. We used to have these dances on Sunday nights where I used to go to school at. That's where I first met Nick.

"I should have known better. Nick was . . . he was okay, but he wasn't really a good person because, you know, he was smoking marijuana, and at some point or other he had started selling it. So I think when I left Durban with you, I think Nick was in the hospital 'cause them police dogs had bit him or something—because of him smoking and selling that stuff.

"Now, when we go to Durban, we gonna walk around some, right? One thing I want to do is go to that market—they built a new market-place over there. I wanna go over there and show you the school I went to and the church where Nick and I got married. They still have the old marketplace, but it's not like the one they built. That's on Grey Street. There used to be a big hotel called the Himalaya that was on Grey Street. When Nick and I got married, we were supposed to stay at the Himalaya, but he was so drunk they wouldn't accept him.

"So we got married and left Durban and went to Cape Town. Now, when I was in Cape Town, we were living in Athlone with Nick's mother. That's when Nettie came along. And when the second baby, Adrienne, came along, we were still living with his mother. And he just abused me there.

"During the time when I lived in Cape Town, a lot of different stuff was going on. Nick was going with this girl over there, and he would come home and beat me, you know, and I would have black and blue eyes and stuff like that. And his mother never said anything to him about abusing me. So I just decided, when I found out that I was pregnant with Adrienne—that's when I decided I was gonna leave. I remember one day we were in the car, and while the car was going, he threw me out of the car. He just abused me. That's why I had to get away from him.

"But when I came to Durban, I thought I was gonna stay with my foster mother. She had a place, but her place was little, and she was renting out the one room to this man, you know. I tried to go over to a friend's house, but she couldn't take me, either. I didn't have no place to stay, no money, no nothing. And so I left to go stay with one of Nick's cousins in Wentworth. She lives there now; her name is Ann. So I went to Ann's house, and I slept on the floor. Me and Antoinette and Adrienne—we slept on the floor. And then I found out that I was pregnant with Geraldine. Nick's cousin didn't even give me a mattress or nothing, didn't even give me a blanket.

"Nick came to Durban and got Esme's mother to give us a room in her house. This was over there at a place off of Carlisle Street. But then Nick started messing around with Esme, who was my best friend from school. So I left him there with Esme and her mother and went back to my adopted mother's house until I got me a little job. Then Nick started coming around again. So I moved and got this little room of my own.

"But so many other things were going on that I ended up staying over at Bessie's house. And I eventually got me a job, back at the factory where I had worked before, and I got myself back on my feet. It was a government uniforms place, prison uniforms and stuff like that, that's what we made. The company would start you off cutting off the threads from the uniform. I had been about sixteen or seventeen when I had first started at the factory.

"This time, of course, I was pregnant with Geraldine, so I had to leave the job. But now I had gotten a place, a flat. I only had one bedroom and a living room, bathroom, and all that kind of stuff. But it was enough for us.

"And that's where Nick came and got the children. That was in 1962.

"They ganged up on me the day they took those children away from me. Nick's mother came and took them from Durban to Cape Town, you know, and that was the last time I saw them. Geraldine was, like, maybe two years old. Adrienne was maybe three. They were right behind one another. And Antoinette, she was four. You know they were all born in the same month, October—Antoinette, the fifteenth; Adrienne, the twenty-third; and Geraldine, the twenty-fifth.

"See, Nick told me that he was gonna let his mother take the children for awhile until we got ourselves together. He had just got off the trawler, the fishing boat—and he said we was gonna try to work things out between us, even though I didn't really want to because he used to beat me all the time.

"Now, I met your father through a guy named Dennis, who used to drive a cab. He brought Dave over to Katie's house. Katie was Bessie's mother. You know, Katie had a shebeen. So that's how I met him. I was reluctant to deal with him, but he was really persistent, and that's how him and I got together. Whenever he would be in town, he would get Katie to call me to come over to her house so he could see me. I started seeing him every time he came to Durban. And he would write me letters when he was away.

"I had been staying with Bessie then, up until the time I got you. And then after I got you, I moved again from Bessie's house over to Mariah's house. She was Raymond's mother, and she had a two-family flat. So she had one room, and I had the other, with a balcony, a closed-in balcony.

"Your father was in the country when you were born. Bessie, you know, she really didn't think that it would get that far, that we would get married. Why? I don't know. You know, Bessie has always been kind of jealous of me, for some reason or other. I don't know why. But I ignored that.

"I had this little girl that was working for me who would take care of you while I was working. I think her name was Tombe. She was an African girl, about fifteen or sixteen years old. She would take care of you and clean my apartment and stuff like that. She stayed right there with us. The balcony was closed in like a room, so I had a bed in there, and she would stay there with me.

"I remember one time she took you to the park. And when we looked around, here you come walking back home by yourself. I don't know how you got across the street or nothing like that. But you came on home and left her down there. So Katie scolded her real good and told her she was probably down there talking to some man.

"After I had you, Nick wanted to come over to Bessie's mother's house and claim you as his baby. But before that, what he wanted to do was—he didn't tell you the part where he wanted me to give you up for adoption, did he? But, you see, I wouldn't have no part of that. So he just tried to cause a whole lot of trouble, you know. Your daddy was in the States during this time. He didn't know anything about it; I didn't tell him about it.

"I was looking into trying to get the girls to come to the States with us. And I found out from the American embassy that they would have to have Nick's permission to leave the country. And I knew that Nick wasn't gonna sign—he wasn't gonna sign nothing for them to leave South Africa to go to the United States. I knew he wasn't gonna do that.

"Your father and I talked about it. He said he would look into it, and, you know, he went back to South Africa from the United States twice after we had left. He tried to find out from the American embassy what we would have to do. They told him that he would have to go to court, and he would have to adopt them. But Nick wasn't going for that stuff, he really wasn't.

"But what was interesting was that after your daddy and I got married, and I was getting ready to come to the States, I didn't see Nick no more. When he found out, I had already left. But when you were born, Nick had already taken the girls away to Cape Town.

"I had to go through a lot to get ready to go to the States. You know, they put you through a process where you have to have a lot of physicals done, chest X-rays, and all kind of stuff before they can clear you. It took nearly two years. Then, after they cleared me, I had to get a passport and visa. And you know what the visa was? Nothing but some chest X-rays that they give to you and you bring them with you. Those were at your grandmother's house. I don't know what she did with them. She destroyed a lot of my stuff—a lot of pictures and stuff that I really treasured.

"Anyway, when we left, we took the plane from Durban to the Ivory Coast. From the Ivory Coast we went to Paris.

"Your father met us at the airport in New York. He said, 'At last you're in New York.' And it was so cold. You know, I'm coming from a hot climate; Durban was so hot. And he had brought us coats. But I had never been so cold in my life.

"Your father was coming up and down to Durban all the time. But we met in New York after you and I left South Africa. Then, when we left New York, we had to stay over in Atlanta because the weather was so bad before we came to Mississippi.

"So we stayed in a hotel out by the airport. It was snowing, and the airlines paid for us to stay in the hotel because the weather was just so bad. That's the first time I had ever seen snow, and that's the first time I had ever seen a TV. And I'll never forget the program that Mr. Green Jeans used to come on. That was the first program I had ever seen, at the airport hotel.

"Now, when we got to Mississippi, your grandmother came over to Jackson to pick us up. She just said, 'Pleased to meet you,' and shook my hand. Your dad was really mad with her, because she was keeping his car, and he told her, 'At least you coulda bought some new tires for the car.'

"To me, when you came out of the life that I came out of, where everything wasn't that good, I always thought stuff would be better in the United States. And when I got to your grandmother's house, I thought to myself, 'Oh, my God, I just jumped out of the frying pan into the fire.' That's what I thought, because here was this house leaning to one side. All them other houses on that street was leaning, too.

"Now just imagine, you coming from another country, and you think you coming to a better place. Here you come down to these broken-down houses, leaning to one side, you know? And your grandmother was never—how can I say?—she was never a good housekeeper. She could cook, but she never kept a really clean house.

"Right then, I made up my mind that I am not gonna stay with this lady long. I'm gonna go to school.

"Pretty soon, I met Inez. Your father and Inez had been neighbors—and that's how they became friends.

"After I met Inez, I met this lady, she was a professor down at the school, Meridian Junior College. So I inquired about enrolling in school. I didn't have a high school education. But I heard about this college down in Ita Bena; they had a program over there where you could test out for the G.E.D.

"When I got my G.E.D., I started going out to the junior college, and right across the street was this hospital, Mattee Hersee Hospital. I went over there, and they were testing for nurse's aides. I took the test to be a nurse's aide, and I started working at Mattee Hersee.

"I didn't have my citizenship while I worked at Mattee Hersee. In the meanwhile, I had gotten a place, and I moved out of your grandmother's house. The place was like a two-bedroom, living room, kitchen—you know, it was a nice place. So I moved there and I was working.

"There was a store down the street, and a man there was selling a Ford Falcon for three hundred dollars, and I bought it. I didn't know how to drive, but I started teaching myself. I was going into one ditch after the other. But I started getting brave and going a little bit at a time on the highway, until I got to where I was driving right on to the hospital. I was working at night, the eleven to seven shift. And I was still going to school.

"One day, this policeman who used to work at the hospital—that was his moonlight job—stopped me. About once a month, they would check the cars and people's registration over at the city line. Anyway, he checked me, and I didn't have no license. He say, 'I want you to go tomorrow and get your license.' Because I had been driving for a while without a license. So the next day I went and got it.

"And I drove that old Falcon until you could see the road through the floor. Then I got a job at Rush General Hospital because they were paying more money. After that, they sponsored me into the LPN program. But I couldn't work while I was in the program.

"Just to show you how prejudiced those folks was, the lady that ran the program told me that I couldn't take the nursing board exams unless I was a citizen. During that time, I had already started working on my citizenship. When we started in the program, there were ten blacks, but by the time the program ended, there were only four of us who graduated. And this white lady—an old cracker woman—just knew that I wasn't gonna make it, but I had passed all my classes and everything. We had to drive over to Jackson so I could take the state exam to get my nursing license. When we returned, I went back to Rush Hospital. And that was when your father died.

"Now let's talk about Xavier. Xavier was born in 1968. I really didn't know something was wrong with Xavier until he was up to a year old. I thought it just took him longer to walk. But I didn't know anything was wrong when we brought him home from the hospital. You know, at that time you couldn't sue no hospital or nothing like that. But we had heard of this program that they had in Jackson; your daddy found out about it some kind of way. So we took him to Jackson for evaluation. We were supposed to go back to Jackson, but that's when your daddy died, so I don't know . . . just, you know . . . it just became where, I don't know, everything fell apart for me.

"Your grandmother wasn't no help to me. She thought I'd got a lot of money, but your daddy did not leave no whole lot of money. He left enough money for him to be buried—and that's basically all I had. And what I did was—he had mortgaged the trailer and that land—so what I did was, I gave the bank back the trailer, and I got another one, the double wide. And like I say, it just seemed like everything went downhill for me after that.

"Before—when my Falcon had went bad on me—I had bought a car. Your daddy signed for me. It was a Firebird. So when he died, my car was paid off. Your grandmother just thought that I had a lot of money. I had a bedroom set, and when we moved into the first trailer, we couldn't take it with us because it was so big. We stored it at your grandmother's house.

So after I got the big trailer, I wanted my bedroom set back. Do you know, that woman said your daddy had gave it to her. I got my bedroom set back. And that's when we really became enemies.

"Then I had a big refrigerator and a stove and washing machine in the new trailer. They thought I had sold stuff—I don't know what it is I was supposed to have sold. And your grandmother was telling Alma a lot of stuff. Your grandmother wanted to let Dave Jr. have your daddy's car. Then she wanted to let Dave Jr. have your daddy's watch. I don't know if he still has it. Then, see, your father had some cattle. He had sold them in the stockyard, and I know he had so much money from the sale. But he put the money in your grandmother's trunk or something. But when the folks came down there to look in her trunk for the pictures and the money—I had the lawyer to look for them—they never could find them.

"Then your father had a hunting gun, and I kept that and gave it to Frank, your grandfather, to keep for you. But I believe he fooled around and gave the gun away, and it ended up with Dave Jr.

"Oh, they treated me real bad. Your grandmother treated me real bad. And Dave Jr. treated you real bad, 'cause he would push you out the bed and stuff like that. He was really selfish. But your grandma treated me real bad.

"But when I left Mississippi to go to Georgia, your grandma told me that I could leave you there until I got myself together—I had got a job before I went there—and had a stable place to stay and then you could come.

"Me and your dad had some rough times before he died, some of it from that family. I know one time I left—it was when your dad had beat me up real bad because of Dave Jr. I was getting on Dave Jr. for mistreating you. I wouldn't let him mistreat you and not say anything. That wasn't right. So your dad beat me because I was saying something, and he didn't want me to say anything to Dave Jr.

"We tried to get Dave Jr. and Alma to stay with us, but Alma—well, both of them were rebellious toward me. When they were staying with us, it was always something. And, like I say, he was always trying to beat up on you and stuff like that. I wasn't gonna take that.

"So that one day, I just left. I went to the bank, and I bought some underwear and some deodorant and other stuff. Your daddy had an aunt that lived in St. Louis. I got on the bus and went to St. Louis. I stayed there about two or three months before they knew where I was. But eventually I came back to Mississippi, to Meridian. When I came back, I didn't come back straight home; I stayed with this lady named Hattie for awhile, and then eventually I went back. By the time I went back, your dad had got Dave Jr. and Alma back to your grandmother. And we got along much better then.

"Now, your granddaddy Frank was real quiet, and he stayed to himself. I would go over to see him and Mary Jane, his wife, all the time. He treated me real nice. He was a straight-up white man, I'm telling you. He wasn't white, he was black. But when you saw him, you thought he was white. You know, they had a daughter named Belinda, and she was retarded. So that means that maybe there was some kind of gene in the family, you know, that affected Xavier, too.

"Now back to Xavier. He would go over there to the railroad tracks. One thing that I have always said to myself, wasn't no use in me bringing him out of that place where he is and I can't take care of him. That would be abusing him. You know what I'm saying? It's best for him to be in a place where he gets twenty-four-hour care, because he needs constant supervision. The doctor had told me that he would need twenty-four-hour supervision. And your grandmother, for some reason or other, this wouldn't click in her head. She had gotten to where she stopped taking him to school, to the programs that was gonna help him. Instead, she was giving in to his demands.

"And he didn't need that. He needed a disciplined environment. As I understand, they took him from the railroad tracks, I guess, and took him up to that asylum place—East Mississippi. See, they took him to a crazy house, and them people over there evaluated him and said he didn't need to be there. That's when they sent him to Boswell, where he is now.

"The doctor diagnosed Xavier as microcephalic—that his head was smaller than the average child. The doctor told me that because of that, microcephalic children always have a problem. That's why they need twenty-four-hour supervision. So I wanted him to go into a place like Boswell, but your grandmother didn't. I had already looked into all of that.

"I'm not saying I was right in leaving him there for all these years, and sometimes I think I could have done more for him than I did. And I used to think about how things woulda turned out different if your daddy hadn't died.

"So, I was thinking that maybe when we get back to the States, we can go see Xavier down in Mississippi. You think that'll be okay?

"You see, I was really young when your daddy died. I was only thirty-five years old. I never remarried. I had so many problems in my marriages, both of them, that I said, hey, if it don't work twice it ain't gonna work again.

"You know, a lot of things I just had to try to block out of my mind because I went through so many things and—"

The sound of a door slamming shut intruded on the extraordinary flow of revelations coming from my mother. We both cringed at the noise, and I got up to make sure the door was locked. "What was that?" she said. I shrugged it off because my mind was elsewhere, veering back into the past over dark terrain suddenly illuminated. The television blared, and a woman choosing lottery numbers on a game show distracted us.

"Oh, I didn't know they had the lottery over here," my mother said.

We were firmly rooted again back in Kokstad, in South Africa.

I returned to my room shortly afterward and fell onto my bed and began to cry. I cried for all the years I had misunderstood my mother. I cried for all the pain and abuse she had endured over the years. I cried because of the seemingly unbridgeable chasm of misunderstanding separating my mother from her daughters. I cried for my brother Xavier and her inability to help him. Mostly, though, I cried because I had spent my entire life believing the worst about my mother. Now that I knew the truth about her life and her situation, I understood why it had taken so long to hear it. Deciphering her story required not only knowledge of South African history but also an appreciation of what it must have been like for her to go, as she put it, "from the frying pan into the fire."

Understanding her story depended on grasping the displacement and exile fostered by South African society and the effects on its nonwhite population. From its origins as a remote mercantilist outpost, to its colonial incarnation with attendant wars between Europeans and against native African tribes, to the fateful installation of apartheid and the consolidation of white supremacy—South Africa had demonstrated its utter disdain for the people entangled in its dystopian social vision.

Apartheid in all its monstrous machinations had established a society steeped in humiliation, perceived inferiority, and degradation as expressed in its laws and institutions. Displacement of entire communities by the apartheid social engineers—blacks into Bantustans, coloureds and Indians into stark locations—disrupted families and shattered individual self-esteem. While many had no choice but to stay and struggle through apartheid's long night, others saw no way out except exile, involuntary or otherwise. Some left South Africa for political reasons, some for economic imperatives, and others, such as my mother, in the hope of escaping a life of abuse and poverty, seeking refuge in a country that embodied the promise of a new beginning.

Parents and siblings often left without a word of farewell, leaving in their wake sentiments unspoken and motives misunderstood. Those left behind in South Africa only added to the exiles' sense of guilt and guaranteed a future in which they would always second-guess their decision to leave: *What will happen to my family once I am gone? Should I have left my babies behind?*

And rather than realizing their dreams of freedom in exile, many found themselves unable to escape their past. Every effort they made to assimilate into new countries reminded them of the strangeness of their situation: they were permanent outsiders, thrust into families and relationships with people who could not fathom what they had escaped by leaving South Africa.

And since exiles were completely dependent on their hosts in their adopted countries, they were often unable to connect more than superficially with those around them. South Africa had infected their lives and tortured their dreams. My mother, for example, had been reliant on my father when she arrived in Mississippi. Certainly, she had begun to carve out a sphere of independence as she pursued her educational and career goals; but the extent to which she remained an alien in an unfamiliar society was revealed when my father died. She was essentially pushed into a world among people to whom she had no connection and with whom she had no shared experience. In the eyes of her new Mississippi family, she would always be the other, the exotic, the unknown. It had taken me years to contextualize my mother's journey through apartheid to the cauldron that was Mississippi in the 1960s—and the long-term effect her journey had had on me and my sense of life. I could only hope that I could get my sisters to understand our mother as I now did.

✳

When we returned to Durban the next evening, I called Robbie from the bus depot. I had contacted him before leaving Atlanta, hoping to enlist him in my attempt to reconcile my mother and her daughters. Now he sounded less than enthusiastic about this prospect, as I explained that my mother and I needed a place to stay for the night; I had again failed to make hotel reservations, and my mother was exhausted after the whirlwind trip to Kokstad. Robbie and Geraldine had weathered a bitter divorce several years earlier, and Robbie now had sole custody of their daughter, Roberta. When I reached him on his cell phone, we managed to get past the awkwardness, and he told me, "Just stay there at the station, and I'll make a plan."

I returned to Yvonne, who was sitting on a bench talking to a woman she had befriended on the bus. "What he say?" she asked me.

"They're coming soon," I told her. I knew how much she wanted to visit with Roberta, whom she hadn't seen in eight years. I hoped that we would also get a chance to contact Geraldine, whom I hadn't seen in more than ten years.

The bus depot was surprisingly busy for a Sunday night. A steady stream of buses discharged passengers at the station, while people crowded around timetables posted in the ticket office windows. Muslim men and women chatting away on cell phones, white students hoisting backpacks, entire African families huddled around boxes and parcels—all manner of people relied on buses to travel to cities such as Cape Town and Johannesburg as well as the more remote areas of South Africa. "One of the consequences of the decades of white government paranoia," observed Paul Theroux in *Dark Star Safari*, "was the ambitious road-building program, for military purposes to keep order. This road network meant that the army could go anywhere, and now civilians could do the same." Looking at the multicultural swirl of people jamming the station caused me to reflect on the remarkable social changes that had taken place in the country over the past ten years. Unlike air travel, which was still out of reach for the vast majority of citizens, travel by bus demonstrated the staying power of the young democracy. People of all races and religions jostled one another in the bus station and headed off to different parts of the country while sharing a common destiny.

Robbie and Roberta showed up a little while later to take us to Sydenham for the night. Roberta was now a startlingly beautiful teenager with long, sandy brown hair and green eyes. My mother embraced her, and I shook Robbie's hand. "Howzit, David?" he greeted me. He hadn't changed much over the years, with his lean frame and runner's physique. "How are you, Roberta?" my mother was saying. Roberta just smiled as Robbie herded us all over to his bakkie.

He and Roberta and my mother sat in the front while I crouched in the back compartment of the truck. As the lights of downtown Durban receded and we entered the streets of Sydenham, I thought back to my first visit and all that had happened since then. Robbie pulled into the garage at the house on Sparks Road, and we retrieved the bags from the truck. Robbie and his mother had traded quarters, and he now occupied the front of the house while she lived in the rear.

After Robbie showed my mother the room where she would be sleeping—I would get the couch—the four of us settled in, sitting around the living room, drinking tea, eating cookies, and talking about everything from the highlights of our trip to American politics.

"Roberta, how is school?" my mother questioned her. "Do you like it?"

Roberta answered shyly, "Yes, I like it very much. We have a nice teacher."

"*Ja,* she is good in school, but she can also be naughty sometimes," Robbie interjected, playfully poking her in the arm.

"No, Daddy, I am very nice in school," she protested. My mother and I laughed. Roberta was twelve, and Robbie seemed to be doing a good job of rearing her.

Of course, I wanted to know about Geraldine. I waited until Roberta left the room before asking Robbie, "So, do you hear from Geraldine? We'd really like to see her before we leave."

"Well . . . ," Robbie paused, "we see her sometimes. You know, she lives near here, and I try to let Roberta see her whenever I can. But she is in very bad shape at the moment—drinking and so forth. I really don't know what happened to Geraldine. I just don't know. . . . "

"Does she still teach at the school?" my mother wanted to know.

"No, she doesn't teach anymore," Robbie sighed. "And at the moment I think she's unemployed."

"Oh, no," my mother shook her head. Robbie went on to tell us that Geraldine had recently gotten into a shouting match with Adrienne and Nettie, who had come to Durban for a holiday trip. "Adrienne said she was cursing them and drinking and just out of control. So I really don't know what to tell you about Geraldine."

"Does Roberta ask about her mother?" my mother quizzed him.

"*Ja,* she does ask about her, and I try to let her visit whenever I can. But, like I said, Geraldine needs some help right now. Listen, sometimes Roberta will call her, and Geraldine just picks up the phone and won't say anything; she just holds the phone. Roberta asks me, 'Daddy, what's wrong with mummy?' and I don't know what to tell her."

Yvonne looked worried. As a nurse in a drug clinic, she recognized the symptoms of addiction. I learned later that she and Geraldine had clashed over this same issue during her 1994 visit to Durban. I could tell that Robbie found this line of conversation uncomfortable and that he didn't want Roberta to overhear us, so I asked him for Geraldine's phone number. While he went to fetch the number from his bedroom, Yvonne just looked at me and shook her head. I hoped that we'd be able to locate Geraldine in the two days we had left in Durban.

In the morning, I awoke on the couch to the screeching of the hadada birds outside. My mother came into the living room. "David, are you up?" I righted myself on the couch and wiped my eyes. I craved a shower but decided to wait until we checked into our hotel later that morning. Roberta emerged from the kitchen.

"Do you want coffee or tea?" she asked us.

"Let me help you, Roberta," my mother offered, and the two of them managed to produce a modest breakfast of eggs and toast for the three of us. Robbie had already left for the butcher shop but had promised to return to give us a lift to a hotel on the beachfront, where I hoped we could secure rooms. I appreciated his hospitality, but I was wary of leaving the impression that my mother and I were freeloaders, that we had nowhere to go.

Meanwhile, my mother and Roberta were getting along famously, clearing the table while laughing and talking in whispers. If nothing else comes of this trip, I thought, this scene of my mother interacting with one of her grandchildren after all these years made everything worthwhile, made all the pain worth enduring.

"Roberta, go back to the room and get that bag on the bed and bring it here," my mother directed. Roberta dutifully returned with the bag, and a slight smile flitted across her mouth.

"Do you like basketball?" Yvonne pulled her closer, put a Detroit Pistons cap on her head, and took a Pistons World Championship jersey from her bag. Roberta giggled and squirmed. "Now you'll be the only one at your school to have a Pistons basketball jersey."

Just then Robbie walked in. "Look, Daddy," Roberta cried out, "Grandma gave me a basketball jersey."

"Ja," he said approvingly, "the Pistons won the NBA championship."

Robbie helped himself to a cup of tea and a cigarette, and then we packed the truck and left for the hotel. Roberta was still wearing the Pistons cap when we said good-bye to them in front of the Holiday Inn at South Beach.

"If you hear from Geraldine, please tell her that we're trying to get in touch with her," I told Robbie.

"*Ja,* I'll tell her you're staying here on South Beach, and maybe she'll call you," he said before he and Roberta left us to the bellmen at the hotel.

✳

Over the next couple of days, Yvonne and I explored downtown Durban, returning to places she had known as a teenager. We went to the old train station, now converted into a cavernous shopping complex. We walked along Grey Street, which teemed with crowds of Africans and Indians, some of whom hustled all sorts of fruits, vegetables, and various other goods. Buses and taxis dashed up and down the streets, where more people walked and mingled dangerously with the onslaught of the incessant traffic.

We continued walking down Grey Street and then ventured over to the Victorian Indian Market, which was housed in a huge building near city hall. The old Indian market had been destroyed in a fire several years earlier. Vendors surrounded us the moment we set foot in the market, coming right up to us, beckoning.

Come just take a look at these beautiful scarves. Only ten rand!

We give you real good deal over here!

Although I felt a momentary pang of guilt about how steeply the vendors were willing to discount their wares, I followed my mother's lead, for she was now seriously immersed in the experience of shopping at the market. We emerged with several bags of gifts about an hour later.

We made our way toward the school my mother had attended as a teenager and the church where she and Nick were married. From the outside, the school resembled a union hall or community center. We stood outside a gated door in front of the staircase that led into the two-story building. We paused there while Yvonne seemed to conjure memories of her adolescent years in 1950s Durban.

"This place sure done changed," she said, pointing to still more vendors on the trash-choked sidewalk outside the school.

Ten years into democracy, much had changed in South Africa—and much remained the same. F. W. de Klerk, in his book *The Last Trek—A New Beginning*, criticized the ANC government for not completely fulfilling the promises its leaders had made in the 1994 election:

> Workers still rise before dawn and pile into minibus taxis, buses and commuter trains to make their way to their jobs in the city, those who are lucky enough to have jobs. They return in the evenings to their crowded matchbox houses, those who are lucky enough to have houses. There has been some progress. There are more houses—but not nearly as many as the ANC promised. More people have access to electricity and telephones, and a lucky minority is beginning to benefit from their greater access to public service jobs. But apart from that, most of the old problems—crime, poverty, inadequate services, poor education and unemployment—remain.

By all appearances, the country and its people certainly seemed busier, more optimistic, and filled with purpose, that is, if the incredible crowds rushing about were any indication of progress. By all accounts, however, whites still controlled the vast majority of wealth and land, the result of a political bargain struck between the government and the ANC a decade earlier. Put simply, the whites agreed to cede political power while holding onto economic hegemony. It was a bargain that had doubtless saved the country from anarchy and continued bloodshed, but it was also a bargain that seemed increasingly untenable, as nonwhites demanded more accountability and justice for the wrongs perpetrated during the apartheid era. Apart from the extreme economic inequality still endemic in the country—most blacks and coloureds, I noticed, still labored for white shopkeepers and landowners—South Africa also faced the formidable challenges of AIDS, crime, unemployment, persistent racism, and corruption.

All these issues and more were on my mind as we retreated to a café, where I asked the waiter for a newspaper. The headline in *The Mercury* read, "Winnie Walks Free Again." Winnie Madikezela-Mandela, former wife of Nelson Mandela, had appeared in the Pretoria High Court, where a judge had reduced her earlier sentence for fraud to a suspended sentence. Dressed in a gold-and-black turban and cape, Madikezela-Mandela emerged from the court, surrounded by her bodyguards, to announce, "I'm fine, as I have always been," before being whisked away in a silver

Mercedes-Benz. Thirteen years earlier, the fiery populist leader had also escaped a jail sentence for kidnapping a teenage activist, who was later found dead.

Another story detailed efforts by the ANC government to limit foreign ownership of land. Since 1994, Europeans and Americans had raced to buy up most of the coastal property around Cape Town and Durban; the countless business concerns and the amount of urban real estate controlled by non–South Africans had also become an issue. The article indicated that the ANC was concerned more about "absentee landlordism" than about a complete ban on foreign ownership of land.

Oddly, I saw only a six-paragraph article on AIDS, buried on page four of the newspaper. The Department of Health and the Democratic Alliance, the official opposition political party, were at odds over a deadline for supplying antiretroviral drugs to fifty-three thousand AIDS patients. The Democratic Alliance was critical of what it perceived as the government's failure to provide a definite timeframe—whether December 2005 or March 2005—for tackling the AIDS crisis. A Health Department spokesman confirmed, "The facts are as they were stated in the president's state-of-the-nation address—the deadline is March 2005."

I put down the newspaper and sipped a cup of Rooibos tea while my mother picked at a salad. The absence of AIDS-related stories in the newspaper surprised me because of what I knew about the existing public health crisis. Durban was part of what researchers termed the AIDS belt, an area "where South Africa faces the full fury of the AIDS pandemic and its social, economic and political devastation." The scourge of AIDS had turned out to be the greatest and cruelest irony of the end of apartheid: now that South Africans were free to exercise civil and political rights, they had to reckon with a pandemic that threatened to wipe out current and future generations.

South Africa had the world's highest number of people living with HIV, the virus that causes AIDS—5.3 million, more than half of them women. Some analysts predicted that AIDS would account for 5 million deaths by 2011 and perhaps 9 or 10 million by 2021. By 2010, life expectancy could fall from sixty-eight years to thirty-six. Some progress had been made in stemming the tide of death, however. The Department of Health had recently begun distributing antiretroviral drugs to HIV-infected pregnant women in order to stem transmission of the virus to newborns, and the government had just implemented a national treatment program only weeks before the national election that solidified the ANC's and Thabo Mbeki's grip on power.

But many people still faulted President Mbeki and his health minister, Manto-Tshabalala-Msimang, for the government's unconscionable delay in tackling the crisis head-on. Bewilderingly, Mbeki had been in denial about the connection between HIV and AIDS. He and Tshabalala-Msimang recommended a diet of garlic, lemon, olive oil, and cassava to combat a disease killing an estimated six hundred people a day. Both of these highly educated people relied on the pseudoscience of a couple of researchers from the University of California at Berkeley who had built reputations as AIDS deniers. Implicit in the government's reluctance to provide free antiretroviral drugs was the conspiratorial belief that AIDS had been developed and engineered by whites to kill off black people and, oddly, that antiretroviral drugs actually shortened lives rather than saving them.

While the government was trying to play catch-up, estimates put the number of infants infected with HIV at forty-five thousand—more than the estimated number of people killed during the tumult of the apartheid era. In a survey conducted by the *Washington Post,* the Henry J. Kaiser Family Foundation, and Harvard University, the majority of South Africans (57 percent) blamed the government for its inaction; and almost 80 percent of survey respondents, across racial and color lines, indicated that they were very worried about contracting HIV.

A subtext of the criticism of Mbeki and his initial dithering and tetchiness in the face of the AIDS crisis was the view held by many long-time analysts that these events revealed the emergence of a troubling authoritarianism in government policy. Critics pointed to the ANC's electoral dominance and the use of proportional representation in parliament, whereby members are selected from party lists. Under proportional representation, the potential for dissent within a party is diminished, and the president has free rein to choose parliamentary posts and other top government jobs. Some observers had even gone so far as to question whether South Africa was really a democracy. James Myburgh, for example, an Oxford University scholar, analyzed the forces shaping the direction of the ANC government and the impact on the country's ten-year experiment with democracy:

> Apart from the ideological hostility to any alternation in government, the collapse of the distinction between party and state provides both motive

and means for the ANC to subvert the democratic process, were their majority ever to be seriously threatened. If one day South Africans try and change their government through the ballot box, and find they can't (as the Zimbabweans did), they will realize that ours was a democracy which never was.

To their credit, the Democratic Alliance and a handful of minority voices within the ANC pushed the government for answers on issues such as its handling of the crisis in Zimbabwe, the HIV/AIDS pandemic, corruption, affirmative action, and racial reconciliation. In response, Mbeki, who was considered more Africanist than his predecessor, Nelson Mandela, consolidated ANC power under the guise of his vision of the "African Renaissance." In a 1998 speech in Johannesburg, then–Deputy President Mbeki described his vision of the revitalization of the African continent:

> The new African world which the African Renaissance seeks to build is one of democracy, peace and stability, sustainable development and a better life for the people, non-racism and non-sexism, equality among the nations and a just and democratic system of international governance. None of this will come about of its own. In as much as we liberated ourselves from colonialism through struggle, so will it be that the African Renaissance will be victorious only as a result of a protracted struggle that we ourselves must wage.

Some critics accused Mbeki and others in the ANC of race-baiting— charging whites with inveterate racism and sending confusing and conflicting messages to the minority coloured and Indian populations, who had become increasingly worried about issues of equity and affirmative action. Among those particularly critical of the government's role in this racial debate was Patricia de Lille, leader of the Independent Democrats (ID), who charged that there was "a tendency on behalf of government to equate African and black, and ID rejects this notion outright. We also need to ensure that our laws do not only reflect African as being black. Anyone in this country has a right to call themselves African, and they then have the choice to take on any other identity they choose." Whites were not entirely blameless: many of them seemed to develop amnesia when it came to apartheid and disavowed any responsibility for its after-effects, even after the deliberations of the country's Truth and Reconciliation Commission in 1996–1998; and a small right-wing group of whites known as the Boeremag had even attempted to stage a coup (quite unsuccessfully). But many had higher expectations for Mbeki, a genuine freedom fighter and an esteemed economist, who should have been leading the nation in a debate about racism. Instead, many observers viewed some of his statements as polarizing and unbecoming for the successor to Nelson Mandela, who had inspired hope for racial reconciliation among the majority of South Africans.

Tom Lodge, a veteran political scientist at the University of the Witwatersrand, cautioned that the concept of the African Renaissance had the potential of masking a movement based on racial sentiment, not unlike the program of white Christian nationalism undertaken by the ideologues of apartheid. "All too easily," he cautioned, "the idea could become debased into a series of self-congratulatory maxims in which the recollection of the African identity of ancient civilizations . . . becomes the founding myth for a new imagined community in which racial sentiment rather than political principle is the animating idea."

So far, the South Africa that my mother and I had encountered presented a model of geniality and goodwill, but I knew that the reality was far different. South Africa had a legacy of violence, and it was still a dangerous place. Carjackings, armored car robberies, deadly home invasions, rape, murder, assault, bank robberies, organized crime, the killing of white farmers on rural outposts—the newspapers were filled with accounts of brutality inflicted on innocent people of all races and colors. Although the country was making great strides in reforming its police services to bolster public safety, the potential for violence and crime had driven people—not only whites but blacks, Indians, and coloureds as well—into gated and walled compounds protected by private security companies.

In contrast to my first stay in Durban, however, I didn't notice a lot of people walking around with guns. Parliament had just passed the Firearms Control Act, which was aimed at reducing the country's murder rate of nearly twenty thousand people annually. To its credit, the government had also embarked on an intense crackdown on criminal activity, motivated in part by the increasing numbers of European and American tourists who were discovering the beauty of the country, which was made more attractive by a favorable exchange rate.

Underlying the soaring crime rates was a stark fact: South Africa has perhaps the greatest degree of economic inequality in the world. The country's unemployment rate was estimated variously between 29 and 40 percent. Whites still dominated the professional and business sectors, and they still owned most of the country's land, though the ANC government had instituted a Land Claims Court after the 1994 election that had some limited success in adjudicating a few tribal and individual claims. The government also boasted that it had built over a million new houses for the black underclass and provided upgraded water, electricity, and sewer service to township dwellers. For the most part, however, the ANC government had fallen short of satisfying the pressing, almost overwhelming—and, in some cases, unrealistic—needs and expectations of the mass of poor South Africans.

The government's remedy for this situation rested on a black empowerment program and an aggressive affirmative action policy. Lately, large white corporations and institutions such as Standard Bank had been transferring shares to small groups of black investors to meet the requirements of the government's black empowerment program. Critics of the program pointed out that it invariably enriched the same group of black businessmen while neglecting the mass of ordinary South Africans. Instead of narrowing, the economic and racial divide yawned even wider. According to journalist Adrian Guelke, "apartheid's legacy of low economic growth and of massive inequalities of income and wealth has proved much more difficult to shake off than white minority rule. Further racial political polarisation has also persisted in the new South Africa, contrary to the image of the 1994 elections as the birth of non-racial politics in the country."

Corruption posed an even greater challenge to the new South Africa. In fact, one of President Mbeki's deputies, Jacob Zuma, was facing corruption charges. Considered by many observers to be next in line to succeed Mbeki in 2009, Zuma had been implicated in a bribery and fraud scheme involving a French arms dealer. The newspapers were also filled with allegations concerning corrupt government officials in the Home Affairs ministry. The police had formed an anti-corruption unit called the Scorpions, modeled after the FBI, that investigated members of parliament for the misuse of travel vouchers.

In addition, immigrants from other African countries were flooding into South Africa and tapping into a shadowy network of government officials who sold passports, work permits, marriage certificates, and immigration documents. Since the end of apartheid, the government had taken a dim view of the mostly unregulated flow of immigrants that poured across the country's borders. Most of these immigrants were poor, black, and unskilled and were perceived as burdensome; whereas whites, some of whom had left in the initial brain drain of the early to mid-1990s, were urged to return (even though some of them were both welcomed and denounced).

These issues of citizenship, identity, and nationality made me reflect on my own situation: because of a legal loophole, I had been able to claim South African citizenship in 1997, so now I was a dual U.S./South African citizen. One of my friends, an immigration attorney, had joked that I was now half South African, half American. The joke, however well meaning and anodyne, struck me to the core as I, inevitably, deconstructed its implications: I was half South African, half American; also a half-caste—since what, after all, was a coloured?—and I was a half-brother to three sisters whose validation I desperately sought; the same three sisters who needed to reconcile with and finally hear the truth from their mother.

✳

We returned to the hotel, and I went to my room, determined to get down to the business of contacting my sisters. My mother retreated to her room for a nap. First, I called Auntie Bessie. She and I had talked before this trip, and she had essentially agreed to tell me everything she knew about the circumstances surrounding my mother's departure from South Africa. Since she had cared for the three girls as children and teenagers, she promised to fill me in on the details of their lives, details they had been reluctant to share with me.

On the phone, however, she seemed surprised that I had actually returned to Durban—and even more surprised that I had brought my mother along. I asked her when we could come for a visit; our time was short, because we were leaving Durban for Cape Town the next day.

She paused for what seemed an unusually long time before saying, "Well, David, I don't know . . . I haven't been feeling well lately. I've just got so much pressure on me right now with the house and Raymond and all."

Her mother had died, she explained, and she had been dealing with the disposition of her mother's house. She was also caring for her husband, who was recovering from a stroke. I was sympathetic, but also a little irritated because I had relied on talking to her to try and make sense of my mother's and sisters' stories.

"Now, Auntie Bessie," I said, before catching myself and realizing that this woman wasn't really my aunt, after all; she and my mother had simply been best friends. "I've come all this way just to talk to you, and I was really counting on you to help me figure out what my sisters' lives were like."

She said, with a touch of weariness in her voice, "Oh, David, I know, and I am sorry; truly, I am. But I just need to rest for a while, and then maybe you can come for a visit. Why don't you call back in about an hour, and I'll try to pull myself together, and we'll go from there. Is that all right?"

I accepted her proposal and promised to call back, while emphasizing that my mother and I were leaving for Cape Town the next day.

"Okay, my baby," she said before ringing off. I replaced the telephone receiver and sat on the edge of the bed, feeling listlessness and a sense of resignation creeping up on me.

Once I recovered, I picked up the phone and called Adrienne on her cell phone, the only number I had for her. She and I had also communicated by e-mail before this trip; based on our exchange, I wasn't too hopeful about getting to see her, either. When I had written that my mother and I were returning to South Africa and wanted to see her and Nettie and Geraldine, Adrienne had replied that she would check with the others to gauge their reaction. A few weeks passed before I sent her another e-mail, asking whether she had spoken with her sisters.

She wrote back, "I'm sorry, David, but they say they want nothing to do with the two of you."

Her response devastated me, and I didn't share this information with my mother. I knew that they were upset—that had been evident from my first trip in 1992—but I had no idea that they still harbored such bitterness after all these years. Of course, they had every reason to be hurt: they had grown up without a mother, who, for one reason or another, stopped communicating with them not long after we arrived in Mississippi.

When Adrienne answered the phone, the first words out of her mouth were, "How did you get this number? Who gave you this number?"

I was a little perturbed by this, and it gave me some indication of what to expect from our stilted conversation. Nevertheless, I persisted, trying to be as cordial and solicitous as possible, because I still had some small hope that I'd be able to orchestrate a reunion or meeting, even at this late stage of this hastily planned trip. I wanted to tell Adrienne how sorry I was that Nick had died; Bessie had given me the news several months before. But I didn't want the conversation to become even more painful, so I told her about the trip to Kokstad and then asked about Angelo and Nettie and Kim. She told me in clipped, somewhat impatient, sentences that everyone was doing well. I felt more like an interrogator than a long-lost brother.

Then I got to the reason for my call.

"So do Nettie and Geraldine still say that they don't want to have anything to do with us?" I asked.

"*Ja,* I told you, that's how they feeling. I don't know. . . . "

"Huh?" I asked stupidly.

"Yes, that's how they're still feeling," she repeated, her voicing crinkling with irritation.

Ever the masochist, I plowed ahead: "So, after all this time, they still don't want to . . . they're still holding on to all that anger?"

"You know, David, I don't want to go there." She was now clearly perturbed. "You know what I mean? I can't change their minds. They got reasons for why they're feeling like that. We're all individuals. And there's nothing I can do about it."

"Okay," I said lamely.

"I tried to speak to them," she continued, "but they've made their minds up. There's nothing I can do about it."

"Is that how you feel also?"

"No, I don't feel like that," she replied, her voice rising and falling with exasperation. "What happened in the past, happened. Life goes on. You can't live in the past, you know. But, David, let me tell you, the ways that Nettie's got, she's got the ways of her mother."

I perked up at this last sentence, expecting some new revelation, any tidbit of information that could help me make sense of my family's tangled story.

"They're both so set in their ways, and there's nothing anyone can tell them." Adrienne had warmed to the conversation. "But, you know, David, our mother must be sorry for what she's done. Has she ever said that to you, that she's sorry?"

After hearing my mother relate what had really happened—that the girls' father had taken them from her and that she and my father had tried to bring them to the United States—I didn't think she needed to apologize. Could she have done more for them over the years? I had asked myself this question countless times, usually with no satisfactory answer. The bottom line was that, when given the opportunity to escape with me from

South Africa for the dream of a better life in America, my mother had taken an incalculable risk. She had left South Africa with a black American for the Deep South, which was mired in the turmoil of the civil rights movement, taking with her the residual trauma and debilitating baggage of apartheid. But even before she stopped communicating with her daughters—and this is what I wanted to tell them—she *had* tried to get them out of South Africa: she and my father had gone to the American embassy for assistance, only to be told that the girls could not leave the country without permission from Nick—permission he would not have granted after an acrimonious divorce from my mother.

"Nettie was the firstborn," Adrienne was now saying, "and so they're one of a kind. Both of them, Nettie and mother, are stubborn and stuck in their ways. That's why they can't understand one another. But life goes on, David. So there's nothing I can do about it."

"You're basically like me." I tried to reach out. "You're kind of caught in the middle."

"I feel bad, though, because you're welcome here in my home," she responded. "I have no hard feelings."

"Yeah, I-I-I can totally understand that." I was beginning to stutter. "I-I-I mean, all I can do is try to try to reach out to Nettie, and, and, you know, she'll just have to treat me as she wants to."

"You know what I'm trying to say to you, David?" Adrienne persisted. "Mother has got things to work out from her life."

"None of us have lived perfect lives," I said defensively.

"You know, David, when her husband—your father—was alive, I still remember when I was a little girl, she always called, she always cared. But I think when that man died, she also died. She forgot she had children."

All I could do was say, woodenly, "Yeah, yeah, I think you're right, yeah."

"I'm telling you, she always called, she always stayed in touch, we always knew we had a mother. Then there was a time when—I don't know what happened. We just lost contact, and I don't know . . . when he died, she died—that's what I say."

I decided to end the call. I now knew that there would be no grand reunion.

"But listen," I said, "our mother is resting right now. We're going to Cape Town tomorrow, and we'll definitely be in touch with you from there. It's good to hear your voice."

"What?" she asked.

"It's good to hear your voice," I repeated.

"Okay, bye," she said.

It hadn't occurred to me to rouse my mother to talk to Adrienne, maybe because I was now confident that Adrienne had made peace with the past—and she had obviously reconciled herself to the fact that we had different fathers, though we had never explicitly discussed this since my first trip in 1992. I put down the phone and walked to my window overlooking the Durban beach. The Vodacom Beach Africa festival was in full swing, and the beachfront was swarming with surfers and holiday revelers. I was craving a beer and wished that I could join the festivities.

Instead, I went to my mother's room to check on her. When I told her that I had tried to call Bessie and had talked to Adrienne, she asked, "Well, have you tried to call Geraldine yet?" I hadn't, so we went back to my room to try to reach her. I dialed the number and gave her the receiver.

"Hello," she began. "Geraldine, how are you? Do you know who this is?"

I could hear Geraldine reply, "No."

"You *don't?*" my mother said, incredulously.

Again Geraldine said that she did not.

"Are you *sure* you don't know who this is?" my mother repeated. "You know who it is. This is Yvonne."

"Oh, okay. I didn't recognize your voice. How are you?"

"I'm good. How about you?"

I breathed a sigh of relief and leaned back on the bed, waiting to see how the conversation would go.

"Well," my mother was saying, "I'm here in Durban, and I'm getting ready to leave again. We were trying to contact you yesterday."

I could no longer make out what Geraldine was saying. My mother was mostly listening and interjecting an occasional "uh-huh" and "yeah." I was surprised that Geraldine was having this conversation, especially since Adrienne had emphasized that she and Nettie wanted nothing to do with us.

"Well, how are you?" I overheard Geraldine ask.

"Well, everything is okay, it's all right," my mother told her. "I was sorry to hear that your father passed away."

I got up to open the window to let the sea breeze into the warm room.

"We're down here at the Holiday Inn, on the beachfront," my mother explained. "We're leaving in the morning, going to Cape Town. We went to Kokstad. Yeah, we went there, and we stayed overnight, and then we came back."

"What's in Kokstad?"

"That's over there near where I was born. We went there, and when we came back, we spent the night at Robbie's, and then we came here to the Holiday Inn. In fact, Robbie brought us to the hotel. And we leaving tomorrow, yeah. What time the plane leave, David?" she turned to me.

"Noon," I whispered.

"Yeah, I came with David. I leave on Saturday from Cape Town, going back home, and David is gonna stay for a few more days."

"So you're leaving tomorrow at twelve? I'm going to try and get by there to see you before you leave, then. I have another commitment, though, you see," Geraldine said.

"Well, why don't you just come to the airport? We'd really like to see you. We came here because we wanted to talk to you," my mother told her.

I could hear Geraldine exclaim, "Why just me?"

"Well, not just you, everybody: Adrienne and the children, Nettie and Kim. Everybody. And Roberta has just gotten so big. She's such a pretty girl."

The two of them laughed and exchanged more small talk.

"Well, we'll look to see you tomorrow if you can come by the hotel or the airport," my mother said. "Bye-bye."

After she rang off with Geraldine, I tried to call Bessie again. This time, someone else answered and said that she was asleep and wasn't feeling well. I couldn't help thinking that Bessie didn't want to be bothered with me or my mother, who said, "Ain't nobody got time for her either. Don't worry about her no more."

I decided to forget about the lady I had known as Auntie Bessie. I was actually feeling better now that we had talked to Geraldine. Nettie was a lost cause, as far as I was concerned, and I had decided that I wouldn't let her bitterness ruin this trip. If we were lucky, my mother and I would see Geraldine tomorrow and maybe lay the groundwork for a return trip to visit her and Adrienne and their children. I wanted desperately to stem the contagion of acrimony so that it wouldn't spread to my mother's grandchildren. Reconciliation, as I'd learned from the example set by this country, takes time and sincere effort—and sometimes things didn't work out as planned. But, as Adrienne had said, life had to go on.

We checked out of the hotel the next morning, expecting to see Geraldine turn up as she had promised. But, as the taxi driver loaded our bags, there was no sign of her.

As we pulled off from the hotel and headed to the airport, my mother said simply, "I knew she wasn't gonna come."

I was shattered by Geraldine's failure to meet us at the hotel, but I said nothing. We arrived at the airport and checked in an hour and a half before our noon flight to Cape Town. I found a café in the terminal, and we sat down to have some breakfast. Neither of us said anything. I tried to read a newspaper. My mother nibbled on a piece of toast. I couldn't suppress a feeling of utter despair and of having been duped by Geraldine. I leaned back in the chair and turned the pages of the newspaper. And that's when I saw her walking toward us. At first, I thought I might have been imagining her, but as she drew closer, I said to my mother, "Look, it's Geraldine."

"Where?" she started, swiveling in the direction I was pointing. I sprang out of my chair as Geraldine approached and greeted her with a hug, and my mother came around the table and hugged her as well. A few people in the café turned to stare at us as I pulled up a chair for Geraldine.

As happy as I was to see her, I was also shocked by her appearance. She had dark spots under her eyes, and her face was drawn, etched in an interminable weariness. The red polish on her fingernails was chipped. I wondered how she was coping with losing custody of Roberta. Once we got past the small talk, she talked about her life. She had accepted a teaching contract in Mozambique and was getting ready to leave. She specialized in teaching students with learning disabilities. She was no longer interested in South Africa, she said. She wanted to go where she felt there was the greatest need.

"Roberta is such a big girl now," my mother commented, "and so pretty, too."

Geraldine chuckled. "Yes, but she is very naughty, too." She explained that although Robbie had complete custody of Roberta, he allowed her occasional visits.

The three of us sat briefly in awkward silence until Geraldine said, "Tell me, David, are there teaching jobs in the States? I want to come and teach over in the States."

There were plenty of opportunities for teachers, I told her. I wrote down my e-mail address, urged her to send me her resume, and promised, with a hint of self-importance, that I'd try to put her in contact with the appropriate resources—though I was hardly in a position to offer career guidance to anyone.

Inevitably, the conversation turned to Adrienne and Nettie.

"They were both here in Durban about a week ago," said Geraldine, "and we really got into a big fight, you know."

"What happened?" my mother asked.

"*Ag*, we were having a good time. Everyone was getting along, and then Nettie just flipped out. I don't know what her problem was. She just started insulting me and saying very bad things about me. I just left them because I couldn't stand her anymore."

"What was the problem?" I inquired.

"You really want to know what Nettie's problem is, David?" Geraldine fumed. "Nettie wants to be white—that's her problem. She's got this whole thing where she thinks she's—what's this white lady who used to be on American television?—yes, Alexis Carrington, or something like that. She's got another white man taking care of her, and she thinks she's white."

My mother shook her head.

I looked at my watch; we needed to get to the departure gate. I grabbed the bags and urged my mother and Geraldine down the terminal. The two of them followed me, talking and laughing until we reached the security lane leading to the departure area, where the world intruded.

"Well, it was really good seeing you again," my mother said, hugging Geraldine. "I love you. I always have and always will."

"That's right," I told Geraldine, taking my turn to embrace her. "We need to stay in touch. I'm going to wait to hear from you, and I'll definitely call you when I get back to the States. I love you. We want us to try to be a family. Okay?"

"Okay, David," she said.

My mother and I waved good-bye to her before being swept through the security gauntlet and onto the plane. I was euphoric as we prepared for take-off. I was now more hopeful that two of my sisters, Adrienne and Geraldine, were open to reconciliation and a relationship with our mother. As the plane rose from the runway, I thought that, considering the journey so far, two out of three wasn't bad.

✳

Our arrival in Cape Town was to be the last leg of our journey—my mother was slated to leave South Africa in two days' time, and I would depart shortly after that. I suppose I could have persisted in trying to arrange a meeting of some kind with my mother and Adrienne and Geraldine—I had given up on reaching out to Nettie—but the truth was that we were both exhausted. Besides, the trip to Kokstad, the chance for my mother to revisit her childhood home, had become an end in itself.

My sisters' stubborn refusal over the years to countenance a more nuanced version of events that explained our mother's motivation for leaving South Africa—and her failure to maintain contact with them—didn't bother me nearly as much now. In fact, I no longer found it so easy to criticize my sisters, either, and the pain and loss they had endured. And though it had once seemed like an excuse, I now understood that my family's predicament—my sisters' lives under apartheid and my mother's escape from that life—had been shaped by the vicissitudes of history, rendering us all victims seeking redemption and a chance at happiness and normalcy.

After we checked into the Holiday Inn on Eastern Boulevard, the sight of Table Mountain and Table Bay rejuvenated us. From the hotel parking lot, we had a breathtaking view of the waterfront. In the distance, we could see the faint outline of Robben Island. Table Mountain, like a silent and ancient sentinel, loomed over the city. Hugged on one side by Devil's Peak and on the other by Lion's Head and Signal Hill, its presence was powerful, all-encompassing—magical, even—and set Cape Town apart from other South African cities. The traffic on the busy M3 Highway below the hotel droned on while my mother and I took in the panoramic view.

"You know, I never been to Cape Town—I mean, downtown Cape Town," my mother admitted.

"But you lived here for awhile, right?" I said.

"Yeah, but I never left Athlone; that's where I stayed the whole time when Nick and I were living with his mother."

This revelation surprised me; even I had been to Cape Town before, during the 1994 election and again in 1998 as a law student at the University of Cape Town.

Though the sun had started to bleed the afternoon into evening, I proposed that we take the hotel shuttle into town and walk around a bit.

The shuttle first dropped us at the waterfront. We walked around the harbor and headed into the Victoria and Albert shopping mall, where tourists toting cameras and backpacks jostled with Cape Town's more affluent residents. Outside in an amphitheater, a choir of African children belted out harmonies. Across the courtyard, a band of coloured musicians twanged through traditional Cape Town banjo music and melodies. Sea gulls, emboldened by the proximity of the ocean, perhaps, swooped in to snatch food from people eating at picnic tables outside the mall's food court. Blacks, whites, coloureds, foreigners, natives—all mixed well here along the waterfront, embodying the country's ideal of the rainbow nation.

We drifted back out to the main road and caught a bus downtown to the central station on Strand Street, across from the World War II memorial. Table Mountain loomed ever larger over the city. Whereas everything at the waterfront had been sweetness and light, the central station provided a decidedly less glamorous view of Cape Town. Peddlers and street merchants crowded the front of the station, and several disheveled men approached us trying to sell batteries, assorted snacks, and socks. A couple of filthy street urchins sat on the curb, breathing into a brown paper bag; their eyes were bloodshot red, their bare feet crusted with muck.

"Oh, my God, what are they doing?" my mother whispered to me.

"I think they're sniffing glue," I said. A few other boys sat beside shops and in the gutter near the station. None of the people streaming in and out of the station seemed to notice this human detritus. No festive choirs or upbeat traditional Cape music here—instead, the atmosphere was tinged with fear and desperation and hopelessness.

We walked over to the St. George's mall and made our way past the rows of shops, banks, and hotels to Wale Street before crossing over to the site of the parliament building and the Company Gardens, where Jan van Riebeeck had planted fruits and vegetables in 1652 to supply the ships passing around the Cape en route to the East Indies. All the benches were occupied in the compound of lush greens, towering oaks, fountains, and soothing shadows, so we kept walking until we wound up in front of Tuynhuis, one of the president's official residences in Cape Town. What amazed me most about this ornate building with its traditional Cape Dutch architecture was its accessibility; only a padlocked fence separated passersby from the place where the president received international dignitaries and lived while parliament was in session. Compared to the intensity and layers of security surrounding the White House, Tuynhuis, though steeped in history and tradition, seemed to be simply a rather ornate building in a gated community, not even a stone's throw away.

Since the daylight was seeping away, and we wanted to be off the streets by nightfall, we headed back toward Adderley Street and the central station. Along the way, we passed a huge statue of the Boer War general and international diplomat Jan Christian Smuts. Not far from this monument to Afrikaners was the South African National Museum and the Slave Lodge, the area of Cape Town where slaves had been auctioned. The port city had been founded on slavery and over the years had become a waystation, and sometimes a permanent home, for immigrants and refugees. All of these disparate peoples had commingled and helped produce the coloureds, masses of whom now lined the sidewalks selling freshly cut flowers, cheap leather goods, shoes, clothing, spices, and other gewgaws. The women wore brightly colored dresses and scarves; the men were invariably dressed in coveralls or workmen's clothes. Almost everyone cradled a cigarette or dangled one from their mouth and flashed a smile littered with broken or missing teeth.

Cape Town was a coloured city in culture and politics alike. For years under apartheid, the city had been designated as a Coloured Labour Preference area; coloureds were given precedence over Africans and other racial groups when it came to employment in the city and its environs. The Nationalists, in their ploy to divide and rule the nonwhite people of South Africa, had crudely manipulated coloureds. In return for their allegiance to the apartheid government, coloureds were exempted from certain aspects of the racist legislation promulgated after 1948. Unlike Africans, coloureds never had to carry passes such as the hated *dompass* (stupid pass); coloureds, while uprooted from their neighborhoods, weren't dumped into townships like Khayelitsha and Guguletu; and coloureds enjoyed marginally better educational opportunities.

In the beginning, most coloureds were seduced by these scraps from the table of the apartheid government because, as painful as it was to acknowledge, coloureds believed that their place was with the whites of South Africa. They spoke the same language; attended, for a time, the same church, the Nederduitse Gereformeerde Kerk (Dutch Reformed Church); and aspired to a Western way of life and values. The Population Registration Act of 1950 solidified the creation of the coloured people; it also signaled their descent into grinding poverty, unemployment, homelessness, and manic confusion over their identity and role in the affairs and future of South Africa. With the exception of those coloured anti-apartheid activists who identified with the Black Consciousness Movement, most coloureds had been duped. Now, ten years into a government dominated by the African National Congress, coloureds were having to reconfigure and renegotiate their place and identity in the new South Africa.

✳

I had journeyed to Cape Town in 1998 to study law at the University of Cape Town. At that time, Adrienne lived in the city with her husband, Wes. He was an officer in the South African air force and had coaxed Adrienne into giving their marriage a second chance. Since I knew no one else in Cape Town, I spent quite a lot of time with them. One of the people I met during that period was a bon vivant named Vernon, the brother of Adrienne's husband. Vernon helped me navigate the city's train system and locate an apartment in Rondebosch, near the university. When I dropped out of the law program after a few months, Vernon also introduced me to life in Athlone, a predominantly coloured community just outside Cape Town, as well as to some of the seamier attractions the city disguises beneath its veneer of tourist-style entertainment.

Vernon and I had maintained sporadic contact through e-mail after I left South Africa. I called him when my mother and I arrived in Cape Town, and he arrived at the hotel the next day.

"Howzit, Dave?" he called when he spotted me in the hotel lobby. My mother was resting in her room, and he and I retired to the bar to talk about old times. We ordered a couple of Castle lagers and whiskies and settled into our chairs. Vernon was an architect, and he was busy building houses and other structures all over Cape Town.

"*Ja,* things are really jumping, Dave," he reported. "And we've got our hands on some other projects. What have you been up to?"

I recounted the trip to Kokstad with my mother and my failed efforts to forge some kind of meeting or reconciliation between her and my sisters.

He drained his whiskey glass and listened intently.

"*Ja,* you know, I was thinking about you when I formed my company," he said. "Don't you think you might want to come back to South Africa for awhile to work or something?"

I shrugged and killed off my beer. I had often thought of returning to South Africa but always dismissed the idea: I was in a hell of a lot of debt in the United States, especially from student loans, and felt trapped.

"Come on," Vernon urged, seeming to read my mind, "how can you live in a country with that fucker George Bush? He's a warmonger, man."

I didn't want to get Vernon started—he had always been critical of America—so I offered to get the next round of drinks.

"So, what are you and your mom doing tomorrow?" he asked when I returned with the beer and whiskey. I told him that I wanted to take her to Cape Point and maybe a couple of other places before she left.

"Tell you what," he offered. "Why don't I come around in the morning to fetch you guys and take a drive out to Cape Point and wherever else she wants to go, hey?"

"Hell, yeah, let's do it," I agreed. "Can you believe she's never been anywhere in Cape Town, that she never left Athlone when she lived here years ago?"

Vernon said, "Shame," which was sort of the national catchall expression used to indicate sadness, astonishment, or amusement, depending on the circumstances. As usual, Vernon and I stayed in the bar for several more hours laughing about previous adventures and losing count of the beers and whiskies we guzzled.

Early the next morning, my mother and I waited in the lobby for Vernon to fetch us. He and another man soon pulled up in an SUV and came in to greet us. I introduced Vernon to my mother, and he introduced his friend, John, who had insisted on coming along for the ride.

"Both Dave and his mom were born here in South Africa," Vernon told John.

"Oh, is that so?" said John. "I'm sure we'll have an interesting visit, then."

John had lived in England for twenty-seven years and had returned to South Africa in 1996. I was anxious to talk to him about his experiences as an exile. The four of us piled into the SUV with Sam Cooke blaring on the CD player. Vernon eased the truck out onto the M3 Highway, and we headed out on the long journey south to Cape Point.

We passed Groote Schuur Hospital, where Christian Barnard had performed the world's first heart transplant in 1967, and continued on through the suburbs of Observatory and Mowbray. The next stretch of the M3 took us through the exclusive area of Bishops Court and a bevy of other estates built around the vineyards of Constantia, which were South Africa's oldest.

Our first glimpse of the ocean came as we approached Muizenberg and its spectacular white sand beaches. We were now in the area known as False Bay, so named because ancient seafarers often mistook it for Cape Town's main Table Bay. From here, you could view miles and miles of pristine beaches and the undulating surf. Not far from Muizenberg, we entered Kalk Bay, a fishing village whose streets were lined with colorful shops selling antiques, furniture, and curios.

Simon's Town, with its double-story Victorian buildings and narrow streets lined with more shops and restaurants advertising prawns, kingklip, and other delicacies, was the last town on False Bay before the final stretch to Cape Point. Several huge artillery guns pointed out toward the ocean. The South African navy maintained a huge base in Simon's Town. According to John, the guns had never been used but remained as a visible reminder of the isolation and paranoia the country had endured. Simon's Town was also home to Boulder's Beach, the site of a huge penguin colony.

"Remember the beach, Dave?" Vernon called out.

Vernon and I and a couple of friends had hung out at Boulder's Beach during my brief career as a law student. I recalled the incredible stench of the penguins and how they ignored us as we swam in the sheltered pools around the beach.

The last leg of our trip—through Rambly Bay, Switswinkel Bay, and Buffels Bay—was just one long, uninterrupted view of the ocean, the undisturbed beaches, and the mountains beyond. Cape Point Road took us right into the Cape Point Nature Reservation, a huge sweep of land completely uninhabited but for a cluster of buildings straight ahead. Vernon pulled the truck into one of the lanes and spoke to a man in a booth.

"Good day, how much is it for all of us?" asked Vernon.

The attendant peered into the car and asked, "Are you all citizens?"

John spoke up, "Yes, we are all South Africans here."

The attendant charged us a reduced rate of admission and gave us brochures describing the history of Cape Point and the incredible variety of flora and fauna in the surrounding reserve. Vernon steered the truck through the toll lane. We had traveled only a few hundred yards before someone spotted baboons playing on the side of the road.

Several tour buses whizzed past us as we entered the parking lot at Cape Point. Up ahead were three more packs of baboons wandering through the area. Some sat on cars and others scurried around looking for food.

My mother said with a chuckle, "They just do what they wanna do, don't they?"

The four of us laughed and cautiously got out of the truck and walked toward the reserve complex, which housed a funicular that carried visitors up to the landing just below the old lighthouse. The more adventurous souls could walk the steep ascent up the slope of Cape Point.

Vernon said, "You and your mother go on up. We're gonna go to the restaurant for a drink, and we'll wait for you there."

The funicular soon delivered my mother and me, along with a small group of other tourists, to the promontory just below the old lighthouse, the ultimate destination. From here, you could witness a magnificent landscape of ocean, dramatic cliffs, and serene, ancient mountains. I wanted to go up to the lighthouse, although my mother declined. For me, this place had become a ritual site I had to visit with each trip to South Africa.

I fought against exhaustion and made it up the narrow steps to the lighthouse. To the left lay the tranquil Indian Ocean with the titanic Hottentot Holland Mountains purple in the distance. And to the right was the mighty Atlantic. Directly beneath the parapet of the lighthouse, the waves crashed and churned ferociously. It was easy to understand how ancient ships had foundered and wrecked in the relentless pounding of the oceans on the jagged outcrops and boulders surrounding Cape Point. Cape Algulhas, just to the east, was the actual tip of Africa, but the mystery and stillness of this place nevertheless resonated and evoked visions of primordial struggles of humanity against nature—struggles that, in the case of Cape Point, nature invariably won.

I took a deep breath and tried to etch the panoramic view onto my memory before descending the slope and finding my mother in the souvenir shop below.

※

John and Vernon were perched at a table outside the Two Oceans Restaurant, which offered sweeping views of False Bay.

"How was it?" Vernon asked as my mother and I sat down across from them. "Very good," my mother smiled. "It's so beautiful here."

We ordered some lunch; it was typical tourist fare at inflated prices. Tiny wisps of fog had started to gather about the water and across the mountains.

"If you guys aren't busy tomorrow," John offered, "I'd like to take you to a place with authentic food from the Cape, Malay food."

"Oh, yes," my mother spoke up. "That's what I've been wanting since I've been here. You know, the Malays cook the best food."

Vernon smiled at me over his food. I had told him how important it was that my mother enjoy herself in Cape Town.

"*Ja,* this is *kak* food," said John, describing our lunch as "shit food." "We'll go tomorrow and have a proper meal."

We were well into our meal when I turned to ask Vernon a question. I turned my head back toward John, who was seated diagonally from me, just in time to see the red ass of a baboon walking away with his steak. Apparently, the animal had come from the ledge below the restaurant and patiently scoped out John's food before stealthily, and rather nonchalantly, lifting it from his plate.

"What the hell!" John sputtered.

All of us turned to see the baboon leap out of reach and out of sight.

"Did you see that bugger?" John exclaimed, standing up and leaning over the ledge.

My mother said, "Oh, my God, he just came over and took your food!"

Vernon and I cracked up with laughter, and so did the people at the tables scattered around us.

"I don't believe it," John cried, motioning for the waitress. All she could do was apologize, and eventually John calmed down as we all speculated on how the baboon must have laid plans to swipe John's food. The sky had darkened, and a mesh of fog began unraveling across the bay. On the way out of the reserve, we kept returning to the spectacle of the baboon stealing John's food.

"This really is their world," my mother observed. "We're just intruders."

✳

One of Cape Town's most enduring colonial traditions is the daily firing of the noon gun at Signal Hill on the slopes of Table Mountain. At its inception in 1864, the cannon-shot ritual helped citizens in the city and the shipping community below check the time and adjust their timepieces; the British navy also thought it a wonderful way to synchronize the society of the Cape Colony. Directly below Signal Hill lay an area called the Bo Kaap, the Malay Quarter, where the city's Malay Muslim community had lived for several centuries. This was a neighborhood of brightly painted nineteenth-century homes fronted by white picket fences, with mosques and macadam streets built along vertiginously steep streets. The four of us were climbing Longmarket Street—with the car unnervingly pitched backward—to have lunch at the Noon Gun restaurant, located just below Signal Hill and its cannon.

Vernon pulled into the garage of a modest house just when I believed the car could go no farther up the street.

"This is it," announced John.

My mother and I looked at each other quizzically and then got out of the car. Other than a small cardboard sign with the name of the restaurant printed in crude, uneven letters, the house blended in with its surroundings. Two women sat on a stoop outside the house and got up as we approached the small gate.

"Hello," John called to the women, both dressed in traditional Muslim scarves and modest dresses. "I've brought some friends for lunch."

The women smiled and opened the door of the restaurant. We walked through, to a covered verandah that revealed a stunning view of Cape Town.

John, who had been here numerous times, smiled. "That's only the beginning. Wait till you taste the food."

After one of the women seated us, Vernon, my mother, and I rose to take in the view from the porch: the whole of Cape Town was before us, from Table Mountain to the waterfront, and the city center in between, with its skyscrapers, hotels, and jumble of commercial and residential blocks. The only imperfection in this magnificent diorama was a deserted area just north of the city center. It was a wound, a gash, an area that had once contained a community of freed slaves, artisans, laborers, immigrants, and other social misfits: District Six.

This boisterous and spirited center of multicultural and multiracial harmony became an affront to the white apartheid government's obsession with racial purity. In 1966, District Six had been declared a white area. By 1982, its houses and buildings had been destroyed, and an estimated sixty thousand people had been forcibly removed to the hinterlands of Cape Town. The area had remained vacant over the years, considered by some whites to be cursed. Now the government had initiated an effort to resettle families in the area and pay restitution to others for the devastation wreaked on the community and its people.

The dining room was empty except for us. The walls were decorated with color photographs of children and more than a few withered black-

and-white pictures that seemed to be earlier generations of the people who operated this restaurant. One of the women came over to the table and engaged in light banter with John, who introduced my mother and me as Americans.

"But they were both born right here in South Africa," he hastened to add.

"Oh, is it!" the woman said and smiled broadly. "Welcome back to South Africa."

"I was born in Umtata," my mother offered, "but I was raised in Kokstad."

"Oh, that's nice," the woman commented in a tone that conveyed both respect and genuine interest. "Shall I bring you some cool drink, then?" She disappeared behind a curtain that separated the dining room from the kitchen and the rest of the house.

"There are no menus here," John explained. "You must just eat what they bring. Simple as that."

"O-oh, this is gonna be really good," my mother breathed. "I can just tell."

"The real deal," John affirmed.

"Yes, the real deal," echoed my mother.

And they were both right. Over the next two hours, we were treated to a lunch that started with small plates of pappadum, thin deep-fried crisps dusted with curry powder; and delicate samoosas, triangles of savory pastry stuffed with potatoes, onions, peas, and minced beef. Soon after followed dishes of chicken brejane, lamb curry, bowls of steaming yellow rice, and cucumber and tomato salad. The table was crowded with food made from recipes that had been passed down through generations of Muslim Malays, who had first been brought from Indonesia as slaves, adding to the mélange of coloured culture in Cape Town. While we savored the meal, John told a steady stream of stories, and we all laughed and talked.

When the final course arrived, my mother leaned over the table.

"Oh, my God, is that bobotie?" she gushed. "I've been wanting some of that, o-oh, for so long!"

Our host laughed and returned to the kitchen.

John said, "Yes, Dave, now you will see the real deal, my son. This is a famous Malay dish."

Vernon also perked up. "*Ja,* Dave, your mother knows about this."

"I sure do," said my mother, already digging into the dish, which is a kind of custard and meat pie seasoned with onion, curry, fruit chutney, and nuts and stuffed with minced lamb. Bobotie is traditionally eaten with yellow rice. Its nearest American equivalent would be a really fancy meatloaf.

As tasty as all these dishes were, they were not meant for light eaters or those who are persnickety about calories or fat. This was rich, sumptuous food steeped in the culture of the Malay slaves at the Cape—not unlike the soul food originated and popularized by African slaves in the American South. After a while, we all sat back in our chairs. No one could eat any more. The woman cleared the table without protest from any of us. Then she brought out a dessert of warm bread pudding studded in raisins and drizzled with rum sauce. When my mother saw this, I thought she was going to lose it.

"Oh, this is really good," she asserted. "You did *really* good, David."

We all nodded toward her. I was especially happy to be able to provide her with this experience. For most of my life, I had felt like a failure as a son. Now I wanted to do whatever I could to bring some joy into her life, especially since she was leaving South Africa that afternoon. She was right: it was time for her to stop beating up on herself about events that had happened years ago over which she had had no control. At this moment, sitting here in this restaurant above Cape Town, relaxing with my friends Vernon and John, and witnessing my mother actually enjoy herself, I realized that there was only one reunion that really mattered right now: the one between my mother and me after so many years of misunderstandings and reticence and adversity.

When we got back in the car, my mother asked Vernon, "Do you think we could go to the casino? Don't they have a casino somewhere over here?"

"*Ja,* not a problem, we can go there," Vernon answered. We crept down the hill back through the Bo Kaap and headed over to the Grand West, a huge gambling and entertainment complex in the suburb of Goodwood. Palm trees lined the driveway of the elaborate complex of faux Victorian buildings. The parking lot was filled, and a shuttle ferried passengers to the front door of the casino. Here, everyone was subject to a security check: everyone had to empty all their pockets, remove their hats, and endure a pat-down search. Once inside the cavernous main room of the casino, my mother headed straight for the slot machines.

After agreeing to meet her in an hour, John, Vernon, and I found a sports bar and joined a crowd watching a rugby match. We ordered a round of beers and sat back to take in the scenery.

"Listen, Dave," said John, "why don't you move out of the hotel and just stay at my place when your mother leaves today? What's the point in spending all that money? I have a room at my place, and you can stay there until you leave Cape Town."

I agreed and, with that settled, we had another round of beers and went to look for my mother. It took a few minutes to find her among the rows and rows of mostly women shoveling coins into the machines. When I spotted her, I walked up and said, "We were looking all over for you. I told John and Vernon that all y'all coloureds look just alike."

"Oh, boy, get out of here," she laughed. "Look, I won two hundred rand."

Later that afternoon, Vernon drove us to the airport, and I helped her check in for her flight back home. Vernon said good-bye to her and drifted back toward the airport entrance. My mother and I walked to the point of no return, the security barrier, and stopped. I hugged her and said, "I love you, Ma."

For some reason, I had always stuttered when uttering those words; now they flowed with a new conviction and a renewed resolve to appreciate my mother and the hardships she had endured largely as a result of her upbringing under apartheid. Though she had escaped South Africa, I understood that the cancer of apartheid had tinged all of her choices, her sense of life, and her life chances.

She kissed me on the neck and said, "I love you, too, David."

And the next thing I knew she was gone, swept up in the machinations of the departure area of the airport. I stood outside the security cordon until I couldn't see her anymore and then went outside to find Vernon.

✳

John's house was located in Claremont, which had excellent views of Table Mountain. Like so many of the other southern suburbs of Cape Town, it had the look and feel of one vast gated community: large family homes hunkered down behind steep walls, with signs warning of armed response security patrols, and few people lingering on the streets. Many of the houses featured large verandahs and lavish gardens, including palm trees and jacarandas. Claremont was a world away from the desolate wasteland of the Cape Flats, where the apartheid government had dumped thousands of coloureds during the forced removals of the 1960s.

John's wife and son had recently left for London, so he was alone in the drafty three-bedroom house. After Vernon and I returned from the airport, I dragged my bags into a room off the back courtyard area, which contained the garage and a separate servants' quarter. John and Vernon were in the living room rearranging the furniture and emptying overflowing ashtrays and whiskey bottles.

"*Ja,* we're going to have a little joll, Dave," John said as I entered the room.

The house had a distinct Mediterranean feel: tiled floors, a rustic fireplace, a thatched braii area off the living room, a huge plate glass window looking into a front yard dominated by a variety of trees and plants. The front room was tastefully furnished with bookshelves and heavy, hand-carved furniture. A television and stereo system took up one wall. Paintings, photographs, and other artwork dotted the walls, including a photo of the poet James Matthews, one of South Africa's legendary anti-apartheid writers who had come of age with the likes of Dennis Brutus, Ezekiel Mphalele, and Richard Rive.

A small Muslim man John introduced to me as his driver, Hakim, was now hauling boxes and boxes of booze and food into the house. As I learned later, Hakim had been John's chauffeur and assistant for many years and had doubtless seen many jolls at the house.

"Shall we have a couple of brewskis, Dave?" said Vernon.

"Absolutely," I replied, joining him on the verandah while John and Hakim sorted out the supplies for the party.

The house was starting to fill up with people. Some of them sat around watching a rugby match on television; others listened to music blaring from the stereo system and drifted through the house, stopping occasionally to talk with friends. I found myself at the center of a group that included Vernon and John and a couple of other guys. Most of the talk dealt with sports—South Africans were mad for sports—and the country's recent selection as host of the 2010 World Cup. Inevitably, though, the conversation turned to politics, and the men couldn't resist the opportunity to rip into the American-led war in Iraq and what they saw as a rising tide of American imperialism and hubris in the world.

"The Americans and their idiot George Bush are fuck-all," spat Vernon. "Dave, you must return to South Africa where the people are humane. I've never been to America, but I can tell you that it is one fucked-up place."

The other men all agreed with Vernon's critique of America, expecting me to come to its defense. But I had no intention of spending my evening apologizing for or attempting to justify American actions in Iraq and the world.

Instead, I took advantage of the break in the conversation and asked John about his artwork and the photograph of James Matthews in the living room. John, I learned, had been active in the South African Coloured People's Congress during the 1960s. He had been forced into exile in England in 1968, shortly after the death of his friend Basil February, one of the unsung heroes of the anti-apartheid struggle, who had been killed while leading a group of insurgents from what was then southern Rhodesia back into South Africa. Before that, John told me, he and February mostly painted political graffiti on walls in the coloured community of Athlone. Though he never explained the extent of his involvement in the anti-apartheid insurgency, I sensed that John somehow blamed himself for February's death.

"So, John, do you think there is such a thing as coloured culture?" I asked. The group went silent, as if I had declared that all the booze was gone and the party was over.

"Well," he began tentatively, "this issue of coloured culture is very complicated, you know. It's not so easy to answer in the affirmative that there is or isn't such a thing."

"I don't believe in it," Vernon spoke up. "Coloured culture is nothing but an apartheid invention, that's all. Why must we have all the 'coloured' this and 'coloured' that, hey? We are all South Africans. If apartheid taught us anything, it's that. *Voetsek* coloured culture!" he exclaimed, "fuck coloured culture!"

The other two gentlemen shifted in their seats, perhaps not wanting to get involved in the discussion. A shout rose from the group watching the rugby match in the living room, and a potentially awkward moment passed. Like so many other topics in South Africa, coloured culture and identity were controversial, especially now that everyone was supposed to be getting along and blurring their differences for the common good. But I had come to South Africa to grapple with this issue as well as with my personal history, and I found it hard to let it go.

Of course, the debate over coloured culture and identity had a long history and was, as John intimated, confounding. No one could deny that coloureds had contributed to the cultural mosaic of South African society through writers such as Alex La Guma, Peter Abrahams, James Matthews, Dennis Brutus, Arthur Nortje, Adam Small, Richard Rive, and Bessie Head, just to name a few. Coloured musicians such as Abdullah Ibrahim (Dollar Brand), Henry February, Sammy Moritz, Johnny Gertse, and others adapted American jazz to the peculiarities of South African culture. But beyond these and other aesthetic contributions, I was looking to interrogate the link between culture and identity. Did coloured culture and identity add up to a separate ethnic makeup? In short, were coloured people for real or an invention of apartheid?

The answer was that no one seemed to know—though I had come across a few intriguing theories. A few years after the Nationalists had taken power and implemented their program of apartheid, a scholar with the South African Institute of Race Relations wrote: "The Coloured people are so diverse in origin, in economic attainment and in individual characteristics that they cannot be easily classified. Today it is probably true that they are gradually becoming a distinct race, and that a community sense is growing among them." Likewise, during the tumult of the 1970s, Al J. Venter affirmed the existence of a distinct coloured culture, commenting that "any society able to produce writers of the stature of Alex La Guma or Peter Abrahams . . . has both the ingredients and the potential with which to build a culture as rich and varied as any in the world." It was sometimes difficult to distinguish the defense of coloured culture from the emergence of a kind of coloured nationalism that had its roots in the founding of the African Political Organization, established in 1912 to safeguard coloured interests.

The theory about coloured culture that I found most captivating, however, flatly denied its existence and posed an alternative explanation of this phenomenon. Beginning with the plethora of names used to identify coloureds, author R. E. Van Der Ross debunked the myths about coloured culture perpetrated by its defenders and detractors alike. Coloureds, he argued, have no special homeland or ancestral lands in South Africa where they are dominant, either demographically or politically. The argument for coloured culture, he asserted, could be made only in a country in which the preservation of identity—whether white or black—has been so fiercely, and bloodily, contested. What has passed for coloured culture, he concluded, is based on a subculture of poverty, in which coloured people have been depicted as "dirty, drunk, noisy and unattractive." Just as stereotypes of African Americans as lazy, unreliable, raping criminals constituted what some whites think of as black culture, Van Der Ross reasoned that the negative image of coloureds had morphed into the belief "that

Coloured people are 'different' and have their own culture." But, he surmised, "Coloured people have no special, peculiar, typical culture which is so different from that of White Afrikaans- or English-speaking South Africans that it could be called 'Coloured culture.'"

By this reckoning, it would seem, coloureds were nothing but the creation of and an extension of whites; they weren't quite white and they weren't quite black—they were, indeed, the nowhere people, the twilight people without a culture, stuck in the proverbial middle.

A couple of nights later, Vernon and I visited some of his friends in Observatory, a bohemian neighborhood just east of downtown Cape Town. He introduced me to a man named Bertram, who had lived in Australia and the Netherlands before returning to South Africa in 1996. From all appearances, Bertram was a white man: he had straight, black hair, angular facial features, and extremely fair skin. He seemed eager to weigh in on the issue of coloured culture.

"The story of coloureds is that of displacement," he began. "But I don't give the theory of coloured culture any credibility at all. Yes, it was raised a number of times when I came back, and people sometimes didn't think that I was coloured: they thought I was white, with the straight hair and all that."

"Did they perform the pencil test on you?" I asked in a mock deadpan that made us both burst out laughing.

Having recovered from my lame attempt at humor, he went on. "You know, people just have expectations of what a coloured person is, especially if you don't fall into that type. In my professional life as well, people assumed that I was a visiting expert from overseas. They said, 'Where you from?' I said, 'I'm from Athlone.'"

We shared another laugh at his mention of Athlone, a coloured community in Cape Town.

"Why does there seem to be such controversy over this whole issue of colouredness?" I asked.

"I think it's just the result of all these years of apartheid, you know—just divide and rule," he observed. "You know, they sort of lumped us all together, even though we were all completely different, and just called us coloureds and imposed distinctions of class and color even within that."

"Is there such a thing as coloured culture?" I persisted. "Or is it just a myth?"

He paused for a moment. The pungent smell of dagga drifted through the house.

"Well, that's an interesting question," Bertram began again. "There are things that are synonymous with 'coloured'—I don't want to use 'coloured culture'—conditions here. It's about the way that we live and how we cook and what we're interested in. But it's not really that important to most people, those things, because we want to be part of the bigger world. We don't want to be locked up in tribalism, which comes along with the classification of being coloured, because then immediately there are preconceived ideas about what you think. And to a certain extent it was true, because you must remember that the coloureds always voted for the National Party, but that's changed now.

"So, for me, I mean, the ten years of democracy and all that rubbish about what we've achieved, has actually meant that in the Western Cape, where we live, people's perceptions have changed. The master-servant relationship has somehow moved a little bit, and now coloured people for the first time are voting for the ANC. That's historic."

*

As much as I appreciated John's hospitality and having the run of his home in Claremont, I was aching to get out on my own during the last couple of days I had left in the country. John's idea of a good day consisted of watching Lance Armstrong conquer the Tour de France on television, but I wanted to get into Cape Town and reacquaint myself with its pubs and shops and sights. When I inquired about public transportation from Claremont into downtown, John said, "Don't worry. I'll make arrangements for you. Cape Town is not safe; you mustn't walk around by yourself."

John's driver, Hakim, began to ferry me wherever I wanted to go in John's white BMW. We drove through Wynberg, Athlone, Rondebosch, and an area called Kew Town, a coloured area that looked like a slum straight out of Mississippi or Atlanta. Hakim swung by and picked up John and drove us both to Camp's Bay. We had lunch at one of the beachfront's trendy restaurants and walked on the beach, where a whale was stranded near the shore. A crowd had gathered to catch a glimpse of the creature.

"Can you see him?" asked John, squinting into the sun toward the beach. I thought I saw the whale's fluke rise out of the surf, but I couldn't be sure. Regardless, I was just happy to be out and about. Cape Town is a city that must be experienced; too often I'd found that its inhabitants took the city and its attractions for granted.

On the morning of my last day in the city—my plane was leaving at midnight—I got Hakim to drop me downtown so that I could pick up a few gifts for friends. I really wanted some time alone, too. A terrific rainstorm had invaded the city, and clouds shrouded Table Mountain.

"You must be very careful, Dave," Hakim advised me when he dropped me downtown near the train station.

"Don't worry," I assured him, "I know my way around." I told him that I'd call him in a few hours to fetch me and set off into the pelting raindrops. I had explored these streets as a student at the university, so I wasn't too concerned about my personal safety.

The rain had driven most people inside, and the sidewalks of St. George's mall were mostly deserted. I was headed to the huge outdoor flea market in Greenmarket Square, where I knew I'd get some good deals on souvenirs. Despite the rain, the merchants were there, perched under blue and green tarps, beckoning tourists to inspect their wares. I had emptied my book bag to make room for all the t-shirts and gifts I began accumulating at the market. When it became obvious that I was spending a lot of money among the merchants' stalls, young boys began coming up to me begging for change. When I rebuffed them, they skittered away to the edges of the muddy market and made faces and fists at me. I was beginning to feel like a piece of raw meat among the merchants and street children, and I was relieved to be done with my shopping.

After securing my treasures in my book bag, I turned to leave the market area and was immediately set upon by a couple of urchins.

"Please, mister," one of the boys mewled, holding out his grubby hands, "we need money for food. Please."

The boys traveled in packs, so three more soon surrounded me. And then I did something totally stupid, something I should have known would get me into trouble: I took out a handful of coins and began passing them around to the street children. Even though I knew it was unwise to give money to these mini-predators, I did it anyway, mainly because I was determined to get rid of all my South African currency before leaving. Now there was no turning back as I doled out the money. Another pack of boys descended on me, pushing, arguing, cajoling, and pleading for money.

"Over here, mister," one of them yelled.

"Sir, you didn't give to me!" another boy at the back of the bunch cried. Most of the boys who had gotten coins grabbed them greedily and ran off into the streets beyond Greenmarket Square. But I wasn't going to be let off that easily, because now a group of about ten boys surrounded me.

Then I did something even more foolish: I took out a roll of paper money and began tossing it out to the boys—because by now I just wanted them gone. A few passersby looked at me with a mixture of sympathy and derision, as if to imply that I was a goddamn fool for having gotten myself into this predicament. I couldn't have agreed with them more, and now I was starting to panic as more and more of the street children showed up, demanding money. I had become a target, and I began moving away from the area and into St. George's mall, hoping to run into a police officer or security guard. The boys trailed me, shouting and screaming, "Over here, mister! Please, give us money, sir!" I had probably given away about a hundred rand, and I knew the situation was getting dangerous.

I ran into a Wimpy's restaurant with two of the boys on my tail. The restaurant workers looked at the boys with contempt and stared at me as if I had lost my mind. Meanwhile, a security guard shooed away the rest of the boys outside the restaurant. The other two boys inside the restaurant continued to hound me, however, until I handed the cashier some money and instructed her to feed them. I was causing a scene and needed to get out of there and to a telephone to call Hakim.

I fled the restaurant and began walking back to the train station. I guess the word had gotten out, though, because soon two more ragged boys were following me. Despite my best efforts—I didn't want to give in to my panic and break into a run—they caught up with me and began pleading for money.

"Please, sir, money, please," the taller of the two moaned.

"I don't have anything," I insisted, with a note of desperation in my voice that disturbed even me.

The other boy wailed, "Please, mister, can you help us? We have no shoes. We have no food. Can't you please help us?"

The taller boy started in again, this time in a more menacing tone: "Now, sir, we have asked you nicely. We are trying to be respectful, sir, but we need you to give us money."

I turned to look at the boy. He was barefoot, and his pants and t-shirt were filthy and tattered. Then I saw that he was carrying a small stick that appeared to be sharpened at one end. I knew at that moment that these boys planned to attack me with the improvised weapon and rob me here on the deserted streets of downtown Cape Town.

I saw a newspaper vendor up ahead, and I crossed the street to escape the boys, who continued to hound me. I bounded toward the vendor's kiosk, hoping that he and his helpers would come to my aid.

I turned to the boys and said, "Please leave me alone. I don't have any more money. Just go away."

I looked at the old man selling the newspapers. He mumbled something, and I leaned closer to hear. "They are going to rob you," he whispered.

"I know," I said, "but what do I do?"

"Just stay here a while, and they will go," he advised. But by now I was terrified and just wanted to get to a safer place. The vendor muttered something to one of his helpers, and the man approached me.

"Where do you want to go?" he asked, keeping an eye on the two young predators.

"I need to get to a telephone and the train station where there are policemen," I told him. The station was just across the street, but I didn't want to risk being attacked.

"Just stay close to me, and I will take you there," the man said.

He made threatening gestures toward the boys, but they continued to follow us as we crossed the street to the station. We were now within sight of the busy outdoor market in front of the station, and I began to breathe easier.

My escort turned to me and said, "Haven't you got something for me, sir?"

As I reached into my pocket to retrieve a tip for him, one of the wild boys lunged toward me. I had half expected them to attack me at some point before reaching the train station. Now they were running down the street, one of them holding something aloft in his hand. I panicked at first but then remembered that I always kept my wallet in my front pocket. The boy had grabbed the piece of paper on which I'd written the names of the people to whom I'd promised souvenirs.

A few people stared at me. One man shook his head, whether in disgust at the street kids or in pity for me, the bumbling tourist. One woman mouthed some words that I couldn't make out as I rushed into the comparative safety of the train station. I made it to a telephone, called Hakim, and then wandered around the station until he pulled up outside.

"Are you all right, Dave?" he asked. "Did you find everything you needed?"

"Oh yeah," I told him, "everything's fine, and I got what I needed."

The attack made me realize that, in the minds of these street kids, I was just another American, a ripe target stupid enough to give them money. They didn't give a damn that I had been born in South Africa and obsessed over the country's history and politics. They couldn't have cared less about my pretensions to South African citizenship and my anxiety about fitting into South African society. They weren't interested in my story and the pains I had suffered to try to bring my mother and her daughters together. None of that mattered to them. So I was happy when Hakim turned the car around and drove back to John's place in Claremont. I had had enough of South Africa for now.

As If This Were Brightness

Clearing a path
NOW covered by dry pods
shaken free from the old trees

All around
discarded fires
dead as soot

I'll work in this half-light
as if it were brightness

Voices

Beckoning
beneath the bark
the sap rising
in the mangled trees

A need to break
what is tangled
and useless

Like this
to be awake forever
to the headlong thrust

the inch by inch
struggle for a clearing
where I'll find
the voice I clearly hear
the only voice I want
of an up-moving sun
breaking my horizon

JENNIFER DAVIDS
Searching for Words

EPILOGUE

Several months after my mother and I returned to the United States from South Africa, we met in Atlanta to embark on another journey to settle some unfinished business. My mother hadn't seen my brother Xavier in thirty years, and now we were driving down Highway 59 South through Hattiesburg to visit him at the Boswell Regional Center in Sanatorium, Mississippi. In contrast to the difficulties and uncertainties we faced in locating and reconciling with my sisters in South Africa, we would have no trouble finding Xavier. He had been at Boswell since my grandmother's death in 1997.

For most of the drive through Mississippi, my mother was silent. Only the sound of the radio punctuated the landscape of pine trees, empty fields, rusted-out gas stations, and remote roadside fruit stands as we traveled deeper into the state. It was hard to tell whether being back in Mississippi after three decades affected my mother at all. I now understood that she was much more complicated than I had ever imagined. Although I found it hard to decipher her expressions or her silence at times, I knew that she was now engrossed by two unspoken concerns: she had been diagnosed with cancer since our return from South Africa, and she was agonizing over the way she had treated Xavier over the years.

We had been traveling down Highway 59 for about fifteen minutes when I became concerned that we might be lost. I got off the highway and pulled into a gas station to ask for directions. The place was crowded with workmen, both black and white, waiting to place orders for burgers and fried chicken at a makeshift grill set up in the corner of the rundown store. Rather than waiting to ask the cashier—a white woman—for directions, I approached a black man in dirty coveralls who was standing in line to pay for gas. My anxiety level was high when I approached the man—my mother was waiting in the car, and I wasn't sure what would happen when we saw Xavier—so I stuttered like a fool.

"Excuse me," I said to the man, "do you know where, uh, uh, uh, it's a place called, uh, uh—" I couldn't get out the word "Sanatorium."

The man just looked at me without a trace of malice or impatience until I was finally able to sputter out that I was looking for Sanatorium.

"Yeah," he said, "just keep on headed down the highway, down 59, until you git to 49 North, and then you gonna take that all the way out 'til you git into Magee. Now when you git into Magee, just start lookin' for the signs for Sanatorium, 'cause it's real easy to miss."

I thanked the man, cursed myself for stuttering, and returned to the car.

"Everything all right?" my mother asked, as I backed the car out of the parking lot.

"Yes, I just needed to make sure we were going the right way," I said.

A car pulled up beside us, and a woman dressed in a chador got out and entered the store.

"Look at that, David," my mother remarked. "They even got Muslims down here now. They didn't have all that back when I was down here, I know that."

I just nodded my head and turned the car around. We resumed our journey down the highway. Mississippi had definitely changed in many ways, but in other ways the state had remained frozen in the past.

The most notable improvements had been in race relations. Whites and blacks had largely buried the hatred and enmity that roiled the state for most of its history. In fact, in a curious twist, Mississippi was now hailed as a model of racial reconciliation for the country, largely through the efforts of organizations such as the William Winter Institute at the University of Mississippi and Mission Mississippi, an evangelical group that preached racial unity. On a personal level, most of the whites I had dealt with in the state's stores and businesses were unfailingly congenial and warm. And Mississippi had more black elected officials than any other state.

Nevertheless, two issues contributed to racial disquiet among the state's citizens: the ongoing controversy over flying a Confederate battle flag over the capitol building in Jackson, and the election of Haley Barbour as governor in 2003. The flag controversy had presumably been settled by voters in 2001, who opted to retain the Confederate symbol, but the issue was slated to be debated again in the Mississippi legislature. Barbour had drawn fire for his affiliation with the Council of Conservative Citizens, an offshoot of the earlier White Citizens Councils and the State Sovereignty Commission, which had championed segregation and spied on its enemies. Further, during his campaign, Barbour had endorsed the continued use of an 1894 Confederate battle emblem on the state flag and lambasted affirmative action programs in a state where blacks suffered from some of the nation's highest poverty rates. Although individual attitudes had changed, the perquisites of white supremacy—the privileges enjoyed by white people as a group—were entrenched in Mississippi. White people still reacted defensively to any issue or group that threatened their dominance in the political and economic realms.

The state still certainly had room for open racists and bigots, such as white rights activist Jim Giles, who had recently lost a bid to unseat incumbent Representative Chip Pickering in the state's Third Congressional District. Considered a long shot, Giles told the *Jackson Free Press* why he opposed the incumbent: "Pickering has total disregard for what's truly best for America. And [the] America that I'm talking about is White America, a white nation, that's what I'm talking about. That's what I want. We started out a white nation; we no longer are. I want it to be a white nation again. I'm advocating separation of the races. I'm a white separatist. . . . Mississippi hasn't changed; my people are still out there."

For the most part, however, whites seemed ready and eager to move forward on the more pressing issues of economic prosperity and business development. The *Jackson Clarion-Ledger* had recently run a five-part series on saving the state's small towns in an economic climate of plant closings and job losses. "The jobless rate in some Mississippi small towns has inched up over the years, mainly because of dwindling factory jobs," the first article in the series reported. "In the past 10 years, the state has lost 67,000 manufacturing jobs, the types of jobs long considered the economic lifeblood of small towns." Like other southern states, Mississippi was struggling with the challenges of attracting industry and new businesses. The state had scored some successes in the tourism and gaming industries. Casinos drew in busloads of people every year, and labor market analysts predicted an increase in jobs for cooks, museum workers, bellhops, concierges, and other low-level service positions.

On other issues, however, such as health care and education, the state continued to fare poorly. The poverty rate had dropped to 17.9 percent in 2003, from 18.9 percent in 2002, but it was still one of the highest in the country, behind only Arkansas and New Mexico. On May 26, 2004, Governor Barbour approved a law mandating significant cuts in Mississippi's

Medicaid program, prompting *New York Times* columnist Bob Herbert to refer to the state's "long tradition of keeping the poor and the unfortunate in as ragged and miserable a condition as possible." In a statement on the Governor's Office Web site, Barbour defended the cuts, arguing that "the best route to quality health care is through job creation, better pay and economic growth." In the meantime, according to Herbert, "the 65,000 seniors and disabled individuals who will lose their Medicaid eligibility have incomes so low they effectively have no money to pay for their health care."

On the education front, in 2003 the state had been ranked forty-eighth, near the bottom, in categories such as per pupil expenditures, public school graduation rates, and student proficiency in reading, writing, and math. And Mississippi, along with rural areas in Alabama, Georgia, and South Carolina, had also become a major battleground in the fight against AIDS. The virus flourished in small, isolated areas trapped in the miasma of drug use, chronic unemployment, teenage pregnancy, and hopelessness.

As if these challenges weren't enough, the state had not yet escaped its bloody past. The U.S. Justice Department had recently reopened the investigation into the murder of Emmett Till, whose death had helped to spark the civil rights revolution. Harking back to the words of Mississippi's most famous literary son, William Faulkner—"The past is not dead. In fact, it's not even past"—prosecutors were now examining many of the state's unsolved murders from the civil rights era, including the killings of Ben Brown, a student activist shot in the back by a police officer during a protest at Jackson State University in 1967; and Charles Moore and Henry Dee, whose shackled bodies were found bobbing in the Mississippi River around the time of the disappearance of Michael Schwerner, James Chaney, and Andrew Goodman. "Blacks have steadily gained political power and have pushed for these cases to be heard before today's racially diverse juries," according to reporter Emily Yellin of the *New York Times*. "At the same time, more witnesses, perhaps with less fear of retaliation and with heavy consciences they want to unburden, are coming forward."

To its credit, Mississippi had pursued convictions in several other civil rights–era murders, prosecuting Byron De La Beckwith for murdering Medgar Evers and former Imperial Wizard Sam Bowers for the killing of Vernon Dahmer. Now the pendulum of justice was swinging in favor of seeking redress for the murders of James Chaney, Michael Schwerner, and Andrew Goodman, the state's most famous unsolved case.

✳

A few weeks before the trip to South Africa with my mother, I had traveled to Philadelphia, Mississippi, to attend the fortieth annual Chaney, Schwerner, Goodman Memorial Service at Mt. Zion Church in the Longdale community. The three civil rights workers had traveled there on June 21, 1964, to investigate the bombing of the Mt. Zion Church and were kidnapped and murdered by the Ku Klux Klan on their return to Meridian. I arrived at the resilient and storied church, a compact red brick building, with my sister Alma, who was at the wheel of my car. Alma and I had kept in touch over the years, although my other sibling from my father's previous marriage, Dave Jr., and I barely spoke these days.

After Alma pulled the car into the church yard, I had the good fortune to run into John Steele, who was coordinating the memorial service in conjunction with the James Chaney Foundation. Ben Chaney, James Chaney's younger brother, was scheduled to arrive at the service with a bus convoy of students from across the country who had volunteered to participate in what was billed as Freedom Summer 2004. Steele, a well-spoken and resolute man with a gray-speckled beard and intense focus, told me that he had been directing the service for several years, long before the intense media scrutiny the unsolved murders had brought to the state.

But now controversy threatened this year's service: a group of civic, business, and political leaders calling itself the Philadelphia Coalition had planned a separate service at the city's civic center. Their aim, according to Steele, was to upstage the service at the church because they were afraid of how the city and its citizens might be portrayed in the local, national, and, increasingly, international media.

"Suddenly, they've decided they want to control our event," he said, "and we've been doing this for years."

Steele was pulled away by one of his assistants and disappeared for a while. While Alma stood near the car smoking a cigarette, I walked around the church grounds and through the attached cemetery. Groups of people wandered around, some of them obviously perplexed because the memorial service, originally scheduled for one o'clock, two hours earlier, still had not begun. According to Steele, it had been pushed back by the "official" Philadelphia Freedom Summer 2004 memorial service at the civic center. A group of Neshoba County sheriff's deputies stood next to a huge command center trailer beside the church, and four or five close-shaven white officers barred entry to the church itself. More white deputies drove up, and others trampled around the church yard in workmanlike brogans.

When Steele returned, I asked him what he thought about the Justice Department reopening the Emmett Till case.

"Well, I'm optimistic," he said, as sweat rolled down his face in the blazing heat, "but we also need to look at doing something about the case of Schwerner, Chaney, and Goodman. There had to be more people involved in killing these boys, particularly in the case of Chaney. Ain't no way, with the amount of damage done to his body, that only a few people was involved. It had to be a gang of people—some of 'em probably still living around here."

I thought about Anthony Walton's excellent book *Mississippi: An American Journey,* which cited a statement from Dr. David Spain, the former medical examiner for Westchester County, New York, who conducted an autopsy on James Chaney after the official state autopsy: "I could barely believe the destruction to these frail young bones," he reported. "In my twenty-five years as a pathologist and medical examiner, I have never seen bones so severely shattered, except in tremendously high speed accidents or airplane crashes. It was obvious to any first-year medical student that this boy had been beaten to a pulp."

But the only way to deal with the state's past, Steele asserted, was to establish a body akin to the South African Truth and Reconciliation Commission. My ears perked up at this, and Steele explained that at least one other southern city—Greensboro, North Carolina—had received direct assistance from representatives in South Africa in setting up its own Truth and Reconciliation Commission to deal with the unprosecuted murders of five community and labor organizers in 1979. Another group, Southern Truth and Reconciliation, based at Emory University in Atlanta, devoted itself to investigating civil rights–era murders, while "seeking justice and reconciliation for human rights violations."

Steele was called away again, and Alma and I stood outside in the oppressive heat, waiting to see what would happen next. Suddenly Alma pointed down the road at a caravan of buses approaching the church.

"There he go," she said, lowering the cigarette from her mouth.

I looked at the buses pull up and park across the dirt road from where the sheriff's deputies had set up their command post.

"Who is it?" I asked her.

"It's Ben," she said. "There go Ben. C'mon."

It took me a second to realize that she was talking about Ben Chaney—and to remember that they had been childhood friends before his brother was murdered. By now, a pack of journalists and several camera crews were waiting for Chaney and his student volunteers to get off the bus.

Chaney finally appeared and did a few interviews before moving away and toward Alma and me.

"Ben," she called out. "Ben Chaney!"

He stopped in his tracks and trained his eyes on her, behind glasses that seemed to dwarf his round face and bald head.

"Is that Alma?" he said, reaching out and pulling her toward him. The media pack now descended on them while I stood back and marveled at the connection—albeit tangential—I had to a piece of civil rights history. Alma brought Ben Chaney over and introduced us.

"Ben, this my brother David. I don't know if you remember him, 'cause ya'll had moved to New York after your brother got killed." We shook hands and walked toward the church. I was anxious to talk to him and get his reaction to the controversy surrounding the memorial service. When he saw the deputies standing in front of the church door, he said, "Come on. Let's walk down the road a bit."

A couple of people in his entourage appeared to object—apparently wondering who the hell I was—but he shooed them away, and we ambled down the dirt road away from the church. This was the same dirt road, I reflected, on which his brother and Michael Schwerner and Andrew Goodman had traveled to their deaths.

Chaney took out a cigarette, and we stopped on the side of the road.

"So what's going on here?" he asked.

I told him everything I knew about the conflict with the Philadelphia political leaders and business community.

"You know, white folks ain't never gonna change," he sighed. "Don't matter if it forty years or fifty years after they killed my brother—they always gonna be the same dirty racists."

A pickup truck passed by, its white driver staring at us for a long time. I knew I didn't have long with Ben before the media and his entourage started clamoring for his return, so I asked him what he thought about efforts to reopen the case of his brother's murder and all the other unsolved murders in Mississippi. He took a deep drag on the cigarette and squinted into the sun before answering.

Finally he said, "The state of Mississippi has a lot to answer for. You know, it's like the white people in this state have a lot to hide—and the niggers are still just as scared as they was back when they couldn't vote. But today it's inexcusable. It's inexcusable that this state has never conducted a proper investigation into these killings. The government of Mississippi has got to be held accountable—or else it's just gonna hold the people and the state back. But no matter what happens, I intend to get justice for my brother, if it's the last thing I do."

*

Those few words—"if it's the last thing I do"—came back to me now as my mother and I rolled past a sign indicating that we were entering Magee, Mississippi. Other than a stretch of gas stations, a few shops alongside the highway, and a Wal-Mart looming in the distance, we could have been in any small southern town.

"How much farther is it?" my mother asked. The trip had taken longer than I had expected, and I could tell that she was in some discomfort and pain from sitting so long.

Just on the outskirts of Magee, I spotted a sign for the Boswell Regional Center and exited onto a rural road parallel to the highway. We were looking for Sanatorium, and I drove around until I recognized the entrance to the Boswell Center from my previous trips there. I turned off the road over some railroad tracks and into a winding driveway toward the main building where my brother Xavier was housed.

The Mississippi State Sanatorium for Tuberculosis was built in 1916, after the State Legislature appropriated twenty-five thousand dollars and two hundred acres of land for the institution to establish a campus and its own water system to accommodate the increased demands of tuberculosis patients and their families. By 1920, the legislature and other civic organizations had contributed more than two million dollars for buildings and equipment. But as improved public health measures decreased the number of tuberculosis cases in the state, the sanatorium was transformed into Boswell Regional Center in July 1976 and now served patients with mental retardation.

The driveway led past several cottages on the sprawling campus. In the distance, I could see a smokestack and several buildings scattered around the main building where we now parked. I looked over at my mother.

"Are you all right?" I asked.

"Yes, I'm fine," she said. "I just keep thinking that I could have done more than I did for him over all these years. I don't know . . . I could have done something."

"Don't worry about all that," I urged, reaching out to squeeze her hand. "Just concentrate on going forward and on what you can do now. Let's go."

Since I had been here before, I knew what to expect. As we approached the front door, we came upon a male patient smoking a cigarette and shivering in the cold. He was wearing a helmet to protect himself, and he called out "Hey!" to us as we entered the lobby and notified the receptionist that we had come to see Xavier Houze. The place had the familiar and slightly disagreeable fecal smell of a hospital.

A few minutes later, Xavier came bounding into the lobby area. He hadn't changed much since the last time I had seen him, about a year earlier. He wore jeans, a windbreaker, and gym shoes. He was still as wiry as ever, and he appeared healthy. He immediately rushed over and embraced me.

"Dave," he cried out, while jumping up and down. "Home! Home! Yayyyyyy!"

Then he went to the mother he hadn't seen in thirty years and kissed her. "Hey, Ma!" he said. My mother broke out into a smile and hugged her son for a long time. She had been afraid he wouldn't recognize her.

The three of us sat down on a couch in the lobby, and I showed Xavier the Christmas gifts I had brought him. A woman came out and introduced herself as one of his social workers. She asked whether we wanted to take him off campus.

My mother said nervously, "Well, it's kind of late. I don't know if we should go anywhere."

The woman looked at me. "I was thinking about just taking him into town to get a hamburger or something. Is that okay?"

"Sure." She led us downstairs, where we checked him out on a day pass.

My mother pulled me aside while a nurse checked Xavier's blood pressure and other vital signs before he left the center.

"Don't you think it's better to stay here?" she whispered. "We might not be able to control him."

"Don't worry," I reassured her. "He'll be fine."

When we got to the car, I placed Xavier in the back seat and buckled him in. He was so happy when I told him that we were going to get hamburgers and chocolate chip cookies, his favorite foods. Unlike my attitude in my childhood years, when I had been ashamed of taking Xavier out to public places, I had learned to steel myself against the inevitable stares. I really didn't give a damn what people thought about my brother: he had been in the shadows for too long, and I was determined to do everything I could to bring some joy and satisfaction to his life. Surprisingly, though, when we got to the restaurant and ordered our food, no one stared, and the three of us were treated just like any other customers.

Every now and then, Xavier pointed out the restaurant window toward the traffic on the busy highway.

"Truck! Truck!" he called out.

"Yep, that's a truck," I answered him.

Soon, my mother was also answering him and asking him to count from one to ten with her, which he dutifully did, with impressive proficiency.

"He knows his numbers," I said proudly. And for the first time, I realized that I hadn't stuttered, which I was guaranteed to do whenever I felt anxious. Even though the trip to South Africa to reconcile with my sisters hadn't gone as well as I'd hoped—a reality that left me with an incurable sadness mixed with weary resignation—I now felt lighter and more hopeful for the future since I had at least reunited my mother with Xavier.

At the same time, I worried about the future. I knew that at some point I would return to South Africa, possibly to live there. But I agonized over whether I could do that in good conscience while my brother languished in an institution in Mississippi. I also worried about leaving my mother as she struggled through chemotherapy in her fight against cancer; doctors had given her a good chance of recovery, and she needed my support. My brother Rasheid had been recently paroled from a prison in Michigan, and he, too, would need my help getting on his feet.

As for me, while my financial situation had somewhat stabilized over the years and I had a decent if uninspiring job (I had yet to break into journalism), I still felt like damaged goods. For one thing, my obsession with South Africa had made me an emotional cripple. I had used books and other literature to fill the void of self-knowledge I carried around during the years before and after I first traveled to the country. The strategies for survival I adopted were taken straight from my childhood and perhaps had never really been abandoned: I used the fact of my South African birth as a crutch, a tool to carve out a space in which I could feel like a special person, untainted by an ancestry prefigured and disfigured by apartheid and Jim Crow.

Of course, this strategy of survival ran smack up against the racial realities of life in America. My relationships with women constantly reminded me of this. Most of my girlfriends had been white because black women saw me as a freak: I read books and followed politics and liked to do "white" stuff, whatever that meant. White women, however, were drawn to me at first out of curiosity, usually sexual, until the objections of family and friends intervened and put me back in my place. I was too white for black women and eventually too black for white women. After a while, I simply withdrew into the illusion of comfort induced by a singular obsession with South Africa.

In terms of my identity, I was equally confused. While I considered myself black—a true African American—I couldn't deny that a part of me feared certain black people. I often thought of an incident that occurred in the late 1980s, while I was delivering pizzas on a bike in downtown Atlanta for Domino's, before I returned to school at the University of Georgia. One afternoon, a gang of at least a hundred black teenagers, fresh from a rap concert at the nearby Omni auditorium, assaulted me. I was thrown from my bike, kicked, punched, and pelted with bottles and rocks until, seemingly out of nowhere, a man pulled up in a car and brandished a gun at the mob. The teenagers quickly dispersed, and I was able to make it back to the store, not seriously hurt but shaken up and forever scarred by the experience. From that moment, I developed a phobia of sorts about being around a lot of black people, especially those trapped in America's permanent underclass; to my mind they were violent, irrational, and just too unpredictable.

Although I was fearful of those I shamefully called "ghetto niggas," I was equally contemptuous of "white racist dogs"—white people bent on asserting their white skin privilege to the detriment of all others. In the final analysis, I had truly become a coloured, trapped in the middle between black and white, occupying the racial interstices, existentially here and nowhere, a prisoner of the twilight I had set out to explore on my journey from Mississippi to South Africa—two geographic poles between which my family's story would always hover.

But I was also disenchanted with America. The country was mired in a senseless, elective war in Iraq. The reelection of George W. Bush had unleashed a torrent of rancor and recrimination into the public discourse, unmatched in its intolerance of dissent and suspicion of "unpatriotic" behavior. In response to the dark specter of terrorism, the government had adopted a siege mentality, and privacy rights were under assault by the Patriot Act and other insidious legislation. Abortion rights, affirmative action, and gay marriage were once again the all too familiar issues in the ongoing culture wars presaging the death of civility in America. And after the most recent presidential campaign, the empowerment of conservative Christians, their touting of "moral values," and the piecemeal erosion of the separation of church and state, I feared that the country was on the verge of becoming a fundamentalist theocracy.

I wasn't sure I could go on living in a country whose culture Morris Berman likened to "a world of endless promotional/commercial bullshit that masks a deep systemic emptiness, the spiritual equivalent of asthma." I was also troubled by an America that, according to historian David K. Shipler, is fixated on racial classification and "finds comfort in the neat matrix of black and white," a country where "breached walls, swirls of coexisting identities cannot satisfy the passion for orderly definition imposed on our racial landscape." Finally, I was alarmed at what I saw as the country's drift toward white Christian nationalism disguised as neoconservatism—the same kind of fanatical patriotism that had gripped South Africa before its formal adoption of apartheid.

Carol Swain, in *The New White Nationalism in America*, warned that a new wave of better-organized, more sophisticated white nationalists were gaining influence in the country's national discourse and affecting policy on affirmative action, immigration, and other race-related issues. In her persuasive calls for discussion of white identity and race in America, Swain cautioned, "I believe that America is more vulnerable than ever to heightened racial and ethnic tension stemming from the aftermath of September 11 and its potential for exploitation by sophisticated white nationalists who may use the events as proof that governmental officials are not doing enough to protect American interests here and abroad." As a result, she concluded, "the future of America has never been more uncertain than it stands today." Swain's appeal rested on the importance of opening dialogue with white nationalists, many of whom fear their impending minority status.

But another book I had come across, *Whitewashing Race,* questioned the efficacy of dialogue at this stage in American race relations and underscored the danger the country faced. "If white Americans make no effort to hear the viewpoints and see the experiences of others, their awareness of their own privileged racial status will disappear," the authors argued. "They can convince themselves that life as they experience it on their side of the color line is simply the objective truth about race. But while this allows them to take their privileged status for granted, it also distorts their understanding. This error poses serious problems for conservatives' analysis of racial inequality."

While I wasn't naïve about South Africa's challenges—the stygian shadow of AIDS, lingering economic and racial inequalities, and appalling crime rates, especially against women—I was more hopeful about that country's future because, unlike the United States, it had at least confronted its demons and tried to exorcise them. And, ironically, coloureds, the personification of South Africa's schizophrenia and insanity on race matters, were poised, yet again, to play a pivotal role in the country's future, as Robert I. Rotberg noted: "The Coloureds—as a political and human problem—are a microcosm of South Africa. In them . . . is encapsulated the peculiar suffering of a beautiful, developed country with its still unrealized potential."

Further, coloureds had the potential of demonstrating to the world that hybridity, racial mixing, was perhaps key to an understanding of the common humanity of all people. Writing twenty-five years ago, historian Al J. Venter advanced this theory: "it is clear to anyone who has peered beneath the welter of double-talk, hyperbole and malaise which surrounds the future of the Coloureds that it is perhaps they who hold the key to the future racial balance in Southern Africa," and they might also be regarded as "the archetype of the future multi-racial society of the world." Perhaps even in America, arguably the last bastion of white supremacy, its citizens might learn to accept and take pride in the country's inevitable mestizo future—or suffer a fate of increasing racial conflict.

On the way back to the Boswell Center, I stopped at a supermarket and bought several boxes of chocolate chip cookies for Xavier. When we pulled up to the gate of the center, a freight train blocked our path.

"Now why on earth would they put a railroad track across here?" my mother puzzled.

Just then the train jolted into motion and then stopped, leaving us parked there near a tree twinkling with Christmas lights. The sky had lost its luster, trapped in that curious state of half-light known as twilight.

There were two kinds of twilight: morning and evening. As we waited for the train to pass, the slab of cobalt and gray-streaked sky above the car could have been either.

"Dave," Xavier cried out, leaning forward from the back seat. "Home! Home!"

It occurred to me that he could have been talking about his home here at the Boswell Center—or his desire to finally go home with his family.

"Yes, Xavier," I assured him, "we're going home," as I waited for the train to jerk into motion and out of sight, before easing the car over the railroad tracks and into the steadily lengthening shadows.

POSTSCRIPT

On January 6, 2005, the state of Mississippi indicted Edgar Ray Killen, an 80-year-old former Klansman and self-described preacher, for the murders of James Chaney, Andrew Goodman, and Michael Schwerner. Killen had long been implicated in the 1964 murders, but he had escaped conviction along with seventeen other men in a 1967 federal civil rights trial. The jury had deadlocked after one of the jurors, the only holdout, declared herself unable to convict a man of the cloth. Killen had spent the intervening years operating a sawmill, raising a family, and promoting his belief in the God-ordained inferiority of blacks. After the indictment, prosecutors spent months assembling a case based mostly on the transcript of the 1967 trial and the testimony of paid FBI informants. Despite their inability to convince seven of the surviving defendants in the 1967 trial to testify in the new trial, prosecutors were able to persuade a multiracial jury to convict Killen on three counts of manslaughter on June 21, forty-one years after the deaths of the three civil rights workers.

On the Sunday before the verdict was announced, I traveled down County Road 632 toward the Longdale community on the outskirts of Philadelphia; a memorial service for the murdered men was being held there, at the site of a community center destroyed in an unsolved 1982 arson. One of the organizers, John Steele, told me that this year's service had been separated from the one at the Mount Zion church, largely because of the controversy surrounding the 2004 memorial. Steele took a few moments to show me and a cluster of other attendees the empty field that he and other people in the community of dirt roads had cleared for the service. A few rows of folding chairs and an impromptu sound system had been set up in the shadow of the burned-out building. While more people arrived, including Ben Chaney and Rita Bender, the widow of Michael Schwerner, I surveyed the scene, comparing it to downtown Philadelphia, which resembled a ghost town, except for the satellite vans of media outlets hunkered down outside the barricaded Neshoba County Courthouse where Edgar Ray Killen was on trial.

As a crowd of about a hundred people gathered in the sweltering Mississippi heat, doing battle with swarms of flies and mosquitoes, John Steele began the program, which featured the testimonies and songs of, among others, civil rights veterans such as Curtis Muhammad and Hollis Watkins, both former members of SNCC and Freedom Summer volunteers. Ben Chaney, flocked by journalists and students, came forward to say, "It's good that the state of Mississippi finally did the right thing, but Killen didn't kill my brother, Mickey, and Andy by himself. There are others that need to be brought to justice." Rita Bender, who had traveled from her home in Seattle with her adult son, echoed Chaney's sentiment. "This trial is only the beginning," she said. "We want to expose all those involved and open up all the other unsolved murders in Mississippi and across the South." The fact that this service was taking place against the backdrop of a trial for the murder of their loved ones, which effectively closed a loophole in justice that had been opened in 1964, imbued it with infinitely more meaning and importance. And this was amplified when the memorial organizers directed the participants to join hands, form a circle, and, in a manner of tribute, shout out the names of martyrs of the civil rights struggle.

"Emmett Till," someone cried. "Viola Liuzzo," a woman called out. And the names just kept flowing: "Mack Charles Parker," "Ben Chester White," "Medgar Evers," "Vernon Dahmer," "Fannie Lou Hamer," and on and on until the names of James Chaney, Michael Schwerner, and Andrew Goodman were sounded. It was a genuinely emotional moment felt by everyone present—black, white, young, and old—and perhaps a glimpse of the justice that had proved so elusive in Mississippi for so many years.

When the jury convicted Killen on three counts of manslaughter on June 21, I thought about something I'd seen at the memorial service in Longdale. Someone had nailed to a withered tree some poster boards displaying the photos of Chaney, Schwerner, and Goodman, along with newspaper clippings of the 1964 search for the men and the subsequent trial of Edgar Ray Killen and other Klansmen. There was also a poem by Goodman, some information on Schwerner's motivation for joining the civil rights movement, and a snippet of conversation that James Chaney had reportedly had with his mother, Fannie Lee Chaney, about his involvement in the civil rights movement:

James: "Mama, I believe I done found an organization that I can be in and do something for myself and somebody else, too."

Fannie: "Ain't you afraid?"

James: "Naw, mama, that's what is the matter now—everybody's scared."

It had taken the town of Philadelphia and its citizens forty-one years to prove James Chaney wrong and throw off the blanket of fear and shame that had stunted its growth and determined its image in the eyes of a world looking for confirmation that, in the words of Martin Luther King Jr., in his March 25, 1965, speech on the steps of the Alabama state capitol, "the arc of the moral universe is long, but it bends toward justice."

On June 23, 2005, Circuit Court Judge Marcus Gordon sentenced Edgar Ray Killen to sixty years in prison for the manslaughter of James Chaney, Michael Schwerner, and Andrew Goodman in 1964.

ACKNOWLEDGMENTS

I could not have written this book without the support and encourage-ment of Professor Sam Freedman, who believed in this project even when I didn't and whom I cherish as a mentor and friend; and my editors, Naomi Schneider and Sierra Filucci, as well as Mary Severance, Mary Renaud, and Alex Dahne, whose enthusiasm propelled me through the production process.

I am also indebted to numerous other individuals and institutions. My college buddies Wendell A. M. Bryant, Adam L. Smith, and Quintin Meminger all put up with me at one time or another during the writing of this book by giving me shelter, sustenance, and friendship when the end of the project seemed far away. My friends Carla Cail and Kevin Miles helped me out of some tight spots during the writing of this book. Quinn and Andy Brisben, unsung heroes of the civil rights and disability rights movements, also shared their lives and their home. Studs Terkel, after an interview in his home in 2001, unwittingly provided further inspiration for me to complete this project. Professor Mokubung Nkomo and Dean Jonathan D. Jansen at the College of Education, University of Pretoria, hosted me during my visit in July 2004. Professor Mohamed Adhikari of the Department of Historical Studies at the University of Cape Town generously shared his time and thoughts on coloured identity and poli-tics. I am also grateful to my home girl, Seipati Mogotsi, whose generos-ity of spirit and love for South Africa have inspired me since the 1980s, when we were both students embroiled in the anti-apartheid struggle in the Atlanta University Center.

The Philippe Wamba Foundation, named after a promising young jour-nalist taken from us too soon, helped to subsidize my travel to South Africa in July 2004. The libraries of Columbia University, the University of Cape Town, the University of Pretoria, the University of the Western Cape, Georgia State University, and Emory University, as well as the

Meridian, Mississippi, Public Library were invaluable resources, and members of their staffs were unfailingly warm and generous in allowing me access to their facilities for researching this book.

Finally, I want to thank all my friends in South Africa for helping me along this journey. *Mayibuye iAfrika!*

NOTES

1. From Down South to Down South

In 1965, thousands of people had been evicted from District Six: Jacqueline A. Kalley et al., *Southern African Political History: A Chronology of Key Political Events from Independence to Mid-1997* (Westport, Conn.: Greenwood Press, 1999), pp. 345–355. See also John Cope, *South Africa* (Westport, Conn.: Praeger, 1965), p. xi.

A month later, U.S. Senator Robert F. Kennedy toured the country: Robert Kinloch Massie provides an excerpt of Kennedy's historic speech at the University of Cape Town: "I come here today because of my deep interest in and affection for a land settled by the Dutch in the seventeenth century, a land taken over by the British and at last independent; a land in which the native inhabitants were at first subdued and relations with whom are a problem to this day; a land which defined itself on a hostile frontier; a land which was once an importer of slaves and now must struggle to wipe out the last traces of the form of bondage. I refer, of course, to the United States of America." (*Loosing the Bonds: The United States and South Africa in the Apartheid Years* [New York: Doubleday, 1997], p. xi.)

"was as though a lid had been lifted off the bubbling cauldron": Douglas Brown, *Against the World: Attitudes of White South Africa* (New York: Doubleday, 1968), p. 222.

Laing was a victim of the 1950 Population Registration Act: For more information on the Sandra Laing case, see William R. Frye, *In Whitest Africa: The Dynamics of Apartheid* (Englewood Cliffs, N.J.: Prentice-Hall, 1968), pp. 24–25; and Marq de Villiers, *White Tribe Dreaming: Apartheid's Bitter Roots as Witnessed by Eight Generations of an Afrikaner Family* (New York: Viking Penguin, 1987), pp. 373–375.

"Mississippi is the nation's neediest state": Sally Belfrage, *Freedom Summer* (New York: Viking, 1965), p. 106.

"Within its borders the closed society of Mississippi": James W. Silver, *Mississippi: The Closed Society* (New York: Harcourt, Brace and World, 1964), p. 151.

When the Klan arrived on the night of January 10, 1966: For more information on the murder of Vernon Dahmer, see Lester A. Sobel, ed., *Civil Rights: 1960–1966* (New York: Facts on File, 1967), vol. 2, p. 210; and L. C. Dorsey, *Freedom Came to Mississippi* (New York: Field Foundation, 1977), p. 25.

A random tug at the bloodied fabric of Mississippi history: Arthur F. Raper, *The Tragedy of Lynching* (Chapel Hill: University of North Carolina Press, 1933), pp. 85–93. See also Philip Drey, *At the Hands of Persons Unknown: The Lynching of Black America* (New York: Random House, 2002), pp. 22–24, 58, 82, 315–317, 359–360.

"Lynching had always been the ultimate form of social control": John Dittmer, *Local People: The Struggle for Civil Rights in Mississippi* (Urbana: University of Illinois Press, 1994), p. 15.

One of the most gruesome examples of brutality: Stephen J. Whitfield, *A Death in the Delta: The Story of Emmett Till* (New York: Free Press, 1988), pp. 15–23. See also Drey, *At the Hands of Persons Unknown,* pp. 422–423.

This outrage was exacerbated when the men described the boy's murder: William Bradford Huie, "The Shocking Story of Approved Killing in Mississippi," *Look,* January 24, 1956, p. 46.

"The advent of the cotton picker": Nicholas Lemann, *The Promised Land: The Great Black Migration and How It Changed America* (New York: Knopf, 1991), p. 6.

"The Southern civil rights movement didn't become truly galvanized at the small-town level until 1961": Ibid., p. 310.

"Nothing in the American experience has prepared the nation": Thurman Sensing, "Radical Extremists Invade Mississippi," *Meridian Star,* July 9, 1964, p. 7.

"The president and his brother were convinced": Dittmer, *Local People,* p. 94.

"The Republic of South Africa is a friend of the U.S.": "Kiwanians Hear Story of South African Republic," *Meridian Star,* January 18, 1962, p. 12.

"From the beginning, railroads and railroad men dominated Meridian's development": Earl Bailey, "Meridian: An Economic Analysis of a Mississippi Community," Bureau of Business Research, University of Mississippi, 1955, p. 2.

"At its zenith a bustling rail junction": Jack Nelson, *Terror in the Night: The Klan's Campaign against the Jews* (New York: Simon and Schuster, 1993), p. 104.

"We can't accommodate you": "Three Negroes Turned Away at Weidmann's," *Meridian Star,* July 9, 1964, home ed., p. 1.

"horrors of integration": "Carry on the Fight," *Meridian Star,* editorial, August 26, 1964, p. 4.

"Mississippi is the decisive battleground for America": Michael Schwerner is quoted in a biographical sketch provided by CORE-Online; see

"Chaney, Goodman, and Schwerner," available online at www.core-online.org/history/chaney.htm.

"The Jew-boy with the beard at Meridian": William Bradford Huie, *Three Lives for Mississippi* (New York: WCC Books, 1965), p. 106.

"must outmaneuver those who would destroy us and our way of life": Ray Bain, "Segregation Is Way to Peace, Johnson Says at Philadelphia," *Meridian Star,* August 13, 1964, home ed., p. 1.

But the Klan had not finished terrorizing the city: Nelson, *Terror in the Night,* pp. 173–187.

2. Into the Breach

"Armed white policemen in neat uniforms": Mark Mathabane, *Kaffir Boy in America: An Encounter with Apartheid* (New York: Scribner's, 1989), p. 11. See also David B. Coplan, "A River Runs through It: The Meaning of the Lesotho–Free State Border," *African Affairs* 100 (January 2001): 81–116.

"I expected momentarily to be dragged off the plane": Mathabane, *Kaffir Boy in America,* p. 12.

"I had arrived earlier that evening at Jan Smuts Airport": Breyten Breytenbach, *The True Confessions of an Albino Terrorist* (London: Faber and Faber, 1984), pp. 15–16.

"In the departure hall, I became intensely aware of several men": Ibid., p. 16.

"Just so one is delivered into the hands of one's enemies": Ibid.

the government's attempts to kill the Rev. Frank Chikane, an ANC member and an outspoken critic of the regime: David Goodman, *Fault Lines: Journeys into the New South Africa* (Berkeley: University of California Press, 1999), pp. 51–52.

the parcel bombs that killed Ruth First, an exiled anti-apartheid activist, as well as Jeanette and Katryn Schoon: See Jacques Pauw, *In the Heart of the Whore: The Story of Apartheid's Death Squads* (Johannesburg: Halfway House/Southern Book Publishers, 1991), pp. 18, 41, 59, 185–186, 205, 256; and Gavin Cawthra, *Policing South Africa: The South African Police and the Transition from Apartheid* (London: Zed Books, 1993), pp. 122–124.

Most countries had lifted sanctions against South Africa: "South Africa: Toward Democracy," U.S. Army Country Studies/Area Handbook series, Federal Research Division, Library of Congress, available online at http://countrystudies.us/south-africa/36.htm. For more information on the events leading up to South Africa's first nonracial election in 1994, see

T. R. H. Davenport, *The Birth of a New South Africa* (Toronto: University of Toronto Press, 1998), pp. 10–18; and Nancy L. Clark and William H. Worger, *South Africa: The Rise and Fall of Apartheid* (New York: Longman, 2004), pp. 103–107.

F. W. de Klerk and Nelson Mandela agreed to a Record of Understanding: For more on the formation, investigations, and findings of the Goldstone Commission, see Peter Gastrow, *Bargaining for Peace: South Africa and the National Peace Accord* (Washington, D.C.: U.S. Institute of Peace Press, 1995), pp. 45–46; Patti Waldmeir, *Anatomy of a Miracle: The End of Apartheid and the Birth of the New South Africa* (New York: Norton, 1997), pp. 183, 186, 248; and David Ottaway, *Chained Together: Mandela, de Klerk, and the Struggle to Remake South Africa* (New York: Times Books, 1993), pp. 236–244.

"the coming of the Indians to Natal": Mabel Palmer, *The History of the Indians in Natal* (Westport, Conn.: Greenwood Press, 1957), p. 4. See also Haraprasad Chattopadhyaya, *Indians in Africa: A Socio-Economic Study* (Calcutta: Bookland, 1970), chap. 1.

Over time, the Indians in Durban became a prosperous community: For more information on the social and political predicament of Indians in mid-nineteenth- and twentieth-century South Africa, see Iqbal Narain, *The Politics of Racialism: A Study of the Indian Minority in South Africa Down to the Gandhi-Smuts Agreement* (Delhi: Shiva Lal Agarwala, 1962), pp. 80–82, 158–181; P. S. Joshi, *The Tyranny of Colour: A Study of the Indian Problem in South Africa* (Port Washington, N.Y.: Kennikat Press, 1973), pp. 41–53, 165–177; and B. Pachai, *The International Aspects of the South African Indian Question, 1860–1971* (Cape Town: C. Struik, 1971), pp. 184–230.

"In the first place, the European community and the government must face the fact": Palmer, *History of the Indians,* p. 182.

"the forces of law and order": *The Forum,* January 29, 1949; cited in Surendra Bhana and Bridglal Pachai, eds., *A Documentary History of Indian South Africans* (Cape Town: David Philip/Hoover Institution Press, 1984), pp. 208–213. See also F. van der Heever, ed., *Report of the Commission of Enquiry into Riots in Durban,* Union Government 36/1949, Cape Town, 1949; and Chattopadhyaya, *Indians in Africa,* pp. 432–433.

By the time the riots ended the next day: Bhana and Pachai, *Documentary History of Indian South Africans,* p. 208.

"Though they are a tiny minority, Indians have not feared their neighbors": South African Institute of Race Relations, "The Indian as a South African," symposium report, 1956; text cited in Bhana and Pachai, *Documentary History of Indian South Africans,* pp. 238–248. For more information on antipathy to Indian immigration to South Africa, see M. K. Gandhi, *Satyagraha in South Africa* (Stanford, Calif.: Academic Reprints, 1954), pp. 30–32.

Camps like this existed in and around all of South Africa's major metropolitan areas: On squatter camps, see Martin J. Murray, *Revolution Deferred: The Painful Birth of Post-Apartheid South Africa* (London: Verso, 1994), pp. 61–63; and F. H. Toase and E. J. Yorke, eds., *The New South Africa: Prospects for Domestic and International Security* (New York: St. Martin's Press, 1998), pp. 26, 79.

"you were expected to express your hurt, anger, or dismay or whatever by one of the many institutionalized rituals available": Peter Lambley, *The Psychology of Apartheid* (Athens: University of Georgia Press, 1980), p. 128. See also Christopher Saunders and Nicholas Southey, *Historical Dictionary of South Africa,* 2nd ed., Historical Dictionaries of Africa, vol. 78 (Lanham, Md.: Scarecrow Press, 2000), p. 21: "It is impossible in a few words to express the extent of the hardships suffered by the victims of apartheid; it was enormously damaging psychologically, and it led to such atrocities as the forced removal of over three million people in an attempt to remove from white South Africa as many blacks as possible without endangering the labor supply." For more on coloured dysfunction, see Anthony Lemon and Owen Williams, *Apartheid: A Geography of Separation* (Farnborough, U.K.: Saxon House, 1976), pp. 127–140.

drinking was a ritual in South Africa: For information on South Africans and alcoholism, see Joseph Lelyveld, *Move Your Shadow: South Africa Black and White* (New York: Times Books, 1985), pp. 264–270; and Paul La Haussé, *Brewers, Beerhalls, and Boycotts: A History of Liquor in South Africa* (Johannesburg: Ravan Press, 1988), pp. 1–5, 29–38.

" 'Non-whites' were banned from the main beaches": Anthony Hazlitt Heard, *The Cape of Storms: A Personal History of the Crisis in South Africa* (Fayetteville: University of Arkansas Press, 1990), p. 46.

"The only amenity the African beach has": E. J. Kahn Jr., *The Separated People: A Look at Contemporary South Africa* (New York: Norton, 1968), p. 31.

Coloureds, by contrast, were maligned: See R. E. Van Der Ross, *Myths and Attitudes: An Inside Look at the Coloured People* (Cape Town: Tafelberg, 1979); Sarah Gertrude Millin, *God's Stepchildren* (Cape Town: A. D. Donker, 1924); Christian Ziervogel, *Who Are the Coloured People?* (Cape Town: African Bookman, 1944); Zoe Wicomb, "Shame and Identity: The Case of the Coloured in South Africa," in *Writing South Africa: Literature, Apartheid, and Democracy, 1970–1995,* ed. Derek Attridge and Rosemary Jolly, pp. 91–107 (Cambridge: Cambridge University Press, 1998); Mohamed Adhikari, "Hope, Fear, Shame, Frustration: Continuity and Change in the Expression of Coloured Identity in White Supremacist South Africa, 1910–1994" (doctoral thesis, Department of Historical Studies, University of Cape Town, 2002).

Keeping an eye on the Dutch activity at the Cape: Leonard Thompson, *A History of South Africa,* 3rd ed. (New Haven: Yale University Press, 2000), pp. 37–87. See also Saunders and Southey, *Historical Dictionary of South Africa; South*

Africa South of the Sahara, 2004, 33rd ed. (London: Europa Publications, 2003); Jiro Tanaka, *The San, Hunter-Gatherers of the Kalahari: A Study in Ecological Anthropology*, trans. David W. Hughes (Tokyo: University of Tokyo Press, 1980), p. 5; and Edward Roux, *Time Longer than Rope: A History of the Black Man's Struggle for Freedom in South Africa* (Madison: University of Wisconsin Press, 1966).

"slight of build and yellow skinned": Elizabeth Marshall Thomas, *The Harmless People* (London: Secker and Warburg, 1959), p. 6.

"the San have lived in southern Africa for at least 11,000 years": Richard B. Lee and Irene DeVore, eds., *Kalahari Hunter-Gatherers: Studies of the !Kung San and Their Neighbors* (Cambridge, Mass.: Harvard University Press, 1976), p. 5. For further discussion of the arrival of African tribes in South Africa, see Gwendolen M. Carter, *The Politics of Inequality* (New York: Octagon Books, 1977), p. 19.

"as a separate genetic development from the black-skinned peoples of Africa": Laurens van der Post and Jane Taylor, *Testament to the Bushmen* (New York: Viking, 1984), p. 11.

"peoples of San origin who have completely lost their language and culture": Lee and Devore, *Kalahari Hunter-Gatherers*, p. 5.

The Khoikhoi/Hottentots also had been in southern Africa for thousands of years: van der Post and Taylor, *Testament to the Bushmen*, p. 11.

"there is evidence of sexual contact": Al J. Venter, *Coloured: A Profile of Two Million South Africans* (Cape Town: Human and Rousseau, 1974). See also F. P. Spooner, *South African Predicament* (New York: Praeger, 1961), pp. 104–105.

"During the process of the displacement and destruction of the indigenous societies": Monica Wilson and Leonard Thompson, eds., *The Oxford History of South Africa*, vol. 1 (New York: Oxford University Press, 1969), p. 184.

"After the abolition of slavery of 1834": George Golding and Franklin Pybus Joshua, "The Coloured Community," in *The South African Way of Life: Values and Ideals for a Multi-Racial Society*, ed. G. H. Calpin, South Africa Institute of Race Relations (New York: Columbia University Press, 1953), p. 75.

"At the turn of the century": Ian Goldin, *Making Race: The Politics and Economics of Coloured Identity in South Africa* (New York: Longman, 1987), p. 234.

"when [the Orange Free State and the Transvaal] were granted responsible government": R. H. Du Pre, *Strangers in Their Own Country: A Political History of the "Coloured" People of South Africa, 1652–1992: An Introduction*, History for the Layman series, vol. 2 (Johannesburg: Skotaville, 1992), p. 51. See also Gavin Lewis, *Between the Wire and the Wall: A History of South African "Coloured" Politics* (Cape Town: David Philip, 1987).

the founding of the South African Native National Congress, the forerunner of the ANC: For additional information on the history of the South African Native National Congress and the ANC, see Frank Welsh, *South Africa: A Narrative History* (New York: Kodansha, 1999), pp. 356, 368; and T. R. H.

Davenport, *South Africa: A Modern History*, 4th ed. (London: Macmillan, 1991), pp. 226, 236–238.

"The reconstitution of Coloured identity": Goldin, *Making Race*, p. 29. See also John Hatch, *The Dilemma of South Africa* (London: Dennis Dobson, 1952), p. 216.

The most obvious manifestation of the coloureds' new preoccupation with identity was political, legitimized by the activism of the African Political Organization: For further discussion of coloureds and Dr. A. Abdurahman, founder of the APO, see William Beinart, *Twentieth-Century South Africa*, 2nd ed. (Cape Town: Oxford University Press, 2001), p. 90.

"aimed to extend Coloured education and wealth": Goldin, *Making Race*, p. 33.

"Living as they did": S. P. Cilliers, *The Coloureds of South Africa* (Cape Town: Banier, 1963), p. 27.

"the growing preference shown towards Coloured men and women": Goldin, *Making Race*, p. 36.

"the Coloreds are regarded by the Bantu as socially apart": Eugene P. Dvorin, *Racial Separation in South Africa: An Analysis of Apartheid Theory* (Chicago: University of Chicago Press, 1952), pp. 61–62. For further descriptions of coloureds, see Graham Leach, *South Africa: No Easy Path to Peace* (London: Routledge and Kegan Paul, 1986), p. 12.

"The NP had never really intended elevating Coloureds": Du Pre, *Strangers in Their Own Country*, p. 64. See also Pierre Hugo, *Quislings or Realists?* (Johannesburg: Ravan Press, 2001).

"Hertzog and the National Party between 1924 and 1934": Du Pre, *Strangers in Their Own Country*, p. 75. For more on Afrikaner efforts to co-opt coloureds, see C. F. J. Muller, ed., *Five Hundred Years: A History of South Africa* (Pretoria: Academica, 1969); and D. V. Cowen, *The Foundations of Freedom: With Special Reference to Southern Africa* (Cape Town: Oxford University Press, 1961), pp. 6–7.

the leaders of the opposition United Party, mainly the Afrikaner general Jan Christian Smuts, promised to safeguard the coloured franchise: Smuts delivered a speech in London in 1917 concerning the color problem in South Africa; for an excerpt, see J. C. Smuts, *Jan Christian Smuts: A Biography* (New York: Morrow, 1952), pp. 181–182.

Many had adopted notions heralding a *volksgroep*: For further discussion of the influence of German National Socialism on Afrikaner thought, see Leonard Thompson, *The Political Mythology of Apartheid* (New Haven: Yale University Press, 1985), pp. 42–43. Thompson cites J. Albert Coetzee: "The history of South Africa is really the history of the origin of a new nation—of how, from different European nations, groups, and individuals it was separated, cut off, differentiated and specialized to form a new volksgroep, with its own calling and destiny, with its own tradition, with its own soul and with its own body" ("Republikanisme in die Kaapkolonie," in *Ons Republiek,* ed. J. Albert Coetzee, P. Meyer, and N. Diederichs [Bloemfontein, 1941], p. 7). See also Saul Debow, *Scientific Racism in Modern South Africa* (Cambridge: Cambridge University Press, 1995), pp. 13–15, 246–283; and Brian Bunting, *The Rise of the South African Reich* (Harmondsworth, U.K.: Penguin Africa Library, 1964; rev. 1969), available online at www.anc.org.za/books/reich.html, sec. 3, "The Broederbond," and sec. 4, "Followers of Hitler."

the Broederbond, the super-secretive Afrikaner self-help organization: For information on the Broederbond, its ties to Nazi Germany, and its political power, see Charles Bloomberg, *Christian-Nationalism and the Rise of the Afrikaner Broederbond in South Africa, 1918-1948* (Bloomington: Indiana University Press, 1989), pp. 2–4, 150–155; Bunting, *Rise of the South African Reich,* www.anc.org.za/books/reich.html, sec. 3, "The Broederbond"; and Ivor Wilkins and Hans Strydom, *The Broederbond* (New York: Paddington Press, 1978), pp. 108–114.

"the advent of the National Party Government in 1948": Alex La Guma, "Apartheid and the Coloured People of South Africa," available online at www.anc.org.za/ancdocs/history/misc/laguma12.html;.originally published in United Nations Centre against Apartheid, Department of Political and Security Council Affairs, *Notes and Documents,* no. 18/72, September 1972.

Once the National Party assumed power: For additional information on the 1948 election and the mobilization of Afrikaner voters, see Thompson, *A History of South Africa,* pp. 184–186; Welsh, *South Africa,* pp. 400–431; and T. R. H. Davenport and Christopher Saunders, *South Africa: A Modern History,* 5th ed. (New York: Macmillan, 2000), pp. 369–374, 378–398.

"Apartheid, then, was devised as a means of ensuring, forever, that non-Whites would never be able to become equal with Whites": Du Pre, *Strangers in Their Own Country,* p. 75.

"it would be difficult to find a line of demarcation": Christian Ziervogel, *Brown South Africa* (Cape Town: Maskew Miller, 1938), p. 21. See also Z. J. de Beer, *Multi-Racial South Africa: The Reconciliation of Forces* (London: Oxford University Press, 1961), p. 20: "To draw the line between Coloured people and whites is impossible, and the efforts of government officials to do so would be ridiculous if their efforts were not so tragic."

Something had to be done, then, to erase the noxious coloured presence from South African society: For more on the difficulties coloureds posed to the white apartheid government, see Theodor Hanf, Heribert Weiland, Gerda Vierdag, et al., *South Africa: The Prospects of Peaceful Change: An Empirical Enquiry into the Possibility of Democratic Regulation* (Bloomington: Indiana University Press, 1981), p. 147, in which an unidentified National Party MP is quoted in a 1974 survey on the Coloured question: "Of course they are a problem. It is true that they don't have their own language and religion. But it is true above all that until now they have not wanted a separate identity. They want to be white. I'm sorry; we can give them money and buildings and institutions, but not an identity."

"apartheid at its most inhuman": Douglas Brown, *Against the World: Attitudes of White South Africa* (New York: Doubleday, 1968), p. 222.

"The African living in his tribal culture and environment": Sheila Patterson, *Colour and Culture in South Africa: A Study of the Status of the Cape Coloured People within the Social Structure of the Union of South Africa* (1953; repr. New York: Kraus Reprint, 1969), p. 177.

"the Afrikaner was an immovable presence": Lambley, *Psychology of Apartheid*, p. 128.

"From time to time, some Coloureds and Africans found common cause politically": Robert R. Edgar, ed., *An African American in South Africa: The Travel Notes of Ralph J. Bunche: 28 September 1937–1 January 1938* (Athens: Ohio University Press, 1992), p. 29.

Coloureds, and some blacks and Indians, attempted to escape into the white population: See Paul Giniewski, *The Two Faces of Apartheid* (Chicago: Regnery, 1965), p. 270, for a definition of coloureds: "The definition of 'Coloured,' according to the Census Act of 1950, indicates the difficulty of stating positively what these people are. It is completely negative. A Coloured man is a person who is not by his appearance a White man, and who is not, in fact, generally accepted as belonging to one of the aboriginal races or tribes of Africa."

Increasingly, coloureds were thought to be under the control of whites: For more information on coloureds and passing, see Leo Marquard, *The People and Politics of South Africa,* 2nd ed.(Cape Town: Oxford University Press, 1960), pp. 65–74. See John Western, *Outcast Cape Town* (Minneapolis: University of Minnesota Press, 1981), pp. 256–257, on the public perception of coloureds.

"The struggles against the destruction of the franchise": La Guma, "Apartheid and the Coloured People of South Africa."

"In general, three distinct social classes": Cilliers, *The Coloureds of South Africa,* p. 27. See also V. A. (Vernie A.) February, *Mind Your Color: The "Coloured" Stereotype in South African Literature* (London: Kegan Paul International, 1991).

"The African societies of Southern Africa experienced intensified pressures after 1870": Thompson, *A History of South Africa,* pp. 122, 124–132. For an excellent account of the Battle of Isandhlwana, see John Laband and Paul Thompson, *The Illustrated Guide to the Anglo-Zulu War* (Pietermaritzburg: University of Natal Press, 2000), pp. 99–108.

"Jo'burg, Johannesburg, Listen when I tell you": Mongane Wally Serote, "City Johannesburg," in *Poets to the People: South African Freedom Poems,* ed. B. Feinberg (London: Allen and Unwin, 1974), pp. 68–69.

"an urban island in the midst of nowhere": Martin Flavin, *Black and White: From the Cape to the Congo* (New York: Harper, 1950), p. 1. For further description of late nineteenth-century Johannesburg, see Geoffrey Wheatcroft, *The Randlords* (New York: Atheneum, 1986), pp. 1–6; Naomi Musiker and Reuben Musiker, *Historical Dictionary of Greater Johannesburg*, Historical Dictionaries of the Cities of the World, vol. 7 (Lanham, Md.: Scarecrow Press, 1999).

"The wealth of South Africa is gold": Flavin, *Black and White*, p. 4.

The pavements were teeming with vendors: See Musiker and Musiker, *Historical Dictionary of Greater Johannesburg*, p. 150: "Since the 1991 amendment to the Business Act, which removed regulation in all but the food industry, there has been a tremendous increase in the number of informal traders or hawkers. This has led to the congestion of city sidewalks, a lack of storage facilities and a certain degree of environmental degradation."

"The many voices of the new South Africa": Anne Fuchs, *Playing the Market: The Market Theatre, Johannesburg, 1976–1986* (New York: Harwood, 1990), p. 123.

On February 5, 1982, Aggett was found hanging in his cell: For a full examination of the Neil Aggett case, see Shireen Motala, with Frances Potter, "Behind Closed Doors: A Study of Deaths in Detention in South Africa between August 1963 and 1984 and of Further Deaths between June 1984 and September 1985," South African Institute of Race Relations, Johannesburg, 1987, pp. 68–72; and Don Foster, with Dennis Davis and Diane Sandler, *Detention and Torture in South Africa: Psychological, Legal, and Historical Studies* (New York: St. Martin's Press, 1987), pp. 32–33.

Among others killed at John Vorster Square: For more on police misconduct and complicity in the deaths of anti-apartheid activists, see Pauw, *In the Heart of the Whore;* Human Rights Watch, "The Killings in South Africa: The Role of the Security Forces and the Response of the State," Human Rights Watch Report, 1991, available online at http://hrw.org/reports/1991/southafrica1/index.htm; Patrick Duncan, *South Africa's Rule of Violence* (London, Metheun, 1964); and Motala and Potter, "Behind Closed Doors."

And it made me think of Mack Charles Parker: For an account of the lynching of Mack Charles Parker, see Taylor Branch, *Parting the Waters: America in the King Years, 1954–1963* (New York: Simon and Schuster, 1988), pp. 257–258; Ralph McGill, *No Place to Hide: The South and Human Rights* (Macon: Mercer University Press, 1984), vol. 1, pp. 274–275; and Sondra Kathryn Wilson, ed., *In Search of Democracy: The NAACP Writings of James Weldon Johnson, Walter White, and Roy Wilkins, 1920–1977* (New York: Oxford University Press, 1999), pp. 274–275.

"No clearer examples of the advantages to the ruling white clique": Wilson, *In Search of Democracy*, p. 394.

Though the neighborhood had been classified as a white area: Alan Morris, *Bleakness and Light: Inner-City Transition in Hillbrow, Johannesburg* (Johannesburg: Witwatersrand University Press, 1999), p. 3.

the population of Hillbrow: Alan Morris's *Bleakness and Light* offers an insightful history and analysis of Hillbrow. For an account of the crumbling of apartheid and the effects on Hillbrow and other South African urban areas, see S. M. Parnell and G. H. Pirie, "Johannesburg," in *Homes Apart: South Africa's Segregated Cities,* ed. Anthony Lemon (Bloomington: Indiana University Press, 1991), pp. 138–145.

an estimated 1 percent of the population was already infected with the virus at this point. . . . "the HIV epidemic will cause the sickness and death of many young adults": Peter Doyle, "The Impact of AIDS on the South African Population," in *AIDS in South Africa: The Demographic and Economic Implications,* Centre for Health Policy Paper no. 23, Department of Community Health, University of the Witwatersrand Medical School, Johannesburg, 1991, p. 25.

Later, as South Africa entered the twenty-first century, researchers estimated the number of AIDS orphans: Jeffrey D. Lewis, "Assessing the Demographic and Economic Impact of HIV/AIDS," in *AIDS and South Africa: The Social Expression of a Pandemic,* ed. Kyle D. Kauffman and David L. Lindauer (New York: Palgrave Macmillan, 2004), p. 99. See also R. Dorrington, D. Bourne, D. Bradshaw, R. Laubscher, and I. M. Timaeus, "The Impact of HIV/AIDS on Adult Mortality in South Africa," Technical Report, Burden of Disease Research Unit, Medical Research Council, Johannesburg, September 2001.

Some researchers at the time estimated that thousands of street children: Jill Swart, *Malunde: The Street Children of Hillbrow* (Johannesburg: Witwatersrand University Press, 1990), p. 42.

British South Africans, I knew, had held a conflicted position in South Africa: See Lindsay Michie Eades, *The End of Apartheid in South Africa* (Westport, Conn.: Greenwood Press, 1999), p. 37; and Paul B. Rich, *Hope and Despair: English-Speaking Intellectuals and South African Politics, 1896–1976* (London: British Academic Press, 1993).

"to convey the image that it is non-racial": "The New-Look NP Goes for Broke," *Weekly Mail,* February 5–11, 1993, p. 30.

"We are unhappy about both the national and regional leadership's attitude": Paul Stober, "Coloureds May Break from ANC," *Weekly Mail,* February 12–18, 1993, p. 7.

"Shorn of all the double-speak": Farouk Chothia, "Students Stung by the 'Cruel' System of Affirmative Action," *Weekly Mail,* Review/Education, vol. 2, no. 1, February 1993, p. 1.

"Until they learn to smile and shed their bias toward us": Ray Nxumalo, "Sabta Fat Cats Should Take the Blame," *Weekly Mail,* February 5–11, 1993, p. 19.

"probably one of the most dramatic developments since the release of Nelson Mandela": Phillip Van Niekerk, "White Politics, Black Humour," *Weekly Mail,* February 5–11, 1993, p. 3.

"Truth is not a collection of facts which can be narrated": André Brink, *Looking on Darkness* (New York: Morrow, 1974), p. 34.

"Her rich voice came back to me like a bell tolling in the dark": Ibid., p. 109.

"I had thought I could escape": Ibid., pp. 189–190.

"And yet, I look upon the same darkness": Ibid., p. 392.

3. Truth and Reconciliation

the murder of ANC leader Chris Hani, who had been gunned down in his driveway: Clive Derby-Lewis, a Conservative Party member of parliament with ties to the far-right Afrikaner Weerstandbewiging (AWB), recruited a radical Polish immigrant, Janus Walusz, for the assassination. Ironically, Walusz was captured when one of Hani's white neighbors, who had witnessed the killing, reported his car's license plate number to the police. Derby-Lewis and Walusz were sentenced to death for Hani's murder. They later appealed to the Truth and Reconciliation Commission for clemency on the grounds that their crime had been politically motivated, but their appeal was denied in April 1999. Because the Constitutional Court had ruled the death penalty unconstitutional in mid-1995, their sentences were commuted to life in prison without parole. For more on the murder of Chris Hani, see Patti Waldmeir, *Anatomy of a Miracle: The End of Apartheid and the Birth of the New South Africa* (New York: Norton, 1997), pp. 223–224; T. R. H. Davenport and Christopher Saunders, *South Africa: A Modern History,* 5th ed. (New York: Macmillan, 2000), pp. 565–566; and Frank Welsh, *South Africa: A Narrative History* (New York: Kodansha, 1999), p. 508.

And a high-level delegation of Western diplomats: For more on events during the runup to the election, see Waldmeir, *Anatomy of a Miracle,* pp. 249–250; and Anthony Sampson, *Mandela: The Authorized Biography* (New York: Knopf, 1999), pp. 479–482.

After conducting an abortive bombing campaign, the white right wing seemed placated: For additional discussion of Afrikaner political goals, see Sampson, *Mandela,* pp. 473–477.

where the American student Amy Biehl had been killed: For further information on Biehl's killing, see *Truth and Reconciliation Commission, South Africa: Final Report* (Cape Town: Juta, 1998), vol. 7, p. 28.

"formed a community which attempted to discover what their role in

South Africa was": Robert Ross, *Adam Kok's Griquas: A Study in the Development of Stratification in South Africa* (Cambridge: Cambridge University Press, 1976), p. 1.

"All felt bitter toward the Griquas": Ibid., p. 31.

"Consistently, the British supported the colonists": Ibid., p. 48.

"Where there had been a certain degree of fluidity": Ibid., p. 135.

"it could be argued that the Griquas' rejection of the Africans": Ibid.

The remaining Griquas, dispossessed of their land, drifted: *Reader's Digest Illustrated History of South Africa: The Real Story* (Pleasantville, N.Y.: Reader's Digest Association, 1989), p. 190.

Ironically, a woman named Sarah Baartman: Concerning the Sarah Baartman case, see Janell Hobson, "Beauty, Difference, and the Hottentot Venus: Black Feminist Revisions in Performance and Aesthetics, 1810 to the Present" (PhD diss., Institute for Women's Studies, Emory University, 2001), pp. 22–27; and Janell Hobson, *Venus in the Dark: Blackness and Beauty in Popular Culture* (New York: Routledge, 2005), pp. 1–7, 57–86. See also T. Denean Sharpley-Whiting, *Black Venus: Sexualized Savages, Primal Fears, and Primitive Narratives in French* (Durham, N.C.: Duke University Press, 1999), pp. 17–31.

"the Quena are the ancestors of a lot of people in this country": "Bring Back the Hottentot Venus," *Mail & Guardian,* June 15, 1995, available online at History of Race in Science, http://web.mit.edu/racescience/in_media/baartman/baartman_m&g_june95.htm.

Even the ANC government, which argued with the Griquas: Ayesha Ismail, "Griquas, ANC Clash over Saartjie's Remains," *Sunday Times* (Cape Town), August 16, 1998, available online at www.suntimes.co.za/1998/08/16/news/cape/nct11.htm.

"the first indigenous people of our country": Deputy President Jacob Zuma, address to the opening ceremony of the National Khoisan Consultative Conference, March 29, 2001, Cape Town, available online at www.info.gov.za/speeches/2001/010330145p1006.htm. For further discussion of Coloureds, descendants of San and Khoi, as original inhabitants of South Africa, see John Middleton, ed., *Encyclopedia of Africa South of the Sahara,* vol. 4 (New York: Scribner's, 1997), pp. 140–143.

"I began to fantasize that the Africa I traveled through was often like a parallel universe": Paul Theroux, *Dark Star Safari: Overland from Cairo to Cape Town* (Boston: Mariner Books, 2003), p. 273.

"One of the consequences of the decades of white government paranoia": Ibid., pp. 437–438.

"Workers still rise before dawn and pile into minibus taxis": F. W. de Klerk, *The Last Trek—A New Beginning: The Autobiography* (New York: St. Martin's Press, 1998), p. 394.

"I'm fine, as I have always been": Nalisha Kalideen, "Winnie Walks Free Again," *The Mercury* (Durban), July 6, 2004, p. 1.

"absentee landlordism": Makhudu Sefara and Moshoeshoe Monare, "ANC Aims to Limit Foreign Landlords," *The Mercury* (Durban), July 6, 2004, p. 3.

"The facts are as they were stated in the president's state-of-the-nation address": Sheena Adams, "Health Department Retracts Statement over ARV Roll-Out Date," *The Mercury* (Durban), July 6, 2004, p. 4.

"where South Africa faces the full fury of the AIDS pandemic": Richard Morin, "A Wave of Death, Surging Higher," *Washington Post,* April 1, 2004, p. A01.

Some analysts predicted that AIDS would account for 5 million deaths by 2011: Ibid.; *Washington Post*/Kaiser Family Foundation/Harvard University Survey Project, "Survey of South Africans at Ten Years of Democracy," March 2004, available online at www.kff.org/kaiserpolls/upload/Survey-of-South-Africans-at-Ten-Years-of-Democracy-Summary-and-Chartpack.pdf.

Both of these highly educated people relied on the pseudoscience of a couple of researchers from the University of California at Berkeley: For information about Mbeki's position and the researchers on whom he relied, see Bernice Ng, "UC Berkeley Professor Doubts Cause of AIDS," *Daily Californian* Online, July 14, 2000, available online at www.dailycal.org/article.php?id=2796; Jeff Stryker, "California AIDS Dissidents on Global Stage," *California Healthline,* May 15, 2000, California Healthcare Foundation, available online at http://californiahealthline.org/index.cfm?Action=dspItem& ItemID=102336&ClassCD=CL; "SA Appoints AIDS Dissidents," *BBC News,* May 5, 2000, available online at http://news.bbc.co.uk/1/hi/world/africa/737406.stm; Peter Duesberg, *Inventing the AIDS Virus* (Washington, D.C.: Regnery, 1996); and Tom Lodge, *Politics in South Africa: From Mandela to Mbeki* (Bloomington: Indiana University Press, 2003), pp. 255–264.

Some observers had even gone so far as to question whether South Africa was really a democracy: Lodge notes: "One very demanding definition of democratic consolidation is that democracies only become mature when a ruling party in power at the democracy's inception is subsequently defeated in an election and allows the winners to take office. Even if one allows that democracies can mature without such an alteration in office, in the South African case the objection might be that the formal institution of liberal democracy does not mean very much in a situation in which representative politics is overwhelmed by one large party and in which the prospect of alternation of parties in government is rather remote" (*Politics in South Africa,* p. 154). See also Robert B. Mattes, "South Africa: Democracy without the People?" *Journal of Democracy* 13, no. 1 (January 2002): 22–36; and Kogila Moodley and Heribert Adam, "Race and Nation in Post-Apartheid South Africa," *Current Sociology* 48, no. 3 (July 2000): 51–69.

"Apart from the ideological hostility to any alternation in government": James Myburgh, "Ideological Battle over Meaning of Democracy," *Focus* 34 (June 2004), available online at www.hsf.org.za/focus34/focus34myburgh.html.

"The new African world which the African Renaissance seeks to build": Deputy President Thabo Mbeki, statement at the African Renaissance Conference, Johannesburg, September 28, 1998, available online at www.anc .org.za/ancdocs/history/mbeki/1998/tm0928.htm.

Some critics accused Mbeki and others in the ANC of race-baiting: See Tony Leon, "ANC Has Tactics of Bush's Republicans," *Mail & Guardian* Online, November 23, 2004, available online at www.mg.co.za/articledirect .aspx?articleid=142576&area=linsight%2finsightcomment; Marianne Merten, "Playing the Race Card in Battle for Western Cape," *Mail & Guardian* Online, October 31, 2003, available online at www.mg.co.za/articledirect.aspx?arti cleid=32412&area=%2finsight%2finsight_national%2f; "DA Hits Out at Minister's 'Racist Tantrum,'" *Mail & Guardian* Online, May 20, 2005, available online at www.mg.co.za/articlePage.aspx?articleid=241211&area=/breaking _news/breaking.

Among those particularly critical of the government's role in this racial debate was Patricia de Lille: See "De Lille Plays the Race Card," *Mail & Guardian* Online, July 15, 2003, available online at www.mg.co.za/articledirect.aspx?arti cleid=24557&area=%2fbreaking_news%2fbreaking_news_national%2f.

a small right-wing group of whites known as the Boeremag had even attempted to stage a coup: Members of the Boeremag (which means "farmers' force" in Afrikaans) went on trial in 2003 for plotting to overthrow the government and assassinate former president Nelson Mandela. The authorities later revealed the utter incompetence of the coup plotters and judged their campaign to be a farce, albeit a dangerous one. As of the summer of 2005, the trial of the twenty-two Boeremag members, the first prosecution for treason in the new South Africa, continued in Pretoria. Since the government and defense lawyers persisted in pursuing dilatory and technical legal motions, observers expected the case to go on indefinitely. For additional information on the case and the trial, see "Boeremag Trial May Be Delayed Again," *Mail & Guardian* Online, October 18, 2004, available online at www.mg.co.za/articlepage.aspx?articleid=139780&area=/breaking_news/break ing_news__national/; and " 'Responsible' Boeremag Trialists Apply for Bail," *Mail & Guardian* Online, January 12, 2005, available online at www.mg.co.za/articlepage.aspx?articleid=195131&area=/breaking_news/break ing_news__national/.

"All too easily, the idea could become debased": Lodge, *Politics in South Africa,* p. 240.

Parliament had just passed the Firearms Control Act: See "South Africa

Begins Gun Amnesty," *BBC News* World Edition, January 1, 2005, available online at http://news.bbc.co.uk/2/hi/africa/4139961.stm; "S. Africa Moves to Curb Gun Crime," *BBC News* World Edition, July 1, 2004, available online at http://news.bbc.co.uk/2/hi/africa/3857163.stm; "Murder Rates Fall in South Africa," *BBC News* World Edition, September 21, 2004, available online at http://news.bbc.co.uk/2/hi/africa/3676112.stm; and "South Africa Leads the Hand Gun Ownership Figures," SABC News, October 26, 2004, available online at www.sabcnews.com/south_africa/crime1justice/0,2172,90724,00.html.

"apartheid's legacy of low economic growth" Adrian Guelke, *South Africa in Transition: The Misunderstood Miracle* (London: I. B. Tauris, 1999), p. 199.

Corruption posed an even greater challenge to the new South Africa: See Mzilikazi Wa Afrika, "Now Speaker Stands Accused in Travel Scam," *Johannesburg Sunday Times,* August 29, 2004, available online at www.sundaytimes.co.za/Articles/TarkArticle.aspx?ID:1213626; Mzilikazi Wa Afrika, "Travelgate: 31 New Names," *Johannesburg Sunday Times,* September 19, 2004, available online at www.sundaytimes.co.za/Articles/TarkArticle.aspx?ID=1253230; and Lodge, *Politics in South Africa,* pp. 146–150.

"The Coloured people are so diverse in origin": George Golding and Franklin Pybus Joshua, "The Coloured Community," in *The South African Way of Life: Values and Ideals of a Multi-Racial Society,* ed. G. H. Calpin, South African Institute of Race Relations (New York: Columbia University Press, 1953), p. 76.

"any society able to produce writers of the stature of Alex La Guma or Peter Abrahams": Al J. Venter, *Coloured: A Profile of Two Million South Africans* (Cape Town: Human and Rousseau, 1974).

Beginning with the plethora of names used to identify coloureds: R. E. Van Der Ross, *Myths and Attitudes: An Inside Look at the Coloured People* (Cape Town: Tafelberg, 1979), p. 8.

"Coloured people have no special, peculiar, typical culture": Ibid., p. 35.

Epilogue

Nevertheless, two issues contributed to racial disquiet: See Julie Goodman and Patrice Sawyer, "Barbour's Use of State Flag Could Win or Lose Votes," *Jackson Clarion-Ledger,* October 1, 2003, available online at www.clarionledger.com/news/0310/01/m03.html; John Fuquay, "Miss. Flag Issue May Resurface in Session," *Jackson Clarion-Ledger,* November 26, 2004, available online at www.clarionledger.com/apps/pbcs.dll/article?AID=/20041126/NEWS01/411260326; and Donna Ladd, "Haley's Choice," *Jackson Free Press,*

October 29, 2003, available online at www.jacksonfreepress.com/comments.php?id=1885_0_9_0_C.

"Pickering has total disregard for what's truly best for America": Ayana Taylor, "Jim Giles Wants a 'White Nation,'" *Jackson Free Press*, October 14, 2004, available online at www.jacksonfreepress.com/comments.php?id=4236_0_9_0_C.

"The jobless rate in some Mississippi small towns has inched up over the years": Nell Luter Floyd, "Can the State's Small Towns Be Saved? Business Leaders Plot Turnaround," *Jackson Clarion-Ledger*, November 14, 2004, p. 1A.

The state had scored some successes in the tourism and gaming industries: Lisa T. Wilson, "Industry Betting on a Prosperous Future," *Jackson Clarion-Ledger*, February 28, 2004, available online at http://64.233.187.104/search?q=cache:q2_ux8WSqrcJ:www.clarionledger.com/news/special/profilems2004/zt001.html+industry+betting+on+a+prosperous+future+jackson+clarion+ledger&hl=en.

The poverty rate had dropped: See U.S. Census Bureau, *Current Population Survey* (August 2004), Economic Research Service, U.S. Department of Agriculture, State Fact Sheets: Mississippi, available online at www.ers.usda.gov/statefacts/MS.htm.

"long tradition of keeping the poor and the unfortunate": Bob Herbert, "Punishing the Poor," *New York Times,* June 11, 2004, p. 27A.

"the best route to quality health care": Mississippi Governor's Office, "Detailed Summary of Medicaid Reform Bill," available online at www.governorbarbour.com/Summary.htm.

"the 65,000 seniors and disabled individuals who will lose their Medicaid eligibility": Herbert, "Punishing the Poor."

On the education front, in 2003 the state had been ranked forty-eighth: Kathleen O'Leary Morgan and Scott Morgan, eds., *State Statistical Trends: Education* (Lawrence, Kan.: Morgan Quitno Press, 2004), available online at www.morganquitno.com/edpri05.htm. For discussion of these rankings, see "Tennessee Slips in Education Rankings," *Nashville Business Journal,* October 10, 2003, available online at www.bizjournals.com/nashville/stories/2003/10/06/daily52.html.

a major battleground in the fight against AIDS: Jacob Levenson, *The Secret Epidemic: The Story of AIDS and Black America* (New York: Pantheon Books, 2004), pp. 19–22.

"Blacks have steadily gained political power": Emily Yellin, "A Changing South Revisits Its Unsolved Racial Killings," *New York Times,* November 8, 1999, p. 1.

"I could barely believe the destruction to these frail young bones": Anthony Walton, *Mississippi: An American Journey* (New York: Knopf, 1996), p. 190.

"seeking justice and reconciliation for human rights violations": "Southern Truth and Reconciliation: The Road to Justice for Human Rights Violations," available online at www.southerntruth.org.

"a world of endless promotional/commercial bullshit": Morris Berman, *The Twilight of American Culture* (New York: Norton, 2000), p. 54.

"finds comfort in the neat matrix of black and white": David K. Shipler, *A Country of Strangers: Blacks and Whites in America* (New York: Knopf, 1997), p. 112.

"I believe that America is more vulnerable than ever": Carol Swain, *The New White Nationalism in America: Its Challenge to Integration* (Cambridge: Cambridge University Press, 2002), p. 460.

"If white Americans make no effort to hear the viewpoints": Michael K. Brown et al., *Whitewashing Race: The Myth of a Color-Blind Society* (Berkeley: University of California Press, 2003), p. 35.

While I wasn't naïve about South Africa's challenges: For more on the prospects for South Africa, see Guy Arnold. *The New South Africa* (New York: St. Martin's Press, 2000), pp. 2–3.

"The Coloureds—as a political and human problem—are a microcosm of South Africa": Robert I. Rotberg, *Suffer the Future: Policy Choices in Southern Africa* (Washington, D.C.: Howard University Press, 1980), pp. 9–10.

"it is clear to anyone who has peered beneath the welter of double-talk, hyperbole, and malaise": Al J. Venter, *Coloured: A Profile of Two Million South Africans* (Cape Town: Human and Rousseau, 1974).

Perhaps even in America, arguably the last bastion of white supremacy: Gregory Rodriguez, "Mongrel America," *Atlantic Monthly,* January/February 2003, pp. 95–97.

BIBLIOGRAPHY

Abel, Richard L. *Politics by Other Means: Law in the Struggle against Apartheid, 1980–1994.* London: Routledge, 1995.

Adams, Sheena. "Health Department Retracts Statement over ARV Roll-Out Date." *The Mercury* (Durban), July 6, 2004, p. 4.

Adhikari, Mohamed. "Hope, Fear, Shame, Frustration: Continuity and Change in the Expression of Coloured Identity in White Supremacist South Africa, 1910–1994." Doctoral thesis, Department of Historical Studies, University of Cape Town, 2002.

Afrika, Mzilikazi Wa. "Now Speaker Stands Accused in Travel Scam." *Johannesburg Sunday Times,* August 29, 2004. Available online at www.sundaytimes.co.za/Articles/TarkArticle.aspx?ID:1213626.

———. "Travelgate: 31 New Names." *Johannesburg Sunday Times,* September 19, 2004. Available online at www.sundaytimes.co.za/Articles/TarkArticle.aspx?ID=1253230.

Arnold, Guy. *The New South Africa.* New York: St. Martin's Press, 2000.

Bailey, Earl. "Meridian: An Economic Analysis of a Mississippi Community." Bureau of Business Research, University of Mississippi, 1955.

Bain, Ray. "Segregation Is Way to Peace, Johnson Says at Philadelphia." *Meridian Star,* August 13, 1964, home ed., p. 1.

Beinart, William. *Twentieth-Century South Africa.* 2nd ed. Cape Town: Oxford University Press, 2001.

Belfrage, Sally. *Freedom Summer.* New York: Viking, 1965.

Benjamin, Robert C. O. *Southern Outrages: A Statistical Record of Lawless Doings.* Pamphlet. Los Angeles [?], 1894.

Berman, Morris. *The Twilight of American Culture.* New York: Norton, 2000.

Bhana, Surendra, and Bridglal Pachai, eds. *A Documentary History of Indian South Africans.* Cape Town: David Philip/Hoover Institution Press, 1984.

Bloomberg, Charles. *Christian-Nationalism and the Rise of the Afrikaner Broederbond in South Africa, 1918–1948.* Bloomington: Indiana University Press, 1989.

"Boeremag Trial May Be Delayed Again." *Mail & Guardian* Online, October 18,

2004. Available online at www.mg.co.za/articlepage.aspx?articleid=139780 &area=/breaking_news/breaking_news__national/.

Branch, Taylor. *Parting the Waters: America in the King Years, 1954–1963*. New York: Simon and Schuster, 1988.

Breytenbach, Breyten. *The True Confessions of an Albino Terrorist*. London: Faber and Faber, 1984.

"Bring Back the Hottentot Venus." *Mail & Guardian,* June 15, 1995. Available online at History of Race in Science, http://web.mit.edu/racescience/in_media/baart man/baartman_m&g_june95.htm.

Brink, André. *Looking on Darkness*. New York: Morrow, 1974.

———. *Reinventing a Continent: Writing and Politics in South Africa*. Cambridge, Mass.: Zoland Books, 1998.

Brown, Douglas. *Against the World: Attitudes of White South Africa*. New York: Doubleday, 1968.

Brown, Michael K., Martin Carnoy, Elliott Currie, Troy Duster, David B. Op-penheimer, Marjorie M. Shultz, and David Wellman. *Whitewashing Race: The Myth of a Color-Blind Society*. Berkeley: University of California Press, 2003.

Bunting, Brian. *The Rise of the South African Reich*. Harmondsworth, U.K.: Pen-guin Africa Library, 1964; rev. 1969. Available online at www.anc.org.za/ books/reich.html.

Burnham, Louis. *Behind the Lynching of Emmet Louis Till*. New York: Freedom Associates, 1955.

Callinicos, Luli. *A People's History of South Africa*. Johannesburg: Ravan Press, 1990.

"Carry on the Fight." *Meridian Star,* editorial, August 26, 1964, p. 4.

Carter, Gwendolen M. *The Politics of Inequality*. New York: Octagon Books, 1977.

Cawthra, Gavin. *Policing South Africa: The South African Police and the Transition from Apartheid*. London: Zed Books, 1993.

"Chaney, Goodman, and Schwerner." Available online at www.core-online .org/history/chaney.htm.

Chattopadhyaya, Haraprasad. *Indians in Africa: A Socio-Economic Study*. Calcutta: Bookland, 1970.

Chothia, Farouk. "Students Stung by the 'Cruel' System of Affirmative Action." *Weekly Mail,* Review/Education, vol. 2, no. 1, February 1993, p. 1.

Cilliers, S. P. *The Coloureds of South Africa*. Cape Town: Banier, 1963.

Clark, Nancy L., and William H. Worger. *South Africa: The Rise and Fall of Apartheid*. New York: Longman, 2004.

Cope, John. *South Africa*. Westport, Conn.: Praeger, 1965.

Coplan, David B. "A River Runs through It: The Meaning of the Lesotho–Free State Border." *African Affairs* 100 (January 2001): 81–116.

Cowen, D. V. *The Foundations of Freedom: With Special Reference to Southern Africa*. Cape Town: Oxford University Press, 1961.

"DA Hits Out at Minister's 'Racist Tantrum.'" *Mail & Guardian* Online, May 20, 2005. Available online at www.mg.co.za/articlePage.aspx?articleid=241211 &area=/breaking_news/breaking.

Davenport, T. R. H. *The Birth of a New South Africa.* Toronto: University of Toronto Press, 1998.

———. *South Africa: A Modern History.* 4th ed. London: Macmillan, 1991.

Davenport, T. R. H., and Christopher Saunders. *South Africa: A Modern History.* 5th ed. New York: Macmillan, 2000.

Davids, Jennifer. *Searching for Words.* Edited by Jack Cope. Cape Town: David Philip, 1974.

de Beer, Z. J. *Multi-Racial South Africa: The Reconciliation of Forces.* London: Oxford University Press, 1961.

Debow, Saul. *Scientific Racism in Modern South Africa.* Cambridge: Cambridge University Press, 1995.

de Klerk, F. W. *The Last Trek—A New Beginning: The Autobiography.* New York: St. Martin's Press, 1998.

"De Lille Plays the Race Card." *Mail & Guardian* Online, July 15, 2003. Available online at www.mg.co.za/articledirect.aspx?articleid=24557&area=%2f breaking_news%2fbreaking_news_national%2f.

de Villiers, Marq. *White Tribe Dreaming: Apartheid's Bitter Roots as Witnessed by Eight Generations of an Afrikaner Family.* New York: Viking Penguin, 1987.

Dickerson, James. *Dixie's Dirty Secret: The True Story of How the Government, the Media, and the Mob Conspired to Combat Integration and the Vietnam Antiwar Movement.* Armonk, N.Y.: Sharpe, 1998.

Dittmer, John. *Local People: The Struggle for Civil Rights in Mississippi.* Urbana: University of Illinois Press, 1994.

Dorrington, R., D. Bourne, D. Bradshaw, R. Laubscher, and I. M. Timaeus. "The Impact of HIV/AIDS on Adult Mortality in South Africa." Technical Report. Burden of Disease Research Unit, Medical Research Council, Johannesburg. September 2001.

Dorsey, L. C. *Freedom Came to Mississippi.* New York: Field Foundation, 1977.

Doyle, Peter. "The Impact of AIDS on the South African Population." In *AIDS in South Africa: The Demographic and Economic Implications.* Centre for Health Policy Paper no. 23. Department of Community Health, University of the Witwatersrand Medical School, Johannesburg, 1991.

Drey, Philip. *At the Hands of Persons Unknown: The Lynching of Black America.* New York: Random House, 2002.

Duesberg, Peter. *Inventing the AIDS Virus.* Washington, D.C.: Regnery, 1996.

Duncan, Patrick. *South Africa's Rule of Violence.* London: Methuen, 1964.

Du Pre, R. H. *Separate But Unequal: The "Coloured" People of South Africa: A Political History.* Johannesburg: Jonathan Ball, 1994.

———. *Strangers in Their Own Country: A Political History of the "Coloured" People of South Africa, 1652–1992: An Introduction.* History for the Layman series, vol. 2. Johannesburg: Skotaville, 1992.

Dvorin, Eugene P. *Racial Separation in South Africa: An Analysis of Apartheid Theory.* Chicago: University of Chicago Press, 1952.

Eades, Lindsay Michie. *The End of Apartheid in South Africa.* Westport, Conn.: Greenwood Press, 1999.

Edgar, Robert R., ed. *An African American in South Africa: The Travel Notes of Ralph J. Bunche: 28 September 1937–1 January 1938.* Athens: Ohio University Press, 1992.

Erasmus, Zimitri. *Coloured by History, Shaped by Place: New Perspectives on Coloured Identities in Cape Town.* Cape Town: Kwela Books, 2001.

Farred, Grant. *The Midfielder's Moment: Coloured Literature and Culture in Contemporary South Africa.* Boulder: Westview Press, 2000.

February, V. A. (Vernie A.) *Mind Your Colour: The "Coloured" Stereotype in South African Literature.* London: Kegan Paul International, 1991.

Flavin, Martin. *Black and White: From the Cape to the Congo.* New York: Harper, 1950.

Floyd, Nell Luter. "Can the State's Small Towns Be Saved? Business Leaders Plot Turnaround." *Jackson Clarion-Ledger,* November 14, 2004, p. 1A.

Foster, Don, with Dennis Davis and Diane Sandler. *Detention and Torture in South Africa: Psychological, Legal, and Historical Studies.* New York: St. Martin's Press, 1987.

Frye, William R. *In Whitest Africa: The Dynamics of Apartheid.* Englewood Cliffs, N.J.: Prentice-Hall, 1968.

Fuchs, Anne. *Playing the Market: The Market Theatre, Johannesburg, 1976–1986.* New York: Harwood, 1990.

Fuquay, John. "Miss. Flag Issue May Resurface in Session." *Jackson Clarion-Ledger,* November 26, 2004. Available online at www.clarionledger.com/apps/pbcs.dll/article?AID=/20041126/NEWS01/411260326.

Gandhi, M. K. *Satyagraha in South Africa.* Stanford, Calif.: Academic Reprints, 1954.

Gastrow, Peter. *Bargaining for Peace: South Africa and the National Peace Accord.* Washington, D.C.: U.S. Institute of Peace Press, 1995.

Giniewski, Paul. *The Two Faces of Apartheid.* Chicago: Regnery, 1965.

Goldin, Ian. *Making Race: The Politics and Economics of Coloured Identity in South Africa.* New York: Longman, 1987.

Golding, George, and Franklin Pybus Joshua. "The Coloured Community." In *The South African Way of Life: Values and Ideals of a Multi-Racial Society,* edited by G. H. Calpin, pp. 70–78. South African Institute of Race Relations. New York: Columbia University Press, 1953.

Goodman, David. *Fault Lines: Journeys into the New South Africa.* Berkeley: University of California Press, 1999.

Goodman, Julie, and Patrice Sawyer. "Barbour's Use of State Flag Could Win or

Lose Votes." *Jackson Clarion-Ledger,* October 1, 2003. Available online at www.clarionledger.com/news/0310/01/m03.html.

Guelke, Adrian. *South Africa in Transition: The Misunderstood Miracle.* London: I. B. Tauris, 1999.

Haldeman-Julius, Margaret. *The Story of a Lynching: An Exploration of Southern Psychology.* Girard, Kans.: Haldeman-Julius Publications, 1927.

Hanf, Theodor, Heribert Weiland, and Gerda Vierdag, with Lawrence Schlemmer, Rainer Hampel, and Burkhard Krupp. *South Africa: The Prospects of Peaceful Change: An Empirical Enquiry into the Possibility of Democratic Regulation.* Bloomington: Indiana University Press, 1981.

Hatch, John. *The Dilemma of South Africa.* London: Dennis Dobson, 1952.

Heard, Anthony Hazlitt. *The Cape of Storms: A Personal History of the Crisis in South Africa.* Fayetteville: University of Arkansas Press, 1990.

Henry, Neil. *Pearl's Secret: A Black Man's Search for His White Family.* Berkeley: University of California Press, 2001.

Herbert, Bob. "Punishing the Poor." *New York Times,* June 11, 2004, p. 27A.

Hobson, Janell. "Beauty, Difference, and the Hottentot Venus: Black Feminist Revisions in Performance and Aesthetics, 1810 to the Present." PhD diss., Institute for Women's Studies, Emory University, 2001.

———. *Venus in the Dark: Blackness and Beauty in Popular Culture.* New York: Routledge, 2005.

Holt, Len. *The Summer That Didn't End: The Story of the Mississippi Civil Rights Project of 1964.* New York: Da Capo Press, 1992.

Hugo, Pierre. *Quislings or Realists?* Johannesburg: Ravan Press, 2001.

Huie, William Bradford. "The Shocking Story of Approved Killing in Mississippi." *Look,* January 24, 1956, pp. 46–49.

———. *Three Lives for Mississippi.* New York: WCC Books, 1965.

Human Rights Watch. "The Killings in South Africa: The Role of the Security Forces and the Response of the State." Human Rights Watch Report, 1991. Available online at http://hrw.org/reports/1991/southafrica1/index.htm.

Ismail, Ayesha. "Griquas, ANC Clash over Saartjie's Remains." *Sunday Times* (Cape Town), August 16, 1998. Available online at www.suntimes.co.za/1998/08/16/news/cape/nct11.htm.

James, Wilmot, Daria Caliguire, and Kerry Cullinan, eds. *Now That We Are Free: Coloured Communities in a Democratic South Africa.* Boulder: Lynne Rienner, 1996.

Jones, J. J. *Shot, Lynched, and Burned: Speech by Rev. J. J. Jones, Pastor of First Baptist Church [Steelton, Pa.], to the National Citizens' Rights Association.* Pamphlet. J. J. Jones, Reporter Electric Power Print, 1893.

Joshi, P. S. *The Tyranny of Colour: A Study of the Indian Problem in South Africa.* Port Washington, N.Y.: Kennikat Press, 1973.

Kahn, E. J., Jr. *The Separated People: A Look at Contemporary South Africa.* New York: Norton, 1968.

Kalideen, Nalisha. "Winnie Walks Free Again." *The Mercury* (Durban), July 6, 2004, p. 1.

Kalley, Jacqueline A., Elna Schoeman, and L. E. Andor, with Abdul Samed Bemath, Claire Kruger, and Beth Strachan. *Southern African Political History: A Chronology of Key Political Events from Independence to Mid-1997.* Westport, Conn.: Greenwood Press, 1999.

Keegan, Timothy J. *Colonial South Africa and the Origins of the Racial Order.* Cape Town: David Philip, 1996.

"Kiwanians Hear Story of South African Republic." *Meridian Star,* January 18, 1962, p. 12.

Laband, John, and Paul Thompson. *The Illustrated Guide to the Anglo-Zulu War.* Pietermaritzburg: University of Natal Press, 2000.

Ladd, Donna. "Haley's Choice." *Jackson Free Press,* October 29, 2003. Available online at www.jacksonfreepress.com/comments.php?id=1885_0_9_0_C.

La Guma, Alex. "Apartheid and the Coloured People of South Africa." Available online at www.anc.org.za/ancdocs/history/misc/laguma12.html. Originally published in United Nations Centre against Apartheid, Department of Political and Security Council Affairs, *Notes and Documents,* no. 18/72, September 1972.

La Haussé, Paul. *Brewers, Beerhalls, and Boycotts: A History of Liquor in South Africa.* Johannesburg: Ravan Press, 1988.

Lambley, Peter. *The Psychology of Apartheid.* Athens: University of Georgia Press, 1980.

Leach, Graham. *South Africa: No Easy Path to Peace.* London: Routledge and Kegan Paul, 1986.

Lee, Richard B., and Irene DeVore, eds. *Kalahari Hunter-Gatherers: Studies of the !Kung San and Their Neighbors.* Cambridge, Mass.: Harvard University Press, 1976.

Lelyveld, Joseph. *Move Your Shadow: South Africa Black and White.* New York: Times Books, 1985.

Lemann, Nicholas. *The Promised Land: The Great Black Migration and How It Changed America.* New York: Knopf, 1991.

Lemon, Anthony, and Owen Williams. *Apartheid: A Geography of Separation.* Farnborough, U.K.: Saxon House, 1976.

Leon, Tony. "ANC Has Tactics of Bush's Republicans." *Mail & Guardian* Online, November 23, 2004. Available online at www.mg.co.za/articledirect.aspx?articleid=142576&area=linsight%2finsightcomment.

Levenson, Jacob. *The Secret Epidemic: The Story of AIDS and Black America.* New York: Pantheon Books, 2004.

Lewis, Gavin. *Between the Wire and the Wall: A History of South African "Coloured" Politics.* Cape Town: David Philip, 1987.

Lewis, Jeffrey D. "Assessing the Demographic and Economic Impact of HIV/AIDS." In *AIDS and South Africa: The Social Expression of a Pandemic,* edited by Kyle D. Kauffman and David L. Lindauer. New York: Palgrave Macmillan, 2004.

Lodge, Tom. *Politics in South Africa: From Mandela to Mbeki.* Bloomington: Indiana University Press, 2003.

Marquard, Leo. *The People and Politics of South Africa.* 2nd ed. Cape Town: Oxford University Press, 1960.

Massie, Robert Kinloch. *Loosing the Bonds: The United States and South Africa in the Apartheid Years.* New York: Doubleday, 1997.

Mathabane, Mark. *Kaffir Boy in America: An Encounter with Apartheid.* New York: Scribner's, 1989.

Mattes, Robert B. "South Africa: Democracy without the People?" *Journal of Democracy* 13, no. 1 (January 2002): 22–36.

Maylam, Paul. *A History of the African People of South Africa.* Cape Town: David Philip, 1986.

Mbeki, Thabo. Statement at the African Renaissance Conference, Johannesburg, September 28, 1998. Available online at www.anc.org.za/ancdocs/history/mbeki/1998/tm0928.htm.

McAdam, Doug. *Freedom Summer.* New York: Oxford University Press, 1988.

McGill, Ralph. *No Place to Hide: The South and Human Rights.* Macon: Mercer University Press, 1984.

Merten, Marianne. "Playing the Race Card in Battle for Western Cape." *Mail & Guardian* Online, October 31, 2003. Available online at www.mg.co.za/articledirect.aspx?articleid=32412&area=%2finsight%2finsight_national%2f.

Middleton, John, ed. *Encyclopedia of Africa South of the Sahara.* Vol. 4. New York: Scribner's, 1997.

Millin, Sarah Gertrude. *God's Stepchildren.* Cape Town: A. D. Donker, 1924.

Mills, Nicolaus. *Like a Holy Crusade: Mississippi, 1964, the Turning Point of the Civil Rights Movement in America.* Chicago: I. R. Dee, 1992.

Mississippi Governor's Office. "Detailed Summary of Medicaid Reform Bill." Available online at www.governorbarbour.com/Summary.htm.

Moodley, Kogila, and Heribert Adam. "Race and Nation in Post-Apartheid South Africa." *Current Sociology* 48, no. 3 (July 2000): 51–69.

Morgan, Kathleen O'Leary, and Scott Morgan, eds. *State Statistical Trends: Education.* Lawrence, Kan.: Morgan Quitno Press, 2004. Available online at www.morganquitno.com/edpri05.htm.

Morin, Richard. "A Wave of Death, Surging Higher." *Washington Post,* April 1, 2004, p. A01.

Morris, Alan. *Bleakness and Light: Inner-City Transition in Hillbrow, Johannesburg.* Johannesburg: Witwatersrand University Press, 1999.

Motala, Shireen, with Frances Potter. "Behind Closed Doors: A Study of Deaths in Detention in South Africa between August 1963 and 1984 and of Further Deaths between June 1984 and September 1985." South African Institute of Race Relations, Johannesburg, 1987.

Muller, C. F. J., ed. *Five Hundred Years: A History of South Africa.* Pretoria: Academica, 1969.

"Murder Rates Fall in South Africa." *BBC News* World Edition, September 21, 2004. Available online at http://news.bbc.co.uk/2/hi/africa/3676112.stm.

Murray, Martin J. *Revolution Deferred: The Painful Birth of Post-Apartheid South Africa.* London: Verso, 1994.

Musiker, Naomi, and Reuben Musiker. *Historical Dictionary of Greater Johannesburg.* Historical Dictionaries of the Cities of the World, vol. 7. Lanham, Md.: Scarecrow Press, 1999.

Myburgh, James. "Ideological Battle over Meaning of Democracy." *Focus* 34 (June 2004). Available online at www.hsf.org.za/focus34/focus34myburgh .html.

Narain, Iqbal. *The Politics of Racialism: A Study of the Indian Minority in South Africa Down to the Gandhi-Smuts Agreement.* Delhi: Shiva Lal Agarwala, 1962.

National Association for the Advancement of Colored People. "Can the States Stop Lynching?" NAACP, 1937.

Nelson, Jack. *Terror in the Night: The Klan's Campaign against the Jews.* New York: Simon and Schuster, 1993.

"The New-Look NP Goes for Broke." *Weekly Mail,* February 5–11, 1993, p. 30.

Ng, Bernice. "UC Berkeley Professor Doubts Cause of AIDS." *Daily Californian* Online, July 14, 2000. Available online at www.dailycal.org/article.php?id=2796.

Nxumalo, Ray. "Sabta Fat Cats Should Take the Blame." *Weekly Mail,* February 5–11, 1993, p. 19.

Ottaway, David. *Chained Together: Mandela, de Klerk, and the Struggle to Remake South Africa.* New York: Times Books, 1993.

Pachai, B. *The International Aspects of the South African Indian Question, 1860–1971.* Cape Town: C. Struik, 1971.

Palmer, Mabel. *The History of the Indians in Natal.* Westport, Conn.: Greenwood Press, 1957.

Parnell, S. M., and G. H. Pirie. "Johannesburg." In *Homes Apart: South Africa's Segregated Cities,* edited by Anthony Lemon, pp. 138–145. Bloomington: Indiana University Press, 1991.

Patterson, Sheila. *Colour and Culture in South Africa: A Study of the Status of the Cape Coloured People within the Social Structure of the Union of South Africa.* 1953. Reprint, New York: Kraus Reprint, 1969.

Pauw, Jacques. *In the Heart of the Whore: The Story of Apartheid's Death Squads.* Johannesburg: Halfway House/Southern Book Publishers, 1991.

Raper, Arthur F. *The Tragedy of Lynching*. Chapel Hill: University of North Carolina Press, 1933.

Reader's Digest Illustrated History of South Africa: The Real Story. Pleasantville, N.Y.: Reader's Digest Association, 1989.

" 'Responsible' Boeremag Trialists Apply for Bail." *Mail & Guardian* Online, January 12, 2005. Available online at www.mg.co.za/articlepage.aspx?articleid=195131&area=/breaking_news/breaking_news__national/.

Reynolds, Andrew, ed. *Election '94 South Africa: The Campaigns, Results, and Future Prospects.* Cape Town: David Philip, 1994.

Rich, Paul B. *Hope and Despair: English-Speaking Intellectuals and South African Politics, 1896–1976.* London: British Academic Press, 1993.

Rodriguez, Gregory. "Mongrel America." *Atlantic Monthly,* January/February 2003, pp. 95–97.

Ross, Robert. *Adam Kok's Griquas: A Study in the Development of Stratification in South Africa.* Cambridge: Cambridge University Press, 1976.

Rotberg, Robert I. *Suffer the Future: Policy Choices in Southern Africa.* Cambridge, Mass.: Harvard University Press, 1980.

Roux, Edward. *Time Longer than Rope: A History of the Black Man's Struggle for Freedom in South Africa.* Madison: University of Wisconsin Press, 1966.

"SA Appoints AIDS Dissidents." *BBC News,* May 5, 2000. Available online at http://news.bbc.co.uk/1/hi/world/africa/737406.stm.

"S. Africa Moves to Curb Gun Crime." *BBC News* World Edition, July 1, 2004. Available online at http://news.bbc.co.uk/2/hi/africa/3857163.stm.

Sampson, Anthony. *Mandela: The Authorized Biography.* New York: Knopf, 1999.

Saunders, Christopher, and Nicholas Southey. *Historical Dictionary of South Africa.* 2nd ed. Historical Dictionaries of Africa, vol. 78. Lanham, Md.: Scarecrow Press, 2000.

Sefara, Makhudu, and Moshoeshoe Monare. "ANC Aims to Limit Foreign Landlords." *The Mercury* (Durban), July 6, 2004, p. 3.

Sensing, Thurman. "Radical Extremists Invade Mississippi." *Meridian Star,* July 9, 1964, p. 7.

Serote, Mongane Wally. "City Johannesburg." In *Poets to the People: South African Freedom Poems,* edited by B. Feinberg, pp. 162–163. London: Allen and Unwin, 1974.

Sharpley-Whiting, T. Denean. *Black Venus: Sexualized Savages, Primal Fears, and Primitive Narratives in French.* Durham, N.C.: Duke University Press, 1999.

Shipler, David K. *A Country of Strangers: Blacks and Whites in America.* New York: Knopf, 1997.

Silver, James W. *Mississippi: The Closed Society.* New York: Harcourt, Brace and World, 1964.

Simons, Harold Jack. *Class and Colour in South Africa, 1850–1950.* Harmondsworth: Penguin, 1969.

Smuts, J. C. *Jan Christian Smuts: A Biography.* New York: Morrow, 1952.

Sobel, Lester A., ed. *Civil Rights: 1960–1966.* Vol. 2. New York: Facts on File, 1967.

"South Africa: Toward Democracy." U.S. Army Country Studies/Area Handbook series, Federal Research Division, Library of Congress. Available online at http://countrystudies.us/south-africa/36.htm.

"South Africa Begins Gun Amnesty." *BBC News* World Edition, January 1, 2005. Available online at http://news.bbc.co.uk/2/hi/africa/4139961.stm.

"South Africa Leads the Hand Gun Ownership Figures." SABC News, October 26, 2004. Available online at www.sabcnews.com/south_africa/crime1 justice/0,2172,90724,00.html.

South Africa South of the Sahara, 2004. 33rd ed. London: Europa Publications, 2003.

"Southern Truth and Reconciliation: The Road to Justice for Human Rights Violations." Available online at www.southerntruth.org.

Spooner, F. P. *South African Predicament.* New York: Praeger, 1961.

Stober, Paul. "Coloureds May Break from ANC." *Weekly Mail,* February 12–18, 1993, p. 7.

Stryker, Jeff. "California AIDS Dissidents on Global Stage." *California Healthline,* May 15, 2000. California Healthcare Foundation. Available online at http://california healthline.org/index.cfm?Action=dspItem&ItemID=102336&ClassCD=CL.

Sugarman, Tracy. *Stranger at the Gates: A Summer in Mississippi.* New York: Hill and Wang, 1967.

Swain, Carol. *The New White Nationalism in America: Its Challenge to Integration.* Cambridge: Cambridge University Press, 2002.

Swart, Jill. *Malunde: The Street Children of Hillbrow.* Johannesburg: Witwatersrand University Press, 1990.

Tanaka, Jiro. *The San, Hunter-Gatherers of the Kalahari: A Study in Ecological Anthropology.* Translated by David W. Hughes. Tokyo: University of Tokyo Press, 1980.

Taylor, Ayana. "Jim Giles Wants a 'White Nation.'" *Jackson Free Press,* October 14, 2004. Available online at www.jacksonfreepress.com/comments.php?id= 4236_0_9_0_C.

"Tennessee Slips in Education Rankings." *Nashville Business Journal,* October 10, 2003. Available online at www.bizjournals.com/nashville/stories/2003/10/06/ daily52.html.

Theroux, Paul. *Dark Star Safari: Overland from Cairo to Cape Town.* Boston: Mariner Books, 2003.

Thomas, Elizabeth Marshall. *The Harmless People.* London: Secker and Warburg, 1959.

Thompson, Leonard. *A History of South Africa.* 3rd ed. New Haven: Yale University Press, 2000.

———. *The Political Mythology of Apartheid.* New Haven: Yale University Press, 1985.

"Three Negroes Turned Away at Weidmann's." *Meridian Star,* July 9, 1964, home ed., p. 1.

Toase, F. H., and E. J. Yorke, eds. *The New South Africa: Prospects for Domestic and International Security.* New York: St. Martin's Press, 1998.

Truth and Reconciliation Commission, South Africa: Final Report. Cape Town: Juta, 1998.

U.S. Census Bureau. *Current Population Survey* (August 2004). Economic Research Service, U.S. Department of Agriculture. State Fact Sheets: Mississippi. Available online at www.ers.usda.gov/statefacts/MS.htm.

van der Heever, F., ed. *Report of the Commission of Enquiry into Riots in Durban.* Union Government 36/1949. Cape Town, 1949.

van der Post, Laurens, and Jane Taylor. *Testament to the Bushmen.* New York: Viking 1984.

Van Der Ross, R. E. *Myths and Attitudes: An Inside Look at the Coloured People.* Cape Town: Tafelberg, 1979.

Van Niekerk, Phillip. "White Politics, Black Humour." *Weekly Mail,* February 5–11, 1993, p. 3.

Venter, Al J. *Coloured: A Profile of Two Million South Africans.* Cape Town: Human and Rousseau, 1974.

Waldmeir, Patti. *Anatomy of a Miracle: The End of Apartheid and the Birth of the New South Africa.* New York: Norton, 1997.

Walton, Anthony. *Mississippi: An American Journey.* New York: Knopf, 1996.

Washington Post/Kaiser Family Foundation/Harvard University Survey Project. "Survey of South Africans at Ten Years of Democracy." March 2004. Available online at www.kff.org/kaiserpolls/upload/Survey-of-South-Africans-at-Ten-Years-of-Democracy-Summary-and-Chartpack.pdf.

Welsh, Frank. *South Africa: A Narrative History.* New York: Kodansha, 1999.

Western, John. *Outcast Cape Town.* Minneapolis: University of Minnesota Press, 1981.

Wheatcroft, Geoffrey. *The Randlords.* New York: Atheneum, 1986.

Whitfield, Stephen J. *A Death in the Delta: The Story of Emmett Till.* New York: Free Press, 1988.

Wicomb, Zoe. "Shame and Identity: The Case of the Coloured in South Africa." In *Writing South Africa: Literature, Apartheid, and Democracy, 1970–1995,* edited by Derek Attridge and Rosemary Jolly, pp. 91–107. Cambridge: Cambridge University Press, 1998.

Wilkins, Ivor, and Hans Strydom. *The Broederbond.* New York: Paddington Press, 1978.

Wilson, Lisa T. "Industry Betting on a Prosperous Future." *Jackson Clarion-Ledger,* February 28, 2004. Available online at http://64.233.187.104/search?q=cache:q2_ux8WSqrcJ:www.clarionledger.com/news/special/profilems

2004/zt001.html+industry+betting+on+a+prosperous+future+jackson+
clarion+ledger&hl=en.

Wilson, Monica, and Leonard Thompson, eds. *The Oxford History of South Africa.*
Vol. 1. New York: Oxford University Press, 1969.

Wilson, Richard. *The Politics of Truth and Reconciliation in South Africa: Legitimiz-
ing the Post-Apartheid State.* Cambridge: Cambridge University Press, 2001.

Wilson, Sondra Kathryn, ed. *In Search of Democracy: The NAACP Writings of James
Weldon Johnson, Walter White, and Roy Wilkins, 1920–1977.* New York: Oxford
University Press, 1999.

Woods, Donald. *Rainbow Nation Revisited: South Africa's Decade of Democracy.* London: Andre Deutsch, 2000.

Yellin, Emily. "A Changing South Revisits Its Unsolved Racial Killings." *New
York Times,* November 8, 1999, p. 1.

Ziervogel, Christian. *Brown South Africa.* Cape Town: Maskew Miller, 1938.

———. *Who Are the Coloured People?* Cape Town: African Bookman, 1944.

Zuma, Jacob. Address to the opening ceremony of the National Khoisan Consultative Conference, March 29, 2001, Cape Town. Available online at
www.info.gov.za/speeches/2001/010330145p1006.htm.

INDEX

Abdurahman, Abdullah, 129

Act of Union, 127

Adrienne (half-sister): biography of, 73, 219, 220, 250; photograph of, 1, 4, 49, 67; relationship with, 92–93, 157–58, 159–60, 204, 240–42; Yvonne's revelation about, 3

African Americans: black culture and, 87–88, 109–10, 261; identity issues, 69; social class and, 121

African heritage, 34–38, 45–46, 48, 56, 57

African National Congress (ANC): Boipatong and, 80; Chikane and, 77; coloured people and, 178, 200; coup by Boeremag and, 305n; Durban and, 86; history of, 128; housing and, 233; IFP vs., 79, 86, 178; infiltrators and, 201; Khoisan people and, 213; land ownership issues, 79, 234, 238; Luthuli and, 77; Mandela, W., and criticism of, 178; Mbeki and, 206; military campaign against, 80; NP and, 179, 200; PAC and, 177, 179; poverty issues, 238; public relations and, 178; race-baiting and, 236; rallies, and supporters of, 200; recruitment and, 86; right-wing elements vs., 79, 86; Robbie and, 86; SASOL plants and, 186; Schoon and, 77; Sisulu and, 204

African Political Organization, 261

African Renaissance, 236, 237

Afrikaner people, 124–25, 127, 128–32, 297n, 298nn

Afrikaner Weerstandbeweging (AWB, the Afrikaner Resistance Movement), 199, 200, 302n

Aggett, Neil, 152

AIDS crisis, 163, 234–35, 236, 274

Alma Mae (half-sister): biography of, 39, 41, 43, 52, 60, 225, 226; Chaney family and, 43; death of Dave, Sr. and, 55; memorial for murdered volunteers and, 275–77; photographs of, 49; relationship with, 41, 275; Yvonne, and relationship with, 41, 55

America: cultural issues, 282; political issues, 282; racism, 282–83; slavery issues, 12, 249; white supremacy and, 100, 283. See also African Americans

American Friends Service Committee, 198

Anglo Boer War, 125, 126, 146

Antoinette "Nettie" (half-sister): biography of, 73, 113, 219, 220, 246; Cedric and, 138–39; house of, 142; photograph of, 1, 4, 49, 67; relationship with, 83–84, 104, 157, 160–62, 179–80, 185–86, 190; Yvonne, and relationship with, 205, 219; Yvonne's revelation about, 3

apartheid: Boxing Day celebrations and, 115–16; coloured culture and, 260–63, 298–99n; Durban and, 116; effects of, 227–28, 295n; history of, 7–8, 116, 132, 151–52, 291n; Indians and, 90; as role model for MS, 15; South Africa

Freedom Summer of 1964, 17, 18, 43

Freedom Summer of 2004, 275, 276, 286

Freelo (Jerry) (childhood friend), 31–33, 58

Fugard, Athol, 69, 149, 150

Gabriel, Peter, 153

Galaska, Christian (Breytenbach), 75–76

Gandhi, Mohandas K., 90

Georgia, 1, 2, 65, 66, 276

Geraldine (half-sister): biography of, 73, 107, 220, 230–31, 245; photograph of, 1, 4, 49, 67; relationship with, 73–74, 83–84, 190; Robbie and, 107, 137–39, 229, 230; Yvonne, and relationship with, 205, 243–44, 245; Yvonne's revelation about, 3

Gogo Katie (mother of Bessie), 114–15, 221

Goldin, Ian, 125–26, 128, 129

Goldstone Commission, 80, 179

Goodman, Andrew: disappearance and death of, 20, 43, 44, 274, 275, 277; Freedom Summer and, 19; memorial for, 275, 285; trial for murder of, 285–87

grandmother (Henderson, Alma Mae), 10, 22–23, 25–28, 41, 42–44, 52

Griqua people, 208–13

Group Areas Act of 1950, 79, 116, 132–33, 150

Guelke, Adrian, 238

Hani, Chris, 198, 302n

Hard Rock Cafe, 196, 198

Heard, Anthony, 116

Henderson, Alma Mae (grandmother). *See* grandmother (Henderson, Alma Mae)

Henry (uncle), 187–88

Herbert, Bob, 274

Hertzog, Barry, 130

Highpoint, 162–67

Hillbrow, 142

HIV/AIDS, 163, 234–35, 236, 274

Hottentots (Khoikhoi), 122, 123, 125, 209, 211

Houze, David: Adrienne, and relationship with, 92–93, 157–58, 159–60, 204, 240–42; Alma Mae, and relationship with, 41, 275; ancestry, 2, 4; Antoinette "Nettie," and relationship with, 83–84, 104, 157, 160–62, 179–80, 185–86, 190; birth in Durban and, 98; childhood friends, 31–37, 58; Dave Jr., and relationship with, 41, 225, 275; and death, experiences with, 54; departures from South Africa, 8, 190; dreams, about fights between Yvonne with Dave Sr., 41; dreams about fights between Dave Sr. and Yvonne, 41; drugs, illegal, 196, 197; education and, 1, 42, 56, 66, 250; employment, 62–64, 167–74, 196–98; Geraldine, and relationship with, 73–74, 83–84, 190; grandmother, relationship with, 10, 25–28; immigration issues, 9, 222; Johannesburg, trip from Durban to, 139–43; Kokstad, trip to, 205–6; movies and, 59; obsession with South Africa, 1, 2–3, 281; relationships with women, 120, 281; trip to reconnect with family in South Africa, 71, 74, 77–78, 81–82, 205; trip to MS, 8–9, 222; Xavier, and relationship with, 60–61, 66, 279–80, 284; youth activities, 59; Yvonne, and relationship with, 3–4, 55, 258

Houze, Rasheid (brother), 57–58, 65, 66, 112, 281

Houze, Xavier (brother): biography of, 29–31, 45, 52, 224; Boswell Regional Center and, 112, 271, 278–79; Christmas celebration and, 279, 284; diagnosis of, 4, 112, 226; grandmother, and relationship with, 64, 226; Jackson school and, 64, 224, 226; relationship with, 60–61, 66, 279–80, 284; Yvonne, and relationship with, 56, 64, 225, 271, 279

ibabhalazi (hung over), 101
identity issues, 69, 281–82
immigration issues, 238–39
immigration issues, and South Africa, 9. 222, 238–39
Immorality Act, 133
Independent Democrats (ID), 236
Independent Electoral Commission (IEC), 179, 199, 201, 202–3
Indians, history of Durban and, 89–92
Inkatha Freedom Party (IFP): all-race elections and, 198; ANC vs., 79, 86, 178; Zulu ethno-politics of Natal province and, 80, 86, 178–79, 199; Zulu people and, 79, 80
Ivory Coast, 8

Jackson, MS, 14, 16, 272
Jackson Clarion-Ledger (newspaper), 273
Jackson Daily News (newspaper), 13
Jackson Free Press (newspaper), 273
Jackson State University, 274
James Chaney Foundation, 275
Jan Smuts Airport, 74–77
Jews, Ku Klux Klan and threats against, 18, 20–21
Johannesburg: Carlton Centre, 147–48; constitutional negotiations in, 86, 177–79; crime rate and, 142, 144, 172, 178; description of, 141, 144, 145–51, 168, 170, 300n; elections, and political unrest in, 198–99; geography of, 139; gold mining industry and, 141, 145, 146; Hillbrow section of, 142, 156, 158, 160, 162–66; Market Theater, 149–51; squatter camps in, 95; transplanted African workers to, 79; trip from Durban to, 139–43
John (friend of Vernon), 251–60

Johnson, Lyndon, 19
Johnson, Paul, 20
John Vorster Square, 151–54
joll (party), 137, 155–57, 259

Kaffir Boy in America (Mathabane), 74–75
Katie (mother of Bessie), 114–15, 221
Keachie, Bessie, 3, 72–73, 110–14, 239–40, 244
Keachie, Marcell, 73
Keachie, Xavier, 3, 73, 111
Kennedy, John F., 14
Kennedy, Robert F., 7, 15, 291n
Khan, E. J., 116
Khoikhoi/Hottentots, 122, 123, 125, 209, 211
Khoza, Aaron, 153
Killen, Edgar Ray, 285, 286, 287
King, Martin Luther, Jr., 15, 44, 287
de Klerk, F. W.: ANC, and criticism of, 233; burned effigies of, 204; rally for coloured supporters and, 200–201; Record of Understanding and, 80; white supremacy and, 79, 179
Kok, Adam, III, 208, 209, 210, 211, 216
Kokstad: crime rate and, 216, 217; description of, 206; history of, 208–13; trip to, 205–6; Yvonne, and Transkei town of, 11, 195, 205, 213–15
Koresh, David, 189
Kriel, Hernus, 200
Ku Klux Klan: activities of, 15, 17, 44; blacks, and fear of, 17; Dahmer's death and, 11–12; imprisonment of members of, 20; Jews, and threats by, 18, 20–21; Killen and, 285, 286, 287; murders by, 20, 43, 60, 275, 285, 286; threats against volunteers working in Freedom Summer, 18–20; voters, and threats by, 44

Laing, Sandra, 8
Lambley, Peter, 100

Orange Free State, 98, 124, 125, 126–27, 209

Oxford History of South Africa, 123

Palmer, Mable, 90
Pan Africanist Congress (PAC), 177, 179
Paris, poverty and, 9
Parker, Mack Charles, 153, 286
Parktown, 168–70, 174–76
Patterson, Sheila, 133
Paulina (domestic worker), 143–44, 176, 180, 181, 188
Pearl (wife of Dave Sr.), 28, 29, 39
Philadelphia, MS, trials for murders of volunteers in, 274–75, 285–87
Philadelphia Coalition, 275
picketing, experiences with, 60
political issues: America and, 282; Zulu ethno-politics of Natal province, 80, 86, 178–79, 199. *See also political parties*
Polly (aunt), 187
Population Registration Act, 8, 79, 132, 150, 249
poverty issues, 9, 10–11, 164–67, 196, 238
Price, Cecil, 19, 20, 60
Price of the Ticket, The (Baldwin), 193
Prohibition of Mixed Marriages Act, 132
Promised Land, The (Lemann), 13
Psychology of Apartheid (Lambley), 100

race relations, 236, 272, 283–84
racism: in America, 282–83; Durban and, 99–100; economic inequality and, 238; Meridian, MS, and, 15, 103; Meridian and, 15, 103; MS and, 11–13, 153; personal experience, 31–33, 46–48, 137–38; South Africa and, 102–3, 200, 236–37
Rainey, Lawrence, 19–20
Record of Understanding, 80
Reservation of Separate Amenities Act, 133
Riefenstahl, Leni, 201

Roberta (niece), 73, 83, 229, 230
Ross, Robert, 209, 211
Rotberg, Robert I., 283

Salvation Army shelter, 196
San (Bushmen), 122, 123, 212
SASOL company, 186
Schoon, Jeanette, 77
Schoon, Katryn, 77
Schoon, Marius, 77
Schwerner, Michael: disappearance and death of, 20, 43, 44, 274, 275, 276, 277; Freedom Summer and, 17–19, 20; memorial for, 275, 285; trial for murder of, 285–87
Schwerner, Rita, 17
Searching for Words (Davids), 269
Secunda, 185–87, 188
Sensing, Thurman, 14
Separated People, The (Khan), 116
Serote, Mongane Wally, x, 145
shebeen (restaurant with illegal liquor), 114–15, 221
Shipler, David K., 282
Silver, James W., 11
Sisulu, Albertina, 204
skollies (hoodlums), 81
slavery issues, 12, 124, 125, 249
Smuts, Jan Christian, 131, 249
social class issues, 8–9, 121, 135–36
South Africa: geography of, 139–40; indigenous peoples of, 122–23; patriarchy and, 107; race relations and, 272, 283–84; sanctions against, 77–78; unemployment and, 233, 237–38, 249
South Africa Act, 127
South Africa into the 1980s (Bissell and Crocker), 69
South African Coloured Peoples Congress, 260
South African Institute of Race Relations, 91, 261
South African Party (SAP), 130

and, 230, 231; trips to South Africa, 195, 205; Xavier, and relationship with, 56, 64, 225, 271, 279

Ziervogel, Christian, 132
Zulu people: Battle of Isandhlwana in 1879, 139–40; ethno-politics of Natal province and, 80, 86, 178–79, 199; history of Durban and, 89–90; IFP and, 79, 80; secession and, 199
Zuma, Jacob, 213, 238

Text:	10.75/14 Bembo
Display:	Bembo
Compositor:	Binghamton Valley Composition, LLC
Indexer:	J. Naomi Linzer
Cartographer	Bill Nelson
Printer and binder:	Maple-Vail Manufacturing Group